Pastoral Leadership

WEST Theological Monograph Series

Wales Evangelical School of Theology (WEST) has produced a stream of successful PhD candidates over the years, whose work has consistently challenged the boundaries of traditional understanding in both systematic and biblical theology. Now, for the first time, this series makes significant examples of this ground-breaking research accessible to a wider readership.

Pastoral Leadership
A Case Study, including Reference to John Chrysostom

Won Sang Lee

Foreword by
Jonathan J. Bonk

Preface by
D. Eryl Davies

WIPF & STOCK · Eugene, Oregon

PASTORAL LEADERSHIP
A Case Study, including Reference to John Chrysostom

WEST Theological Monograph Series

Copyright © 2015 Won Sang Lee. All rights reserved. Except for brief quotations in critical publications or reviews, no part of this book may be reproduced in any manner without prior written permission from the publisher. Write: Permissions, Wipf and Stock Publishers, 199 W. 8th Ave., Suite 3, Eugene, OR 97401.

Wipf & Stock
An Imprint of Wipf and Stock Publishers
199 W. 8th Ave., Suite 3
Eugene, OR 97401

www.wipfandstock.com

ISBN 13: 978-1-62564-363-6

Contents

Foreword by Jonathan J. Bonk / vii
Preface D. Eryl Davies / xi
Acknowledgments / xiii
Abbreviations / xv

1 Introduction / 1

2 A Case Study of KCPC / 29

3 Pastoral Leadership Principles / 60

4 Conversation with Chrysostom / 94

5 Chrysostom's Pastoral Leadership Principles: On the Priesthood / 132

6 Chrysostom's Pastoral Principles: New Testament Homilies / 165

7 Conclusion / 222

About the Author / 260
Index / 261

Foreword

EVANGELICAL LEADERS ARE NOT known for their recourse to early church fathers, and even less for mining the wisdom of these forefathers for answers to the challenges confronting churches in contemporary society. John Chrysostom is not a name instinctively associated with any Korean Presbyterian Church!

Most evangelical leaders—pastors, mission leaders—are just too busy to do the work necessary to study and apply the teachings of the church fathers. Unlike the Orthodox churches, the names of the Church Fathers are scarcely known in evangelical pews, because they are seldom mentioned in evangelical preaching. Nor have they figured prominently in ministerial training—especially these days when large churches function like corporations with pastors as CEOs and numerical growth and profit the bottom line, and slick marketing the engine that drives the "growth." The resulting growth in numbers may not necessarily be matched by an increasing harvest of the fruits of the Spirit—fruits that are not for self-consumption, but for nourishing others. Self-serving competition for numbers rather than humble service can sometimes characterize a church, no matter what its official statement might assert. That is why this book is a sign of deep hope.

John Chrysostom (c. 347–407) was born in Antioch in privileged circumstances. His father, Secundus—a general in the imperial army—died soon after the birth of his son. His wealthy, highly educated and deeply pious mother, Anthusa, was a devout Christian who devoted her life to the training her gifted only son, ensuring that he received the best of both classical education and training in Christian theology and piety. Chrysostom studied under some of the most gifted teachers of the time, including the celebrated orator Libanius and the noted theologian Diodore of Tarsus. Leaving his life as a hermit in 387 to be ordained a priest, he would come to serve as bishop of Constantinople from 398 until his exile in 403. He was

vii

Foreword

an ardent and effective promoter of Christian missions, mandating and supervising the evangelising of surrounding peoples, including the Goths. He refused the imperial use of force to win converts, insisting that Christ-like living was the most compelling and only authentic argument for the faith.

He was the most famous preacher of the fourth century Syrian church. Nicknamed *Chrysostomos*—"golden-mouthed"—his preaching was pastoral and his writing practical. Both were firmly rooted in a historical reading of Scripture, and his homilies on Genesis, Matthew, John, Romans, Galatians, Corinthians, Ephesians, Timothy, and Titus are still timely, more than sixteen hundred years after his death.

This is the legacy from which the author of this book draws. In some ways, the life of Pastor Won Sang Lee and John Chrysostom are parallel. Both were pastors; both were strong and effective advocates of evangelizing the unreached; both were outstanding Bible teachers and mentors by example. In the case of Won Sang Lee, he served as pastor of the Korean Central Presbyterian Church in Centreville, Virginia from 1977 to 2003. During those twenty-six years, the congregation grew 100 fold, from 30 to 3,000 members, becoming a beacon of ecclesiastical integrity and missionary dynamism.

Although on the surface of things it would seem that a fifth century bishop of an Orthodox Church would have little in common with a twenty-first-century pastor of a Korean Presbyterian congregation in the United States. But this book shows that while the differences in terms of time, context, and ecclesiology are substantial, at the deepest level human needs remain the same, and the spiritual resources available for the reconciling of people are timeless. And so it should not be surprising that Pastor Won Sang Lee has discovered in John Chrysostom a kindred spirit, a wise counselor, and a pastoral exemplar. While the language, culture and social circumstances within which John Chrysostom ministered sixteen hundred years ago contrast sharply with a modern Korean diaspora congregation in the United States, the human dynamics issuing in human crises and church divisions seem to be the same from generation to generation, regardless of time, culture, or place. The parallels are clear in the author's case study. Given the depth of field provided by the author—a leadership approach rooted in almost 1600 years of history—this book should serve as a reliable guide to servant-pastors and Spirit-gifted congregations who yearn to flourish authentically, congregationally, and Biblically within their own contexts, to the glory of God.

Foreword

Poet laureate Robert Pinsky wisely observed, "*A people is defined and unified not by blood but by shared memory. . . . Deciding to remember, and what to remember, is how we decide who we are.*"[1] Readers of this book—and I hope that many of these are congregational leaders and pastors—will be indebted to Pastor Lee for helping us tap into some of the deep memory of our Christian story, so that we can remember where we come from, where we're going, and how to get there as the children of God in Christ, doing his will in his way on his earth. He is like the figure in Jesus' parable, "*a teacher . . . who has been instructed about the kingdom of heaven [and] like the owner of a house who brings out of his storeroom new treasures as well as old*" (Matt 13:52).

Jonathan J. Bonk
Executive Director Emeritus
Overseas Ministries Study Center
New Haven, CT

---

1. Pinsky, "Poetry and American Memory."

Preface

I COUNT IT A privilege to be invited by the author to write a Preface to this book. The *Concise Oxford Dictionary* defines "Preface" as "an introduction to a book stating its subject, scope." For the benefit of readers, however, it may be helpful to explain first of all the background to this book and my personal involvement.

When Rev. Lee was accepted as a student to pursue the PhD program at Wales Evangelical School of Theology (WEST) in partnership with the University of Wales, Lampeter, I was given responsibility for directing and supervising his research.

Within the United Kingdom, the university PhD program consists entirely of research with no taught modules or classroom attendance required, although entrance requirements are of a high standard with one or more Master's degrees required. The university conducts a regular and strict monitoring process in order to assess a student's progress on the program. On the eventual submission of the thesis (80–95,000 words), examination is by means of a *viva voce* before two university academics who are appointed as examiners. One of the examiners at least must be from a different university within the United Kingdom having no contact with the candidate; nor must the examiners have contributed advice to the candidate concerning the research thesis to be examined. It is also required that the external examiner must be a recognized authority within the field of research.

Rev. Lee adapted well to this challenging program. His visits to Wales for supervision, as well as regular email contact, gave me the opportunity to interact extensively and in-depth with him as we explored his subject, clarified the methodology, reviewed relevant contemporary writings and developed further his academic skills. We enjoyed many hours together discussing the content and direction of his thesis. In addition to the

Preface

academic involvement, over a period of four years, I also came to respect Rev. Lee as a genuine disciple and servant of the Lord Jesus Christ. His love of the Lord and commitment to him and his work stood out for me as I observed Rev. Lee's humble servant attitude and the priority he himself gave to prayer. He exemplified the pastoral principles he had identified in his ministry and research. Our times of prayer and fellowship together were most encouraging.

His chosen research subject was "A critical exploration and conversation across the centuries of pastoral leadership principles in John Chrysostom's Antioch and Constantinople and Won Sang Lee's Washington's Korean Central Presbyterian Church." Rev. Lee's reading needed to be as comprehensive as possible, especially in interacting with prominent contemporary pastoral theologians, as well as Patristic scholars.

Reflecting initially on his twenty-six years of pastoral ministry in the Korean Central Presbyterian Church near Washington, Rev. Lee's research was innovative, extensive and self-critical as he identified and evaluated key principles, which he had developed during his long ministry in KCPC. These principles included integrity, humility, and spirituality but especially prayer, preaching, including cross-cultural mission. His case study is intriguing as well as honest; his pastoral principles were sometimes challenged but always wisely applied in his pastorate, resulting eventually in remarkable church growth, both quantitatively and qualitatively. The conversation across the centuries with John Chrysostom, which Rev. Lee undertakes later in this book, is absorbing and comparative, revealing some similarities despite the enormous differences in time, location, culture, and ecclesiology.

I strongly recommend the book to you, especially if you are a church leader with responsibilities for guiding, teaching, and pastoring a local church either in your homeland or cross-culturally. This book will inform you but even more it will challenge you to be a leader with integrity, to seek to know the Lord more and maintain regular fellowship with him, yet at the same time also care for the people both from the pulpit and in visitation. This author, Rev. Lee, provides churches and pastors with an enormous, yet exciting challenge. For this reason, the book ought to be a priority read for you.

Dr. D. Eryl Davies
Research Supervisor, Principal Emeritus (1985–2006)
Wales Evangelical School of Theology (WEST)

Acknowledgments

FIRST OF ALL, I would like to thank God, who called me to pastoral ministry and blessed my service at Korean Central Presbyterian Church (KCPC) for twenty-six years during which time I have learned the importance of pastoral leadership and have desired to explore a biblical model. I am grateful for the Session and Congregation of KCPC, and SEED International and its missionaries who challenged and motivated me to investigate pastoral leadership principles from the perspective of the imitation of Christ for contemporary leadership application.

I am particularly grateful for Dr. Eryl Davies, the former principal of the Wales Evangelical School of Theology, who has been my dissertation director for the past five years. I have been greatly encouraged by his example of excellence as a scholar, theologian and mentor. This dissertation could not have been completed without his supervision as he faithfully guided me throughout the writing process. I would also like to thank Dr. Tom O'Loughlin, Dean of Theology & Religious Studies, University of Wales, Lampeter, who has been my dissertation supervisor at the University of Wales, now professor of Historical Theology at the University of Nottingham.

I am also grateful for those who supported me through their consistent prayers at KCPC and SEED International, as well as the late Elder Byung Ik Lee, the founder of Ezra Leadership Institutes, of which I served as director, for his continuous support.

Finally, I would like to thank Ok Hwa Kim, my mother-in-law, who has supported me with continuous prayer during this process, as well as throughout my life. I also want to acknowledge my son Joseph, his wife Esther, my grandchildren, Caitlyn, Jett, Lauren, Samantha, and Victoria for their encouragement. And also I would especially like to thank my daughter, Eunice, for faithfully editing my dissertation, and David, my son-in-law

xiii

Acknowledgments

with their twins, Nathan and Caroline, and their daughter Colette, for they are a source of my joy. I would like to express my deepest thanks to my dear wife, Young Ja Lee, my greatest champion, for her passionate love for God and her ceaseless prayers and encouragement to me.

Abbreviations

ACW	Ancient Christian Writers
BI	Biblical Interpretation
CBQ	Catholic Biblical Quarterly
CCR	Coptic Church Review
CP	Classical Philology
GOTR	Greek Orthodox Theological Review
ET	The Expository Time
FOTC	Fathers of the Church
HTR	Harvard Theological Review
JECS	Journal of Early Christian Studies
JRS	Journal of Roman Studies
JTS	Journal of Theological Studies
KCPC	Korean Central Presbyterian Church
NIGTC	New International Greek Testament Commentary
NPNF	Nicene and Post-Nicene Fathers
SB	Studia Biblica
SLJT	Saint Luke's Journal of Theology
SP	Studia Patristica
TB	Tyndale Bulletin
TZ	Theologische Zeitschrift
WBC	Word Biblical Commentary
ZNW	Zeitschrift fur Die Neuen Testamentliche Wissenschaft

1

Introduction

THIS BOOK WAS ORIGINALLY written as a PhD dissertation submitted to University of Wales, in Lampeter, UK in collaboration with Wales Evangelical School of Theology, and was accepted in 2010.

My first task is to outline and briefly discuss the three aims that I have chosen in writing this dissertation before defining my terms and then outlining my own pastoral church experience.

AIMS

My first aim is to describe and reflect upon my church ministry at the Korean Central Presbyterian Church (KCPC) in Vienna, Virginia, near Washington, D.C. but with special reference to pastoral leadership. In supporting my choice of this aim, I offer two reasons. First, I completed twenty-six years of ministry in 2003 as the senior pastor of KCPC, a church that is affiliated with the Presbyterian Churches in America (PCA). The PCA denomination was organized in 1973 as a result of the division from the Presbyterian Church in the United States, which originally formed in 1861. The Constitution of the PCA is expressed in its *Book of Church Order*[1], which is, in turn, subordinate to the Old and New Testaments of Holy Scripture. The PCA believes that the major doctrines of Scripture are set forth clearly and faithfully in its subordinate Standard of Faith, which is the Westminster

---

1. Gilchrist, *Book of Church Order*, 21:5. PCA "adopted the Westminster Confession of Faith and the Larger and Shorter Catechism as the doctrinal portion of its Constitution, with only minor changes from the form that was originally adopted by the first General Assembly of PCUSA in 1789." Smith, *Commentary*, 1.

Pastoral Leadership

Confession of Faith. This research has given me the opportunity to further reflect on that period of my ministry and to articulate further the principles and various aspects of pastoral leadership that I wrestled with during my years at KCPC.

I still have a high regard for KCPC and I am delighted that it continues to prosper. This, I believe, is largely due to the pastoral leadership principles that I was able to identify, articulate and practice along with my colleagues during my twenty-six years there. I am increasingly persuaded of the importance of those pastoral leadership principles for churches. My first aim, therefore, captures something of my own personal convictions and reflections that I have given to the subject of pastoral church leadership over many years.

My second aim is to identify and critically discuss key principles relating to pastoral leadership arising from my ministry and to do so with reference to principles and models suggested by other pastoral theologians. I have two reasons for making this the second aim of my research. First, I recognized, articulated, and developed some key principles for my own ministry, but I did this gradually and over a period of time. These early principles of pastoral leadership consisted of developing Christlike character through prayer, caring for the people under my pastoral care through visitation, personal interest in individuals, discipleship training, expository preaching and cross-cultural mission. I continue to embrace these principles with even greater conviction and clarity, but I do so after considerable experience of having seen these pastoral leadership principles applied to church life through many challenging periods and difficulties. A second reason for choosing this aim is that I want to ensure as much objectivity as possible regarding the study of my own ministry. I recognize the inherent dangers of personal bias and subjectivity in this context, especially in reflecting on my own ministry. I will turn to this aspect of objectivity in more detail later, but in short I will be looking briefly at one other model of pastoral leadership at least in order to be both self-critical and to obtain good standards of comparison.

My third aim is also very important to me; namely, I intend to engage in conversation with John Chrysostom (347–407 AD), especially with a sample of his New Testament homilies with relevance to more pastoral concerns and practices in order to identify and explore those major principles that contributed significantly to his pastoral church leadership. I recognize that his situation was vastly different from my own in the twentieth and

Introduction

early twenty-first centuries but are there principles in his pastoral leadership that are consistent with my own? I suggest that there are similar principles, although the expression of these principles was somewhat different and I will pursue this point in later chapters. I want to engage, therefore, in conversation and reflection with Chrysostom. I suggest there are important similarities between Chrysostom's pastoral situations in Antioch and Constantinople and my own in Washington, D.C.

Another reason for choosing this aim is my great respect for Chrysostom and the work he achieved. I had searched for a role model for pastoral leadership from the apostolic period and the Patristics for some time for my own personal benefit and also for the benefit of future pastors. I was delighted to discover Chrysostom, despite many weaknesses both in terms of character and practice. He first ministered in Antioch, the cradle of Christianity, and then later in Constantinople. In regard to the origin of the development of Christianity in Antioch, John P. Meir writes:

> It was Antioch that the disciples were first called Christians (Acts 11:26). What may thus be called the cradle of Christianity was, according to Josephus, the third greatest city in Roman Empire. Situated on the Orontes River and capital of the Roman province of Syria, Antioch was the first important urban center of the Christian movement outside Jerusalem. From Ignatius, the bishop of Antioch in the early second century, to John Chrysostom, priest of that church in the late fourth century Antioch was the home of great theologians and strong bishops, the seat of a celebrated school of exegesis, and a hotbed of heretical tendencies as well.[2]

The Church of Antioch became the first church planted by Christians who had emigrated from Jerusalem and had witnessed the Great Commission of the Lord. It was the center of Christian culture and theology; it was a model for church planting. The Gospel of Matthew was written in AD 80–90, most probably in Antioch of Syria.[3] It is possible that the *Didache*,[4] the primitive Christian instruction of the Apostles was also writ-

---

2. Brown and Meier, *Antioch and Rome*, 12.

3. Ibid., 15. Meier also claimed, "The Antiochene origin of the Gospel of Matthew is confirmed by the fact that Ignatius of Antioch is the first father of the church to use Matthew." For the location of composition, see Slee, "Church in Antioch," 118.

4. Martin and Davids, *Dictionary of the Later NT*, 300–02. *Didache* ("the teaching") is the teaching of the Lord to the Gentiles by the twelve apostles known in ancient times. It is a handbook or manual of Christian ethical instruction and church order. The date of composition and place are unknown, but most likely first or second century in Antioch, Syria.

3

Pastoral Leadership

ten in Antioch, as the *Didache* shares points of contact with the Gospel of Matthew.[5] The Church of Antioch was in the midst of a thriving biblical, theological, and historical heritage, so naturally, Chrysostom was educated in Hellenistic, Judaic, and Christian cultures to serve in Antioch and then in Constantinople.

The Church of Antioch is positioned uniquely in the history of the church in part because of its understanding of the biblical theology of mission from the perspective that the church and mission are inseparable and originated as one.[6] The apostle Paul played a major role as a divinely chosen agent who was converted and received the call to Gentile mission from the risen Christ.[7] I concur with Seyoon Kim that Paul received his apostolic call as well as the gospel itself directly from Christ on the road when he had encountered the Lord[8] (Acts 22:14–21). The Apostle Paul and the Church of Antioch, therefore, are significant in helping us to understand the church's mission and pastoral theology.

Andrew Purves pointed out that Chrysostom's pastoral leadership was to lead the people "not by force but by persuasion."[9] This reflects the distinctiveness of Chrysostom's leadership with its emphasis on character. I agree and found this to be profoundly relevant in my ministry. While Chrysostom was renowned for his preaching, he also prized and sought after, in his own way, the goal of Christlikeness, and in this context frequently referred to Paul's example of imitating Christ. I have come to respect his influential ministry and some aspects of the pastoral leadership he demonstrated in his preaching, writings, and church life. While reading scholarly works on Chrysostom, I recognized that research on his pastoral theology was scarce. There was little, if any, published work on his pastoral leadership principles. Therefore, I wanted to explore this area further and make a

---

5. Slee, "Church in Antioch," 55.

6. Peters, *Biblical Theology of Missions*, 208. In regard to the missionary task of the church Peters wrote that: "Because the church is God's unique creation and not the result of historical and natural process, and because she is God's unique possession through Jesus Christ, it is to be expected that she has been designed for a unique purpose and mission." See also Johnstone, *Church is Bigger*, 23. Johnstone emphasizes, "Scripture, theology, the Church, and even Christians would not exist without mission. Therefore a theology without mission is not a biblical theology, a Church without mission is no longer truly the Church and a Christian without mission is no true disciple."

7. Acts 9:15–17.

8. Kim, *New Perspective*, 157–58.

9. Purves, *Pastoral Theology*, 44. See also Gibbs, *Church Next*, 105–19.

Introduction

small contribution within the boundaries of pastoral theology rather than in Patristics.

Having now outlined and given reasons for my three aims, I want to define a key term in my dissertation title, namely, "pastoral leadership." This is a complex term but I emphasize that it does not solely refer to a Protestant or Presbyterian Church minister. Instead, I intend to use the term more widely to refer to ordained clergy of all denominations. In addition, I include all church officers under the umbrella term "pastoral leadership" including deacons in varying traditions and with various nuances of meaning and significance, local church elders, ministers, and also bishops. Without further weakening this term, I would also like to include missionary agency personnel and leaders who train new generations of preachers and cross-cultural workers for churches.

The term "pastoral leadership" also needs to be discussed within the field of pastoral theology. I am sympathetic with the distinction that Paul Ballard and John Pritchard make between pastoral studies and pastoral theology.[10] For them, the former indicates reflection—which is inter-disciplinary—study, which both supports the pastoral work of the ordained ministry, and also that which stimulates and supports the entire scope of clergy activity. But for them, pastoral theology includes ministerial studies as well as the theological aspect and "underpinning" of pastoral ministry, which embraces the concern of all God's people. Pastoral theology is, therefore, a more comprehensive theological discipline covering all aspects of pastoral ministry. This subject has to do with the clergy who carry out the ministry, the people who are in need of service, and also with the contents of the ministry. In pastoral theology, there are three main entities: the clergy, the congregation, and the ministry. Thomas C. Oden defines the scope of pastoral theology in a way consistent with that of Ballard and Pritchard:

> Pastoral theology is that branch of Christian theology that deals with the office and functions of the pastor. It is theology because it treats of the consequences of God's self-disclosure in history. It is pastoral because it deals with those consequences as they pertain to the roles, tasks, duties, and work of the pastor. Pastoral theology is a special form of practical theology because it focuses on the practice of ministry, with particular attention to the systematic definition of the pastoral office and its function.[11]

10. Ballard and Prichard, *Practical Theology*, 24.
11. Oden, *Pastoral Theology*, x.

Pastoral Leadership

While pastoral theology defines the practical issues regarding the role, function, and the practice of the clergy on behalf of the congregations,[12] pastoral leadership itself has to do with the efficiency and effectiveness of the principles governing the clergy's performance of their duties. According to the manner—but also the theology—of one's pastoral leadership, so the outcome of that particular pastoral ministry is determined. Pastoral leadership is, therefore, important not only from a divine perspective, but also from the perspective of the members of the congregation who are involved themselves in church ministry alongside, and supportive of, the clergy. The quality of the leadership often determines the outcome of what happens church wise and to its people.

The term "pastoral leadership," refers to a recognized role and an authentic ability to influence people under one's care through authentic personality. Regardless of whether the leadership is religious or secular, its function is to powerfully influence others positively. Without the power of influencing the congregation, the development of any kind, whether personal or community-based, cannot be achieved. Donald Dorr, who devoted his life to missionary leadership training within the Roman Catholic Church, and whom I will turn to in more detail later, stated:

> Leadership is the influencing, motivating, guiding, directing, or coordinating of individuals, groups, communities, or organizations in a way that affects their behavior or actions, especially in relation to bring about change or resisting changes.[13]

Dorr classifies that there are four different types of leadership:

1) The lone leader, like St. Francis of Assisi or Buddha, who has a very personal vision and sets out to follow the vision with no intention of persuading others to follow.

---

12. Hiltner, *Preface to Pastoral Theology*, 15–29. In regard to the meaning of pastoral theology, Hiltner writes, "Pastoral theology is defined here as that branch or field of theological knowledge and inquiry that brings the shepherding perspective to bear upon all the operations and functions of the church and the minister, and then draws conclusions of a theological order from reflection on these observations. This means, first, that pastoral theology comes out of inquiry from the shepherding perspective, when the latter is defined as in the previous section. I hold that there are two other perspectives cognate with shepherding which I call communicating and organizing."

13. Dorr, *Faith at Work*, 64–65.

Introduction

2) The emergent leader is the one who demonstrates special leadership gifts and it is evident that the group is able to recognize his leadership ability.

3) The classic leader, like Gandhi of India, has a vision that inspires hundreds, thousands or even millions of others to adopt that vision and follow the leader in working to implement it.

4) The power-hungry leader, like Hitler or Stalin, has all leadership gifts, but they cannot be called wise leaders. They use their gifts for their own benefits and enjoyment, and not for the service of the community and the nation.[14]

Pastoral leadership cannot be defined exclusively in terms of these four categories, but Dorr urges us to follow Christ's example. Essential to Dorr's concept of leadership is the continuing actions influencing the people one serves through example. Only leaders who possess godly moral character can genuinely persuade their followers to respond to their teaching and support the witness and life of the church. A leader's influence without a respectful moral character is weakened, if not undermined and rendered ineffective in the task of leading others. John Gardner, for example, challengingly defines leadership as persuasion:

> Leadership is the process of persuasion or example by which an individual (or leadership team) induces a group to pursue objectives held by the leader or shared by the leader and his or her followers. In any established group, individuals fill different roles, and one of the roles is that of leader.[15]

Leaders can guide people towards a goal through the process of persuasion or by their example. In regard to the law of influence, John Maxwell also observes, "The true measure of leadership is influence—nothing more, nothing less."[16] Influence comes from the authentic character of love, compassionate concern, and clear vision. Without this type of influence upon people, there will be no movement or change in them.

However, the process by which a pastoral leader influences his followers needs to be explored.[17] A leader must earn the power of influence in

14. Ibid., 64–73.
15. Gardner, *On Leadership*, 1.
16. Maxwell, *21 Irrefutable Laws*, 11.
17. Malphurs, *Being Leaders*, 11. In regard to the core concept of Christian leadership Malphurs emphasized the significance of influence, stating: "Leadership is all about

Pastoral Leadership

order to gain followers. Substantial time and practice are required to build one's character throughout life although perfection can never be achieved here. In regard to biblical influence, Donald Dorr explains in a most helpful way that:

> The significant point here is that the kernel of leadership is not simply the power to influence people or the ability to provide effective and efficient governance. Rather the gift of wise leadership has to do above all with moral issues. It is the ability "to discern between good and evil." This is where the biblical position contrasts sharply with that of Machiavelli—and with the attitude of many who hold leadership positions in today's world.[18]

In regards to pastoral leadership, Jesus' example of leadership is the core concept to be explored, including his character, sacrifice, and his leadership style.[19] Because Jesus was the ultimate role model for pastoral leadership during his earthly ministry, I suggest following Christ's model is the most effective way to perform pastoral ministry. In pursuing the bridge between the twenty-first century in Washington, D.C. and Chrysostom in the fourth century, the goal of my conversation is to discover some principles that are also applicable to all generations. I, therefore, regard it as useful to reflect upon and apply, if possible, Christological pattern of pastoral leadership, one that is contained in the concept of the imitation of Christ. From this Christological perspective, Andrew Purves attempts to reconstruct pastoral theology:

> Pastoral work is concerned always with the gospel of God's redemption in, through, and as Jesus Christ. . . . Pastoral work by definition connects the gospel story, that is, the truths and realities of God's saving economy, with the actual lives and situations of the people. In other words, pastoral work is at all points guided by

---

influence, and chapter 5 addresses the leader's style of influence or how leaders influence followers. A leadership tool will help you discover your leadership style and thus how specifically you affect followers."

18. Dorr, *Faith at Work*, 3.

19. Dale, *Pastoral Leadership*, 55–76. Dale emphasizes that there are triangle relationships (leader-follower-situation) in pastoral leadership. He states: "Leadership isn't exercised in isolation. Leaders and followers relate to one another; leaders and situations interact. Leadership in congregations is an interactive triangle. Effective leaders recognize the three elements of this triangle: (1) their own preferred and comfortable leader style, (2) the comfortable relational styles of their followers, and (3) the most productively structured ministry situations for them. Pastoral leaders are alert to the most comfortable and productive combination of these three elements—leader-follower-situation."

Introduction

biblical and theological perspectives, and these biblical and theological perspectives, properly rooted in the gospel of salvation, are discovered to be inherently pastoral.[20]

The purpose of pastoral work is, in principle, to provide not only physical, mental, social, and varied forms of practical help, but also to respond to spiritual needs in order to know Christ personally from the perspective of God's redemptive plan. Christ himself claimed, "I am the good shepherd. The good shepherd lays down His life for the sheep" (John 10:11). Pastoral work, therefore, follows the pattern of Christ as the good shepherd. In performing his redemptive work, which was the ultimate goal of his mission on earth, Jesus demonstrated the example of pastoral leadership through his life and teachings. The origin of the pastoral concept goes back to the Messianic prophecy conveying the ideal shepherd and servant. The Prophet Jeremiah proclaimed, "Then I will give you shepherds after my own heart, who will lead you with knowledge and understanding" (Jer 3:15). The fundamental task for pastoral leadership is, therefore, to explore the original concept of shepherding from the messianic prophecy[21] so the life of Jesus can be explored in order to understand the concept of pastoral ministry. The model for pastoral leadership originates with Jesus and can be applied to all generations. It is important, therefore, to begin with Jesus as the starting point for the foundation of pastoral leadership today. In his *New Testament Theology*, Howard Marshall described the shepherd motif:

> The traditional role of the king or a messianic figure as a shepherd of the people is taken over from Mark; it is to be traced in the motif of compassion for the shepherdless sheep in Matt 9:36 (cf. Mark 6:34 in the context of the feeding of five thousand), and is also present in the description of the last judgment (Matt 25:32–33).[22]

This messianic shepherd motif in the Old Testament was realized in the life of Jesus and demonstrated through his earthly ministry. At the heart of the Christian hymn in Phil 2:5–11, Jesus was depicted as the one who was completely obedient to God in order to care for his sheep.[23] This shepherd motif was revealed throughout Jesus' earthly ministry and

20. Purves, *Reconstructing Pastoral Theology*, xxix–xxx.

21. Marshall, *New Testament Theology*, 72. Marshall identified the shepherds described in Jer 23 and Ezek 34 as the corrupted ones, but the ultimate figure in the vineyard is the Messiah who is the perfect shepherd, namely, Jesus Christ.

22. Ibid., 112.

23. Longenecker, "Foundational Conviction," 475.

Pastoral Leadership

his ascension. Appearing at the Sea of Galilee before his ascension, Jesus commissioned Peter by saying, "Feed my lambs" (John 21:15), "Tend my sheep" (John 21:16), and "Feed my sheep" (John 21:17). It was clearly a pastoral commission, not only to Peter, but also to the other disciples as well as to his followers in future generations. Rudolf Bultmann, for example, stated: "In reply Jesus gives him the charge to feed his 'lambs'; i.e., he entrusts to him the leadership of his community."[24] C. K. Barrett added that, "The interest here lies not in the mission of the church but in leadership and pastoral care within it."[25] In actuality, Jesus commanded his disciples to carry out the Great Commission by exercising pastoral leadership through the pastoral care of his people. Herman Ridderbos also referred to God as our true shepherd, stating: "Shepherding is one of the most frequent and characteristic images for leadership and care of the church. It is rooted in the portrayal of God as shepherd of his people."[26]

Concerning Jesus' strategy for the expansion of the Gospel, he clearly commanded Peter to establish the Church by which Peter and other apostles would fulfill the Great Commission. The core mission is, however, to be carried out through the pastoral commission by caring for his flock. George R. Beasley-Murray's interpretation of the shepherd's mission is sound:

> The one clear connection between the figures employed in Matt 16:19a and John 21:15–17 lies in the aspect of the shepherd's calling to seek the lost sheep and gather them into flock, hence the aspect of mission. By general consent, that is not the primary emphasis of John 21:15–17, where the concern is rather for the care of those who belong to the flock of Jesus.[27]

John 21:15–17, therefore, indicates Christ's commission to his disciples regarding pastoral leadership with an eye to world evangelization. This is also a permanent command to all his followers to obey as Jesus himself demonstrated through his earthly ministry. Even in the secular world, Jesus' life and teachings are honored and observed as illustrating and articulating fundamental leadership principles. Laurie Beth Jones, for example, published a national bestseller entitled *Jesus CEO*:

---

24. Bultmann, *Gospel of John*, 712.
25. Barrett, *St. John*, 583.
26. Ridderbos, *Gospel of John*, 666.
27. Bultmann, *Gospel of John*, 407. Beasley-Murray also reiterated the significance of the pastoral commission in this context.

Introduction

> Jesus CEO: Using Ancient Wisdom for Visionary Leadership is a practical, step-by-step guide to communicating with and motivating people. It is based on the self-mastery, action, and relationship skills that Jesus used to train and motivate his team. It can be applied to any business, service, or endeavor that depends on more than one person to accomplish a goal, and can be implemented by anyone who dares.[28]

Jesus' life example provides significant wisdom for those wanting to pursue successful leadership in all walks of life. Exploring pastoral leadership, therefore, from a Christological perspective may also be fruitful and provide a way to bridge key pastoral leadership principles in different locations, cultures and centuries.

One of the prevalent issues in the twenty-first century, according to Peter F. Drucker, is a lack of leadership, whether in domestic or international communities, regardless of religious or secular backgrounds.[29] There are major issues facing our planet today—the threat of nuclear terrorism, worldwide famine and plague, global warming, the conflict between nationalism and globalism, industrial competitiveness, world recession and the moral degeneration of Western society. On the surface of all of these problems, however, is the question concerning the nature of leadership in our national and global communities.[30] If leadership is critically important in all areas of human institutions, then it is imperative that we develop and improve our leadership skills for the benefits of all. Against this background of the general need to improve leadership skills as a matter of urgency for society, it is my intention to explore principles of pastoral leadership which may be applicable especially to church leadership and have abiding relevance for churches of various denominations.

At this point, in order to introduce my church situation and case study, I provide a brief outline of my own life, ministry and theology.

PASTOR WON SANG LEE[31]

The Keimyung Pioneers is a publication that commemorates the 50th anniversary of Keimyung University, founded by the North America

---

28. Jones, *Jesus CEO*, xi.
29. Drucker, *Management Challenges*, ix.
30. Nanus, *Visionary Leadership*, xiii–iv.
31. Chung et al., "Providence of God," 415–25.

Pastoral Leadership

Presbyterian Mission Board in 1954. Dr. Ilhi Synn, President of Keimyung University, describes the occasion of the publication:

> The Keimyung Pioneer is just a sketch of some of the many whose tireless efforts have made it possible for Keimyung to become what it is today. The twenty profiles include the three founders, Edward Adams, Choi Jaehwa, and Kang Ingoo, and many others who helped with their dedication, encouragement and generosity. This book also retraces the historical footsteps of both Keimyung and Daegu community, as well as of entire Korea over the past half century. I believe this book will also serve to inspire present and future Keimyung students through the exemplary lives of the pioneers present here.

Pastor Won Sang Lee was chosen to be one of the twenty pioneers described in this publication. The following biography is an excerpt from *The Keimyung Pioneers*:

I was born into a devoted Christian family in 1937, in the San Sung Jin village in the Northern Jilin Province of Manchuria. My father, Sung-Bong Lee, was an elder at the San Sung Jin Presbyterian Church. After the end of World War II, my family was forced to move to North Korea in 1945, and then escaped to South Korea in 1947. During this period, my family experienced persecution on account of our Christian faith, and these trials during my childhood prepared me for my later service as a pastor. In 1949, shortly before the Korean War started, my family moved from Seoul to Kyung San, a village in the southern part of Korea, so that we would not be within reach of the war zone.

Having been raised by godly parents, I committed my life to Christ for the ministry and confessed my calling to become a minister of God in front of my class as a sixth grader. This commitment remained firm all the way to my ordination into the Christian ministry. The greatest spiritual influence I received in my life was during my senior high school years, from Reverend Dong Jin Choi who ministered at Kyung-San Presbyterian Church during the period of 1954 to 1957. Pastor Choi later moved to Cho-Ryang Presbyterian Church, one of the oldest churches in Korea, established in 1892. Pastor Choi was a man of prayer who demonstrated spiritual power in his ministry. Through the examples of my father and Pastor Choi's prayer life, I learned that prayer is the key to a successful pastoral ministry. After four years of liberal arts study majoring in philosophy, I graduated with honor

Introduction

from Keimyung University,[32] Dae-Gu, Korea in 1962. Forty years later, in 2002, I also received an Honorary Doctor of Philosophy degree from my alma mater Keimyung University. I continued my study at the Kyung-Pook National University Graduate School and graduated with a Master of Arts in philosophy in 1965. In 1968, I came to the United States to study at the Dallas Theological Seminary, and obtained a Master of Theology degree majoring in the Old Testament in 1972. Subsequently, I went to Philadelphia where I earned a Master of Arts degree in Near Eastern Studies at the University of Pennsylvania in 1981. My diversified education was a great asset in my future pastoral ministry. Upon retiring from my twenty-six years of pastoral ministry in 2003, I immediately began my PhD studies in the area of pastoral leadership.

My first pastoral experience began at Pyung-San Presbyterian Church[33] where I ministered from 1963 to 1967 as an un-ordained pastor[34] while pursuing graduate study in philosophy at Kyung-Pook National University. In addition to these responsibilities, I served as an English and History teacher at the Mennonite Vocational School for junior and senior high school students. During the Korean War (1950–53) the Mennonite Central Committee established this boarding school in order to provide Christian education and vocational training for war orphans. Teaching at this school could also be likened to pastoral ministry in terms of caring for pupils and leading them.

My first pastoral ministry as an un-ordained pastor at Pyung-San Presbyterian Church was an important pastoral experience for me. It provided me with an unceasing desire to develop pastoral leadership skills for the benefit of my ministry. Pyung-San Presbyterian Church was first established for a group of wounded soldiers during the Korean War (1950–53)

---

32. Lee, "Edward Adams," 315–30, 7–29. Keimyung University was established by Dr. Edward Adams, a missionary to Korea from the Presbyterian Board of Foreign Mission in the United States, and two Korean church leaders, Rev. Jae Hwa Choi and Rev. In Ku Kang, in 1954 in order to educate Christian leaders. Dr. Archibald Campbell was inaugurated as the first president and Dr. Edward Adams succeeded him as the second president.

33. Pyung-San Presbyterian Church is located at 168-1 Pyung-San Dong, Kyung-San City, Kyung-Book Province, Korea and the church is affiliated with Kyung-Chung Presbytery of the General Assembly of the Presbyterian Churches (Hap-Dong) in Korea. Currently, Rev. Jong Dae Suh is the Senior Pastor.

34. I was licensed as un-ordained pastor to minister at Pyung-San Presbyterian Church at the 8th Kyung-Chung Presbytery meeting held at Ja In Presbyterian Church on March 15–17, 1966 presided by Rev. Hyun Dal Lee.

Pastoral Leadership

who had been cared for at the House for Homeless Wounded Soldiers, the "Jung Yang Won," in Kyung San, Korea. These soldiers were neglected, uncared for, homeless, and many had become amputees. They were filled with bitterness and complaint because of all the hardships they endured. Korea's economy was devastated during the war, and the government did not have sufficient funds to care for these war veterans in appropriate facilities. When I began my ministry at this church in 1963, there were about twenty members in desperate need of a pastor. They could not call a pastor because they were unable to support him financially nor could the Presbytery send a Pastor to care for them. My first objective was to build a pastoral relationship with the members by earning their trust through love and care. I visited their homes regularly and provided spiritual counseling according to their need. During the course of four and a half years I was able to build up a unity among church members and built a new sanctuary, relocating the church to the main part of town. The church then became an organized church through the ordination of two elders.[35] The memory of this unique pastoral experience has stayed with me throughout all these years, reminding me of the importance of integrity and love in church ministry. This was the only pastoral ministry experience I had prior to becoming the pastor of KCPC in 1977. After I retired from KCPC I continued to serve as president of SEED International, a foreign mission agency[36] and as director of the Ezra Leadership Institute.[37] During service honoring my retirement on September 27, 2003, I received two tributes from federal and local government officials. It was an honor to be recognized by the House of Represen-

---

35. In the *PCA Book of Church Order*, a church without elders is called a mission church; it becomes a particular church when the church establishes a Session by ordaining at least two elders. We elected two elder candidates, namely, Mr. Dong Keun Lee and Mr. Joon Woong Lee for elder ordination in 1965 and they were ordained after elder training sessions.

36. SEED International is a missionary sending agency incorporated in the State of Virginia as a non-profit organization in 2000. It is, however, originally from the Central Missionary Fellowship established by KCPC in 1990 with the purpose of missionary commissioning to the foreign countries. In 2000 C. M.F. was merged with ROW (Reaching to the World) founded by New York Presbyterian Church (Senior Pastor was Rev. Young Hee Lee) in order to become an interdenominational Korean-American mission agency. In 2000, SEED International was awarded to hold the full membership of Missio Nexus (formerly the Evangelical Fellowship Mission Agencies). Currently, eighty missionary families are serving in twenty-seven different countries.

37. Ezra Leadership Institute was founded by Dr. Byung Ik Lee in 2003 for the purpose of retreat, training, and fellowship for missionary candidates, missionaries and their families, lay leaders, pastors, and pastoral candidates.

Introduction

tatives of the United States of America at the 108th Congress, First Session. The Honorable Tom Davis of the United States House of Representative presented Pastor Won Sang Lee with the tribute, entitled "Honoring Reverend Won Sang Lee upon His Retirement" on Tuesday, September 30, 2003.

> Mr. Speaker, I would like to pay tribute to Reverend Won Sang Lee as he retires after twenty-six years as the Senior Pastor of the Korean Central Presbyterian Church in Vienna, Virginia. He had taken a lead role in providing a spiritual center for the Korean-American community in the 11th district of Virginia. Reverend Lee has demonstrated the importance of education with his extensive studies, which began at Keimyung University in Korea where he received a bachelor's degree in philosophy. He went on to complete three master's degrees, first in philosophy from Kyung Book National University, Korea, next in theology from Dallas Theological Seminary, and finally in Near Eastern studies from the University of Pennsylvania. He was also awarded an Honorary Doctor of Philosophy from Keimyung University, Korea.
>
> During Reverend Lee's career, his focus has been community outreach, both local and international. The Reverend has made an impact globally by serving as the President of SEED International, which is a mission agency that provides support for missionary activities both home and abroad, and by holding a leadership position in the Korean World Mission Council for Christ.
>
> On a national scale, Reverend Lee has served as the Moderator for the Coalition of the Korean Churches in the Presbyterian Church in America, and as Chairman of the Korean-American Food for the Hungry. Locally, Reverend Lee has been very involved a bright future for children as Chairman of the Washington Youth Foundation. He also directed the Metro-Washington Council of Korean Churches as its President.
>
> In November 2001, the Reverend's life-long commitment to his fellow human being was recognized when he received the Virginia Governor's Award for Outstanding Religious Institution. This award was granted in honor of his work in the Korean Central Senior Center, where he had served as the Chairman of the Board of Directors since 1994.
>
> Mr. Speaker, in closing, I would like to applaud the efforts of Reverend Lee who has provided spiritual guidance to citizens all across globe, and more importantly right here at home. I ask all my colleagues to join me in paying tribute to this great humanitarian.[38]

---

38. This was recorded in the Congressional Record of the Proceedings and Debates of the 108th Congress, First Session on Tuesday, September 30, 2003 and the plaque was

Pastoral Leadership

I also received a Certificate of Recognition from Mr. Gerald E. Connolly, Providence District Supervisor in whose district KCPC belongs.[39]

The Korean Central Presbyterian Church is located at 8526 Amanda Place, Vienna, Virginia, a suburb of Washington, D.C., approximately fourteen miles from the White House. The church was founded on November 4, 1973 by the Rev. Myung Ho Yoon with an initial congregation of twenty Korean American immigrants.[40] During the next four years, the church grew rapidly under Rev. Yoon's leadership but, unfortunately, the church faced a crisis when some lay leaders challenged Rev. Yoon's personal integrity. On September 25, 1977, two-thirds of KCPC's members left the church with the founding pastor and established a new church named Seoul Presbyterian Church.[41] The thirty members who remained at KCPC experienced considerable distress and frustration on account of this division. This church crisis will be explored in the KCPC case study in the next chapter.

In the midst of the spiritual and emotional struggles of this church, my wife and I, two children, Joseph (three and a half) and Eunice (eleven months), and my mother-in-law came to Washington, D.C. in 1977 to serve KCPC, relocating from Philadelphia, Pennsylvania where I was attending the University of Pennsylvania for graduate studies in the Near Eastern Studies Department. Accepting KCPC's pastoral call, I assumed pastoral responsibility as a non-ordained pastor on December 4, 1977. At that time, the church's membership roll included thirty people from seventeen families. When I retired in 2003 after twenty-six years of ministry, the church had grown to be the largest Korean-American church on the east coast of the United States with an average Sunday attendance of four thousand people, including children.[42] According to KCPC's Annual Congregational Re-

---

presented to Pastor Won Sang Lee.

39. Mr. Gerald E. Connolly, Providence District Supervisor, to which KCPC belongs, presented this plaque to me on September 27, 2003 during the ceremony of my retirement. It reads: Certificate of Recognition in honor of Reverend Won Sang Lee "On the occasion of his retirement as senior pastor of Korean Central Presbyterian Church after twenty-six years of dedicated service to the citizens of Fairfax County during which time his leadership and commitment to community service resulted in the growth of the Korean Central Presbyterian Church to a membership of more than 4,000 and the establishment of church's award winning local and international community outreach program."

40. Paik, *Thirty-Year Anniversary*, 118.

41. Ibid., 137.

42. The Korean Central Presbyterian Church Sunday Bulletin shows that the average Sunday attendance in October 2003 was 3858 including children. The church secretary

Introduction

port (October 1, 2002 to September 30, 2003), on October 12, 2003, there were 2208 family units and 3030 communicant members on the church registry.[43] During this period, 353 new family units joined the church.[44]

KCPC celebrated its thirty-second anniversary on Sunday, November 6, 2005. During the past thirty-two years, the church has grown significantly under three different pastoral leaders. KCPC's growth was documented in Thom Rainer's book, *Breakout Churches*.[45] Before the publication of *Breakout Churches*, Jim Collins published *Good to Great: Why Some Companies Make the Leap and Others Don't*.[46] Collins writes:

> Good is the enemy of great. And that is one of the key reasons why we have so little that becomes great. We don't have great schools, principally because we have good schools. We don't have great government, principally because we have good government. Few people attain great lives, in large part because it is just so easy to settle for a good life. The vast majority of companies never become great, precisely because the vast majority become quite good—and that is their main problem.[47]

Jim Collins and twenty-one research team members investigated twenty-eight good companies spending 15,000 hours during a five-year span in order to discover common principles behind becoming a great company. One of the conclusions that they came to was that the quality of leadership was essential. Collins wrote: "To use an analogy, the 'Leadership is the answer to everything' perspective is the modern equivalent of the 'God is the answer to everything' perspective that held back our scientific understanding of the physical world in the Ark Age."[48] In my estimate, Jim Collins'

reported the statistics of Sunday attendance on the Sunday church bulletin every week. This shows that the Sunday attendance visibly grew each week.

43. "Annual Congregational Report of the KCPC" published by the Session clerk on October 12, 2003. The Annual Report reflects not only the church's numerical growth of Sunday attendance, church finance, but also all other church's ministries in general. Every director of church ministry must report their activities performed during the fiscal year in written form so that the entire congregation can understand the church's vision and goals.

44. Ibid., 5.

45. Rainer, *Breakout Churches*, 259. Thom S. Rainer is a renowned scholar on church growth, founding dean of the Billy Graham School of Missions, Evangelism and Church Growth at the Southern Baptist Theological Seminary in Louisville, KY.

46. Collins, *Good to Great*, 200

47. Ibid., 1.

48. Ibid., 21.

Pastoral Leadership

Good to Great is a masterpiece of research, useful not only to businessmen but also to Christians who are seeking to improve their leadership skills within a church pastoral context. It is estimated that there are approximately 400,000 Protestant churches in the United States. But why do some churches remain static and others grow continually? The answer is complex and multi-faceted but Jim Collins' book written mainly from a business perspective has some relevance for Christian leadership. In regard to how he was motivated by Jim Collins' book, *Good to Great* to write *Breakout Churches*, Rainer writes:

> Good to Great: Why Some Companies Make the Leap and Others Don't by Jim Collins is a masterpiece of research into the business world of America. Collins' team identified eleven Fortune 500 companies that had transitioned from mediocrity to excellence over several years. The book had a profound impact on me.... We saw numerous principles that were biblical in their foundations, even though the book has no explicit Christian focus.[49]

Profoundly impacted by Good to Great, Rainer and his eleven research team members[50] were determined to explore Protestant churches of the United States in order to find key biblical pastoral leadership principles because he discovered that Collins' book contained numerous principles which were applicable to Christian leadership. Out of nearly 400,000 churches in the United States, Rainer's research team was able to examine 52,333 churches and eventually selected thirteen churches as "Good to Great Churches" according to their criteria. On November 10, 2003 Thom Rainer wrote me a letter in which he informed me that:

> We have examined 52,333 churches in America, and your church is one of only thirteen that met our criteria of being a "good-to-great church." I thank God for the work he has done through your ministry.

It was really an exciting moment when I received this news from such a renowned expert in church growth and evangelism. This also motivated me to study pastoral leadership even further by exploring my own pastoral ministry. I believed that this may also be beneficial to others who are in the

---

49. Rainer, *Breakout Churches*, 13.

50. Ibid. The names of the ten research team members are: Doug Whitaker, Joong Shik Kim, Michael McDaniel, David Bell, Laura Cruse, Stuart Swicegood, Chris Bonts, George Lee, Deborah Morton, Elisha Rimestead and Michael O'Neal.

Introduction

ministry of Korean immigrant churches in order to avoid church conflicts and encourage greater harmony and effectiveness.

What I want to do now is to begin to explore Korean Central Presbyterian Church from the perspective of pastoral leadership principles.

BRIEF HISTORY OF KCPC

The first 102 Korean immigrants to the United States arrived in Honolulu, Hawaii on January 13, 1903.[51] As a celebration of the centennial anniversary of Korean immigration to the United State, former President George W. Bush proclaimed:

> From every corner of the world, immigrants have come to America to discover the promise of our nation. On January 13, 1903, the first Korean immigrants to the United States arrived in Honolulu, Hawaii, on the SS Gaelic. Today, Korean Americans live throughout the United States, representing one of our largest Asian-American populations. As we commemorate the centennial anniversary of Korean immigration to the United States, we recognize the individual contributions of Korean Americans to our Nation's rich cultural diversity, economic strength, and proud heritage.

Here is an indication that the contribution of Korean-Americans to the United States is publicly recognized. In addition, on December 13, 2005 the House of Representatives of the Unites States unanimously adopted a resolution to commemorate January 13 each year as Korean Day in remembrance of the first arrival of Koreans in 1903. According to the 2000 national census of the United States, the total U.S. population was 281,421,906 and the Korean-American population was 1,228,427, which indicated that Koreans made up 0.004365 percent of the total population. The proportion of Korean-American churches to American churches is, however, much higher.[52] When KCPC was established in 1973, the Korean-American population in Washington, D.C. was estimated to be about 10,000[53] and there were eight Korean metropolitan churches in existence.[54] At present, there

---

51. Chae, *History of the Korean Community*, 47.

52. Rainer, *Breakout Churches*, 13. Rainer estimated that there are about 400,000 churches in U.S. In comparison, there are approximately 3,000 Korean churches, which is proportionately higher than the number of American churches in proportion to the population.

53. Chae, *History of the Korean Community*, 31.

54. Ibid., 107–12. The six other churches were Korean United Methodist Church

Pastoral Leadership

are approximately 120,000 Korean-Americans living in the Greater Washington area and 300 Korean churches. KCPC has grown to be the largest church within the Korean-American community, not only in the Greater Washington area, but also throughout the entire east coast of the United States. Reflecting on KCPC's forty years, this growth did not come without problems. The worship attendance of the average church in the U.S. declined over the next five years, while the attendance of the churches profiled in *Breakout Churches* increased by 71 percent.[55] At KCPC, we experienced considerable growth even after internal disputes.

KCPC's first thirty-two-year history (1973–2005) can be divided into six stages:[56]

The first stage (1973–81) began with the founding pastor, Rev. Myung Ho Yoon. The church consisted of twenty families and met in Rev. Yoon's residence at 313 Park St. N.E., Vienna, Virginia starting on November 4, 1973. In 1976, internal difficulties arose when some members of the church confronted Rev. Yoon about his personal morality. Rev. Yoon then left KCPC with two-thirds of its members and founded a new church. On December 4, 1977, I came to KCPC as its second pastor and I was soon confronted by some of the elders because of differences in our ministry philosophy. In 1981, one-third of KCPC's members left the church marking the second trial in the church's thirty-year history.

The second stage (1982–85) was characterized by stabilization and construction. The church constructed a new building, 22,000 square feet on 3.5 acres, at 8526 Amanda Place, Vienna, Virginia. The dedication service of the new sanctuary was held on December 7, 1985. This was the period that Thom Rainer calls "Breakout Point."[57] It was the turning point for spiritual and numerical growth in KCPC's history. During this period the congregation recognized my leadership, in particular my sacrificial commitment to the ministry.[58] During the third stage, 1986–90, KCPC witnessed tremendous growth by providing various training programs for the

---

of Greater Washington (1951), Korean Baptist Church of Washington (1955), Korean Presbyterian Church of Washington (1965), United Korean Presbyterian Church (1969), Bethesda Korean Baptist Church (1971), Virginia Korean Baptist Church (1972), First Korean Presbyterian Church of Maryland (1973), Global Mission Church of Washington (1973) and KCPC (1973).

55. Rainer, *Breakout Churches*, 16.
56. Paik, *Thirty-Year Anniversary*, 120–22.
57. Rainer, *Breakout Churches*, 26.
58. Chae, *History of the Korean Community*, 112.

Introduction

congregation such as 2:7 Disciple Training Series by Navigator Mission and Evangelism Explosion; these programs were also offered in the Children and Youth Ministries. The average Sunday attendance in October 1986 was 625[59] including children, while four years later in 1990 it doubled to 1179.[60]

The fourth stage (1991–95) was characterized as the period of KCPC's vision for world mission. I introduced Vision 2020: "Training the Saints to Transform the World" based on Eph 4:12 to the congregation. KCPC commissioned its first missionary family, Rev. and Mrs. John Shin-Wook Park and their children, to Argentina on December 5, 1990 and continued to send out seven additional missionary families to Thailand, China, Mexico, Brazil and Uzbekistan.

The fifth stage (1996–2003) revealed the ministry's diversity and focused on nurturing the congregation, as well as the community and global outreach. KCPC established a Washington, D.C. Community Center for the center-city homeless people, Culpeper Prayer House in Culpeper, Virginia, and SEED International, a world mission agency. These ministries enhanced the diversified character of the church's comprehensive mission outreach strategy for the Gospel. KCPC also organized a building committee and purchased eighty acres of land to relocate the church to Centreville, Virginia, approximately twenty minutes away from the present location. Furthermore, I retired on September 27, 2003 after twenty-six years of ministry and Reverend Danny Chang-Soo Ro succeeded me as the third senior pastor. This was the beginning of a new chapter in KCPC's history.

In 1992, KCPC decided to establish an English-Speaking Congregation in order to provide a worship service for English-speakers as well as other ethnic groups. The session appointed Rev. David Choon-Ho Yang as their first English Ministry pastor. In 1993, Rev. Raymond Chang succeeded Rev. Yang as the second pastor and the board of deacons was also organized. In 1996, Rev. James Kwang-Jin Lee succeeded as the third pastor. After Rev. James Lee left for the mission field, Rev. Hank Hyun-Ku Hahm and Rev. Harold Hyung-Yoon Kim were installed as the English pastoral team in 2001. The English Ministry at KCPC renamed their church the "Christ Central Presbyterian Church" and the church became an organized church in 2008 when they ordained their own five ruling elders according

---

59. The church Sunday bulletin recorded October 5, 1986 (634), October 12 (628), October 19 (629) and October 26 (609).

60. The church Sunday bulletin recorded October 7, 1990 (1106), October 14 (1195), October 21 (1222) and October 28 (1194).

Pastoral Leadership

to their bylaws under the Korean Capital Presbytery of the Presbyterian Church of America. This became a landmark in KCPC's history as the two churches minister independently yet cooperatively for the Kingdom of God.[61]

From October 2003 to June 2012, KCPC has been continuously growing under the new leadership of Reverend Ro, installed as Senior Pastor of KCPC by the Korean Capital Presbytery of PCA. There are many examples of problems that arise in the course of leadership transition, especially when the retiring pastor was successful and respected by the congregation during his ministry.[62] This phenomenon indicates that the effect of pastoral leadership is not only applicable to the period of the retiring pastor's ministry, but also to the process of transition. The pastoral leadership principle, therefore, covers both the retiring pastor and the successor in terms of successful transition. Any church will face struggles and frustration if the senior pastor's transition is not successfully executed. In this respect, KCPC's senior pastor transition can be an example for churches in the U.S. and Korea as the congregation and lay leadership have adjusted well to Rev. Danny Ro and the new leadership since my retirement. KCPC's leadership transition will be discussed later in this dissertation.[63] Rev. Danny Ro, however, resigned KCPC in May 2013 after ten years service in order to accept the call from Sa Rang Presbyterian Church in Los Angeles, which is the largest Korean-American Church in the United States. After eleven months without senior pastor, Rev. David Eungyul Ryoo was installed in April 2013

---

61. Paik, *Thirty-Year Anniversary*, 257–62. See also Ro, *KCPC Handbook*, 6–11.

62. Problems arising in senior pastor transitions are typical among Korean-American churches in the U.S., especially when the outgoing senior pastor has been well respected by the congregation. Oriental Mission Church (OMC) at 424 N. Western Avenue, Los Angeles, California 90004 is an example of the difficulties that can arise during such transitions. OMC is among the largest churches in the United States founded by Rev. Dong Sun Lim, who is one of the most respected pastors among Korean-American Christians. Rev. Lim established OMC in 1970 and retired after twenty years of service in 1990. Rev. Byung Hee Lee, who had ministered quite successfully at the Korean Church of Houston, Texas, was installed as the next senior pastor of OMC in 1990. This arrangement only lasted three years and Rev. Kwang Chul Park, a professor of World Mission at the Seoul Theological Seminary, succeeded Rev. Lee as the third pastor of OMC in 1993. After five years of service, Rev. Park also resigned from OMC in 1998 and the church struggled for three years without pastor. In 2001, Rev. Joon Min Kang became the fourth pastor. He also experienced frustration, as it was difficult to overcome the ongoing church tensions. In spite of all of these problems, Rev. Kang was successful in the ministry and the current average Sunday attendance has reached 7000 including children.

63. See chapter 3.

Introduction

as new senior pastor. This was a new chapter for KCPC, celebrating its 40th anniversary in November 2013.

Based on my reflections on my own ministry, Rev. Danny Ro's ministry, and the fourteen other Korean churches that existed in the greater Washington, D.C. area when I began my pastoral ministry in 1977, I have concluded that good pastoral leadership is the essential element in church growth.

When I began my pastoral ministry at KCPC in 1977, it had the lowest church membership, Sunday attendance, and annual budget among the fourteen Korean churches in the greater Washington, D.C. area.[64] Exploring these fourteen churches from a pastoral leadership perspective from 1977 to 2007, it is evident that pastoral leadership influenced the life of the congregations and the churches growth or otherwise in the community. From 1951 to 1977, these fourteen Korean churches were established as the Korean community grew through the arrival of new immigrants, students, diplomats, journalists, business-related people, and others to the area. Observing the changes in these fourteen churches over the past thirty years, I have identified the following data from each church in order to identify principles for church growth and health.

1. The Korean United Methodist Church of Greater Washington, D.C. (1951)
2. The Korean Baptist Church of Washington (1955)
3. The Korean Presbyterian Church of Washington (1965)
4. The Korean United Presbyterian Church of Washington (1969)
5. Virginia Korean Baptist Church (1972)
6. The Korean Presbyterian Church of Maryland (1972)
7. The Korean Central Presbyterian Church (1973)
8. The First Korean Presbyterian Church of Maryland (1973)
9. Global Mission Church (1974)
10. The Korean Presbyterian Church of Northern Virginia (1975)
11. The Korean Nazarene Church (1976)[65]

64. Kang, *History of the Korean Community*, 70–81.
65. Ibid., 78. The Korean Nazarene Church was founded by Rev. James Young-Yong Kim in 1977 and Rev. Kwang Ho Yang became the second pastor in 1992. The church's name was changed to The Korean Church of Fairfax.

Pastoral Leadership

12. The Korean Baptist Church of Montgomery (1977)[66]

13. Seoul Presbyterian Church (1977)[67]

14. McLean Korean Presbyterian Church (1977)

Studying these fourteen churches, Yoo Kyung Ko compiled a report, entitled "A Comparative Analysis of the Interrelation of the Pastoral Leadership and the Church Growth."[68] This research surveyed all fourteen churches and he spoke with all the pastors or church leaders individually. He collected the following data from each church for comparison. This survey indicates that the senior pastor's pastoral leadership principles play a significant role in a church's health and growth.

	Present Senior Pastor[A]	Average Sunday Attendance[B]	Annual Budget (Units: $10,000)	Year Established	Number of Pastoral Transitions[C]
1.	7th (2)	1,400 (400)	250	1951	4
2.	9th (9)	260 (60)	50	1956	5
3.	5th (1.5)	430 (90)	80	1965	5
4.	4th (6)	150 (35)	20	1969	4
5.	4th (4)	330 (110)	85	1972	3
6.	5th (6)	135 (20)	25	1972	5
7.	3rd (4)	4500 (1500)	600	1973	3
8.	2nd (4)	220 (30)	50	1973	2
9.	3rd (14)	2100 (500)	400	1974	3
10.	2nd (4)	150 (50)	30	1975	2

66. Ibid., 79. The Korean Baptist Church of Montgomery was founded by Rev. Seung Hak Kim in 1977 who retired in 1989 after twelve years of ministry.

67. Ibid., 80. The Seoul Presbyterian Church was founded on September 18, 1077 by Rev. Myung Ho Yoon who was the founding pastor of KCPC in 1973 and left KCPC with two-thirds of the members. After founding Seoul Presbyterian Church he also left that church within six months. The Seoul Presbyterian Church underwent many difficulties without a pastor. Until the current pastor Rev. Jae Dong Kim was installed as the seventh pastor, the church had not settled. Now under Rev. Kim's pastoral leadership the church has been experiencing new vitality and growth.

68. Ko, "Comparative Analysis." Ko is currently serving as Director of Midwest University Washington, D.C. campus, Vice President of China Aid Association (CAA) since 2004. He received his PhD from the School of Law, Kyungpook National University, Korea in 1999.

Introduction

11.	2nd (15)	300 (100)	75	1976	2
12.	4th (5)	100 (20)	22	1977	3
13.	9th (18)	850 (250)	120	1977	8
14.	3rd (1.5)	310 (50)	83	1977	2

A. This number indicates the number of years the senior pastor has served the church and the senior pastor's order since the founding of the church.

B. This number indicates the average Sunday attendance including children. The number in parenthesis indicates the number of children attending on Sundays.

C. This number indicates number of senior pastor transitions since the founding of the church.

I have established that there were no sociological, political, or environmental catastrophes of major significance that may have caused unusual church growth or activity in the community between 1977 and 2007 and during my active pastoral ministry at KCPC. Evaluating the data surveyed from the fourteen churches, KCPC stands out from the other thirteen churches in terms of church growth. In 1977, KCPC had the lowest church membership and annual budget compared to the other thirteen churches. KCPC multiplied 100 times during the length of my pastoral ministry. Besides KCPC (7), the Global Mission Church (9)[69] and the Korean United Methodist Church of Greater Washington (1)[70] also stand out among the 14 churches. Both of these churches also recognize the contributions of their outstanding senior pastors who served with exceptional pastoral leadership. Rev. Dong Won Lee[71] of Global Mission Church (GMC) was one of the most prominent preachers among Korean pastors both in Korea as well as in the United States. Rev. Lee served GMC for ten years (1983–93) during which time the church has rapidly grown under his pastoral leadership. His spirit-filled and fresh expository preaching satisfied people searching for a dynamic, biblical spirituality. Rev. Lee also initiated training for lay

69. Kang, *History of the Korean Community*, 76–77. The GMC is affiliated with the Southern Baptist Convention in the United States and was established in 1974 and is located at 13421 Georgia Avenue, Silver Spring, Maryland. Rev. Dong Won Lee served the Church from 1983 to 1993 during which time the church has grown amazingly.

70. Ibid., 70–71. The Korean United Methodist Church of Greater Washington was the first Korean church to be established in the Greater Washington, D.C. area in 1951. Rev. Young Jin Cho was installed as the sixth pastor in 1983 and retired in 2005. During his ministry for 22 years (1983–2005) the church has expanded by dedicating a new sanctuary in 1990 and became a model church in the Korean community under Rev. Cho's pastoral leadership.

71. Ibid., 76–77.

Pastoral Leadership

people through his unique inductive Bible studies. In 1993, Rev. Lee went back to Seoul to plant Global Mission Church with the same vision he had at GMC. Now, GMC in Seoul has grown to twenty thousand members under his leadership.

Regarding the Korean United Methodist Church of Greater Washington (KUMC), Rev. Young Jin Cho[72] was recognized as a humble person with a godly character because of his exemplary life, serving the church and community. Rev. Cho was a quiet man, but his life demonstrated exceptional power and influence, not only to his own congregation but also to the leadership of his denomination. Retiring from KUMC after 22 years of service, he was appointed Bishop of the Arlington District of the United Methodist Church 2005. Observing GMC and KUMC from the perspective of church health and growth, Rev. Lee's outstanding preaching ministry and Rev. Cho's humble character both were recognized as two fundamental principles in their fruitful pastoral ministries. The results from this survey also support the relevance of my dissertation, which explores my own pastoral leadership principles at KCPC and which I believe may provide core values for effective pastoral leadership.

In the field of business management, leadership principles are also important for success just as they are in pastoral ministry. In search of excellence in business management, James Collins and Jerry Porras published a book, entitled *Built to Last*, which discloses the successful habits of visionary companies. This book was the outcome of a six-year research project at Stanford University's Graduate School of Business. Throughout the research process, Collins and Porras sought to identify the attributes that make truly exceptional companies different from others. They discovered one of the qualities for a successful and long-lasting company:

> Ultimately, the only thing a company should not change over time is its core ideology—that is, if it wants to be a visionary company. This brings us to the central concept of this book: the underlying dynamic of "Preserve the core and stimulate progress" that's the essence of a visionary company.[73]

The key issue was how to preserve the core value, the company's identity, while constantly making progress with new vision. Without innovative progress an organization cannot grow. A company's core value and its

---

72. Ibid., 70–71.
73. Collins and Porras, *Built to Last*, 82.

Introduction

progress are the constant elements for maintaining its life and identity. During the company's life cycle, leadership plays a significant role. Collins concluded that the principles for *Built to Last* are not only applicable to the business world, but also to all types of organizations, such as universities, churches, governments, non-profit organizations, and even families and individuals.[74] Leadership plays a decisive role for the enduring success and health of any organization, whether religious or secular and the unchanging core value and innovative progress are interwoven together in principle through the leadership exercise.

It is, therefore, exciting for me to explore my ministry at KCPC as well as enter into conversation with John Chrysostom in order to identify the enduring principles of pastoral leadership so that other clergy and leaders in the contemporary Global Christian Community can benefit. My intention is to explore the pastoral leadership principles that I have developed and practiced at KCPC for twenty-six years and then to do so in conversation with John Chrysostom and the practice of his leadership principles at the Churches of Antioch and Constantinople.

METHODOLOGY

I make clear early in the next chapter that this research falls within the scope of pastoral theology rather than in Patristics or church history. As such, recent developments in pastoral theology, including Congregational Studies[75] and the contemporary interest in general as well as more specifically in leadership principles encourage me to explore the leadership principles that governed my own pastoral ministry at KCPC.

In chapter two, I provide a case study of my KCPC ministry. This case study is descriptive and analytical. In order to provide greater objectivity, I have used Thomas Rainer's outline and assessment of KCPC under my ministry but not in order to foster personal pride but rather to provide an external and more objective evaluation of my ministry there.

Because the term "leadership" remains ambiguous and fluid in the varied ways in which it is used today, I return to a further discussion of its nature and expression in chapter three. In this same chapter, I introduce

74. Ibid., xviii.

75. Chambers, *Religion Secularization*, 42–74, 199–229. In this congregational study, Chambers demonstrates the changes of religious population in Swansea, Wales, which is the second largest city in Wales, due to the social and religious changes. As a result, he could also inform an understanding church growth and decline.

Pastoral Leadership

an alternative but extremely popular model of church leadership as it is expressed in varied ways among the Emerging Churches, particularly in the United Kingdom and the United States. I have found this alternative model stimulating but deficient, yet I also insist that my pastoral leadership principles can still apply within this radical model while expressing the principles more corporately rather than initially through a group of church elders and a pastor. The "cell" approach is also considered and it is an approach that I have used myself and advocate.

Methodological questions relating to my "conversation" across the centuries with John Chrysostom are discussed in some detail in the relevant place early in chapter four, while the "gaps" between the two pastoral situations are identified, acknowledged and addressed at the beginning of chapter five.

2

A Case Study of KCPC

IN ORDER TO INTRODUCE my case study in this chapter, I want to comment further concerning my Presbyterian model, as well as my purpose in providing the case study before emphasizing the helpfulness of a congregational study like the one I am providing here on KCPC. I emphasized in the previous chapter that the model which is being used to describe my pastoral experience in KCPC is a Presbyterian model of a Minister and Elders, appointed by the membership, who rule over, and minister to, the church in all areas of its life and witness. I draw attention to this model again, not in order to exalt it over all other possible models but because as a Presbyterian minister in a Presbyterian denomination this is the major model which needs to be used in describing my pastoral experience. While acknowledging this fact, I do not believe that it is the only possible model and I assume that my pastoral leadership principles which I identified and developed during my ministry in KCPC could function well within almost any form of church government whether Episcopalian, Methodist, Independent or Pentecostal. In chapter three, I will discuss in more detail an alternative model of leadership advocated among the Emerging Churches. However, what I do emphasize here is the fact that I have discovered then tested my pastoral leadership principles and found them to be extremely effective within a Presbyterian model as I hope to illustrate.

Regarding the case study itself, my purpose is two-fold and consistent with my aims, which I described early in chapter one. First of all, I am seeking to describe then explore and evaluate my own pastoral experience by reflecting on my twenty-six years as minister at KCPC. This being so,

Pastoral Leadership

this second chapter will be more descriptive and factual in providing the actual case study. A related purpose in using this case study is to identify and discuss as well as to begin to evaluate key principles relating to pastoral leadership and models suggested by other pastoral theologians. Some of these principles will become apparent in the course of this chapter but will be developed further in chapter three. Here, I want to place my case study in the context of such developments and to do so in two ways.

First, Brynolf Lyon reminds us that recent pastoral theology has become interested in groups and communities, not just individuals. Understandably then in this context, congregational studies has emerged focusing on the life and dynamism of the local congregation in all its complexities and challenges. To be effective, congregational studies needs to be interdisciplinary but essentially theological and pastoral.[1] Second, congregational studies emerged during the 1980s and was linked primarily with a number of writers and publications such as Carl Dudley's *Building Effective Ministry: Theory and Practice in the Local Church* (1983), Denham Grierson's *A People on the Way* (1991), James Hopewell's *Congregation: Story and Structure* (1987), and *Studying Congregations: A New Handbook* edited by Nancy T. Ammerman, Jackson W. Carroll, Carl Dudley and William McKinney (1998). The continuing interest in this area of pastoral theology leads Lyon to make the reasonable claim that "the academy has rediscovered the congregation."[2] This being so, at least to some extent within pastoral theology, in describing congregational church life and history at KCPC in this chapter, I am encouraged that there is a more sympathetic awareness of, and a positive attitude towards, a case study like this one regarding KCPC.

However, studying congregations is valuable socially because the church is a center of religious life and its influence can be significant. The editors of *Studying Congregations: A New Handbook* express this point strongly:

> Congregations are, we believe, essential to the religious health of the United States and central to the religious well-being of a very large portion of this country's population. The Year of American and Canadian Churches reports some 350,000 local communities of faith in the United States alone, with almost 135 million

---

1. Lyon, "Relevance of Congregational Studies," 257. Lyon also explains that "the congregational study is defined as the study of the life of the local congregation. It allows participants to explore a variety of aspects of how a group or congregation works and worship together."

2. Ibid., 258.

members and an average weekly attendance in excess of 65 million adults More individuals belong to congregations than to any other voluntary association, and they provide as much financial support for the work of their religious communities as is given to all other philanthropic causes combined.[3]

Recognizing therefore the importance and influence of a congregation's contribution to a community, it is helpful to probe the composition, nature, dynamism and life of the congregation then to assess its influence and role for members as well as the community in which it functions. Studying a congregation also provides opportunities to re-evaluate the church's mission and vision statements, as well as identifying some of the weak areas in church life and leadership. As in my own case, it provided the opportunity to consider the possibility of relocating the church building and expanding the sanctuary.[4]

In writing my case study, I have been conscious of the dangers of my own subjectivity and bias since I am after all researching at this point my own ministry. I am assuming some key biblical principles and also a confessional theological basis to evaluate my ministry and then to identify and articulate the major pastoral leadership principles, which I have also used in my ministry.

EXTERNAL PROFILE OF KCPC

For an objective description, I would like to introduce a synopsis of KCPC that Thom S. Rainer provided in his book, *Breakout Churches*.

Korean Central Presbyterian Church: Vienna, Virginia

Won Sang Lee pastored Korean Central Presbyterian Church from 1977 to 2003. The church experienced a split in 1977 just prior to Lee's arrival.

---

3. Ammerman, et al., *Studying Congregations*, 8. Since this is a 1998 statistic, the figures may have increased in 2007. In regard to the importance of studying the congregation, the editors added that: "People of faith, gathered in congregations, work every day to make sense of their lives and to devise ways of relating to the divine powers that lie within and beyond them."

4. Ibid., 23–25. For the benefits of congregational study, the editors emphasized that it provides a balance and sense of proportion often absent from self-descriptions of congregations. It also provides problems related to structures of the church and the patterns, and reveals what a congregation does not want to see. See also, Carroll, et al., *Handbook for Congregational Studies*, 7–10.

Pastoral Leadership

Average attendance was about thirty people. By 1979, however, attendance had increased more than fourfold to 130.

By the time attendance had reached the 130 mark in 1979, some of the elders in the church began to question the pastor's leadership style, theology, and preferred worship style. The issues were mostly trivial, such as the pastor allowing members to clap while singing hymns. The power struggle continued unabated for two years. Pastor Lee found himself discouraged and seriously considering leaving Korean Central Presbyterian for another church. Many of the deacons supported him, however, and convinced him to stay. They also made a commitment to pray for him with greater fervency each day.

The problems were not over for the young pastor. The dissenting elders and one-third of the members left the church in 1981. Many of the statistical gains were lost and attendance dropped to 100. As researcher Joong Shik Kim noted, "The attendance of Korean Central Presbyterian church began to grow significantly after the critics left and the crisis was resolved."

By 1982 attendance was up to 207. The growth continued unabated and attendance reached 539 by 1985. In 2003 the average worship attendance was about 4,000. Won Sang Lee retired in September 2003 and was succeeded by Chang Soo Ro.

The growth of KCPC brought about the need for more space. The church has consistently purchased more property over the years, and additional worship services have provided more space as well. In 1986, the church started an English-speaking worship service. By 2003, KCPC had seven worship services on Sunday, beginning 7:45 a.m. and concluding at 3:30 p.m. In 2001 the church purchased seventy-four acres for new facilities and a school.

The church established the Central Missionary Fellowship in 1990 and sent its first missionary that same year. Currently the church has twelve missionary families serving in eight countries. All of the families are fully supported financially by the church. Another forty-one associate missionaries are partially supported by KCPC.

Korean Central Presbyterian Church is also very mission-focused in its own locality. In 2000, the church purchased the Community Service Center in Washington, D.C., to minister the alcoholics, drug addicts, and poor population in downtown area. The congregation also has specific missions and ministries focused on large population of indigent African-Americans in the inner city.

A Case Study of KCPC

Pastor Lee's original plans were to affiliate the church denominationally with the Presbyterian Church, USA. Before that tie was made, however, he began to have concerns about what he perceived to be leftward shift in that denomination. Consequently, the affiliation never took place. In 1985, the church finally did make a formal denominational tie, this time with the more conservative Presbyterian Church in America.

Korean Central Presbyterian Church fits our criteria well for a breakout church. As is common in the churches represented in this book, a crisis precipitated the breakout growth. Also, this church scenario demonstrated the common pattern of the pastor facing severe conflict and considering leaving the church. I would have liked to have had more specific data on conversion growth in the church. The anecdotal evidence, however, is convincing that many people are being reached for Christ in this church. It is a clear case study of a breakout church."[5]

This profile of KCPC describes the qualification for being a "breakout church" and, as mentioned in chapter 1, KCPC was one of 13 churches eventually selected out of 52,333 potential American churches by Rainer and his research team.[6] "Breakout churches" had to fulfill the following five criteria:

1) The church must be evangelistic, responding to the Great Commission of Christ resulting in baptisms, conversions, or professions of faith.

2) Within the previous five years, there must be a minimum of twenty-six conversions, which translates into a conversion of one person every two weeks.

3) The church must have a maximum ratio of 20:1 to conversions, reaching one person for Christ for at least one of the five years.

4) The church has evidence of decline in worship attendance in past years followed by a sustained period of growth of at least five years. The church must also demonstrate that the most recent year represented growth in worship attendance.

---

5. Rainer, *Breakout Churches*, 232–33.

6. Ibid., 214–15. Currently there are about 400,000 churches in the United States and they selected thirteen Breakout Churches through six screening process: The screening can be illustrated as follows: 1) Beginning Database: 52,333 church, 2) Evangelist Screen: 1,936 churches, 3) Received Historical Data: 881 churches, 4) Reported a Decline/Breakout/Growth Pattern: 221 churches, 5) Reported Breakout under Same Pastor: 17 churches, and Verified Data to Qualify: 13 churches.

Pastoral Leadership

5) These details of decline, breakout and growth must have taken place under the same pastor's leadership.[7]

Rainer's primary interest was to discern how the breakout churches overcame their plateaus and continued to grow. The five criteria can easily be criticized, for example, as highlighting quantitative rather than qualitative church growth and they do not focus in any depth on pastoral leadership. Nevertheless, one must acknowledge Rainer's particular interest and his findings and assessment of KCPC do provide some degree of objectivity for my case study and I appreciate that.

KCPC'S First Crisis: 1977

There were only six other Korean-American churches in the Greater Washington, D.C. area when Pastor Myung Ho Yoon founded KCPC with about twenty believers at his house in 1973.[8] Young Ki Lee testified that Reverend Myung Ho Yoon had previously served the Korean United Methodist Church (KUMC) of Greater Washington, D.C.[9] as an associate pastor. When there was an issue regarding Sunday observance, Reverend Yoon, a Presbyterian minister and holding a conservative view of Sabbath observance, decided to establish a Presbyterian church with some of the members from KUMC. He also knew that those who lived in Northern Virginia felt that the current KCPC church location in Washington, D.C. was inconvenient for them. Pastor Yoon, therefore, was encouraged to establish a Presbyterian church in Northern Virginia.[10] On December 2, 1973, eighty-nine people including children attended the Sunday service and the offering amounted to $535.05. During the next four years the church grew rapidly and reached 291 Sunday attendants on January 9, 1977, an increase of more than 100 percent in terms of annual growth. This church growth statistic pointed to outstanding pastoral leadership as well as the congregation's commitment to the church. KCPC's growth rate was vastly greater than that of the other six Korean-American churches in the Greater Washington, D.C. area. Pastor Yoon was a relational leader who embraced the congregation with his unique warm-hearted personality and he was sought after by young

---

7. Ibid., 213–14.

8. Kang, *History of the Korean Community*, 75.

9. KUMC is the first Korean-American church established in 1951 and had been meeting at Foundry United Methodist Church located 1500 16th Street, Washington, D.C. At the first the church was not affiliated with the United Methodist Church because the substantial numbers of the members were Presbyterians.

10. Young Ki Lee, Personal Interview, October 21, 2007.

A Case Study of KCPC

and older church members alike. His gifted musical talent also added to the vitality of the congregation. During this period, there were many new immigrants pouring into the Washington area and some were at KCPC[11] but emotionally and socially needy, experiencing difficulties adjusting to a new society. The church was the only place at the time that provided them with comfort and encouragement. Ki Chan Jin witnessed that Pastor Yoon was very active in caring for these newcomers by meeting their immediate needs, such as helping them find apartments, obtain a driver's license, open up bank accounts, find jobs, enroll their children in school, and in many other particular ways. Pastor Yoon was energetic, selflessly devoted to the ministry, and his preaching was dynamic. His open-minded character was liked by all, young and old.[12] Unfortunately, as the church grew there were some disputes among members in regard to Pastor Yoon's attitude and actions so a church division occurred in September 1977. The majority of KCPC members founded a new congregation under Pastor Yoon called Seoul Presbyterian Church. On September 18, 1977, they conducted their first Sunday worship service at the home of Young Joon Cha[13] who later became an ordained elder.[14] I interviewed three of the lay leaders who founded Seoul Presbyterian Church with Pastor Yoon to ascertain the reason why they left KCPC.

The decision to found a new church was enforced when 46 KCPC members had a separate meeting on August 26, 1977 in order to obtain a congregational meeting for a vote of confidence regarding Pastor Myung Ho Yoon as they contended he had behaved unethically on several occasions. A letter with forty-six signatures was sent to Reverend Edward White, the Stated Clerk of National Capital Union Presbytery, which I have included as an appendix. Although these members made charges against Pastor Yoon, the majority of KCPC members, however, tried to protect him by persuading him to break away from KCPC and found a new church because they realized that they could not get along with those who were against Pastor Yoon. On September 18, 1977, the same Sunday on which the 46 members were planning a congregational meeting to obtain a vote

---

11. The door was open for the immigrants by John F. Kennedy's new immigration law in 1965. By the time KCPC was founded in 1973, many new immigrants from Korea were rushed to the Washington, D.C. area.
12. Ki Chan Jin, Personal Interview, October 18, 2007.
13. 3115 Faber Dr., Falls Church, VA 22042
14. Kang, *History of the Korean Community*, 80.

Pastoral Leadership

of confidence, a group of KCPC members with Pastor Yoon broke away from KCPC and founded Seoul Presbyterian Church. During my interview with In Kyu Chang, Chairman of the Board of Directors of KCPC at that time, Chang stated that the congregational meeting planned for September 18, 1977 was not convened because Pastor Yoon and the majority of KCPC's members had already established a new church. In Kyu Chang also acknowledged that Pastor Yoon had a good character as pastor and that the congregation liked him very much. Even though the majority of the congregation left to found another church with him, Yoon himself left that new church within a few months due to questions yet again regarding his personal integrity and lifestyle. He left for New Jersey and founded another church.[15] Seoul Presbyterian Church was left for some time without a pastor. Reverend Yoon Sam Park was invited as interim pastor and served the church for seven months. In 1978, Reverend Moon Jae Cha was installed as its second pastor and continued to serve for five years until 1984 during which time the church experienced rapid growth. On January 8, 1984, however, Reverend Moon Jae Cha with two elders Dr. Byung In Lee and Chae Gon Park founded a new church called Korean Orthodox Presbyterian Church[16] because some of the lay leaders could not get along with Pastor Cha's strong conservative leadership. On December 22, 1991, Reverend Yong Hoon Kim was called as an associate pastor and later became the senior pastor on November 29, 1992. This church continued to grow under Pastor Kim's leadership and purchased a new facility with sixteen acres and a 90,000 square-foot building[17] on October 21, 2001. They renamed the church the Open Door Presbyterian Church and it experienced tremendous growth under Pastor Yong Hoon Kim demonstrating exemplary church behavior in the Korean-American community.[18] Seoul Presbyterian Church was finally stabilized when Reverend Jae Dong Kim was installed as the eighth Pastor in July 1989. The church purchased twenty-two acres of land and dedicated the first sanctuary; they have an average of 900 in Sunday attendance, including children.[19] Consequently those who left KCPC

---

15. Interviewed with Mr. In Kyu Chang who joined KCPC in 1974 and served as chairman of the Board of Directors. He resides at 25630 Old Hundred Road, Dickerson, Maryland 20842.

16. 1900 N. Glebe Road, Arlington, VA

17. 3001 Centreville, Road, Herndon, VA

18. Kang, *History of the Korean Community*, 87.

19. Ibid., 80.

A Case Study of KCPC

had established two churches in the community. Currently there are 375 churches listed in the Korean Churches Directory of 2007/8.[20] All these 375 churches have experienced division due to leadership conflicts. Reflecting on Korean-American immigrant church history, a common phenomenon is church growth due to a division on account of conflict within the congregation. I will refer to this in more detail in the next chapter.

Won Sang Lee Assumes Pastoral Duty at KCPC on December 4, 1977

After the church split, I assumed pastoral duty on December 4, 1977. Among the forty-six members who signed the petition at the congregational meeting, only twenty-eight people had remained when I came to KCPC. Then eighteen of the forty-six members joined other churches or were inactive. The remaining KCPC members were bitter toward Pastor Yoon and the members who had left. I was hearing nothing but words of hatred and accusations. I was fully aware of my priorities at KCPC and I had to do two things: first, to comfort and encourage the congregation through preaching the Word of God and, second, to safeguard my personal integrity and build congregational trust.

The record from the Board of Deacons Meeting on February 5, 1978 indicates that at that meeting I read Rom 12:9: "Love must be sincere. Hate what is evil; cling to what is good."[21] My goal was to attempt to remove the bad memories of church disputes from their minds. The main activities of the church were focused on promoting fellowship within the congregation. On March 5, 1978, at the monthly meeting of the Board of Deacons, I read 1 Cor 12:25, which says, "So that there should be no division in the body, but that its parts should have equal concern for each other." My intention was to restore genuine love and fellowship to the congregation so that the church would regain strength. At that monthly meeting I organized seven committees for church functions: 1) Visitation, 2) Fellowship, 3) Evangelism, 4) Publication, 5) Pastoral Concerns, 6) Worship, and 7) Christian Education.[22]

---

20. Korean Churches Directory, published by the Council of Korean Churches of Greater Washington, D.C. Byung Wan Lee, President, Pastor of Sekeroh Presbyterian Church, 4401 Muncaster Mill Road, Rockville, MD. The churches include Washington, D.C., Maryland, Virginia.

21. Board of Deacons on February 5, 1978, recorded by Hak Chul Chung.

22. Board of Deacons on March 5, 1978, recorded by Ha Chul Chung.

Pastoral Leadership

On March 18, 1978 the Board of Deacons was convened to discuss the relocation of the church. Before the meeting, I read 2 Tim 2:1-4, emphasizing the importance of personal commitment as disciples of Christ. At each meeting, I selected scriptural passages in order to restore my members' commitment to Christ and the church. Gradually, the lay leaders began to realize their need for rededication to Christ. These board meetings were significant because we decided to relocate the church to Northern Virginia for three reasons:

1) More people were residing in Northern Virginia and it would be more convenient for them to attend church.
2) The facility expenses for the church in Washington, D.C. were more expensive.
3) We had more problems with theft in D.C. during our Sunday worship service.

We organized a committee to search for a new place of worship and appointed five people to report their progress at the next meeting.[23] On April 2, 1978, the Board of Deacons was convened. The scripture reading from 2 Cor 8:1-5 encouraged us to follow a pattern of commitment and sacrificial giving. Through scripture reading, a message, and prayer, I intended to help the deacons capture the spirit of discipleship in the early churches so that KCPC could be restored. Gradually we recognized our weaknesses regarding our congregational unity and biblical stewardship.

The committee dealing with relocation reported that they had contacted four churches but the one chosen was Lewinsville Presbyterian Church, so on June 4, 1978, KCPC relocated to Lewinsville Presbyterian Church.[24] For seven and a half years, from June 1978 to November 1985, KCPC gradually recovered from the 1977 church division and experienced church growth. KCPC Sunday bulletin statistics demonstrate that church growth was apparent after relocation from Washington, D.C. to McLean, Virginia.[25]

Date	Sunday Worship	Children's School	Total Attendance	Offering
July 16, 1978	90	27	117	$472.51

23. The Board of Deacons on March 18, 1978, recorded by Ha Chul Chung.
24. 1724 Chain Bridge Road, McLean, VA
25. The following statistics are taken from the KCPC Sunday Service bulletin from July 16, 1978 to July 27, 1980.

A Case Study of KCPC

July 23, 1978	80	28	108	$1,299.80
July 30, 1978	80	29	109	$474.94
July 15, 1979	103	25	128	$1,551.54
July 22, 1979	120	0	160	$2,037.67
July 29, 1979	102	N/A	N/A	$903.70
July 13, 1980	141	29	170	$1,203.10
July 20, 1980	157	142	199	$1,625.46
July 27, 1980	161	34	195	$1,076.90

This sample of the statistics indicates that KCPC was stabilized under the new pastoral leadership during these three years. Personally, I was devoted to prayer ministry, home visitation, Wednesday evening Bible study, and personal evangelism. Daily Morning Prayer in the church at six o'clock in the morning was invigorating and this practice continues. The Bible study on Wednesday evening was like a discipleship training class that went through consecutively the Old and New Testaments and aimed to teach congregation members how to become more mature Christians.

KCPC's Second Crisis: 1981

Outwardly, KCPC had recovered from the 1977 split. Inwardly, however, as the church grew there was a growing problem. Usually in Korean-American immigrant churches, problems arise during the election of church officers. KCPC was no exception. On October 7, 1979, we had deacon elections for ordination; there were five names on the ballot and we were to choose only four persons. One person was left out for deacon ordination and problems arose because he and his close friends were disgruntled.[26] There were also personal conflicts among the three elders of the Session as well as complaints against some deacons. All these factors and personal conflicts were a challenge to me as pastor. One of the KCPC elders, involved in conflict with another elder, also challenged the validity of my own ordination and claimed, "Pastor Won Sang Lee is a fake minister."[27] He argued that my ordination on June 22, 1978 at the Pennsylvania Presbytery was illegal. The elder proposed two challenges with regard to my ordination: First, he

26. At the annual congregational meeting on October 7, 1979, forty-seven members were present and voted for deacon ordination.

27. The KCPC Session on September 6, 1981 recorded the content of the complaint brought.

Pastoral Leadership

proposed that the Pennsylvania Presbytery was not officially approved by the General Assembly of the Presbyterian Churches of Korea at the time of my ordination. The General Assembly, however, officially approved the Pennsylvania Presbytery as an Overseas Presbytery in 1979. Second, he proposed that I was ordained without licensure procedure. However, the Credential Committee of the General Assembly had allowed me to take the Licensure Examination as an overseas candidate and issued the official licensure, dated January 15, 1979. When the elder challenged me in May 1981, all of his challenges regarding my ordination were cleared.[28] In the end, this elder submitted his resignation at KCPC on May 17, 1981; and this was accepted at KCPC's Session.[29] If it were a judicial case against me in regard to the validity of my ordination then the case should have been brought to Pennsylvania Presbytery and the Credential Committee of the General Assembly of the Presbyterian Church of Korea.

Furthermore, there was disunity between the three elders I had ordained as members of KCPC's Session. One elder brought an official charge against the other on account of a false accusation against him. The content of his complaint entailed the following: 1) On June 6, 1981 he was falsely accused to be planning to establish a new church with another pastor. 2) He was also falsely accused of interrupting the church's building plan by giving the chairman a hard time.[30] This was my first experience in handling a church discipline case, and it was extremely frustrating. Church attendance was also affected as the following statistics indicate.

Date	Worship Attendance	Children's School	Offerings
October 4, 1981	144	N/A	$1885.65
October 11, 1981	136	N/A	$1189.70
October 25, 1981	134	32	$2064.50

28. The official Certificate of Licensure issued to Won Sang Lee by the Credential Committee of the General Assembly of the Presbyterian Churches of Korea dated on January 15, 1979, signed by Chairman of the General Assembly, Reverend Byung Ki Hahn, Credential Committee Chairman, Reverend Joong Sup Ahn, and the Secretary, Reverend Sung Pil Suh.

29. The KCPC Session on May 17, 1981 indicates that his written resignation was accepted.

30. The written complaint against one of the elders, dated on September 6, 1981, was brought to the Session of KCPC. The Session reviewed it and decided to dismiss the charge because the Session believed that the problem was already resolved.

A Case Study of KCPC

November 1, 1981	108	34	$894.43
November 15, 1981	104	30	$2019.05

KCPC church membership was now in decline and the church elected three new elders at the annual congregational meeting on October 4, 1981 and they were ordained on December 12, 1981.[31] The KCPC Session now consisted of five elders and I realized that building up genuine fellowship and unity among the five Session members was the most important task of my pastoral leadership. Without achieving this goal, the KCPC Session could not be a role model for the congregation.

In spite of my efforts to maintain harmony within the Session and the congregation, two other Session members left KCPC. Through the judicial cases at the church court of KCPC's session and the struggles between Session members, I realized that personal integrity and maintaining unity in love and humility were even more important ingredients of pastoral leadership. At the service honoring my retirement on September 27, 2003, I quoted before the congregation 1 Cor 15:10: "But by the grace of God I am what I am." It was a heart-felt confession that by the grace of God, KCPC has been peaceful, growing, and vibrant for twenty-two years since the 1981 crisis.

It took about two years for the congregation to recover from the turmoil of 1981. I devoted myself to prayer, caring for the congregation, teaching the Scripture, reaching out to the community, and training lay leaders. The statistics of the Sunday bulletin over a two-year period indicate KCPC's stability and steady growth.[32]

Date	Sunday Worship	Children's Church	Total	Offerings
October 3, 1982	203	N/A	N/A	$4,141.35
October 10, 1982	182	54	236	$2,608.70
October 17, 1982	213	54	267	$2,867.59
October 24, 1982	270	55	325	$3,136.81
October 2, 1983	285	61	346	$10,494.03
October 9, 1983	274	62	336	$4,783.20

31. The three elders ordained were Phyong Choon Kim, Chi Sun Park, and In Kyu Pak.

32. These statistics are taken from the Sunday bulletins of each date.

Pastoral Leadership

October 16, 1983	277	62	339	$5,900.50
October 23, 1983	279	61	340	$4,905.75
October 30, 1983	235	57	292	$4020.75
October 14, 1984	361	84	445	$8,219.13
November 4, 1984	345	73	418	$19,843.71
November 11, 1984	392	N/A	N/A	$5,272.90
November 18, 1984	389	76	465	$10,733.0

There were no more critical disputes among the congregation and Session members for the next twenty-two years and no challenge against my pastoral leadership concerning my integrity. The crisis of 1981 can be summarized as challenging but then eventually also consolidating the unity of the lay leadership and the integrity of pastoral leadership. Genuine church growth is not possible without these ingredients.

At the time of KCPC's crisis in 1981, there were 119 families in the church directory. Of those 119 families, twenty-nine people died, nine families returned to Korea, twenty-nine families are still KCPC members and the rest either moved to other cities or joined other churches. Reflecting on this incident is not easy. For this congregational study of KCPC, I chose Yoo Kyung Ko[33] who was not in the United States at the time of KCPC's crisis in 1981, to conduct interviews in regard to my pastoral leadership. The interviews were designed to discern how I overcame this crisis, since KCPC has experienced unusual and continued church growth after the 1981. Ko interviewed seven people who were members at the time of crisis in 1981 and still members of KCPC except one person. He asked four questions:

1) When did you join KCPC?

2) Do you remember the crisis in 1981?

3) How did Pastor Lee overcome the crisis?

4) What were Pastor Lee's merits in terms of pastoral leadership?

---

33. Yoo Kyung Ko is an adjunct professor of Virginia Christian University and vice president of China Aid Association. He was also professor and dean of Hyechon Christian College in Daejon, Korea from 1990 to 2003. He obtained a PhD from the Law School of Kyungbook National University, Taegu, Korea in 1995. He was a postdoctoral fellow and visiting professor at the Law School of Freiburg National University, Germany in 1996.

A Case Study of KCPC

Concerning the third question, it is interesting to know that all seven of them answered exactly the same word; through prayer pastor overcame the crisis. In regard to Pastor Lee's merit of pastoral leadership they replied unanimously in highlighting spiritual and Christlike character leadership.[34] Concerning the importance of interviews in congregational studies, Scott L. Thumma reminds us that the congregation's most knowledgeable insiders and a key informant or two can give considerable insight into the life of the church, but a much broader base is also required.[35] But in this case study, one concern has been to avoid subjectivity by adopting more objective and extended evaluation as well as criteria.

Recovery from the 1981 Crisis

One of the common patterns of the Korean-American immigrant churchgoer is "Church Shopping," where people visit different churches for a long time before finally deciding to join a church. Church visitors' concerns are various, including: the quality of the preaching, children's Sunday School,

---

34. Ko interviewed 7 members: 1) Sung Yong Wei (1979–present) remembers that one of the main problem was the issue on the spiritual gifts. They disagreed with pastor Lee who believes in the spiritual gifts. Pastor Lee, however, had been patient through prayer. 2) Sam Hyun Chung (1980–present) was just converted and a new Christian when he joined the church in 1980. He is now a Session member. He remembers that they raised an issue on the validity of pastor Lee's ordination and their plan was to let pastor Lee leave the church. Pastor Lee, however, devoted to prayer. 3) Hae Sun Chung (1980) remembers that some of the elders were not satisfied because pastor Lee was not on their side. Pastor Lee devoted to prayer and was ready to leave the church if it was God's will. Pastor Lee's leadership principle was to imitate Christ and demonstrated example before the congregation. Until the dedication of the new sanctuary he even did not want to buy a new car. 4) Jin Pil Chang (1980–present) also witnessed that Pastor Lee overcame this crisis only through prayer with patience and always was depending on God for solution. 5) Dong Soo Kim (1978–present) observed that Pastor Lee's leadership is to be characterized as integrity. There was no discrepancy found in his word and deed. 6) Kang Hyun Chung (1980–2002) was converted through the ministry of KCPC and was ordained as minister. He had served at KCPC and left the church for church planting in 2002. He described Pastor Lee's pastoral leadership as character leadership. 7) Young Ki Lee was converted through the ministry of KCPC in 1978. She and her husband became faithful in serving the Lord. She witnessed that Pastor Lee devoted himself to prayer and God delivered him from the crisis in 1981.

35. Ammerman, et al., *Studying Congregations*, 196–253. In regard to choosing individuals to interview, Scott L. Thumma expressed some concerns: "Choosing the people you interview is a crucial task in a congregational study. Every faith community has several members who are most vocal about their opinions but whose views may not accurately represent the entire group."

Pastoral Leadership

Sunday worship hours, church facilities, parking, worship style, church location, friendliness, and warmth of welcome. The 1985 KCPC Church Member Directory lists 247 families of which seventy-three families are still attending KCPC, thirty-eight people are deceased, fifty-one families returned to Korea, forty-four families moved to another city or state, and forty-one families joined other churches for various reasons.[36] Out of 247 families in 1985, seventy-three families continued to be members at KCPC until the present. These statistics demonstrate KCPC's stability and strength. Evaluating the membership from year to year, the annual retention rate has been greater than 90 percent, indicating there has been good pastoral care of the congregation.[37]

In the Korean-American immigrant churches at least, the Sunday Worship attendance would drastically drop whenever there is a church split or struggle within the church for the people desire peace and unity as well as integrity on the part of the pastoral leadership. If the tenure of the senior pastor is long and consistent, stability and growth are usually evident. For example, the Korean Baptist Church of Washington, the second oldest church in the Greater Washington, D.C. area, was founded in 1955 and there have been nine senior pastors serving during the church's 52-year history, an average of 5.7 years per pastor. Compared with other Korean-American churches in Greater Washington, D.C., this Korean Baptist Church is not a good example of church growth because the frequent change of pastor militates against church growth. Another example is the Virginia Korean Baptist Church founded in 1972. During its 35-year history, four pastors served the church and the current conflict in the church is due to questions of integrity regarding the senior pastor's doctoral dissertation.[38] This also demonstrates that church growth greatly depends on the senior pastor's personal character. The statistics of KCPC Sunday Worship attendance from January 6, 1985 through December 29, 1985 indicate steady growth and church stability.[39]

---

36. KCPC 1985 Directory.

37. The yearly retaining rate of the members at KCPC is to be calculated by comparing the yearly church directory with the next year directory.

38. *Christian Power Weekly News* on October 12, 2007, 119:A-9.

39. KCPC Sunday Worship Bulletin from January 6, 1985 through January 27 and from October 6, 1985 through December 29, 1985.

A Case Study of KCPC

Date	Sunday Worship Attendance	Children	Sunday Offering
January 6, 1985	359	N/A	$7,666.32
January 13, 1985	406	83	$9,428.25
January 27, 1985	302	59	$5,591.79
October 6, 1985	426	N/A	$16,701.05
October 13, 1985	396	62	$9,057.80
November 3, 1985	408	87	$10,335.13
November 10, 1985	404	94	$9,389.00
December 1, 1985	477	104	$13,532.21
December 29, 1985	539	114	$10,756.56

The average attendance of six weeks in the Sunday worship attendance from October 4, 1981 through November 15, 1981 was 125. Immediately after the 1981 KCPC crisis, there was a substantial decrease numerically. However, the six weeks average in the Sunday worship attendance from November 24, 1985 through December 29, 1985 was 479. The attendance increase from 125 in 1981 to 479 in 1985 demonstrates a 383.2 % growth in four years, an average annual growth of 95.8 percent. The 2007 Yearbook of American & Canadian Church reported that the average annual church growth rate in the United States was 1.63 percent.[40] The 95.8 percent annual growth of KCPC from 1981 through 1985 indicates extraordinary church growth.

KCPC Growth Factors: 1981–85

How does one interpret KCPC's extraordinary numerical growth from 1981–85? I submit that such growth inevitably involves qualitative growth, which involves a robust spirituality, godly living, clear understanding of foundational Christian doctrines, active church involvement and zealous personal evangelism. Donald A. McGavran affirms the important relationship between "revival" and church growth; here the term "revival" is used within the American context to refer to a deeper spirituality and commitment and where this exists people are drawn to the church. Based on a study of the history of "revivals," McGavran identifies seven ways in which such "revival" can impact church growth:

40. Lindner, *American & Canadian Churches*.

Pastoral Leadership

1. Larger congregations who have more contact with unbelievers
2. A constant stream of converts to the Christian faith
3. Converts who spontaneously bring others to faith in Christ
4. Converts who are adequately trained
5. Church leaders who are taught to delegate work to lay leaders in various ways
6. Church leaders who consider the spiritual vitality and life of the church as being of primary importance
7. Church leaders who are instructed about achieving a deeper spirituality or "revival"[41]

Concerning my own leadership, I recognized the need, partly through my reading of authors like McGavran as well as the influence and ministry of Rev. Dong Jin Choi and others in KCPC in 1979, to focus on improving the spiritual life of the church and one significant step was to hold special meetings for this purpose. In 1982, Rev. Jin Kwan Hahn was invited to address KCPC on this subject. One cultural and social benefit of his ministry as well was the fact he identified with some of our church members as a first generation Korean-American immigrant who converted to Christianity while in America then eventually he became pastor of a Korean church in New York. He had a significant influence on the lives of KCPC church members. Other similar pastors addressed my people during 1982 and in March 1983.

One of the most useful and fruitful ministries in affecting the spiritual life of KCPC was by the Rev Sang Keun Lee of Taegu, Korea in May 1983. A number of other preachers were carefully selected to minister at special meetings at regular intervals in KCPC. For example, the messages of the Rev Yong Jo Ha expounding and applying the Sermon on the Mount (Matt 5–7) in January 1984 contributed to what I would call a silent but deep spiritual revolution in the lives of many church members.

Another key factor in contributing to qualitative and quantitative church growth in KCPC between 1982–85 was my endeavor to establish a closer and warmer relationship as pastor to the church members. This was a deliberate policy and I was assisted in various ways in this. For example, my wife, Young Ja Lee, always accompanied me for the visitation of church members and joined me in devoting ourselves to prayer. Without

---

41. McGavran, *Understanding Church Growth*, 141–43.

A Case Study of KCPC

her help and companionship in the work, my ministry would have been less effective in this crucial period. My wife also kept a register of those members attending services on a Sunday (a task she did from 1977–2003) and appropriate visits were made and the Sunday Church bulletin was mailed to absentees, which was greatly appreciated. Eventually, this care ministry was delegated to cell leaders and other small group leaders but a substantial part of this ministry continued to be carried out by Chang Ho Lim and my wife for the sick, new members or those requiring emergency care. Hospitality was also another way in which we were able to get closer to the church members. The goal of the Annual Spring and Fall Visitation Ministry was to visit each member in their homes. Home-cell leaders, assistants, elders, and other visitation team members—alongside my wife and me—participated in this visitation. Culturally for Koreans, it is an honor to receive the church minister or leaders into their homes and this has helped enormously in deepening the unity and love of the people for one another and for the church leadership. Again, I must emphasize my wife's role in supporting me daily at home and joining me for a fasting-prayer retreat each January since 1982. I have also felt accountable to her as we shared our lives and ministries together.

Pastoral and Lay Leadership

I concur with Donald J. MacNair that there are four functions required for a healthy church, namely, worship, nurture, mercy and outreach.[42] Assuming the deepening spirituality of the church members and their unity, these functions can consolidate and strengthen the life and witness of the church. But how does one achieve these functions and plan for them? Edward P. Hahnenberg warns, for example, against a sharp divide between clerical and lay leadership. For him, a lay leadership "keeps the church from becoming too self-absorbed, too focused on internal issues and structures to the detriment of its responsibility to transform the world in the light of Christ."[43] My personal experience and conviction was that, assuming the Trinitarian model, it is more effective to reduce the barriers between these two groups in order to achieve church growth so that the whole church can be encouraged to contribute to, and participate fully in, the mission of the church I was also persuaded that as church membership is voluntary, members need to be encouraged and persuaded rather than commanded to be

42. MacNair, *Practices*, 39–43.
43. Hahnenberg, *Ministries*, 27.

Pastoral Leadership

involved in the church's wider ministry. It was, therefore, my responsibility to encourage the entire laity to participate in ministry but this depends to a large extent also on the warmth of the relationship between pastoral leaders and members as well as their personal integrity.

Peter Wagner confirmed me in this conviction when he placed dynamic pastoral leadership as the first requirement for church growth and a well-mobilized laity as the second requirement.[44] Is the pastor competent to do this and does he have the moral character and integrity to do it? This is a major issue. And coupled with moral integrity is the need for humility and spirituality in order to create a dynamic synergy within the congregation. Interestingly, Eddie Gibbs suggests five leadership models which the pastor or priest may be called upon to adopt: 1) competent expository ministry, 2) a loving and encouraging father role, 3) a supporting brother who expresses the bond of spiritual kinship uniting the congregation, 4) a faithful, wise manager helping the congregation to participate in ministry, and 5) an obedient servant who serves while exercising leadership, forging fraternal relationships with each member of the congregation.[45] While no one person may possess or excel in all five roles, what unites these different models is humility and the willingness to encourage and allow different people to be part of, and involved in the one body of the church.

For these reasons I tried as pastor to encourage and place members in the most appropriate ministry according to their gifts and availability. Aware that younger generations are unimpressed by authoritarian leadership and that there is a profound distrust on their part in institutions and churches,[46] even politics, yet I wanted to maintain a firm, biblical but gentle

---

44. Wagner, *Your Church Can Grow*, 187–88. The Seven Vital Signs for Church Growth are 1) pastor's dynamic leadership, 2) well-mobilized laity, 3) church facilities, 4) the proper relationship between celebration, congregation and cell, 5) homogeneous unit, 6) evangelistic methods, and 7) biblical priorities. Concerning the diagnosis of a healthy church Wagner says, "Vital signs were identified by medical science to describe what happens inside a healthy human being. Vital signs are also useful to diagnose ill health. Churches also have vital signs-seven of them. A recognition of these signs and their implications leads to an understanding of what happens within healthy, growing churches."

45. Gibbs, *I Believe*, 264–74. Gibbs believes that all leaders are not adequately equipped with all five models, but may have one or more gifts of leadership models. He writes, "Within the church context there are a number of leadership models which the minister or priest may be called upon to adopt. Different individuals will feel easier in one role than in the other, and some personality types are more adaptable than others."

46. Gibbs, *Church Next*, 25. Gibbs identified that modern people prefer centralized hierarchies, while the postmodern model prefers a decentralized network.

A Case Study of KCPC

leadership that was characterized by love and humility. I was convinced people would respond to this kind of leadership, and that it would help to mobilize the laity for active involvement in the church. The philosophy of Emerging Churches emphasizes relationships rather than activities and authoritarian leadership structures.[47] I am in sympathy with some of their dissatisfaction with current Christendom, especially the point that church should be viewed essentially from a relational rather than a hierarchical and institutional perspective within the family of God.

One of my goals, then, as pastor was to mobilize the laity as co-laborers in the church's fellowship and witness. The church elders were also co-workers with me and members respected them. In addition, my pastoral staff was faithful and shared the burdens of the work with me. In January 1985, KCPC published its Annual Member Handbook in which 243 families were listed and the average Sunday attendance for worship was 359 adults and 75 children. Under the supervision of the "Session," that is, the three elders, four associates and myself, thirty-four deacons and forty-four deaconesses were appointed in 1985. Twenty members taught in Sunday school, two in the adult department and some in the junior high or senior high with eleven serving in the Korean Language School. Fifty-two participated in the church choir and there were also seven Mission groups organized by age with their own officers and responsibilities to support cross-cultural workers and also rural churches in Korea. There were also seventeen home-cells with leaders who cared for an average of fourteen families in each cell. From October 1984, KCPC was sponsoring six missionaries overseas and eight rural churches in Korea. In these ways, the whole congregation was mobilized to serve the church in the areas of worship, fellowship, caring, discipleship training, evangelism and missions.

A New Church Building

It became necessary in 1982 for KCPC to find a new and more appropriate place to conduct its worship and activities. A building committee was immediately established. This building project further contributed to church growth rather unexpectedly by providing members with a sense of belonging and ownership through praying, giving and supporting the

---

47. Gibbs and Bolger, *Emerging Churches*, 96–101. Emerging churches are group of people who are missional communities arising from within postmodern culture and consisting of followers of Jesus. They believe that "church as family is primarily about relationships. It is not about meetings, events, or structures."

Pastoral Leadership

project. A greater love was expressed amongst, and between, the members and they were spontaneously inviting more of their friends to church. The whole church was involved and mobilized enthusiastically in this and other aspects of church life. Recognizing that any church building can assume excessive importance over the spiritual life of that community, on January 1, 1985, I announced that the theme for the church during that year would be the "dedication of the New Sanctuary" and I outlined five specific goals for KCKC: 1) the Word of Truth, 2) Evangelism, 3) Worship, 4) Peace and Harmony, and 5) Service and Humility.[48] Eventually, the new church building was dedicated on December 7, 1985, preceded by the church's first Holy Communion service on the new premises on November 15, 1985; this was a landmark in KCPC's history and demonstrated that it had recovered from the 1981 crisis.

Sociologically and culturally, Korean immigrants long to have their own buildings for church worship/activities and to feel freedom in using those facilities according to their own vision and goals. The following sample of KCPC Sunday attendance statistics shows that there was substantial church growth after the dedication of the new sanctuary:[49]

Date	Children Sunday School	Adult Sunday Worship	Offerings
October 6, 1985	N/A	426	$16,701.05
October 13, 1985	62	396	$9,075.80
October 20, 1985	97	394	$9,574.52
October 5, 1986	125	509	$9,122.48
October 12, 1986	124	504	$25,246.74
October 4, 1987	152	567	$11,617.56
October 11, 1987	166	609	$12,735.29
October 2, 1988	160	663	$13,407.66
October 9, 1988	169	691	$15,038.36
October 1, 1989	147	836	$17,099.21
October 8, 1989	172	839	$21,130.02

48. *KCPC Members Handbook*, January 1985

49. The following Sunday worship statistics were taken from KCPC Sunday Church Bulletins. The following statistics are the Sunday worship attendance for October of each year.

A Case Study of KCPC

| October 7, 1990 | 167 | 939 | $21,825.30 |
| October 14, 1990 | 201 | 997 | $24,261.09 |

From October 1991, the classification of the statistics for Sunday attendance was modified from the previous year. There were several other needs for youth and English-speaking young adults so the ministry was adjusted to meet their needs. The youth ministry was also divided into English-speaking youth and Korean-speaking youth ministries because recent immigrants preferred a Korean-speaking youth service. The English-speaking young adult group also became independent as the KPCC English Ministry. Living in a bilingual culture, two different ministries were necessary.

Korean-American immigrant history is comparatively shorter than that of other ethnic groups such as the Chinese and Japanese who have lived in the States for several generations. The first Chinese immigrants to the U.S. arrived in San Francisco in 1848. In 1870, their number increased to 60,000. In 1900, there were 25,000 Japanese living on the West Coast.[50] However, the Korean United Methodist Church of Greater Washington—the first Korean Church in Washington, D.C.—was founded only in 1951.[51]

English Language Ministry Provision

Aware of the cultural needs of Korean-American immigrants, including second generation young people, the leadership at KCPC resolved to provide a bi-lingual Korean-English youth service under the supervision of two new church elders; this project was launched on June 28, 1992 and David Yang briefly became the first Pastor of this English ministry. The goal of KCPC leadership was to develop this provision into an independent English language church in the Presbyterian Church in America. Pastor Raymond Chang then became the next English pastor and under him his congregation gradually became an independent church, although in fellowship, and co-operating, with KCPC. My vision was for this second-generation Korean-American Congregation to cease being one of KCPC's ministries and to become independent from its Korean parent as I anticipated that as an English language church it would mobilize itself well for world mission. Its members were well-trained professionals, financially secure and skillful in administration. However, in the area of spiritual maturity, they

---

50. Fong, *Pursuing the Pearl*, 52–54.
51. Kang, *History of the Korean Community*, 70.

Pastoral Leadership

still had much to learn from their Korean first-generation Christian leaders with regard to commitment and spirituality in the church. Culturally, there is often tension between first-generation Korean pastors in America and younger, second-generation Korean-American pastors with the latter wanting more independence and clearly viewing situations and thinking in radically different ways from that of their seniors. My response to resolving this tension was to achieve a highly functioning church system with both first and second-generation churches residing under the same umbrella. While each would be independent in governing its people, they would nevertheless co-operate where possible in fellowship together, although being within different presbyteries in the PCA. For example, a covenant is being established between KCPC and the English church with a willingness to serve together on the same campus and with mutual respect.

In these ways, some of the cultural and language tensions, even the question of identity for second generation Korean-Americans, were eased considerably and KCPC has been kept from unnecessary conflict and even division over these matters.

KCPC's Ministry: 1991-2003

KCPC had an annual growth rate of 29.42% from 1985 to 1990, an explosive growth rate that took place after the dedication of the new church building. *The Yearbook of American & Canadian Churches* from 2007 records the top 25 churches' annual growth rates, but the highest annual increase among these top ten denominations was 1.86 percent from the Assemblies of God and the highest decrease was 2.84 percent from the Presbyterian Church. Compared to these annual church growth rates in the United States, KCPC's annual church growth of 29.42 percent from 1985-90 was extraordinary. As the congregation reached higher numbers, the annual growth rate of KCPC was, however, minimized. The following sample and the average Sunday worship attendance according to KCPC's Sunday Worship Bulletin indicate the progress made by KCPC:[52]

Date	Children	Youth	Korean Youth	English Service	Korean Service
October 11	223	151	132	70	1061
October 10	N/A	185	112	167	1153
October 16	351	178	192	182	1192

52. KCPC Sunday worship bulletin of October 1992-1995.

A Case Study of KCPC

October 8	356	168	110	218	1421
October 13	470	164	117	193	1509
October 12	388	227	126	201	1540
October 11	425	211	118	197	1859
October 10	435	242	84	175	1923
October 8	517	242	105	345	2035
October 14	530	270	138	421	2565
October 13	480	248	109	436	2217
October 12	515	316	132	453	2507

October is the beginning of KCPC's fiscal year and is a special time for KCPC families because the Session appoints new church officers and announces any changes in church operations. Every church activity officially commences in October. Thus, I have deliberately chosen to take statistics from the month of October each year. The Sunday worship attendance statistics may not correctly reflect the health and the growth of the church but, however, they demonstrate the church's movement toward growth. The following statistics give a glimpse of KCPC's comprehensive activities and its growth:[53]

Year	Total number of Attendance	Growth Rate from the Previous Year
1993	1855	14.22% Increase
1994	2098	13.09% Increase
1995	2239	6.72% Increase
1996	2431	8.57% Increase
1997	2415	0.0066% Decrease
1998	2796	15.77% Increase
1999	2868	2.57% Increase
2000	3243	13.07% Increase
2001	3689	13.75% Increase
2002	3487	5.47% Decrease
2003	3862	10.77% Increase

---

53. All statistics were taken from the Sunday church bulletins of the appropriate Sunday in October of each year from 1993 through 2003.

Pastoral Leadership

The average annual growth rate between 1993 and 2003 was 8.45%; according to the 2007 *Yearbook of American and Canadian Churches*, the Catholic Church in the United States had a 1.94 percent increase which is the highest increase in church membership among all other denominations in the United States of America.

Peace and Unity in the Church

After the restoration of peace and unity following 1981, KCPC's congregation began to grow and take ownership of the church. The editorial committee of *The Thirty-Year Anniversary of KCPC* also emphasized unity and peace as one of the significant elements for the growth of KCPC:

> The Thirty-Year Anniversary of KCPC demonstrates that there has been some apparent characteristics for the church growth in the congregation: 1) Preaching the Word of God based on the evangelical theology of faith and training the Saints, 2) Strong emphasis on the long and short-term mission as the priority of the church's ministry, 3) Spiritual personal relationship between the senior pastor and the lay people, 4) Commitment of the lay people, 5) The unity and commitment of the Session members with Senior Pastor, and 6) Other elements like location of the church and growth of the immigrants.[54]

From 1981 to my retirement in 2003 and until the present time, I have experienced unity and the dynamic power of the Session together with the congregation through which the church has been continually growing. Especially in Korean immigrant churches in the United States, the process of change in receiving the senior pastor's successor often creates turmoil in the church and results in church divisions. If the retiring senior pastor has served the church for many years and been successful, three problems are likely to occur during the process of succession: the first may occur during the process of calling a new senior pastor, the second problem may be conflict between the new senior pastor and the retired pastor, and the third may be a struggle between the new senior pastor and the lay leadership.[55]

---

54. Paik, *Thirty-Year Anniversary*, 101–2.

55. One typical example is the case of the Oriental Mission Church. The church was founded by Rev. Dong Sun Lim, one of the most respected pastors among Korean immigrant churches, on July 26, 1970. Pursuing mission, education, and service as the church's essential goals, the church had grown to be one of the largest the Korean immigrant churches under Rev. Lim's outstanding pastoral leadership. Having been a greatly respected pastor, Rev. Lim did not have any problems in appointing his successor at his

A Case Study of KCPC

It is an unusual phenomenon for KCPC that the church has been continually growing after the leadership transition. Other Korean immigrant churches in the United States have been curiously watching the development of KCPC's transition of leadership to observe any negative impact. However, the statistics of the average Sunday worship attendance of October of each year demonstrate that KCPC has been continuously growing from 2003 to 2007 after the leadership transition.[56]

Date	Children	Youth	Agape	E. M.	K. M.	Total
October 12, 2003	515	316	132	453	2507	3923
October 10, 2004[A]	553	330	86	450	2755	4174
October 9, 2005[B]	591	328	108	511	2743	4281
October 8, 2006[C]	583	365	80	494	2825	4347
October 14, 2007[D]	654	332	105	509	2859	4459

A. The average Sunday attendance of October 2003 was 3863 and October 2004 was 4053. The growth rate from 2003–04 was a 4.9 percent increase.

B. The average Sunday worship attendance of October 2005 was 4217. The growth rate from 2004–05 was a 4.04 percent increase.

C. The average Sunday worship attendance of October 2006 was 4316. The growth rate from 200506 was a 2.34 percent increase.

D. The average Sunday worship attendance of October 2007 was 4313. The growth rate from 2006–07 was a 0.07 percent decrease.

After my retirement in 2003, the growth rates of Sunday worship attendance saw a 4.9 percent increase in 2004, 4.04 percent increase in 2005, 2.34 percent increase in 2006, and a 0.07 percent decrease in 2007 under the new senior pastor Danny Ro. The average annual growth rate from 2004–07 was, therefore, a 2.80 percent increase.

---

retirement in 1990 after twenty years of ministry. Rev. Byung Hee Lee became the next senior pastor after Rev. Lim's retirement. Rev. Lee was also an outstanding minister in his preaching, evangelistic training, and spiritual caring ministries. However, his tenure was terminated after three years in 1993. Dr. Kwang Chul Park was installed as the third senior pastor of Oriental Mission Church in 1993. He was also an outstanding preacher, scholar, and pastor. He, too, resigned from the church within six years. After Rev. Dong Sun Lim's successful retirement the church struggled for ten years until the current pastor, Joon Min Kang, became the fourth senior pastor in 2001.

56. These statistics are taken from the Sunday worship bulletin attendance report of each Sunday in October.

Pastoral Leadership

The ordered procedure of electing a pastor for the congregation is prescribed in the *Book of Church Order*,[57] in which the church needs to elect a pulpit committee by a congregational meeting before proceeding with electing a pastor. Often, churches experience congregational disputes and struggles during the process of pursuing the necessary steps for the election of the senior pastor. According to the *Book of Church Order*, there is no mandatory retirement age for ministers. The KCPC bylaw 6:19, however, designates that the senior pastor and associate pastor must retire by the age of 65. Realizing the difficulty of leadership transitions and my approaching retirement date, I had been carefully preparing a plan for my retirement to avoid any confusion before the Session. To the Session's surprise, on January 15, 2000, three years and eight months before my official retirement, I presented the issue of my retirement by recommending Pastor Danny Ro as the next senior pastor at the monthly Session meeting. I presented five ideal characteristics for my successor: 1) spiritual leader, 2) an evangelical, biblical, and powerful preacher, 3) bridge-builder between the first and second generations, 4) respected leader who possesses godly character, and 5) a pastor proven by previous ministries. I defended my reasons for my recommendation of Pastor Danny Ro:

a) He was equipped with all five conditions above

b) He would be a good mediator between the first and second generations

c) He could resolve the issue of the 5th Service on Sundays

d) He could handle the new sanctuary building and church relocation

e) He had great potential to form a good team with the current pastoral staff

f) He would be able to recruit pastoral staff for team ministry

g) He could solve the current problems within the Christian Education Department

h) He was 40 years old with 13 years of pastoral experience

It was difficult to find a single pastor who fulfilled all of KCPC's needs.[58] Pastor Danny Ro[59] had served KCPC from June 1987 to September 1991 as

57. Gilchrist, *Book of Church Order*, 23:2
58. KCPC Session, recorded on January 15, 2000.
59. Pastor Danny Changsoo Ro was born on January 15, 1960 in Korea and came to the United States as an immigrant with his parents when he was in junior high school. He belongs to the 1.5 generation among Korean immigrants in the United States. During his

A Case Study of KCPC

Education Pastor during which time he demonstrated his passion for youth ministry and was respected by parents and Session members for his devoted commitment and passionate preaching of the Word of God. On January 29, 2000, the Session passed a unanimous resolution to recommend Pastor Danny Ro as the next senior pastor at the annual congregational meeting.[60]

It was very unusual that all eighteen Session members unanimously approved the decision to propose Rev. Ro as the next senior pastor. The typical procedure in pastoral selection is to organize a pulpit committee according to the *PCA Book of Church Order* and have meetings for several months.[61] With the help of Christian newspaper announcements and recommendations from other sources the committee would make a list of candidates to review. Going through this laborious process the committee would most likely face frustrations and disputes. Even if the committee agrees to recommend a candidate to the congregational meeting, their request may not be granted.

On October 20, 2002, a year before my expected retirement, the Session recommended Pastor Danny Ro to the congregational meeting to elect him as the next senior pastor. Out of 559 members that attended the meeting, 554 members voted for Pastor Ro to be elected, a 99.1 percent approval rate. This is certainly an unusual outcome for the election of a senior pastor from a congregational vote. There are several reasons that explain this result. First of all, the Session was united under my leadership. Without unity and support of the Session, the new senior pastor cannot fulfill his potential in his pastoral ministry. Secondly, Pastor Danny Ro had already commended himself to Session members and the congregation during his service at KCPC from 1987–91, especially that he was a caring pastor and an excellent preacher. Thirdly, Session and congregation trusted and relied on my recommendation. For the past six years, Pastor Ro has been able to establish a trusting relationship with both the Session and congregation, allowing KCPC to continue to grow without any struggles.

---

undergraduate study at the University of California at Los Angeles (UCLA) he became a Christian and transferred to Biola University. After completing his undergraduate study he went to the Dallas Theological Seminary and graduated with a ThM degree in 1987.

60. Upon the KCPC Session's unanimous decision to recommend Pastor Danny Ro to the congregation as the next senior pastor after my retirement, Wayne Kim, the Session clerk, wrote an official letter of the Senior Pastor invitation to Pastor Ro on behalf of the Session members dated on February 5, 2000.

61. *The Book of Church Order* 20-2 allows that the Session can function as the pulpit committee.

Pastoral Leadership

Pastor Ro did not pursue a drastic change from my pastoral philosophy but modified its emphasis. Pastor Ro is continuing with KCPC's theme of Vision 2020, "Training the Saint to Transform the World" (Eph 4:12), which I presented first to the Session in 1994. Pastor Ro, however, emphasized worship and the small group as the two basic principles in his pastoral ministry. He presented "A Community of Disciples Soaring on Wings" to the congregation as KCPC's theme for 2008, reflecting that KCPC's community will be revitalized by the emphasis on worship and small groups.[62] For the past four years since my retirement, Pastor Ro has focused on training lay leaders for small groups. These leaders will become the main task force for the care ministry at KCPC, as well as his preaching ministry.[63] These two main focuses of his ministry have prevented other problematic issues. Under his new leadership, KCPC has been steadily growing because there is no conflict in his relationship with the former senior pastor.

In conclusion, this case study of KCPC demonstrates that pastoral leadership plays a key role in church life and growth. During KCPC's history from 1973 to 2007, three pastors, Myung Ho Yoon (1973–77), Won Sang Lee (1977–2003), and Danny Ro (2003–present), have served the church in their distinctive ways. There were three critical moments in 1977, 1981, and 2003, but each of these church crises, however, became a platform for church growth through steady pastoral leadership. The unity of the congregation, and harmony between the lay leaders and senior pastor created a strong synergy that allowed the congregation to be vitalized and to grow. The unity in the Holy Spirit through prayer was the key element for KCPC's exceptional growth. Building the sanctuary and education building in 1985 and 1994 provided a unique motivation for unity and commitment through which KCPC has been building a spirit of community and discipleship for evangelism and world mission. This study leads me to conclude that church growth depends on the pastoral leadership that brings unity between the

---

62. "The Disciples" is KCPC's monthly newsletter (October 2007, 26:1).

63. Pastor Danny Ro's Pastoral Letter to the Congregation included in the KCPC Annual Report on October 21, 2007. He stated that in preparing for the church relocation to Centreville, Virginia, he is going to emphasize two areas of KCPC's ministries in 2008. The first area of emphasis is worship. He will devote his time and energy to enhance spiritual worship through the ministry of the Holy Spirit so that the congregation may experience the full grace of God. The second area is to train the lay leaders for small group ministry, which will be an ongoing effort. He will be devoted to establishing KCPC's philosophy, strategies, and lay leader training.

lay leaders and the senior pastor through prayer, in order to achieve the essential mission of the church.

3

Pastoral Leadership Principles

HAVING DEFINED SOME KEY terms, including "pastoral leadership" in chapter one and then provided a case study of KCPC in chapter two, I now want to identify and discuss those key principles that influenced my ministry at KCPC. These principles, which are four in number, emerged gradually in my ministry and the pastoral problems experienced served to strengthen and articulate further these principles in my own mind.

LEADERSHIP

Before reflecting on these principles, it is necessary to refer again to the term "leadership" for it is a rather fluid and ambiguous term. Donald Dorr illustrates how the term can refer to a person empowered with directing a nation, a community, an organization or, more specifically, to the ability and performance of that person or persons.[1] Dorr's working definition of the term is precisely the way in which I have understood "leadership" in my ministry, namely as "the influencing, motivating, guiding, directing, or coordinating of individuals, groups, communities or organizations in a way that affects their behavior or actions, especially in relation to bringing about change or resisting change."[2] However, a warning is in order here. Steven Croft suggests that the term leader is often being used as a substitute for

---

1. Dorr, *Faith at Work*, 64; See also, Sanders, *Spiritual Leadership*, 27: "Leadership is influence, the ability of one person to influence others to follow his or her lead." See also, Gardner, *On Leadership*, 1: "Leadership is the process of persuasion or example." See also, Malphurs, *Being Leaders*, 11: "Leadership is all about influence."

2. Ibid., 64–65.

Pastoral Leadership Principles

terms such as priest, presbyter, minister or pastor and he advises that this should give us pause for thought because there are two dangers involved. One danger in substituting the word leader is that of creating a distance between a popular perception of what ordination involves and the church's own understanding of that ministry. A second danger is using a term that does not have any deep roots either in Scripture or in tradition. This would be misleading for the early church leaders used a number of titles but did so carefully and significantly to describe the varied aspects of the ordained minister's work. The title leader was not one of those terms they chose or favored.[3] Concerning the management models adopted by the church leaders, Croft expressed a warning:

> But when the insights gained from these worlds are adopted uncritically by the church, there are dangers. Pendulum swings are not always healthy. Today's under-emphasis easily becomes tomorrow's overstatement and broken dream. Uncritical adoption of management insights is not the answer to our need for a new paradigm of Christian ministry.[4]

Croft is not alone among contemporary theologians in warning against the danger of adopting secular models for pastoral leadership uncritically. I acknowledge, however, that there are different kinds of leaders as well as different styles and models of leadership; we can also learn, in varying degrees and ways, from most models. One of these models I want to refer to now for Gibbs and Bolger describe a model of pastoral leadership that is radically different from the one I used in KCPC.[5]

This model is common to that used in emerging churches. The latter title is often used as a general umbrella term to refer to numerous diverse churches and movements so it is far from easy obtaining a precise definition. Emerging churches do represent a rather fluid group of churches that are innovative, contemporary, developing, radical, postmodern, and reactive with regard to traditional and even newer churches. Gibbs and Bolger describe these emerging churches more precisely as "missional communities

---

3. Steven Croft, *Ministry in Three Dimensions*, 170–73.

4. Ibid., 27. In comparison of church size with industrial skill level in the secular world management Croft illustrated that church size of 1, 2–65, 66–150, 151–450, 451–1,000, and 1,000+ may correspond to unskilled worker, foreman, supervisor, middle management, top management, and chairman of the board accordingly. Croft, however, could not agree this idea as a biblical. See also, Gerkin, *Introduction to Pastoral Care*, 27.

5. Dorr, *Faith at Work*, 74–84.

Pastoral Leadership

arising from within postmodern culture and consisting of followers of Jesus who are seeking to be faithful in their place and time."[6] Their leaders do not always find it easy to identify themselves as they are rebuilding but in an open creative manner. Gibbs and Bolger for that reason are possibly correct in understanding these churches as being fragile and belonging to a disparate movement, which is so diverse and fragmented. Gibbs and Bolger remind us that emerging churches avoid all types of control in their leadership formation and there has been experimentation in developing leaderless groups.[7] One feature of this model is the radical re-interpretation of power and power structures within a church. Acknowledging the headship of Christ alone, and the absence of patriarchs in the New Testament churches, there has been a reaction to the hierarchical approaches to ecclesiastical power in many traditional churches and the emphasis on an individual minister or a group of elders who are able to wield power over the community of believers. Gibbs and Bolger claim that such an approach to control is a primary tool of modernity;[8] during modernity, the concept of believers actively participating with God was replaced by that of a commanding, powerful God who demanded complete obedience together with submission to his officers. On this new model, the priesthood of believers is applied without any hierarchical implications with consensus and persuasion as the dominant features of leadership. One emerging church leader in London undergirds this model theologically with reference to the intra-Trinitarian relations of the Father, Son, and Holy Spirit where he argues there is no hierarchy but complete equality and active, communal participation in decisions and activities[9] Theologically, however, what this leader does not take adequately into account is that within the equality and activity of the divine persons within the Holy Trinity there is also a principle in orthodox Trinitarian theology of subordination with regards to redemption in which the Son of God became incarnate and humbled himself to become a suffering and obedient servant while the Spirit of God functioned to glorify Christ in his person and work. Ecclesiastically, however, for the Emerging Church leader the equality of the intra-Trinitarian relations

6. Gibbs and Bolger, *Emerging Churches*, 28.

7. Ibid., 29.

8. Ibid., 193.

9. Ibid., 194. One of the leadership styles of the emerging churches is sharing the leadership with many rather than a few in the leadership group. They are opposed to any hierarchical understanding of leadership and claim that collective leadership produces a better result. They shift from the vision of the leader to the vision of all.

Pastoral Leadership Principles

means that all church members contribute significantly to the decision-making process. There is also emphasis on networking between members. Some emerging churches have even attempted what can be referred to as leaderless groups, which are strongly democratic, possibly originating in the 1960s counterculture and its deconstruction of hierarchical power structures.[10] Other factors contributing to such an approach would include bad experiences with "cultic" leaders with a heavy shepherding approach to members. Some emerging church leaders view this approach as being over-reactionary to experiences of poor leadership. Perhaps what is meant with regard to leaderless groups is the fluidity and flexibility of leadership rather than the absence of leaders.[11]

However, leadership in one form or another does emerge within these churches and that is acknowledged by numerous emerging church leaders like Paul Roberts in Bristol, Andy Thornton in Glasgow or Kester Brewin in London.[12] But what is different from modernity's control of power is that this type of leadership is not vested exclusively or permanently in one individual and changes are made in various local situations in terms of sharing the leadership but this is based on gifting, not power. Servanthood is at the root of this radical approach to pastoral leadership so that the power remains with the people. The practicalities in implementing this type of leadership are far from easy within a church context and reaching a consensus decision by the community requires patience, discipline and can involve agreement but also disagreement at varying levels. Similarly, even a team leadership will make their decisions in the community. Once a church grows numerically then there is a further problem of bridging the principle of consensus with that of representational leadership or delegated decision making. Networking, maximum sharing, and generous communication between members of the community are key factors in this context, if the church continues to grow without spinning off to form smaller congregations. Gibbs and Bolger then identify a wide range of functions that belong to pastoral leadership. Such leaders are facilitators of ministry rather than mediators, they use a "relational, decentralized approach" rather than a centralized one; they also create space for others to serve.

10. Ibid., 197.
11. Ibid., 198.
12. Ibid., 198. Paul Roberts, for example, states, "The leaderless idea came in part from Glasgow's Late Service, which was fiercely democratic, reflecting the Scottish Presbyterian model, and partly arose from the postmodern culture of the people who set it up." Andy Thornton also experienced this: "Shared leadership kept most people happy."

Pastoral Leadership

In addition, they equip missionaries rather than members, and emphasize spiritual direction rather than structures and authority with the aim of obtaining maximum participation in the community and its mission. There are significant differences in the emerging churches' concepts of leadership from that which belongs to the Presbyterian model; such differences include a strongly democratic, de-centralized emphasis, an open and fluid understanding of leadership where "authority" and structures are much less important. However, these differences can be exaggerated, too. For example, a classical Presbyterian model assumes and encourages the rights of church members to elect individuals to the offices of deacon, elder and minister. There is extensive corporate involvement in this process of such elections, which I will illustrate later with regard to KCPC. In addition, all members need to vote on a wide range of issues and matters relating to church life and ministry, including finance, building projects and the direction or development of the church's ministry. Presbyterian eldership ought always to encourage this maximum participation on the part of the church's community in this decision-making process. Again, Presbyterian elders and ministers ought to be elected on the basis of their gifting and integrity, not their social or financial status and as also having a proven attitude of servanthood in their lives, families and church involvement. A Presbyterian "session" of elders/minister will also understand their people well and win their willing support in pursuing appropriate policies. What is also pertinent within the Presbyterian model is that the eldership should not be hierarchical in allowing the minister unlimited powers of leadership; rather, within the session the elders will share responsibilities of oversight so that a team dynamic operates yet with respect for the gifting of the pastor as the servant set aside for public preaching of the Word and administration of the sacraments. Again, in Presbyterianism the Session or elders hold the key for leading and caring for the church as it is the governing body of the local church with the pastor, sometimes referred to also as a senior pastor, functioning within the Session as team leader. Unity and mutual respect as well as acceptance of each other's gifts are essential within the Session and after KCPC's 1981 crisis the Session became very supportive of the ministry and also united in their oversight of the church.

In contrasting the Presbyterian and emerging churches' models of pastoral leadership, I conclude that there are major differences but also similarities. Again, while my purpose in this comparison is not to disparage models of leadership that are being tested among the emerging churches,

Pastoral Leadership Principles

I want to stress that whether Presbyterian, Episcopal or Congregational models of leadership are used, what is of crucial importance are the principles which govern those appointed to leadership within those different structures and models.

I now turn to a discussion of those principles that I identified and used in my Presbyterian Church situation to meet the needs of the people committed to my pastoral care. The first principle will be that of caring for people. Sociologically, any society or institution will face problems due to the nature of people. The church is an assembly of imperfect people, and the church should therefore be constantly renewed and find ways to experience breakout growth. C. Peter Wagner also pointed out that the pastor's role is of utmost importance for a healthy and growing church. In regard to the seven vital signs of ecclesiastical good health, Wagner writes:

> 1. The pastor. What kind of a role must the pastor play if the church is to grow? 2. The People of the church. Is it possible for a church to grow if it has a perfect kind of pastor, but the wrong kind of people? How can the wrong kind of people become the right kind of people? 3. Church size. How big does a church need to be in order to be healthy and growing? 4. Structure and functions. 5. Homogeneous unit. 6. Methods. What kind of methods have proved to be effective instruments for evangelism in America today? 7. Priorities.[13]

These seven vital signs indicate that church growth depends to a large extent on pastoral leadership and the pastor's ability to identify and deal with any problem in the church by motivating and encouraging the congregation to actively participate in the ministry of God. The objective of this chapter is to explore my pastoral leadership principles by reflecting on my twenty-six years of pastoral ministry at KCPC.

1. Caring for People

As I articulate this first pastoral leadership principle, I am aware of Charles Gerkin's repost that pastoral care in the twentieth-century "must find new ways to give equal emphasis to concerns for the individual and concern for the larger social environment that surrounds the individual."[14] In other words, the earlier sharper division between an exclusive type of pietistic individualism and the so-called Social Gospel committed primarily to the

---

13. Wagner, *Your Church Can Grow*, 35.
14. Gerkin, *Introduction to Pastoral Care*, 90.

Pastoral Leadership

relief of humanitarian needs by churches must be reduced but preferably removed. In this respect, Gerkin draws attention to the need for two essential features, namely, the art of listening and also the "capacity to observe," particularly with regard to the social environment of those subject to our care in the churches. Even more exciting for me was Gerkin's reminder of the contemporary "rediscovery" of the congregation as a major context and agent for the care of God's people.[15] It is for Gerkin a "rediscovery" because of changing emphases in pastoral care and also the fact that individual pastoral care has been the main emphasis in recent decades. The communal aspect, therefore, is important and new studies of the congregation are welcomed so I am more encouraged to articulate from my experience this principle of caring for people.

I began my ministry at KCPC with fourteen families who had just experienced the trauma of a church division. They were angry, disillusioned, emotionally wounded and in desperate need of encouragement and pastoral care. James P. Wind and James W. Lewis remind us that this is a natural and common response to conflict. They write:

> The pain of a congregational schism, the feelings of betrayal remaining after a pastor suddenly resigns, the cynicism lingering after a congregational scandal, and many other memories often go unmentioned in daily congregational discourse. Yet those repressed memories, hiding under the façade of amnesia, can powerfully shape a community's life.[16]

In the aftermath of conflict and division with lingering and painful memories and attitudes on the part of the remaining members, my convictions concerning the necessity of caring for people both within and outside the church were strengthened and tested.

Pastoral care, however, should be understood as a comprehensive term in pastoral ministry.[17] In regard to the care-giving aspect of pastoral ministry, Paul E. Johnson stated, "A pastor is a religious leader who understands and individually cares for his (or her) people to whom they

---

15. Ibid., 91–92.
16. Dudley et al., *Carriers of Faith*, 26.
17. Bloede, *Effective Pastor*, 86–87. Bloede defines the term pastoral care and counseling that: "Pastoral care should be seen as a broader, more comprehensive ministry than the traditional counseling relationship in which one person counsels another. All pastoral counseling is a form of pastoral care, but not all pastoral care involves counseling. For example, the worship life of the congregation may be seen as a form of pastoral care, but it is quite different from a counseling session in the pastor's study."

Pastoral Leadership Principles

return for the health of their souls."[18] Pastoral care involves caring for the well-being of the congregation physically as well as spiritually. Concerning people-centered ministry, Derek Tidball rightly stated:

> The minister is a servant. This minister is person centered. He is always available and much loved. He has a profound influence on the community, since in his frequent visiting nothing ever seems too much trouble for him and his interests and patience seem to know no bounds. Some aspects of his ministry may suffer. For example, he may not devote sufficient attention to sermon preparation and therefore deliver half-baked ideas from the pulpit from time to time. But his people are willing to overlook that deficiency in the light of his excellent pastoral skills. His sustenance comes from being wanted and his support comes from fellow ministers.[19]

The core concept of pastoral ministry is relational and people-centered. Ministry starts from one's heart, building genuine friendships with congregation members through love and compassion. Creating intimate relationships allow for genuine understanding between the pastor and the congregation, allowing the pastor to effectively reach the hearts of those he serves. Pastoral ministry is essentially relational—paradoxically both people-centered and Christ-centered, and then practical and compassionate. Like Andrew Purves, I agree that shepherding is a key biblical model for pastoral ministry and central to it is tender, solicitous care directed toward healing in some regard. The parable of the Good Samaritan is, therefore, a fundamental theological explanation of pastoral care. Caring for people as a pastor involves visitations and face-to-face communication. Purves defines pastoral care in the following way:

> The essential meaning of shepherding is given in the parable of the Good Samaritan. The mode of response to need is appropriate to the situation; thus when healing is required, shepherding is an appropriate response. The biblical base is secured for Hiltner[20] by illustration of the shepherd who goes in search of the one sheep

---

18. Johnson, *Psychology of Pastoral Care*, 21.
19. Tidball, *Skillful Shepherds*, 320.
20. Hiltner, *Preface to Pastoral Theology*, 64. Hiltner states that "the traditional aspects of shepherding have been three: discipline, comfort, and edification." Contrary to these traditional view he suggests that "we shall propose the substitution of: healing, sustaining, and guiding."

Pastoral Leadership

that is lost. Central to shepherding is tender, solicitous care directed toward healing in some regard.[21]

Shepherding is a comprehensive ministry, which involves providing spiritual as well as spiritual care so that the whole person can recover. Pastoral care starts with immediate visitation of those in need as exemplified by Christ's earthly ministry. In light of this basic assumption regarding pastoral care, I developed the Home-Visitation Ministry (HVM) at KCPC when I assumed my pastoral duty in 1977. This ministry continued for twenty-six years until my retirement in 2003.

Seward Hiltner argues that pastoral theology arises from an exploration using the shepherding perspective; communication and organizing are two other perspectives that are "cognates" with shepherding for Hiltner.[22] Emphasizing the important concept of shepherding in pastoral theology, Hiltner explains, "Pastoral theology is a formal branch of theology resulting from study of Christian shepherding, that it is just as important as biblical or doctrinal or historical theology."[23] I will refer later in the chapter to the shepherding model. In addition to having to care for the families following immediately the 1977 church division, there was the complex factor of a Korean immigrant community in the United States with all its variegated struggles and problems. Some background is necessary at this point in order to appreciate the "social environment" of those I cared for in the church and community.

The Korean immigrant churches in the Unites States were very unique from the start. On January 13, 2003, Korean-Americans celebrated the centennial Korean immigration to the United States, and President George W. Bush proclaimed:

> Now, therefore, I, George W. Bush, President of the United States of America, by virtue of the authority vested in me by the constitution and laws of the United States, do hereby proclaim January 13, 2003, as the Centennial of Korean immigration to the United States. I call upon all Americans to observe the anniversary with appropriate programs, ceremonies, and activities honoring Korean immigrants and their descendants for their countless contributions to America.

---

21. Purves, *Reconstructing Pastoral Theology*, xxxi.
22. Woodward and Pattison, *Pastoral and Practical Theology*, 28–29.
23. Ibid., 28.

Pastoral Leadership Principles

During the course of one hundred years, Korean immigrants have had to persevere through many struggles and difficulties. Of the first 102 Korean immigrants who arrived in the U.S. to work on a Hawaiian sugar plantation on January 13, 1903, 50 were Christians from Naeri Methodist Church founded by Rev. Henry G. Appenzeller who went to Korea as the first Protestant missionary on April 5, 1885. Naeri Methodist Church commissioned Seung Ha Hong as their first missionary to care for the first immigrants to Hawaii.[24] The early immigrants did not work under pleasant conditions. "Between 1900 and 1905, in hopes of making enough money to return to Korea and enjoying relatively comfortable lives, approximately 7,000 Korean immigrants found work laboring under harsh conditions for long hours on sugar plantations or as cooks, janitors, and launderers at subsistence wages within the confines of the plantations."[25]

Currently, there are about two million Korean immigrants living in the United States and about 3,800 Korean churches; it represents one Korean church per 500 Koreans in the United States as compared with one church per 750 Americans. However, seventy percent of Korean churches in the United States have fewer than one hundred members who usually all experience difficulties in adjusting to the language, culture, employment and even have problems raising their children due to the generational and cultural gaps. However, Korean immigrant churches in the United States tend towards rapid church growth. One sociological reason for this is that Koreans belong to a unified race rather than diversified ethnic groups. Another reason is that the Korean church normally serves as a community and cultural center where people can relax using their native language and following their own customs in an alien situation. The danger, as I have seen, is that of majoring on these aspects to the neglect of biblical teaching and discipleship training. I will refer to this aspect of the problem later in the chapter.

Returning to the immediate challenge of facing up to the consequences of the 1977 church division on my small Korean congregation, I began to work out in detail my principle concerning pastoral care for the people.

Home-Visitation Ministry

In retrospect, I find encouragement from what Gerkin affirms concerning those involved in pastoral care within a congregation. While the care given

---

24. Kim, *Naeri Methodist Church Handbook*, 6–118.
25. Jo, *Korean Immigrant*, 2.

Pastoral Leadership

by the pastor is essential and influential, Gerkin rightly emphasizes that in many ways it is "secondary to the care informally given and received among fellow believers within the community of faith. It is the work of all members of the community."[26] I endeavored to develop the communal model of pastoral care within my church.

One immediate decision made in assuming my duties as pastor in 1977 was to develop the Home-Visitation Ministry (HVM) and this continued throughout my ministry there. Initially, I visited each of the fourteen families at least on alternate weeks to encourage and develop a close pastoral relationship. I then needed to prioritize in terms of emergencies—new members and those who were known to have spiritual or more practical and pressing needs. Initially, only my wife and I undertook this work but as the church grew, other team members were added. Before long, due to steady numerical growth in the size of the congregation, HVM was undertaken more by other team members and I was involved in more specialized as well as seasonal visitation. To assist me, Lay Visitation Teams (LVT) were organized and trained. Within Korean culture, home visitation by the senior pastor is highly welcomed and so I continued in HVM alongside, and complementary to, the LVT. Within this context of on-going pastoral care, there was a steady increase in the number of family units and baptized members in the church. For example, 175 new families were added in 1995 alone with as many as 281 families added in 2001 and 355 families in 2005. Because of this phenomenal growth, HVM was expanded and the church appointed a visitation pastor to specialize and direct in this aspect of ministry. A further development was the creation of smaller groups into which members of the congregation were placed for purposes of fellowship and encouraging missionary support. For example, in 2007 there were fifty-one groups organized by age and consisting of thirty to fifty people or more in each group, which had its own committee, but with support from the church Session. These groups helped to vitalize the whole church through improving personal relationships between members, providing a further network of spiritual support as well as fostering missionary prayer and interest. Creating, supervising, training, and enriching these mission groups became one of KCPC's main pastoral responsibilities. I was aware that Christian A. Schwarz advocated holistic small groups within churches as an important ingredient for church growth. His extensive research revealed that small group activity is a crucial element in church growth because it

---

26. Gerkin, *Introduction to Pastoral Care*, 102.

Pastoral Leadership Principles

promotes multiplication of groups. His *Natural Church Development: A Guide to Eight Essential Qualities of Healthy Churches* gave special attention to the pastors in the United States. The sixth principle out of the eight is "Holistic Small Groups." Schwarz stated:

> Our research in growing and declining churches all over the world has shown that continuous multiplication of small group is a universal church growth principle. Furthermore, it has also disclosed what life in these small groups should be like if they are to have a positive effect on both quality and numerical growth within a church. They must be holistic groups that go beyond just discussing Bible passages to applying it message to daily life. In these groups, members are able to bring up those issues and questions that are immediate personal concerns.[27]

Holistic small groups is considered to be the most important ingredient for church growth because they encompasses worship, Bible study, fellowship, counseling, evangelism, service, discipleship, missions, cell division, as well as other church activities. If the holistic small group is sound and mature, church growth follows naturally. Schwarz's research group processed 4.2 million surveys and discovered that small group activity is the most crucial element for church growth because the church grows through the multiplication of small group (cell) division.[28] Emphasizing the importance of the small group, Schwarz also points out "the quality of the small group depends literally on the qualification of its leader"[29] in the process of implementation. A pastor's task is, therefore, to discover laypersons with the gift of pastoring. I agree with Schwarz when he stated:

> The most important gift that a small group leader should bring to this ministry is the gift of pastoring. This gift enables people to shoulder the long-term responsibility for the spiritual and personal welfare of a group of people. Our research indicates that this is one of the most widespread spiritual gifts, but it is often not exercised because of misconception that pastoral ministry belongs to the classical tasks of a pastor.[30]

For the continuing growth of the small group ministry, the main task is to install ongoing training program: "The best method for continually raising

27. Schwarz, *Natural Church Development*, 32.
28. Ibid., 33.
29. Schwarz, *Implementation Guide*, 97.
30. Ibid.

Pastoral Leadership

up leaders for future groups is to first appoint possible candidates as apprentice leaders."[31]

According to Peter Wagner's three functional divisions of the whole church, (Celebration + Congregation + Cell = Church), the cell (small group) is the foundation of the church. If the foundation is not strong enough, the entire structure is at danger of collapsing. Concerning the function and necessity of the cell group, Wagner also emphasized:

> It is possible to fellowship with eighty other people, but it is not possible to enter into the deeper kind of interpersonal relationships that are necessary to meet another important set of human needs. The cell, sometimes called a small group, is a very special relationship. It is so close to a family situation that I like to call it a kinship circle to contrast it from the membership circle and the fellowship circle.[32]

The small cell group is foundational for Wagner because it is a very special relationship; it is so close to a family situation. This encouraged me in further promoting these smaller groups in KCPC; currently, the Home-Cell groups are organized on the basis of locality but they have been reduced to no more than five to ten family units each in order to provide even more intimate and effective fellowship and support for one another. They meet once or twice a month for a worship as well as intimate fellowship with one another. However, alongside these smaller groups, I recognized the need also to disciple and train the laity even more and I decided to introduce the Discipleship Training for the Laity (DTL), which continued until I retired. My successor continued this program and he re-affirmed Vision 2020: "Training the Saints to Transform the World," which I had initiated in 1994.[33]

---

31. Ibid., 98.

32. Wagner, *Your Church Can Grow*, 123.

33. During my fasting retreat in 1994, God placed in my mind Vision 2020: "Training the Saints to Transform the World" based on Eph 4:12 which states, "To prepare God's people for works of service, so that the body of Christ may be built up." The best way to care for people is to train them to become mature disciples of Christ. The church should be a training center for lay people as well as for the clergy. Vision 2020 has a double meaning, which indicates the year 2020 as well as 20/20 perfect eyesight. Jesus first demonstrated this vision through his three years of training the twelve disciples: "Follow me and I will make you fishers of men" (Matt 4:19). I had a clear vision of caring for people, my first pastoral leadership principle, by training the committed disciples of Christ, and in turn, letting them care for their own flocks in the Home-Cell ministry.

Pastoral Leadership Principles

Different Ministries of Caring

I recognized that caring for people requires meeting, as far as possible, the practical, social, emotional, cultural and spiritual needs of the people and so a number of different ministries were established in KCPC to meet these varied needs.

Biblical Counseling Foundation (BCF) was introduced to KCPC in 1991 with the purpose of training biblical counselors to become even more mature Christians; it offers a basic study course of twenty-four weeks with opportunities and guidance in self-reflection. Care for the church needs to be expressed in other ways, as well as the fact that some members require friendship and support. After the initial training of six persons in the church, KCPC initiated the Stephen Ministry for laypersons. Following fifty hours of training in the church, thirty-five Stephen Ministers were assigned to practice within the congregation in September 1997. This was an exciting ministry in which the trained individuals functioned as careworkers listening to, and encouraging lonely, needy people.

In addition, the pastoral care was extended to the elderly in even more detail. For first generation immigrants, it is a normal work pattern to be away from home for many hours while aged parents care for the grandchildren. They too have needs and, after consultations with members, KCPC launched "Central Senior Center" initially for church members on a one-day weekly basis. Because of the considerable needs among the aged in the community, this service was extended and numbers attending increased considerably. While there was a didactic element to the program, many other practical subjects and activities were included in the program with lunch provided. About seventy volunteers from the church were involved in this ministry and in November 2001, the KCPC received the Virginia Governor's Award for Excellence in Service and also the presidential Award of the Republic of Korea for outstanding service in the community at the Washington Korean Embassy in January 2003. Between 1994 and 2000, numbers attending the Center had increased from 134 to 547. Regular attendees consist of only 35 percent from KCPC and the others are from the community and some other churches. For this reason, Fairfax County also recognized and supported us by providing six Fast Tran Buses for the seniors and meal service aid.

Another unique caring ministry in KCPC is the "Mutual Aid Association," which organizes aid for the funeral expenses of members. For immigrants in the United States especially, the funeral is a very important issue

Pastoral Leadership

for the family as funeral expenses can be high in the country. As at September 2007, the total membership in this Association reached 1,220 members and averaged ten thousand dollars to the deceased family, which covers all funeral expenses, and to date 180 families have benefited. In this way again, the church has gained a reputation of caring for people. A similar program for the aged is to offer a burial lot on a site that KCPC purchased, which is a great comfort for the aged and their families.

I have illustrated the way in which my major principle of pastoral leadership involved caring for people in a genuine, practical way which covered all major areas of human need which a church can be legitimately and realistically involved in. Above all, and through all these practical ministries, the aim is to provide Christian teaching from the Word and to indicate the relevance of the Christian gospel for contemporary Korean immigrants in the United States. The expression of my principle of caring for people has developed significantly during the ministry so it has been expressed in many different ways. Initially, in the early months, I did most of the caring for the few families in the church with the help of my wife and slowly the circle of people involved in visitation and caring increased as the church grew. The principle of caring for people was with me throughout as I initiated new avenues to express that care and engage with people in their different and rather urgent needs. I regard this as a foundational principle and without which the public teaching ministry would have been far less effective.

Although I disagree with the radical definition of church in Eddie Gibbs's *Emerging Churches*,[34] I do agree that the church is a family, not merely an institution and the church family is primarily about relationships. He writes:

> Church as family is primarily about relationships. It is not about meetings, or structures. Such rubric questions do not make sense when discussing relational issues. The alternative family structure of emerging churches seeks a sort of family commitment. People are part of a kingdom community even if they don't get their needs met and often whether they feel like it or not. "I believe the commitment is relational more than institutional. Emerging people commit to one another and to God, and that commitment is deep and lasting. We are stuck together as family, even if we don't like one another" (Andrew Jones, Boaz, UK).[35]

---

34. Gibbs and Bolger, *Emerging Churches*, 27–34.
35. Gibbs and Bolger, *Emerging Churches*, 97.

Pastoral Leadership Principles

Theologically, I am unwilling to reject traditional church forms and structures as the emerging churches suggest for the change of such forms may only be a product of a cultural and even generational bias. However, emerging churches do raise questions about the nature of the church, which are relevant today, whatever structure or polity is accepted. They do not have the monopoly of working for genuine and close relationships between members within the congregation and pastoral care should, whatever its form or structure, work hard to build a community of believers who are cared for, not only by the clergy, but by the whole church.

2. Pastor's Character: Integrity and Spirituality

My second principle relating to pastoral leadership in KCPC concerns the integrity of character, as well as the spiritual, prayerful, and humble lives of church leaders. I want to discuss this principle in three related ways in order to highlight its importance.

Context

By this, I am referring to the context of Korean-American churches and here one is able to recognize more clearly the necessity and relevance of integrity and spirituality amongst pastoral leaders. This context relating to integrity can be illustrated in several ways. First, among Asiatic peoples there is a growing and general lack of respect and honor shown towards leaders. In Korea, for example, this is surprising for the general cultural attitude traditionally has been to respect the elderly and those in authority. Confucianism has also served to enforce this principle. For example, Confucianism encourages courtesy alongside its feudal ethic of three bonds or principles involving ruler/subject, parents/children/husband/wife, and young/old people. This ethic is partly expressed in the considerable status accorded to the senior pastor of a Korean Protestant church, especially Presbyterian and the authority he exercises. However, the more recent history and culture of Korea and other Asiatic countries reveal the constant changes and divisions that have occurred due to unstable or corrupt leadership. To some degree, Korean-American congregations have developed the same critical attitude and this is illustrated in the regular conflicts and divisions of Korean-American churches in the Greater Washington, D.C area from 1974 to 2007.

Suk Hee Yoo, publisher of *Hankook Ilbo* (a daily Korean newspaper), informed me that from his examination of these churches he is able to

Pastoral Leadership

identify two main reasons for all the conflicts that have occurred within them. One reason is the undiscerning attitude of those who support the pastor; they tend to support the pastor out of personal loyalty rather than with a good understanding of principles. This in itself contributes to confusion and conflict in churches. A second reason he identified is that many pastors are unqualified theologically for leadership and they also have numerous character failings. According to Yoo, the pastor's personal integrity, both in the church and the community, is the most important factor in maintaining the stability and growth of a Korea-American church. I agree with Yoo—Korean immigrants struggle for survival in the community, at home, and in the church and they are searching for leaders whom they can trust and respect as good models. If the people are disillusioned in this respect and lose respect, then divisions and related problems normally occur within those churches. I want to add to Yoo's analysis by broadening it and referring to the church situation in Korea itself and its religiously pluralist context, which has contributed significantly to the Korean mindset. Shamanism, for example, existed in Korea from the earliest days and it was the religious context in which foreign religions like Buddhism, Confucianism, and Christianity emerged. Although it was influenced by these other religions, Shamanism continues to influence peoples' lives—especially the lower classes—and forms the strata of the Korean mindset.[36] One influence of Shamanism on Christianity in Korea has been the emphasis on present blessing, which in turn encourages selfishness and introspection with a tendency to regard lightly group or church interests in the desire to obtain short-term gain and success. Again, Korean Buddhism has tended towards introspection with little interest or desire to contribute to, and transform, society. On the other hand, Confucianism's ideal of filial piety has engendered a family orientated egotism, which increasingly disregards the greater interests both of the church and society. This has also given rise to what is referred to in Korea as church individualism. This is a reference to the prioritizing of local church needs and activities over other churches, even its own denomination. Not only does this result in competitiveness, which is a serious problem among Presbyterian churches in Korea and also among Korean-America congregations, but it also has contributed to the emergence of mega-churches inheriting pastorates (from father to son or nephew) and church divisions.[37]

36. Song, "Analysis of Schism," 222.
37. Ibid., 228–38.

Pastoral Leadership Principles

Stephen Warner, in his research into Korean immigrant churches in the U.S., points to several key factors that contribute significantly to problems within these churches. He draws attention to the fact that 70 percent of U.S. Koreans are church members. This in itself need not be a negative factor. However, Warner's research reveals that a large proportion of these church members are only nominal Christians and have no vital Christian testimony and commitment to Christ or desire to show integrity of character in church life. He also refers to their high educational attainments and expectations, an aggressive survival spirit, a proud individualism that lacks concern for the church as a group in favor of individual preferences. Warner also discerned amongst these immigrants an aggressive competitive attitude, which often does not hesitate to divide a church and further the interests of some individuals, possibly a leader within the church.[38] In addition to these factors mentioned by Warner, I want to refer also to the distinctive trait of hastiness conveyed by the Korean words *palli-palli* ("quickly, quickly"). This hastiness is applied to all areas of life and the aim is to finish a task quickly, and often despite inferior workmanship or lack of careful thought and planning. I would add another factor, namely, "church shopping" which is popular among Korean immigrants. This is a common pattern in which Korean-American immigrant churchgoers visit different churches for a long period of time before finally settling in a church. Their concerns are various. For example, the quality of the preaching and pastoral care, church facilities and location, warmth of welcome, worship style, and provision for children and young people. Korean immigrants can therefore be quite mobile and lack commitment to a local church. Unless there is a clear example of integrity by the pastor and elders then the leadership cannot survive within this type of immigrant community. Interestingly, there are no recorded instances of Korean-American churches that have not had at least one division since their formation.

Another difficult area is the relationship between the retired minister and his young successor because there are few role models to follow. This has been a common problem in many Korean-American churches, namely, that the retired pastor continues in the church but contributes significantly to a breakdown in the relationship or even a church division over their respective opinions and attitudes. Rev. Danny Ro, my successor, and I have been aware of this danger and we continue to pursue a biblical model like Timothy and Paul's relationship in the New Testament, despite

---

38. Warner, "Korean Immigrant Church," 30.

Pastoral Leadership

my twenty-six years ministry in the church and the warm relationship I have with many of the church members. We are monitoring the relationship carefully in a genuine, mutual desire to maintain the good relationship Pastoral leadership must be transparent as an example to the whole church.

Brief Ministries

Reflecting on the fourteen Korean-American churches in the Greater Washington, D.C. area when I began my pastoral ministry in 1977, I suggest that, in particular, pastoral leadership and personal integrity have been essential factors contributing to church growth. When I began my pastoral ministry at KCPC in 1977, it had the lowest church membership, Sunday attendance, and annual budget among the fourteen Korean churches in the Greater Washington, D.C. area.[39] Analyzing these churches from a leadership perspective from 1977 to 2007, there is compelling evidence that pastoral leadership influenced the congregations extensively. From 1951 to 1977, these fourteen Korean churches were established as the Korean community grew through the arrival of new Korean immigrants, students, diplomats, journalists, business-related people and others to the area. Observing changes in these fourteen churches over the past thirty years, I have identified the following data relevant to pastoral leadership principles and for church growth both quantitatively and qualitatively:

1. The Korean United Methodist Church of Greater Washington, D.C. (1951)
2. The Korean Baptist Church of Washington (1955)
3. The Korean Presbyterian Church of Washington (1965)
4. The Korean United Presbyterian Church of Washington (1969)
5. Virginia Korean Baptist Church (1972)
6. The Korean Presbyterian Church of Maryland (1972)
7. The Korean Central Presbyterian Church (1973)
8. The First Korean Presbyterian Church of Maryland (1973)
9. Global Mission Church (1974)
10. The Korean Presbyterian Church of Northern Virginia (1975)
11. The Korean Nazarene Church (1976)[40]

39. Kang, *History of the Korean Community*, 70–81
40. Kang, *History of the Korean Community*, 78. The Korean Nazarene Church was

Pastoral Leadership Principles

12. The Korean Baptist Church of Montgomery (1977)[41]
13. Seoul Presbyterian Church (1977)[42]
14. McLean Korean Presbyterian Church (1977)

Note that the dates in brackets after each church refers to the year in which the church was first established. Analyzing statistics from these fourteen churches, Yoo Kyung Ko compiled a report, entitled "A Comparative Analysis of the Interrelation of the Pastoral Leadership and the Church Growth."[43] This research surveyed all fourteen churches and involved field interviews with all the pastors/church leaders individually and confidentially. This survey confirms that the senior pastor's pastoral leadership principles and also length of service in the pastorate played a significant role in a church's health and growth or otherwise.

	Present Senior Pastor[A]	Annual Budget (Units: $10,000)	Number of Attendance[B]	Year Established	
1.	7th (2)	250	1,400 (400)	1951	4
2.	9th (9)	50	260 (60)	1956	5
3.	5th (1.5)	80	430 (90)	1965	5
4.	4th (6)	20	150 (35)	1969	4
5.	4th (4)	85	330 (110)	1972	3
6.	5th (6)	25	135 (20)	1972	5
7.	3rd (4)	600	4500 (1500)	1973	3
8.	2nd (4)	50	220 (30)	1973	2
9.	3rd (14)	400	2100 (500)	1974	3
10.	2nd (4)	30	150 (50)	1975	2
11.	2nd (15)	75	300 (100)	1976	2
12.	4th (5)	22	100 (20)	1977	3

---

founded by Rev. James Young-Yong Kim in 1977 and Rev. Kwang Ho Yang became the second pastor in 1992. The church's name was changed to The Korean Church of Fairfax.

41. Ibid., 79. The Korean Baptist Church of Montgomery was founded by Rev. Seung Hak Kim in 1977, who retired in 1989 after twelve years of ministry.

42. Ibid., 80. The Seoul Presbyterian Church was founded on September 18, 1077 by Rev. Myung Ho Yoon who was the founding pastor of KCPC in 1973 and left KCPC with two-thirds of the members of the church. After founding Seoul Presbyterian Church, he also left within six months; this church underwent many difficulties without a pastor. Until the current pastor Rev. Jae Dong Kim was installed as the seventh pastor, the church has been experiencing new vitality and growth.

43. Ko, "Comparative Analysis."

Pastoral Leadership

| 13. | 9th (18) | 120 | 850 (250) | 1977 | 8 |
| 14. | 3rd (1.5) | 83 | 310 (50) | 1977 | 2 |

A. This number indicates the number of years the senior pastor has served the church and the senior pastor's order since the founding of the church.

B. This number indicates the average Sunday attendance including children. The number in parenthesis indicates the number of children attending on Sundays.

I also have established that there were no sociological, political, or environmental catastrophes of major significance, which may have contributed to unusual church growth or activity in the community between 1977 and 2007. Evaluating the data surveyed, KCPC stands out in terms of church growth and multiplied 100 times during the this period. Besides KCPC (7), the Global Mission Church (9)[44] and the Korean United Methodist Church of Greater Washington (1)[45] also stand out among the fourteen churches. Both churches recognize the contributions of their senior pastors who served with exceptional pastoral leadership. For example, the Rev. Dong Won Lee[46] of Global Mission Church (GMC) was one of the most prominent preachers among Korean pastors both in Korea and in the United States. He served GMC for as long as ten years (1983–93) during which time the church grew rapidly. His fresh, powerful expository preaching satisfied people who were searching for a biblical but dynamic spirituality. In 1993, Rev. Lee returned to Seoul to plant the Global Mission Church, which now has grown to over ten thousand members under his leadership. His current ministry there spans fifteen years.

Regarding the Korean United Methodist Church of Greater Washington (KUMC), Rev. Young Jin Cho[47] was recognized as a humble person

---

44. Kang, *History of the Korean Community*, 76–77. The Global Mission Church is affiliated with the Southern Baptist Convention in the United States and was established in 1974. Rev. Dong Won Lee served the Church from 1983 to 1993 during which time the church has grown amazingly.

45. Ibid., 70–71. The Korean United Methodist Church of Greater Washington was the first Korean church to be established in the Greater Washington, D.C. area in 1951. Rev. Young Jin Cho was installed as the sixth pastor in 1983 and retired in 2005. During his ministry for twenty-two years (1983–2005) the church has expanded by dedicating a new sanctuary in 1990 and became a model church in the Korean community under Rev. Cho's pastoral leadership.

46. Ibid., 76–77.

47. Ibid., 70–71.

Pastoral Leadership Principles

with a godly character; his exemplary life was a great challenge to people, as he served the church and community. He was a quiet man, but his life and integrity influenced not only his own congregation but also the leadership of his denomination. Retiring from KUMC after as much as twenty-two years of service, he was appointed Bishop of the Arlington District of the United Methodist Church in 2005. Analyzing the history of GMC and KUMC, Rev. Lee's outstanding preaching ministry and consistent character and Rev. Cho's humble, gracious character were the two fundamental principles in their fruitful pastoral ministries. The results from this survey also support my own pastoral leadership principles at KCPC, and particularly here integrity of character. I also want to emphasize in this context that very few Korean-American church pastors have continued their pastorates for a lengthy period; in fact, their short-term ministries have not been helpful to the churches. Thomas S. Rainer's research, for example, discovered that the average tenure recorded from the national survey of Protestant pastors in the United States is only 3.6 years, while pastors of the "break-out" churches, referred to in chapters one and two, had an average tenure of 21.6 years.[48] This statistic is especially relevant to Korean-American churches. For example, Pastor Yoon, who founded KCPC, left the church under four years but also left his next church, which he had established under sad circumstances, after only five months. Other examples can be given of this trend for some pastors to serve only briefly in a pastorate before moving elsewhere.

Integrity

This context of relational issues between pastors and congregations demands integrity of character on the part of pastors and church elders, if they are to care for the church and lead it in a helpful, biblical manner. Charles V. Gerkin draws attention to this fact and argues that the theme of pastoral care throughout church history has "consistently been paralleled with another theme, namely, that of the pastor as caretaker of the moral life of the people."[49] He reminds us that this was the primary self-image of the Old Testament prophets then of both Jesus in the Gospels and Paul in his pastoral writings. I have observed that the congregation honors and respects its pastor not because of his skill or eloquence, but rather his consistently godly character and his own care for their moral welfare. I realized that my

---

48. Rainer, *Breakout Churches*, 56–57.
49. Gerkin, *Introduction to Pastoral Care*, 85.

Pastoral Leadership

congregation did not remember what I preached, but did remember and respect my personal character. In regard to a leader's character, personal integrity is the most important part in relation to the trust of the congregation. Henry Blackaby, in confirming this point, states that:

> The fact that integrity is mutually desired by both employers and employees should come as no surprise. Leadership is ultimately based on trust. Since people choose to follow leaders they trust, their confidence must have a foundation. The foundation is honesty.[50]

Croft expresses the point even more strongly: "At the heart of becoming a Christian leader is integrity: a wholeness of life and consistency between the faith we profess and the lives we lead. Integrity is more important than any gifts or skills that we might have been given."[51]

In recent years, the integrity of the clergy has become an important issue in the United States because of the sexual immorality and corruption of well-known preachers and tele-evangelists. In one particular case, he was pastor of a 14,000-member church and President of the National Association of Evangelicals since 2003. On November 5, 2006 he admitted sexual immorality and confessed, "I was a deceiver and liar."[52] Many Americans were greatly disappointed at the news but this is one of many such incidents and shows that the trust relationship in pastoral care is based on integrity. The core concept of character building, I suggest, is to imitate the character of Christ. This is both biblical and confirmed in church history, as I will illustrate later in conversation with John Chrysostom. Integrity is the foundation of the Christlike character upon which we have to build by imitating him; especially in Korean culture, the pastor is understood as being a "father figure." A pastor with a fatherly love and compassion coupled with integrity of character is expected. Donald Dorr emphasizes that integrity of character—coupled with the expression of the love of God—influences people both in and outside the church. In regard to a spiritual leadership, Donald Dorr argues that character with the love of God influences the hearts of the people, even unbelievers. He rightly describes:

---

50. Blackaby, *Spiritual Leadership*, 104.

51. Croft, *Ministry in Three Dimensions*, 77.

52. On November 4, 2006 the Overseer Board of the New Life Church have concluded that their investigation and the pastor's public statements have proven without doubt that he had committed sexually immoral conduct. He resigned from his senior pastor's position.

Pastoral Leadership Principles

Is it possible for somebody who has little or no explicit relationship with God to experience what Ignatius calls "consolation without cause"? I have no doubt the answer is yes. This implies that the experience can be described in more secular terms than those used by Ignatius. In taking this view I am encouraged by Bernard Lonergan's remark to the effect that the experience of the love of God poured into our hearts is interpreted differently in the context of different religious traditions. In our modern, rather secularized culture it may be that the experience is articulated by the use of some or all of the following terms: a sense of deep abiding peace, fulfillment, love, joy, gratitude, benevolence, or loving-kindness.[53]

Ultimately the experience of God in human minds is only through the work of the Holy Spirit. I agree, however, with Dorr that it is character that influences the hearts of the people for transformation. People are persuaded by a person's character of love, gratitude, benevolence, or loving-kindness. Throughout my twenty-six years of pastoral leadership experience, I discovered that a leader's character is constantly challenged by the people—including Session members, individual congregations, and pastoral staff. Authentic leadership needs to be proven by the leader's character, which persuades people to follow with respect and honor. Undoubtedly, people are profoundly influenced by, and kindly disposed towards, those who live consistently Christlike.

Humility

Humility, as illustrated in Christ, is the core feature of integrity. Without humility, pastoral leadership will be ineffective. Robert H. Gundry emphasized, with regard to Jesus' teaching in Mark 10:42–45, that "The Son of man provides a model, which because of his authority is also a reason, for this sort of behavior on the part of the Twelve."[54] Such servant leadership was a new model based on humility, not only for the twelve disciples, but also for all Christians, especially church leaders. Jesus demonstrated humility in many ways, such as by washing his own disciples' feet on the night before his crucifixion. He said, "I have set you an example that you should do as I have done for you" (John 13:15). The humility of Christ in serving people is the new paradigm in pastoral leadership.

I submit that servant leadership is, therefore, nothing less than the humility of Christ. The character of the coming Messiah was revealed as a

53. Dorr, *Faith at Work*, 149–50.
54. Gundry, *Mark: A Commentary*, 581.

Pastoral Leadership

servant in Isa 42:1–3: "Here is my servant, whom I uphold, my chosen one in whom I delight." The servant, ultimately, is the Messiah, as described in Isa 61:1, also: "The Spirit of the Sovereign Lord is on me, because the Lord has anointed me to preach good news to the poor. He has sent me to bind up the brokenhearted, to proclaim freedom for the captives and release from darkness for the prisoners."[55] The Messiah was portrayed as a humble servant, and yet the task executed to him was the sovereign mission commissioned by the Lord God himself. Consistent with the servant songs of Isaiah, Paul presents Christ as a servant in Phil 2:5–8. For Paul, this is the perfect example of humility. In this respect, Gerald F. Hawthorne remarks, "The Christ-hymn presents Jesus as the supreme example of the humble, self-sacrificing, self-denying, self-giving service that Paul has just been urging the Philippians to practice in their relations one toward another."[56] Jesus surrendered his divine power in order that he might serve. Gordon D. Fee's interpretation of this passage is appropriate:

> But in the present context the emphasis does not lie on Jesus' messianism or on his fulfilling the role of the Servant of the Lord. Rather it lies primarily on the servant nature of Christ's incarnation. He entered our history not as kyrios (Lord), which name he acquires at his vindication (2:9–11), but as doulos (slave), a person without advantages, with no rights or privileges, but in servanthood to all.[57]

For clergy, this is the ultimate example to imitate Christ's model and I will return to this theme in later chapters.

Spirituality

There are varied, traditional Catholic, Orthodox and Protestant spirituality as well as newer ones like New Age Spirituality, which are attracting

---

55. Young, *Book of Isaiah*, 3:111. By citing John Calvin's interpretation, Young interpreted that this is clearly Messianic and said: "This judgment the servant will bring to the Gentiles, who know not Israel's God. His work, therefore, is missionary. "Christ," says Calvin, was sent in order to bring to the whole world under the authority of God and under obedience to him."

56. Hawthorne, *Philippians*, 79. See also O'Brien, *Commentary on Philippians*, 205. O'Brien observes, "The Christ-hymn presents Jesus as the ultimate model for Christian behavior and action, the supreme example of humble, self-sacrificing, self-giving service that Paul has just been urging the Philippians to practice in their relations one toward another."

57. Fee, *Paul's Letter*, 213. Fee associates Phil 2:5–11 with Isa 53 in order to describe Christ's condescension and the spirit of servanthood.

Pastoral Leadership Principles

attention today. The latter are distinctive in producing hybrid spirituality.[58] New Age spirituality combines the essence of Eastern religious thought but includes some elements of Western, Judeo-Christian thought like optimism and belief in progress, which are alien to traditional Eastern religions. Detailed discussion of New Age spirituality and its varied, contemporary expressions lies beyond the scope of this research, but I am using the term here to refer to Protestant—especially Presbyterian—spirituality in which the Word is central and determinative in terms of belief. This spirituality—also sometimes referred to as Reformed Spirituality[59]—tends to be the means by which, through the Holy Spirit, believers enjoy access to God in a vital, dynamic relationship.

In this tradition, the Word, along with the sacraments, prayer, and fellowship are regarded as the means of grace by which Christians enjoy God and his presence. I will refer to preaching of the Word next, but here I wish to underline the importance of prayer for pastoral leaders. David Cornick stresses that reformed Christians are a praying people, and that doing theology, whether pastorally or academically, is impossible without prayer.[60] There is an essential, inseparable link also between prayer and a Christlike, humble character. Profoundly, prayer is the expression of humility as believers themselves acknowledge their need of God and of his blessing and grace. I concur with Gerkin's criticism of pastoral care practitioners who have too often made a "biased distinction" between pastoral care dealing with their real, daily-life problems and "spiritual direction," which was assumed to be encouraging merely introspection and a type of Gnosticism in a remote search for the reality of Christ. Gerkin recognizes "signs" today that these two pastoral traditions, which have been "long-separated," are being viewed as allies and partners.[61] For example, throughout my ministry at KCPC, I increasingly recognized the importance and necessity of prayer as part of the spiritual direction of pastors and the church community; in this my wife has been an active prayer-partner and encourager. In addition to daily, early morning church prayer meetings, which I encouraged church members to attend, I gave priority to prayer in my own life. I agree with Chrysostom: "Prayer is our invincible weapon."[62] My father also taught

58. Groothuis, *Unmasking the New Age*, 131.
59. Cornick, *Letting God Be God*, 11–21.
60. Ibid., 53.
61. Ibid., 86.
62. Chrysostom, *Baptismal Instructions*, 115.

Pastoral Leadership

me and exemplified the importance of prayer and thus it became an integral part of my spiritual life from childhood.[63] During my senior high school period, between the 1954 and 1957, I was also deeply influenced by Pastor Dong-Jin Choi of Kyung-San Presbyterian Church, Kyung-San Korea.[64] Pastor Choi took us to Mt. Sung-Am regularly for prayer-vigils and provided me with spiritual mentorship and discipleship. He demonstrated leadership through his exemplary prayer life and his preaching was so powerful that the church experienced considerable numerical and qualitative growth. Moreover, Ok Hwa Kang, my mother-in-law, who was known as a woman of prayer, taught me the significance of prayer through her prayer-centered life. She influenced me to consider prayer as the priority in my pastoral work.

Furthermore, Jesus Christ's prayer life during his earthly ministry provided me with the most fundamental example that I should follow, particularly during the period of 1977–2003 at KCPC. From 1992 to 2003, prayer meetings were a crucial point for the whole congregation. I instituted the fast-prayer retreat on the first weekend of January and daily prayer meetings every morning at 5:30 a.m. during the month of October.[65] This month-long prayer meeting in October was subsequently divided into two meetings: the first in October and the second during Passion Week. Daily Morning Prayer meeting at 5:45 a.m. continued throughout the year without a break. Morning Prayer has been effective in my own ministry.

An important congregational survey of my pastoral leadership was held on January 7, 2006 during KCPC's annual fasting-prayer retreat at Potomac Park Camp.[66] To achieve more objectivity regarding my pastoral leadership principles, I delegated the administration of the survey to Ju Yong Park, KCPC's Director of Network Ministry.[67] He reported the following results:

---

63. Kim, *Keimyung Pioneers*, 246–47.

64. Reverend Dong-Jin Choi began his ministry at Kyung-San Presbyterian Church on January 1, 1954 as the 15th pastor of the church and ended on September 25, 1957 in order to accept the pastoral call from Cho-Ryang Presbyterian Church, Pusan, Korea.

65. Yearly the *KCPC Handbook* (1993–2003): the fast prayer and Morning Prayer meeting were scheduled at the beginning of the new fiscal year.

66. The KCPC has practiced the annual fast-prayer retreat for twenty years on the first weekend of January every year. This year there were more than 700 members attended. They are the core members of the KCPC.

67. Ju Yong Park is Senior Financial Officer at World Bank, Washington, D.C. and obtained PhD from Wharton Business School, University of Pennsylvania.

Pastoral Leadership Principles

This group is the core of our church, and out of about 700 in attendance that morning, 446 people responded to the survey, of which 430 surveys were valid. The survey interviewees were asked to rank the five areas that you (Won Sang Lee) had been most effective and the five areas that you paid most attention to during your twenty-six years tenure as Senior Pastor at KCPC, from 1 to 5, with 1 being the most important. Here are highlights from the survey—total rank scores are in brackets.[68]

Five areas where Reverend Lee was most effective:

1. Praying (752)
2. Character (Personality) (920)
3. Pastoral Leadership (1,376)
4. Preaching (1,439)
5. Personal Relations (1,963)

Five areas that Reverend Lee paid most attention to:

1. Worship Service (824)
2. Evangelism/Missions (887)
3. Discipleship Training (1,293)
4. Home Visitations (1,656)
5. Mercy Ministry/Relief (1,790)

It is not with any sense of pride that I read of the Survey conducted by the Evangelical Alliance in the UK in 1990. The Alliance surveyed three thousand evangelical clergy from a number of different denominations and discovered that seven in ten felt overworked, twenty hours on average were spent weekly by each in administration while only thirty eight minutes per week were spent in personal prayer.[69] Integrity, sacrificial love, faithfulness, and humility in Christlike character are essential for pastoral leadership;

---

68. The result of the survey for this case study was reported in the letter to me written by Ju Yong Park on January 30, 2006.

69. Croft, *Ministry in Three Dimensions*, 17–18. "A survey conducted on behalf of the Evangelical Alliance in 1990 of 3000 evangelical clergy" across different denominations makes sobering reading: 7 out of 10 clergy feel overworked, 3 in 10 feel their families suffer because of their work, only 2 in 10 have received training in management or leading teams, out of a typical 60-hour week, an average of 22 hours is spent in administration, and in contrast to this just 38 minutes per week are spent in personal prayer."

Pastoral Leadership

however, spirituality—especially personal and corporate prayer—is the key for building these characteristics through the ministry of the Holy Spirit.

3. Preaching

My third principle of pastoral leadership is preaching the Word, which for Protestants, is the central focus and climax of public worship. Croft confirms this and views preaching of the Word as "the central part of the vocation of the presbyter."[70] For David Cornick, "the Bible is the heart of reformed spirituality and it remains dominant in Reformed worship. Furthermore, he writes:

> To be Reformed is to be caught in the dynamics of the Word, because Scripture is one of God, appointed trysting places, where the Word spoken before all time, the Word incarnate and the words written about the Word become, through the activity of the Spirit, the living Word.[71]

I agree with Cornick; I increasingly regarded the preaching ministry as my most important duty as a Reformed Presbyterian pastor. Biblically, the Lord Jesus commissioned Peter to "Feed my sheep" (John 21:15) and scholars generally regard these words as Jesus' commission to Peter as leader of the Church of Christ with responsibility for its total pastoral care.[72] Herman Ridderbos, agrees with this idea regarding shepherding:

> It is one of the most frequent and characteristic images for leadership and care of the church. It is rooted in the portrayal of God as shepherd of his people (Ps 23; 77:20; Ezek 34) and of Jesus as the good shepherd (John 10:1, 26, Heb 13:20; 1 Pet 2:25).[73]

---

70. Ibid., 114.

71. Cornick, *Letting God be God*, 55.

72. Bultmann, *Gospel of John*, 712. Bultmann writes, "The story rather is a variant of Peter's commission to be a leader of the community, Matt 16:17–19." See also Barrett, *St. John*, 584–85. Barrett stated that: "For Christian ministers as shepherds see Acts 20:28; 1 Pet 5:2–4. It is because Peter can answer Jesus' question affirmatively that he can be appointed shepherd of the flock."

73. Ridderbos, *Gospel of John*, 666. Ridderbos writes, "As such it is not typically 'apostolic' but rather characteristic of every task or ministry in the church (Acts 20:28; Eph 4:11; 1 Pet 5:1). Accordingly, there is in Jesus' repeated designation of Peter as shepherd nothing unique. Peter is not charged with the care of the entire flock as Jesus' earthly vicar, and he is not the chief shepherd to whom all the other shepherds are subordinate. Peter's commissioning here is not different from that of all the disciples in 20:21–23, 66.

Pastoral Leadership Principles

Charles V. Gerkin rightly emphasizes that the model of the pastor as shepherding the flock has been a "prototypical image" from the earliest Christian era. He draws attention to the fact that this model also appears regularly in the writings of Early Church fathers as the "organizing metaphor par excellence for the work of the pastoral leader."[74] The words, "Feed my sheep" are then a symbolic description of the pastoral duty, but in practice the ministry of the Word is the ultimate task, and the highest responsibility, of pastors.

When I realized the call to pastoral ministry, my first reaction was my inadequacy to fulfill the task. For me, a good theological training was essential so I pursued several courses after 1968, and majored in the Old Testament as well as in Near Eastern Studies. It is encouraging that Croft insists that those called to preach the Word "should build faithful and lifelong habits of study and reflection around and upon and within and under the text of the Scriptures."[75] My mentor for expository preaching was the Reverend Sang Keun Lee who served the First Presbyterian Church of Dae-Gu, Korea, 1957 to 1991; he devoted himself to pastoral ministry of this church, writing expository commentaries on the entire New Testament. He was a respected pastor, biblical scholar and expository preacher, and elected as the moderator of the General Assembly of the Presbyterian Churches of Korea (Tong-Hap) in 1974. Haddon Robinson, in particular, introduced me to expository preaching. His book, *Biblical Preaching: The Development and Delivery of Expository Messages*[76] was recognized as the standard textbook for expository preaching in the United States as well as abroad. For over thirty years, I have practiced expository preaching and it became one of my main pastoral leadership principles.

Weekly congregational assemblies included Sunday Worship, Mid-Week Wednesday Service, and Daily Morning Prayer Service at six in the morning. Except for special occasions, expository preaching was delivered as a sermon series from the Old and New Testaments.[77] Through basic,

---

74. Gerkin, *Introduction to Pastoral Care*, 27.

75. Croft, *Ministry in Three Dimensions*, 111.

76. Robinson, *Biblical Preaching*.

77. For example, at daily prayer meeting at 6 a.m. the whole congregation read one chapter from the Bible in order all year round and the preacher delivered the expository preaching from the text congregation read. The congregants then continued their personal prayers. Twice a year, however, there were special prayer week at 5:30 a.m. in October and March or April during the Passion Week.

Pastoral Leadership

relevant biblical teaching, the congregations grew in their knowledge and understanding of Scripture. I agree with Mark Dever's statement:

> The first mark of a healthy church is expository preaching. It is not only the first mark; it is far and away the most important of them all, because if you get this one right, all of others should follow.[78]

In my experience, sermon preparation requires considerable discipline and good study habits with much prayer and meditation on the text. Like Chrysostom, I maintained that the source of power in preaching is not derived from human ability, but from Christ, the author of the Word.[79] Examining the Greek and Hebrew text provided clearer understanding of the meaning intended by the original authors in the text. In particular, the lexicographer's interpretation from other cognate languages and cross-references were an indispensable help for grappling with the text before giving its contemporary relevance and application. Reading commentators' works and other theological as well as historical writings were also essential for preparing the homilies. I learned at KCPC that the pastoral leadership gains respect by diligently prepared preaching and the personal practice of what is preached.

However, the pastoral and preaching ministry cannot be accomplished by the clergy alone, but through cooperative team work with laypeople. KCPC's Vision 2020: "Training the Saints to Transform the World" was a reflection of the principle in which the ministry of the church is given to the entire body of Christ and everyone is a minister. The clergy's duty is to equip God's people for ministry in, and through, the church. At KCPC, therefore, one of the main ministries was to train the small group Bible study leaders to communicate the Word and I determined that the central focus of KCPC's Vision 2020 would be the training of cell-group leaders. The uniqueness of this study is that it was organized, operated, and taught only by lay people. In order to strengthen the lay people's participation in the ministry of the Word of God, I also proposed to the Session the establishing of the "Timothy Bible Institute" in KCPC. We adopted "Bible

---

78. Dever, *Nine Marks*, 39. Dever believes that there are nine marks for becoming a healthy church: 1) Expository Preaching, 2) Biblical Theology, 3) The Gospel, 4) A Biblical Understanding of Conversion, 5) A Biblical Understanding of Evangelism, 6) A Biblical Understanding of Church Membership, 7) Biblical Church Discipline, 8) A Concern for Discipleship and Growth, 9) Biblical Church Leadership.

79. Chrysostom, *Homilies on Second Corinthians* (NPNF1 12:301).

Pastoral Leadership Principles

Training Centre for Pastors"[80] as our main curriculum for training. Dennis J. Mock writes concerning BTCP's purpose:

> The Bible Training Centre for Pastors and Church Leaders (BTCP and BTCL) is designed for the specific purpose of providing trans denominational basic Bible training for national pastors and church leaders which will adequately and effectively equip them with the necessary knowledge and practical skills for the work of local church ministry. Most BTCP/BTCL students have not been to Bible College or seminary character.[81]

The KCPC Session appointed Pastor Jin Myung Chang as the pastor in charge. In January 2000 KCPC launched BTCP with twenty-three students and all twenty-three graduated on December 14, 2002 after three years demanding training.

So far, I have explored the three principles of my pastoral leadership and I turn now to my fourth principle, which I developed in KCPC, namely, cross-cultural mission.

4. Cross-Cultural Mission

By cross-cultural mission, I am referring primarily to the Great Commission of Christ in Matt 28:18–20 which directs the church to communicate his Word and disciple those who profess faith; the scope of the commission is universal and continuous as well as corporate so the church has the enormous task of reaching all people throughout all generations. Penetrating these people often involves adaptation in terms of culture, language, location and resources. Biblically, the church is the prime focus in redemptive history. Jurgen Moltmann rightly insists that: "The church participates in Christ's messianic mission and in the creative mission of the Spirit."[82] For Croft, the local church "has very little choice" regarding mission. He and Robert Warren emphasize that "the call is for the whole church to be changed and to become a missionary congregation."[83] Local churches should set their missional goals to become a church engaged in mission, whether cross-cultural or mono-cultural, at home and at a dis-

---

80. Mock, *Bible Training Centre*. Mock designed to train lay people and pastors in the mission field with equivalent to two years of Bible College study.

81. Ibid., 11.

82. Moltmann, *Church in the Power*, 65.

83. Croft, *Ministry in Three Dimensions*, 7. See also Warren, *Building Missionary Congregations*.

Pastoral Leadership

tance. From the beginning of my ministry at KCPC, this was my perspective for the church because I was persuaded it was biblical. This was also my perspective based on the reason my father became a Christian—through an American missionary in Korea. My country owes much to those who engaged in cross-cultural mission there from the late nineteenth-century onwards.

My first step in KCPC was to encourage personal evangelism through "Evangelism Explosion (EE),"[84] a movement founded by James Kennedy. Increasingly at KCPC, mission became the main focus of our ministry and our Session resolved to send ten families to cross-cultural mission from our congregation by 2000.[85] KCPC endeavored to fulfill this vision statement by sending out career and short-term missionaries, and summer-mission teams; KCPC established a mission agency called CMF (Central Missionary Fellowship).[86] After 1990, thirteen other career missionary families have been commissioned to cross-cultural mission.[87] Seven short-term missionaries have also been commissioned to seven different countries and more than a thousand summer mission teams have been sent out since 1987. Instituting a professional mission agency, called SEED International, further developed KCPC's cross-cultural mission; it was founded on September 1, 2000 as an independent, interdenominational mission agency for churches. Since September 2000, as president of SEED International, my main duty has been to promote cross-cultural mission in local churches and recruit candidates. In November 2005, SEED International had sixty-six missionaries (thirty-four family units) serving in twenty-one countries and collected $2,176,795.[88]

The ultimate goal of Vision 2020 of KCPC was to reach out from our community to the world with the gospel; more specifically, the main purpose

---

84. James Kennedy, *Evangelism Explosion*. Evangelism Explosion is a training program for local church leaders and laypersons equipping churches for friendship, evangelism, discipleship, and healthy growth.

85. The KCPC 1989 Annual Report, 1. The Pastoral Report noted that the KCPC Session adopted a resolution to send ten missionary families by the year 2000. Rev. Peace Sung-Sik Ahn was already commissioned by the Session to Global Missionary Fellowship and Rev. John Shin-Wook Park was scheduled to be commissioned to Argentina in 1990.

86. Paik, *Thirty-Year Anniversary*, 217.

87. Thirteen other missionary families were commissioned to East Asia, Thailand, Central Asia, Brazil, Mexico, Japan, Middle East and Cambodia.

88. SEED International 2005 Annual Report, 4–12.

Pastoral Leadership Principles

for world missions was to work among un-reached people groups.[89] In response to the Adopt-a-People Clearinghouse and the AD 2000 and Beyond Movement, KCPC adopted the Charm people in Cambodia on March 2002. The Session appointed Daniel & Esther Baeq as non-resident missionaries to the Charm people and later they were commissioned to the Charms in Cambodia on August 14, 2004.[90] On March 8, 2003, KCPC adopted the Kurdish people in Turkey and also sent out a short-term mission team.

Realizing the importance of the cross-cultural mission committed to the church, it was necessary for me to provide a theological foundation for mission for the whole congregation. I proposed to my session the creation of the position of mission pastor to be responsible for mission operations in the church, and consequently Kang-Hyun Chung was appointed. The session also authorized the organizing of the KCPC Mission Board for overseeing the mission operation of the church and also adopted KCPC mission policy, which became a manual for the church's mission.[91] The session's goal was to increase the cross-cultural mission budget by 20 percent of the total KCPC annual budget; it reached $495,000 in the fiscal year of 2003, which constituted 12.54 percent of the total annual budget. KCPC's summer mission teams have built church buildings in areas such as Central Asia, East Asia, Mexico, Honduras, Bolivia, Chard, and others. This type of mission work is continued annually.[92]

Throughout my pastoral ministry, I acknowledge that these four principles have been strengthened and developed; at times, one or the other of the principles received greater attention for a period due to the different phases of church development and particular problems encountered. Caring ministry, Christlike character, preaching, and cross-cultural mission have been my core values and pastoral leadership principles, which I believe are unchanging in their importance and relevance. The ultimate goal of these four pastoral leadership principles is to fulfill the divine plan for world mission and church maturity. The pastoral role is, therefore, to care for the people through effectively and prayerfully preaching the Word but with a Christlike character so that God's people may be equipped for witness in the community and beyond.

---

89. Yates, *Christian Mission*, 244.
90. *KCPC Members Handbook*, 11.
91. Paik, *Thirty-Year Anniversary*, 216–32. KCPC Mission Policy, 1–22.
92. Paik, *Thirty-Year Anniversary*, 290.

4

Conversation with Chrysostom

HAVING IDENTIFIED, ILLUSTRATED, AND discussed four pastoral leadership principles relating to my own ministry in KCPC, I now want to begin to enter into conversation with John Chrysostom, an outstanding church leader and preacher in the fourth century. First, I want to discuss my methodology and reasons for this type of conversation with Chrysostom.

As a way of proceeding with theological reflection on pastoral work and church life, Stephen Pattison commends the model of "critical conversation" as a useful and helpful starting point. For Pattison, this critical conversation involves a three-fold interaction between the Christian tradition, the student's own faith presuppositions, and a specific contemporary situation. While not claiming originality or exhaustiveness for this approach, Pattison makes the modest claim that it is "a starting point" at least.[1] Somewhat differently, Paul Ballard and John Pritchard suggest four possible models for doing theology, maintaining that these can be interwoven rather than regarded as being mutually exclusive. One such method is that of critical correlation which can, for example, encourage and bring together pastoral concerns and ethics or, as for Tillich, establish a dialogue between a question and answer.[2] However, for Stephen Pattison, his proposed meth-

---

1. Woodward and Pattison, *Pastoral and Practical Theology*, 1–19. They insisted that both deductive and inductive methods could be applied for the practical theology. The inductive approach is, however, preferred for the principles of the practical theology.

2. Ballard and Prichard, *Practical Theology*, 57–70. For practical theology Ballard and Pritchard suggest the four models; the first one is applied theory resulted from the social sciences to the pastoral situation. The second model is the method of critical correlation, which is the emergence of the social sciences and their related professions like education,

Conversation with Chrysostom

od invites a dialogue between a tradition or a theological perspective and a contemporary situation or issue. Pattison proposes that theology should be viewed essentially as being *contemporary enquiry*, involving a "quest" for satisfactory and legitimate responses to real life situations and experiences, including religious experience.[3]

Unlike Pattison, I want to emphasize the importance of the core doctrines of the Christian faith. These doctrines must be reflected on and wrestled with in order to understand and relate them to contemporary life. I concur with Pattison that competent theological reflection "deepens our experience of the world and of our own assumptions,"[4] thus preventing us from being satisfied with superficial and unwarranted answers and attitudes. In my own situation, my theological training, exposure to postgraduate studies, a deep engagement with church history such as a sustained study of Chrysostom's life and work together with the challenges of cross-cultural ministry have all contributed to my personal "quest" for an appropriate theological response to the nature of pastoral leadership. I have been deeply challenged in this quest and agree again with Pattison that Christians have addressed many contemporary questions about human life, as well as church leadership, in the past. That is what I have discovered in my "conversation" with Chrysostom across the centuries. However, I want to employ the model which Pattison recommends as a starting point for theological reflection, namely, that of "critical conversation," in which one thinks of oneself as being in a three-way conversation between a) one's own assumptions, feelings and beliefs, b) those beliefs and perceptions provided by Christian tradition, including the Bible and c) the specific contemporary situation which is being analyzed.[5] I am seeking to establish this kind of interaction in "critical conversation" between my own beliefs, perceptions, and a wider Christian tradition as represented in Chrysostom and the contemporary church pastoral situation in KCPC during my recent ministry there.

---

social work, nursing, and other groups. The third one models practical theory, and the fourth one is the habitus model which the training the mind and heart. See also Anderson, *Shape of Practical Theology*, 35–46. Anderson demonstrates a Trinitarian model.

3. Woodward and Pattison, *Pastoral and Practical Theology*, 137.

4. Ibid., 138. Pattison also says that the value of theological reflection has "the effect of ensuring that faith and religious ideas do not become encapsulated and cut off from our experience of everyday life."

5. Ibid., 139.

Pastoral Leadership

Pattison argues that employing this model of conversation has as many as ten advantages.[6] For example, it allows what he calls "heuristic clarity" in which one becomes more skilled and enabled to explore and discover for oneself. There is also the identification of starting points from different perspectives. This model also allows for changes. I have been challenged in my research by these three benefits of Pattison's method for participants themselves to change in various ways, as they are willing to listen to others and see themselves in a new or different light. Pattison suggests another advantage in using his model: acknowledging the enormous gaps between some contemporary situations and the religious tradition involved in the conversation. While acknowledging this, one must go forward with Pattison and see theological reflection as a diligent enquiry, which involves exploring and living with gaps as well as with similarities. I find this reassuring because in my own conversation with Chrysostom I am aware of numerous "gaps" as well as "similarities." Nevertheless, the exploration is useful, illuminating, challenging, and humbling in so many ways. However, as Pattison suggests, "the important thing is to find a way into critical conversation" in which each participant is questioned in turn by the other, namely, the student's assumptions, tradition and the contemporary reality. My own way into this critical conversation comes in the form of a conversation between John Chrysostom's pastoral concerns and leadership and my own pastoral leadership at KCPC. While adapting Pattison's method, I nevertheless acknowledge with Swinton and Mowatt that "the model of mutual critical correlation opens up the opportunity to challenge the interpretations of Scripture and tradition that may have become distorted, forgotten or deliberately overlooked."[7] The latter is too ambitious for my purpose here and lies strictly outside the scope of this dissertation to major on the interpretations of Scripture but nevertheless I am deeply challenged and humbled in my conversation with Chrysostom from an entirely different culture, tradition and historical period.

Why enter into conversation with John Chrysostom when there are so many "gaps" as well as "similarities" to cope with? I have chosen Chrysostom because I have come to respect and appreciate his influential ministry,

---

6. Ibid., 139–40. The ninth among ten is that "an important part of conversation may be that of silence, disagreement or lack of communication. This element is very important in theological reflection; many people suppose that if they understand the Christian tradition properly, they can then apply its eternal truth easily to the contemporary reality."

7. Swinton and Mowatt, *Practical Theology*, 82.

Conversation with Chrysostom

and theology. Again, he has much to say about pastoral leadership and many of his writings have been preserved. I especially would like to explore ways in which Chrysostom's pastoral teaching may relate to, and enrich my own and be applied to contemporary church leadership. Another reason is that pastoral leadership demands the holistic practice of the Christian faith and requires transformation and movement through example. My reading of Chrysostom leads me to think that "conversation" with him will be beneficial and challenging, especially with regard to pastoral leadership. I have another reason for choosing Chrysostom in that not much research has been undertaken on the subject of Chrysostom's pastoral leadership, even though there is great need for this focus as well as its contemporary application. I am aware that I am unable to fill this gap in Chrysostom research but, more modestly, by focusing on Chrysostom in this conversation and his pastoral leadership principles that other scholars will be encouraged to undertake more detailed research on this aspect of the contribution of this outstanding Patristic leader.

Finally, I have chosen Chrysostom because of his integrity of character, which I hope to describe later in this chapter. Such integrity of faith and practice, even during times of hardship and persecution, is a profound challenge to me. It is my conviction that, for these reasons, to enter into conversation with a person of Chrysostom's integrity and gifts will be helpful for a further understanding of pastoral leadership principles.

CHRYSOSTOM'S LIFE (347–407)

The majority of Chrysostom scholars accept 347 AD as the year of his birth[8] in Antioch, the capital of Syria and where the followers of Christ were first called "Christians."[9] His father, Secundus, was a distinguished military officer in Syria's imperial army but died during his son's infancy. His widowed mother, Anthusa, was only twenty years of age at this time.[10] She was a pious woman, refusing all offers of remarriage because of her ardent devotion to raise her son in Christian truth and piety. She felt she was called of God to devote herself wholly in the training of her son and to shield him from the contaminating influences of the pagan city of An-

---

8. Carter, "Chrysostom's Early Life," 357. Carter suggested that the date of Chrysostom's birth is 349 AD.

9. "The disciples were called Christians first at Antioch" (Acts 11:26 NIV).

10. Socrates, *Ecclesiastical History*, 303. See also Palladius, *Life of St. John Chrysostom*, 34–35; Philip Schaff, *Saint Chrysostom*, 13; Kelly, *Golden Mouth*, 4–5.

tioch.[11] Thus, the tenderness of his character and his insight into domestic life can be attributed to his mother's influence and were reflected later in his preaching.[12] Chrysostom received a liberal and excellent education, studying rhetoric under Libanius and philosophy under Andragathius.[13] He became the most distinguished student under Libanius[14]; the latter greatly respected his student for his remarkable oratorical ability and also his moral character. When Chrysostom was eighteen, he left the school of Libanius and developed a close relationship with Meletius, the archbishop of Antioch.[15] Under his influence, Chrysostom began to show interest in studying the Sacred Scriptures.[16] Palladius writes how Meletius discovered Chrysostom's unusual character and finally led him to be baptized:

> At that time the blessed Meletius the confessor, an Armenian by nationality, ruled the church at Antioch. He took notice of the bright lad and was impressed by the beauty of his character so he had him almost constantly near him. He observed him with prophetic eye as it were, and he could envisage the young man's brilliant future. He was admitted to the mystery of the washing of regeneration.[17]

Completing the usual period of probation and instruction for three years as a catechumen, Chrysostom was baptized by Meletius in about 367.[18] Chrysostom's baptism was delayed until he was about twenty years old and he may have considered baptism to be a stepping-stone toward a renunciation of a secular life-style.[19] "Chrysostom's baptism was, as in the case of St. Augustine, the turning point in his life, an entire renunciation of this world and dedication to the service of Christ. The change was radical and permanent."[20] Although an outstanding student with the

---

11. Attwater, *Pastor and Preacher*, 18–19; Anderson, *Power as a Preacher*, 53. Baur, *John Chrysostom*, 1:3–4.
12. Chase, *Chrysostom*, 12
13. Socrates, *Ecclesiastical History* (NPNF2 2:303).
14. Sozomen, *Ecclesiastical History* (NPNF2 2:13).
15. Baur, *John Chrysostom*, 1:80.
16. Attwater, *Pastor and Preacher*, 20.
17. Palladius, *Life of St. John Chrysostom*, 35.
18. Attwater, *Pastor and Preacher*, 21.
19. Vandenburghe, *John of the Golden Mouth*, 4.
20. Schaff, "Prolegomena" (NPNF1 9:6).

Conversation with Chrysostom

potential for a successful legal career,[21] Chrysostom turned from a secular career initially because of two celebrated monastic teachers, Diodorus and Carterius whom he had met.[22] Diodorus was the founder of the second theological school of Antioch and helped to influence Chrysostom's theological development. Lucian preceded Diodorus and was considered the founder of the first theological school of Antioch. It was Diodorus, however, who influenced Chrysostom to turn away from secular interests and led him into Scriptural studies at the school called the Asceterion.[23] The school was managed by Diodorus, who as a priest had been ordained by Meletius, and he subsequently became bishop of Tarsus.[24] It is uncertain whether the Asceterion was a proper monastery because there is no literary or archaeological evidence for its existence as a monastery within the walls of Antioch at that early date. However, the Asceterion must have had certain unmistakably "monastic" features.[25] Socrates explicitly states that the turning point of Chrysostom's entrance into the sacred profession came through the influence of Diodorus.[26] Chrysostom was not an outstanding or original thinker as some of his peers were but through Diodorus's teaching, he became an eminent preacher, pastor and theologian.

After his mother's death,[27] Chrysostom left for monastic solitude in the mountains south of Antioch; there, he spent four years learning to subdue his passions under Syrus, an elderly Syrian ascetic;[28] he strove to imitate Syrus' great self-discipline and austere lifestyle.[29] According to the philosophy of Syrian asceticism, monks were required to take a vow of vir-

---

21. Downey, *Ancient Antioch*, 197.

22. Sozomen, *Ecclesiastical History*, 376. Sozomen writes, "He (Chrysostom) learnt rhetoric from Libanius, and philosophy from Andragathius. It was expected that he would have embraced the legal profession, but he devoted himself to the study of the Sacred Scriptures, and to a life of ecclesiastical philosophy, under the guidance of Carterius and Diodorus, two celebrated presidents of monastic assemblies."

23. Meyer, *Palladius*, 171.

24. Mayer and Allen, *John Chrysostom*, 5.

25. Kelly, *Golden Mouth*, 19.

26. Socrates, *Ecclesiastical History*, 303

27. Schaff, "Prolegomena" (*NPNF*1 9:9).

28. Mayer and Allen, *John Chrysostom*, 6.

29. Meyer, *Palladius*, 35. D'Alton states that it is not certain who the Syrian ascetic was; George Alexander says the monk was called Hesychius; some identified him with Carterius. D'Alton, *St. John Chrysostom*, 4; See also Mayer and Allen, *John Chrysostom*, 2:1139.

Pastoral Leadership

ginity that forbade them from ever speaking with women. If a monk could not avoid meeting women, he at least averted his eyes from their faces and listened only to their speech. The monk's cell was also kept extremely sparse so that the desire for possessions would not arise.[30] In an effort to imitate the life of Christ, monks practiced fasting regularly, sometime all day and eating in the evening after sunset.[31] Besides fasting, the most prominent parts of daily life included meditation, prayer, and daily lections and recitation of the Scriptures.[32] After spending four years in the monastery, Chrysostom settled in a cave where he stayed for two years. Even though Chrysostom became physically weak during these years, while in the monastery and cave he experienced extraordinary opportunities for prayer and memorizing Scripture.[33] For these two years Chrysostom lived alone in a cave, slept little, and studied the Bible day and night, practicing the mortification of the flesh.[34] Not surprisingly, during this period his health was adversely affected. Chrysostom's six-year monastic experience probably deepened his own understanding of the kenosis of Christ and aided him in his pursuit of living a Christlike life void of earthly pleasures. Practicing this type of self-denial as a monk provided Chrysostom with new opportunities for serving others later in the priesthood. His experience in the monastery served as a stepping-stone toward leadership roles as a preacher and priest.

Chrysostom returned to Antioch after six years of living the ascetic life and was immediately ordained as a deacon by Bishop Meletius in 381.[35] Meletius probably influenced Chrysostom's spiritual formation, because he had baptized Chrysostom in 367. As a deacon, Chrysostom had great opportunities to serve people by caring for the poor and sick, and thus entered the active ministry stage in his life.[36] Until he was ordained as a priest in 386, Chrysostom served the congregation in Antioch for five years as a deacon, ministering to people in the Antioch Church and also responsible for tending to three thousand people who depended on the local church for meeting their material needs. This proved a good opportunity for him to know, and love the ordinary people, for many of the poor and oppressed

30. Voobus, *History of Asceticism*, 257–59.
31. Ibid., 261.
32. Ibid., 278–89.
33. Mayer and Allen, *John Chrysostom*, 6.
34. Willey, *Early Church Portraits*, 111.
35. Meyer, *Palladius*, 36.
36. Schaff, "Prolegomena" (*NPNF* 9:10).

Conversation with Chrysostom

people were disillusioned with the rich who misused their wealth.[37] Besides fulfilling the practical needs of others, he also performed ecclesiastical and liturgical duties as a deacon; the principal office of the deacon was the service of the altar.

Chrysostom wrote his celebrated treatise, *On the Priesthood* probably during his ministry as a deacon between 381 and 386. In his treatise, he discussed the theoretical and practical qualifications, exalted duties, responsibilities and honors of the priesthood.[38] Chrysostom had higher standards for the qualifications of the priesthood than for any other occupation. He was fully aware of the responsibilities and commitment of the priesthood even though he wrote this book prior to ordination. Through prayer and contemplation he finally made his decision to be ordained a priest and never regretted his decision because he was convinced that his call to priesthood was a divine calling, similar to the experience Paul had on the Damascus road. He expressed admiration for Paul, stating: "The blessed Paul, in whose honor we are assembled today, was a light to the entire world."[39]

Chrysostom was ordained to the priesthood by Bishop Flavian on February 26, 386 in Antioch.[40] For twelve years in Antioch, from 386 to 397, he ministered to the congregation as preacher and pastor, firmly establishing himself as one of the greatest of Christian pulpit orators.[41] Because of his rare gift of eloquence, the title "Chrysostom"—meaning "Golden Mouth"—was awarded to him in the sixth century, possibly by Facundus de Hermiane.[42] From the first day of his priesthood, Bishop Flavian entrusted the ministry of the Word to Chrysostom and he preached almost uninterruptedly for twelve consecutive years in Antioch with great passion and uncompromising integrity.[43]

The overwhelming praise and fame Chrysostom received from the people in Antioch was due to his brilliant skills in communicating the Word, and also to his personal integrity. Regarding his character, Donald Attwater writes:

37. Attwater, *Pastor and Preacher*, 33.
38. Schaff, *History of the Christian Church*, 3:253.
39. Chrysostom, *In Praise of Saint Paul*, 53.
40. Baur, *John Chrysostom*. 180.
41. Quasten, *Patrology*, 3:425.
42. D'Alton, *Selections from St. John Chrysostom*, 1.
43. Puech, *Saint John Chrysostom*, 33.

Pastoral Leadership

> Its potential effectiveness owed much to its direct practicality and solid thought that lay behind it, but its actual success was due to Chrysostom as a man of God, to the holy personality of one who was ever trying to "practice what he preached," whose love and disinterested concern for the welfare of those whom he addressed was evident to all.[44]

Although he was frail, shabby, and unimpressive in outward appearance, those that heard him preach in Eucharist services were amazed by his insights and speaking ability. The simplicity of Chrysostom's lifestyle, regardless of his distinguished position, also gave evidence of his integrity, humility, and Christlike character. Chrysostom had earned respect from the people whom he served on account of his guileless attitude and deeds. During Chrysostom's twelve years in pastoral ministry in Antioch he was never charged with unethical behavior, with the exception of "the Synod of the Oak in 403"[45] in Constantinople.

Greatly admired by the congregation in Antioch for his exposition of the Word, he sought to testify to the truth of the doctrines by practicing those very principles in his own life. Furthermore, the homilies that he delivered had a sanctifying influence on Chrysostom himself.[46] His ministry had a great impact upon the daily lives of people in Antioch, as exemplified in the riot of 387.[47] In February of 387, during the Lent season, Chrysostom began his series of homilies but at the end of February, it was known that Emperor Theodosius had imposed a rather oppressive tax.[48] The riot at Antioch has been described by two eyewitness accounts.[49] The new tax was imposed in order to cover the expenses of foreign and civil wars, and large donations for the army in celebration of the Tenth Anniversary of Emperor Theodosius. All classes and ages of people complained against the new taxes, and a riot broke out in the city.[50] They first pulled down portraits of emperors painted with wax colors on wooden panels that were distributed to the cities of the empire, and then went to the bronze statues of the imperial family, breaking them up and dragging them through the

---

44. Attwater, *Pastor and Preacher*, 43.
45. Liebeschuetz, "Friends and Enemies," 85–111.
46. Neander, *Life of St. Chrysostom*, 111.
47. Baur, *John Chrysostom*, 1:259–78.
48. Ibid., 259.
49. Browning, "Riot of AD 387," 13–20.
50. Bouchier, *Short History of Antioch*, 164–65.

Conversation with Chrysostom

streets. The people then set fire to the house of a prominent citizen, and were ready to burn the imperial palace.[51] The statues of the emperor were thrown down and defaced; after the riot was brought under control, many citizens were imprisoned and executed. In addition, a great portion of their private property was confiscated. The people waited in terror to hear of their fate but when Bishop Flavian returned from the imperial city bringing a message of reconciliation from the Emperor, Chrysostom delivered his twenty-first homily of the series. This affair of the statues was a crucial point in Chrysostom's life because he genuinely related to the citizens of Antioch and communicated his message effectively to them during this time. Until he moved to Constantinople in 398, Chrysostom's influence was significant, even in the Eastern Empire's political sphere. The years 387 to 398 were the most fruitful period in his preaching career, which consisted of two elements: scriptural and dogmatic exposition.[52]

The first Ecumenical Council, held at Nicaea in 325, recognized the three principal Episcopal sees of the Church to be Rome, Alexandria and Antioch, in that order. However, at the second Ecumenical Council in 381, the fathers decreed that the bishop of Constantinople should have the first place of honor after the bishop of Rome, because Constantinople had become very prosperous. Therefore, the order of the Eastern Churches was changed to Constantinople, Alexandria and Antioch.[53] The political importance of Constantinople created many problems among the bishops because of religious corruption after Patriarch Nectarius of Constantinople died on September 27, 397. Threatened by the rise of Constantinople, the Archbishop of Alexandria, Theophilus, was frustrated at the rivalry that he knew he could not avoid. Theophilus favored Isidore, the aged priest who was ordained by Athanasius the Great in Alexandria, to become the new archbishop of Constantinople.[54] However, Emperor Arcadius, having been informed of Chrysostom's great reputation with regard to his preaching and pastoral ministry in Antioch, sent for Chrysostom, and ordered the bishops to install him as the pastor of Constantinople.[55] The emperor, the

51. Browning, "Riot of AD 387," 15.
52. Attwater, *Pastor and Preacher*, 53.
53. Ibid., 78.
54. Baur, *John Chrysostom*, 2:19.
55. Theodoret, *History of the Church*, 5:235. See also Quasten, *Patrology*, 3:425; Meyer, *Palladius*, 5:36. Palladius witnessed that the eunich, Eutropius, was the one who persuaded the emperor Arcadius to write a letter to the governor of Antioch that he should send Chrysostom to the imperial city quietly so as not to disturb the people in

Pastoral Leadership

bishops, and the people of Constantinople greeted Chrysostom with honor and rejoiced to see him elevated to the patriarchal throne. Theophilus, however, did not share the same sentiments.

Why did Chrysostom face so much opposition in Constantinople and why could he not overcome it? Chrysostom faced the problem of dealing with different classes of people; namely, the common people, as well as the religious hierarchical bishops, and the imperial officers. The challenge before him was to preach to these different audiences effectively and exercise his authority appropriately, while always maintaining his integrity. Even though the same social and moral conditions also existed in Antioch, differences between the rich and the poor, poverty and luxury, high and lower classes, were much more pronounced in Constantinople than in Antioch. Therefore, Chrysostom began to preach to the rich, urging them to help the poor and cease behaving arrogantly towards them.[56] His efforts to rebuild morality and piety in the city through reformation of both clergy and laymen were courageous. Palladius, "who was present at the Synod of the Oak, where Chrysostom was deposed by Theophilus"[57] witnessed how Chrysostom fulfilled his mission as archbishop of the imperial city and chief hierarch of the growing Byzantine church:

> Now that he was ordained John began the proper care of his affairs. First of all he tried his flock by playing the pipe of reason. Sometimes he used the staff of correction as well. He reprimanded very strongly that way of life that went under the fictitious name of "living together as brother and sister." After this he began to speak about injustice, condemning avarice, that metropolis of evil, with the intent of building a firm foundation for righteousness. For it is a characteristic of good builders to pull down first of all the structure of falsehood and to erect later the firm foundation of truth, as it was said by the prophet. "I have set you this day over nations, and over kingdoms, to root up and to pull down, and to waste and to destroy and to build."[58]

Chrysostom's strong reprimand of the church stemmed partly from the ascetic life he had known and the influence of his godly mother.[59] He

---

Antioch. Because John was well received by the people in Antioch and it may create a riot again if it is noticed of his moving out of the city.

56. Baur, *John Chrysostom*, 2:82.
57. Meyer, *Palladius*, 3.
58. Meyer, *Palladius*, 38.
59. Chrysostom, *On the Priesthood*, 1:5.

Conversation with Chrysostom

began church reformation through his supervision of the church's finances, personally intervening in the use of church funds by abolishing Episcopal banquets and cutting out all unnecessary expenses in the bishop's household in order to provide hospital funds for the poor.[60] This action contributed to his unpopularity among the clergy and the rich. Chrysostom's high regard for ministry to the poor was also depicted in his preaching. One example is his preaching on Matt 25:31-41 where he stated, "Unto this most delightful portion of scripture, which we do not cease continually revolving, let us now listen with all earnestness and compunction, this wherewith his discourse ended, even as the last thing, reasonably; for great indeed was his regard for philanthropy and mercy."[61] B. H. Vandenburghe pointed out that, theologically, almsgiving is giving restitution to God in the person of Christ who became poor for our benefit. When a Christian gives alms, it is as to Jesus Christ as declared in Matt 25:40. Possibly no one has expressed this essential Christian doctrine with more persuasion than Chrysostom.[62] The conflicts between Chrysostom and the monks as well as bishops in Constantinople were unavoidable, as the nature of monasticism at Constantinople was radically different from what Chrysostom had experienced and practiced. Living without any regard for ecclesiastical authority, monks moved in and out of monasteries and retired from monastic life as they pleased with little discipline exercised on them because of misbehavior. Therefore when Chrysostom came to Constantinople, he pursued the integrity of the religious order in public and private arenas.[63] Concerning the unethical practices of bishops in Constantinople, Sozomen writes:

> John, having been informed that many of the bishops of Asia and of the neighboring churches were unworthy of their office, and that they sold the priesthood for money, or bestowed that dignity as a matter of private favor, repaired to Ephesus, and deposed thirteen bishops of Lydia, Phrygia, and Asia, and elected others in their stead.[64]

60. Ibid., 39. Palladius states that " He built more hospitals and over these he delegated two devout priests in addition to doctors, cooks, and other workers from unmarried state to look after them. In this way strangers coming from afar to the city and becoming ill could receive proper medical care. This hospital was not only a good venture, but it served for the glory of God as well." See also Liebeschuetz, "Friends and Enemies," 89.

61. Chrysostom, *Homilies on Matthew* (NPNF1 10:474).

62. Vandenburghe, *John of the Golden Mouth*, 49.

63. Liebeschuetz, "Friends and Enemies," 92.

64. Sozomen, *Ecclesiastical History* (NPNF2 8:384-85). Sozomen states, "The enmity

Pastoral Leadership

All dependable historical evidence witnesses that Chrysostom was an innocent victim of the harsh actions taken by Empress Eudoxia and Theophilus, Bishop of Alexandria, and he willingly accepted their condemnation to become exiled.[65] From the start, Theophilus had opposed Chrysostom's ordination as Patriarch of Constantinople and was eventually successful in persuading the emperor and his followers to depose Chrysostom and send him into exile. One particular instance of conflict between Chrysostom and Theophilus was due to the unjust excommunication of the Tall Brothers and Isidore by Theophilus.[66] Without investigating their confession of faith, Theophilus accused the four Tall Brothers and Isidore to be adherents of the heresy of origin and expelled them from Alexandria. Chrysostom argued that it was not proper for a bishop to be tried outside of his province[67] but he received the Tall Brothers and Isidore with kindness, treated them with honor, allowing them to pray in the church and gave them quarters in the Church of Resurrection but did not admit them to Holy Communion. The Empress Eudoxia became hostile towards Chrysostom because she assumed he had deliberately insulted her by calling her "Jezebel." Even though Chrysostom may not have intended to denounce her, those who heard him preaching, however, interpreted it in that way and there may have been a lack of wisdom on his part. Because of his integrity, however,

---

of the clergy against John was greatly increased by Serapion, his archdeacon, a man naturally prone to anger, and always ready to insult his opponents. The feelings of hostility were further fostered by the counsel, which Olympia received from John. Olympia was a widow of illustrious birth, zealously attached to the exercises of monastic philosophy. John had several disputes with many of the monks."

65. Historical authenticity of John Chrysostom's integrity is absolutely relied on the ancient writings of Palladius (363–431), Socrates (born 380), Sozomen (born 447), and Theodoret (393–466). All of them witnessed the integrity of John Chrysostom who unjustly was deposed from the seat of the bishop of Constantinople.

66. Sozomen, *Ecclesiastical History* (*NPNF2* 3:392–93). See also Meyer, *Palladius*, 6:42–43. Isidore was a priest in Alexandria who was in charge of a hospice for the care of strangers. He was ordained to the priesthood by St. Athanasius the Great, Patriarch of Alexandria. Theophilus became angry toward Isidore because he defended the Alexandrian priest Peter whom Theophilus had intended to deprive from his priesthood. Palladius also recorded another instance on Theophilus' greediness. A noble widow of the city brought one thousand gold pieces to Isidore that he would purchase clothes for the poorer women of Alexandria, and asked not to share with Theophilus lest he take the money and waste it on stones rather than the poor women. However, being confronted by Theophilus on the occasion, Isidore confessed the account of the whole matter. After that, Theophilus excommunicated Isidore with false accusations.

67. Liebeschuetz, "Fall of John Chrysostom," 11.

Conversation with Chrysostom

Chrysostom chose his own fate of exile because he did not want to participate in religious politics.[68] After being persuaded by the Empress Eudoxia, "the emperor therefore authorized Theophilus to convoke a Synod without delay against John."[69] Chrysostom appeared at the Synod of the Oak to respond to twenty-nine accounts of charges given by the deacon John whom Chrysostom himself expelled from the rank of the clergy for manslaughter.[70] These twenty-nine charges against Chrysostom were all groundless. Palladius,[71] as well as Socrates, expressed the opinion that "all were intent on urging a variety of criminations, many of which were ridiculous."[72] Furthermore, Isaac, the leader of monks, came forward with seventeen more accusations against Chrysostom that could not be validated.[73] Theophilus cleverly took advantage of this situation; at the conclusion of the Synod of the Oak, thirty-six bishops voted to depose Chrysostom. The Synod sent the verdict to the Imperial Majesty for ratification, who commanded that he should be immediately sent into exile.[74] When the people realized what had happened, they were angry and ran to churches and market places,

---

68. Baur, *John Chrysostom*, 2:238. Baur describes Chrysostom's integrity in character by saying that "It is a brilliant proof of the irreproachable conduct of Chrysostom, in whose life and dealings one would not have been able to find anything which, to a reasonable man, would have sufficed for an accusation. Here a criminal must be brought in against the innocent."

69. Socrates, *Ecclesiastical History* (NPNF2 6:324). See also Sozomen, *Ecclesiastical History* (NPNF2 8:399).

70. Baur, *John Chrysostom*, 2:246–47. All twenty-nine charges cannot be validated for criminal cases by prosecutors, nor reasonably persuaded by general public. For example, he had sold marble, which the Patriarch Nectarius had intended for the adornment of the Church of Resurrection. Naturally, Chrysostom, by the same right with which Nectarius had bought it, could sell it again, and use the money for the building of his hospitals.

71. Meyer, *Palladius*, 8:56.

72. Socrates, *Ecclesiastical History* (NPNF2 6:324). Sozomen also stated that the Council decided to depose Chrysostom from the Patriarchate of Constantinople without substantial ground of the accusations except his refusal to obey the summons of the council.

73. Baur, *John Chrysostom*, 2:249. See also Liebeschuetz, "Friends and Enemies," 90.

74. Socrates, *Ecclesiastical History* (NPNF2 6:325). See also Meyer, *Palladius*, 8:57. Concerning this unjust sentence of the Synod, Palladius compared him with Daniel who underwent persecution by the plot of officers under king Darius period and said, "For there the lions were subdued and spared Daniel, but the men turned wild and did not spare the prophet. However, God conquered the wild nature of men once the nature of the beast was subdued."

Pastoral Leadership

even to the palace of the Emperor, demanding their bishop's restoration. Therefore, the Empress persuaded the Emperor to bring him back.[75]

On June 20, 404, Chrysostom began his second exile, a journey to Cucusus, Armenia from which he would not return; Emperor Arcadius had sent a court order to exile Chrysostom. But the exiled bishop took advantage of this opportunity for ministry to the poor. The cruel Empress Eudoxia then ordered Chrysostom to be transferred first to Arabissus, then to Pityus on the shores of the Black Sea. Two brutal guards rushed him along at high speed instructed; the soldiers had been promised promotion if he died on the way. He was in a seriously weakened state as he continued his journey. On September 13, 407, just one day before his death,[76] they continued their journey to the small city of Comana, Pontica about five miles from Dazimon. In Comana the guards again refused to rest and insisted on marching further until they arrived at the chapel of the martyr St. Basiliscus, where they spent the night. Chrysostom, nearing death, pleaded with the soldiers to delay travel but they forced him to continue the journey yet only for very briefly. Chrysostom died on September 14th, 407. His enemies and many others were all later removed from office.

CHRYSOSTOM'S WRITINGS

I now intend to identify Chrysostom's main writings then indicate briefly the quality and extent of recent research on Chrysostom. Chrysostom was known as one of the four preeminent Doctors of the Church along with St. Basil, St. Gregory Nazianzen, and St. Athanasius in the Eastern Church. He was a king among preachers as well as a caring pastor and a writer who produced more than seven hundred homilies,[77] 236 letters,[78] and many other theological works. It is now necessary to refer to a sample of his literary work relating to pastoral leadership before exploring and engaging in conversation with Chrysostom regarding this subject. "Chrysostom was a prolific writer, albeit many of his writings are actually transcriptions of his sermons,"[79] writes Duane Garrett. His writings were influential and his gifts as a writer were described by H. B. Swete: "He is at once a true exegete and

75. Sozomen, *Ecclesiastical History* (NPNF2 8:403); Socrates, *Ecclesiastical History* (NPNF2 6:325).
76. Baur, *John Chrysostom*, 2:420.
77. Attwater, *Pastor and Preacher*, 43.
78. Questen, *Patrology* 3:469.
79. Garrett, *Analysis of the Hermeneutics*, 12:31.

Conversation with Chrysostom

a true orator, a combination found in such perfection perhaps nowhere else."[80] No Greek Father has produced as extensive a literary legacy as Chrysostom.[81]

A turning point in Chrysostom's writing career was his ordination as deacon.[82] Socrates witnessed that "Meletius, having not long after conferred on him the rank of deacon, he produced his work *On Priesthood*."[83] From 380 to 386, Chrysostom performed the full range of pastoral duties in looking after the poor, the sick, the demon possessed, widows and orphans.[84] He also practiced every pastoral duty except preaching, and was aware of the ministries of the Church of Antioch in regard to caring for people. Through his practical experience, he developed a heart for pastoral ministry through his direct contact with different types of people. For example, he had three thousand widows and virgins under his care at the church of Antioch.[85] Methodologically, the limitations of space and the aims of this book demand that in focusing on Chrysostom's pastoral leadership, I will major on and only sample his *On the Priesthood*, some of his homilies on Pastoral Epistles, and a selection of New Testament homilies. I acknowledge that this is a significant delimitation but one which is necessary due to my focus and the vast extent of Chrystostom's writings. I suggest also that this sample of the homilies gives me at least a reliable foundation for identifying his pastoral leadership principles. Regarding his writings, Philip Schaff wrote:

> The best have been preserved and have already been noticed in chronological order. They may be divided into five classes: (1) Moral and ascetic treatises, including the work on the priesthood; (2) About six hundred Homilies and Commentaries; (3) Occasional, festal panegyrical orations; (4) Letters; (5) Liturgy.[86]

The first attempt to produce a scientific edition of the complete works of John Chrysostom, known as *Saint Johannis Chrysostomi Opera Omnos*, was published by Sir Henry Savile (1549–1622) in eight volumes.[87] The next edition of Chrysostom's works, entitled *Fronton le Duc, Sancti Joanis*

80. Swete, *Patristic Study*, 104.
81. Hamell, *Handbook of Patrology*, 115.
82. Schaff, "Prolegomena" (*NPNF1* 4:10).
83. Socrates, *Ecclesiastical History*, 2:139.
84. Kelly, *Golden Mouth*, 39.
85. Chrysostom, *Homilies on Matthew* 61 (*NPNF1* 10:407).
86. Schaff, "Prolegomena"(*NPNF1* 4:5).
87. Garrett, *Analysis of the Hermeneutics*, 32–33.

Pastoral Leadership

Chrysostomi Opera omnia in 12 tomos didtributata, was published in Paris from 1636 to 1642 and called, the "Morel Edition," published by Frederick and Claude Morel.[88] The third edition, the "Benediction Edition of Bernard de Montfaucon," entitled *Sancti Joannis Chrysostomi Opera omnia quae extant vel eius nomine circumferunter*, was published from 1718 to 1738 in Paris in thirteen volumes. This remains the standard edition of Chrysostom's works.[89] The complete set of Patristic texts can be found in the greatest and most important collection of all by Jacques Paul Migne.[90] I accept Schaff's division of Chrysostom's life into five periods and though some of his works cannot be dated, it is still useful to explore his writings chronologically.

I now explore a sample of writings from each period of Chrysostom's life from a pastoral leadership perspective. His homilies from 386 to 398 in Antioch and also from 398 until his final exile in Constantinople are vital to the exploration of his pastoral leadership principles. As already indicated, his *On the Priesthood*, written before 386, has also significant value because it reveals his general views on the priesthood. During the early period, AD 347-70, there is little evidence that Chrysostom produced any literary writings, but the years AD 370-81 formed his first period of literary activity.

His first work, entitled *A Comparison between a King and a Monk*, marks a significant turning point in his philosophical life, describing his personal departure from worldliness to the religious life; it was probably composed shortly after his return to Antioch from the monastic life in 378.[91] As a Christian apologist, he defended his Christian philosophy of life, arguing against the relative and temporary views of the visible world from the perspective of the ideal of Christian perfection. From the same period, he wrote another important literary work, entitled *Against the Enemies of Monasticism*,[92] which is composed of three books. In it, he attacks the enemies of monasticism and refutes their accusations. Chrysostom persuades Christian fathers to send their sons to monks for higher education and moral training[93] as they were known to provide good education for children in Antioch. Often, the young men did not wish to return after-

---

88. Ibid., 33.
89. Schaff, "Prolegomena" (*NPNF1* 4:3).
90. Hamell, *Handbook of Patrology*, 13-18.
91. Chrysostom, *King and a Monk*, 39.
92. Quasten, *Patrology*, 3:463.
93. Ibid.

Conversation with Chrysostom

wards to their families because they were attracted to the monks' way of life so many people in Antioch mistreated the monks in the streets and markets. Chrysostom wrote the aforementioned book to advocate the values of a monastic life.[94] He continued to persuade pagan and Christian parents in order to help them understand the value of Monasticism, encouraging parents to honor the work of monks. It was apparent that his main motif was to provide pastoral care rather than giving a harsh rebuke.

In his *Two Letters: An Exhortation to Theodore after His Fall*, Chrysostom's pastoral heart was demonstrated by persuading his friends to turn to the Christian faith, even before he himself received holy orders. The period of AD 381–98 represents his work as a priest and preacher at Antioch. Ordained as deacon, he had various opportunities in serving as many as 3,000 people who depended on the local church for their material needs.[95] During this time, he produced his most important literary works, which I identify below. His *Letter to a Young Widow* was a consolatory letter to a young widow whose husband had died after five years of happy marriage.[96] This letter must have been written before 382 when Chrysostom consoled and encouraged the young widow to remain a pure bride of Christ. *On Virginity and Widowhood* was produced when Chrysostom returned from the Mountain around 381–82. J. N. D. Kelly appears to be correct in affirming:

> It was addressed, apparently, to women who had already embraced the virgin state. Its aim was to demolish the doubts of critics of virginity by highlighting its special dignity, and to impress on dedicated virgins both its demands and its signal rewards.[97]

The treatise was mainly intended as a detailed interpretation of Paul's statement in 1 Cor 7 regarding marriage.[98] In *On Vain Glory*[99] and *How Parents Should Bring up Children*,[100] Chrysostom communicated strongly that people needed a spiritual awakening so he attacked the luxury and immorality that prevailed in Antioch; in *On the Education of Children*, he

---

94. Baur, *John Chrysostom*, 1:118.
95. Attwater, *Pastor and Preacher*, 33.
96. Baur, *John Chrysostom*, 1:164.
97. Kelly, *Golden Mouth*, 45.
98. Quasten, *Patrology*, 3:464.
99. In Greek, *kenodoxia* means "vanity, conceit, holding emptiness without reality."
100. Malingrey, *Sur la vaine glorie*, 188. There are only two surviving MSS and the first published in 1656 by the Dominican F. Combefis under the more apposite title (in Latin) *St. John Chrysostom's Golden Book on Bringing Up Children*.

Pastoral Leadership

"intends to protect the youth from such vices by teaching the right way for parents to bring up their sons and daughters."[101] Kelly points out that Chrysostom emphasized the provision of spiritual and moral training for children as the most important parental duty and as the foundation of Christian pedagogy.[102] His *On the Priesthood* was the product of Chrysostom's experience at the Antioch Church and it became one of the most important works written on the priesthood at that time. Meletius' kindness in welcoming Chrysostom to the church by appointing him deacon also contributed to his ability to write this monumental work.[103]

Discourses against Judaizing Christians consists of eight homilies delivered at the Church of Antioch from 386 to 387, after Chrysostom's ordination. These homilies were especially directed at Christian Jews in his congregation.[104] Chrysostom was not an anti-Semite, but assailed specifically nominal Christians in his congregation only because they were jeopardizing their Christian faith by participation in Jewish ceremonies and festivals. Paul W. Harkins added the word "Christians" to the original title when he translated this discourse because he believed that Chrysostom delivered these eight homilies only to Christian Jews in the Antioch Church, not to all the Jews.[105] Chrysostom's impolite descriptions of the Jews, such as "the Judaizing disease," "pitiable and miserable," or "the Jews, the most miserable and wretched of all men,"[106] added to the antagonism expressed against Chrysostom personally. His *Baptismal Instruction* is an important element in Chrysostom's literary writings when exploring his pastoral theology. This aspect of his pastoral practice came into focus when Pere Antoine Wenger published the complete series of Chrysostom's catechetical *Instructions* in 1955. Through these twelve instructions for baptism, Chrysostom envisioned the ideal of the committed disciple of

---

101. Quasten, *Patrology*, 3:465.

102. Kelly, *Golden Mouth*, 85–87. Kelly believes that Chrysostom is a strong believer of parents' Christian education at home training them as athletes for Christ.

103. Neander, *Life of St. Chrysostom*, 38. Neander explains how Chrysostom could produce many important writings during his ministry under Meletius. He writes, "While he performed the duties of this office, which did not require his exclusive attention, he devoted his leisure hours to compose, on various occasions, treatises, in which he strongly enjoined the practice of Christian virtues."

104. Quasten, *Patrology*, 3:452.

105. Harkins, "Introduction," in Chrysostom's *Discourses against Judaizing Christians*, 68:xxi–xxxix. See also Wilken, *Chrysostom and the Jews*, 72.

106. Chrysostom, *Discourses against Judaizing Christians*, 3, 5, 71, 95, 214, 225.

Conversation with Chrysostom

Christ overcoming Satanic-like temptations. He concluded by charging: "Therefore, teach yourself now, so that when you receive the sign, you will be a ready soldier, and that after you raise the trophies of your rout of the devil, you will receive the crown of justice."[107] Chrysostom's instructions may be considered an ancient manual of discipleship training because "it highlights the change of character of a preacher's audience."[108]

Twenty-One Homilies Concerning the Statues were delivered at Antioch on Saturday, March 27, 387 in the course of the Lent that followed the riots.[109] Hearing of the imposition of an extraordinary tax upon the people, the mob mutilated the Statues of the Emperor Theodosius and the Imperial family. Theodosius was so outraged that he considered destroying the city and the people were terrified at the prospect of their impending punishment.[110] During this critical time, Chrysostom assumed a pastoral role and preached to console and prompted the people to repentance. He felt that "the present troubles are to be viewed as a penance for one's sins, and that it is by deepening one's spiritual union with God that one may hope to win his forgiveness."[111] On the return of Flavian the Bishop who brought the message of the Emperor's reconciliation with the city, Chrysostom preached his twenty-first sermon.[112] *Seven Homilies on Wealth and Poverty* is the only collection taken from the gospel of Luke.[113] Chrysostom preached these homilies after the Riot in 387, sending a message to people that the reward of the afterlife is better than life in this present world. He delivered a series of sermons on the parable of Lazarus and the rich man, either in 388 or 389.[114] Chrysostom expected that his sermons would have a transforming effect on the lives of those in his audience so he began the last sermon:

> I want to start again on my usual instruction and set the spiritual table before you; but I hesitate and draw back, seeing that you have

---

107. Chrysostom, *Baptismal Instructions*, 190–91.

108. Mayer and Allen, *John Chrysostom*, 126.

109. Browning, "Riot of AD 387," 13–20. The Riot at Antioch is described in two eyewitness accounts—that of Libanius and that of John Chrysostom.

110. Quasten, *Patrology*, 3:456.

111. Kelly, *Golden Mouth*, 79.

112. Mayer and Allen, *John Chrysostom*, 105. Mayer and Allen point out in these homilies that Chrysostom exhibited a profound pastoral concern for the people.

113. Chrysostom, *On Wealth and Poverty*.

114. Roth, "Introduction" in *On Wealth and Poverty*, 10.

Pastoral Leadership

> gathered no fruit from my continual preaching. When a farmer has sowed the seeds with a generous hand in the bosom of the earth, and sees that the yield is not worthy of his efforts, he does not undertake his work with the same willingness; for the hope of the harvest always relieves the burden of effort.[115]

He may have been impatient in expecting the moral transformation of his people to occur immediately but nevertheless, his preaching continued to focus on directing peoples' lives towards godliness.

Ten Homilies on Repentance and Almsgiving is an extremely important collection for exploring the ecclesiastical nature of his work. He preached them in Antioch during 386–87. Although some doubt has been cast on the authenticity of homilies five, seven, eight, and nine,[116] they are considered genuine by Constantine Loukakis, the Greek patristic scholar and compiler of Chrysostom's writings.[117] In the nine homilies on repentance, Chrysostom taught his congregation that the most appropriate way to proceed in the presence of God was through repentance. The tenth sermon on almsgiving was delivered after Chrysostom had an opportunity to meet the poor and the beggars when passing through the market place during winter. His preaching was not speculative, but expressed his concern and heartbreaking encounters with the poor. He began his sermon with these words:

> Today, I stand before you to make a just, useful, and suitable intercession. I come from no one else; only the beggars who live in our city elected me for this purpose, not with words, votes, and the resolve of a common council, but rather with their pitiful and most bitter spectacle.[118]

Through his sermon, Chrysostom allowed his congregation to understand what he had experienced and encouraged them to practice generosity towards the poor.

On the Incomprehensible Nature of God consisted of twelve sermons divided into two series. The first series contained five sermons delivered

---

115. Chrysostom, *On Wealth and Poverty*, 125.

116. Aldama, *Repertorium Pseudochrysostomicum*, 34.

117. Christo, "Introduction," in *On Repentance and Almsgiving*, xv. Constantine Loukakis said: "These nine homilies have all the characteristics of the Chrysostomian corpus. They reveal unity of thought and are expressed briskly. They exclude a deep knowledge of the human soul and are well founded in Holy Scripture." Loukakis, *Works of St. John Chrysostom*, 1:144.

118. Chrysostom, *On Repentance and Almsgiving*, 96:131.

at Antioch in order to attack the Anomoeans,[119] the most radical of the Arian parties.[120] "Chrysostom defends the ineffable, and incomprehensible nature of God against rationalistic tendencies, which denied the divine transcendence. At the same time he pointed out the co-equality of the Son with the Father."[121] Using the Greek word for "condescension," Chrysostom attempted to explain the essence of Christ in the flesh. In his seventh homily, he wrote:

> This is why he did not, from the very beginning, assume a mature manhood. He allowed himself to be conceived, born, nourished with milk. He spent so long a time in this world so that he might prove that he was true flesh both by the length of his days and by every other means.[122]

While Chrysostom was interested in social issues, he also wanted to preserve theological orthodoxy like his older contemporaries, Basil of Caesarea and Gregory of Nyssa.[123] He then wrote *The Discourse on Blessed Babylas and against the Greeks* in praise of this martyr, most likely between 363 and 380 at bishop Meletius's encouragement.[124] Babylas was the successor of Zebinus as Bishop of Antioch during the reign of the Emperor Gordianus (238–44). During the Decian persecution (260), he died in prison because of his unwavering confession of faith. Chrysostom praised his apostolic boldness. Chrysostom delivered a great number of panegyrics on the Saints but none were as famous as the *Homiliae 7 de laudibus S. Pauli*.[125] Thomas Halton reports, "It seems certain from references in sermon four to Julian and the Shrine of Apollo at Daphne, a suburb of Antioch that these panegyrics were preached at Antioch sometime during Chrysostom's twelve-year stay there after his ordination (386–98 AD)."[126]

119. The Anomoeans were an extreme sect of the Arians founded by Aetius (fourth century) who believed that the Son was a totally different substance from the Father and was created from nothing. He was a Syrian bishop, originally ordained a deacon at Antioch to teach Christian doctrine. Aetius nevertheless alienated the general membership of Arians by his extreme views on the Son. *Encyclopedia Britannica*, 1:116–17.

120. Quasten, *Patrology*, 3:451.

121. Ibid., 451.

122. Chrysostom, *Incomprehensible Nature of God*, 72:205.

123. Kelly, *Golden Mouth*, 61.

124. Schatkin, "Introduction," in Chrysostom's *Apologist*, 15. See also Baur, *John Chrysostom*, 1:285.

125. Quasten, *Patrology*, 3:456.

126. Halton, "Introduction," in *Praise of Saint Paul*, 9.

Pastoral Leadership

In these seven sermons, Chrysostom described Paul as the exemplar for Christian maturity and following Christ. In comparison with Old Testament Saints, Chrysostom believed "St. Paul was the noblest of men and the most outstanding example of the nobility of human nature and of its possibilities for virtue."[127] Chrysostom confessed, "I love all the saints, but I live most the blessed Paul, the chosen vessel, the heavenly trumpet, the friend of the bridegroom, Christ."[128] He compared St. Paul with a royal procession, which draws crowds to watch a majestic scene. Chrysostom named Paul "a Standard-Bearer of Christ" because he carried the Cross of Christ and invited people to imitate him just as he himself imitated Christ.[129] Paul was Chrysostom's ideal for imitation because of his Christian virtue, his mission to the world, and his bearing of Christ's cross. Scholars in recent years, like Margaret Mitchell for example, have appreciated the historical and theological significance of Chrysostom's understanding of Pauline Theology.[130]

Exegetical Homilies of Chrysostom

One of Chrysostom's strengths was his love of Scripture and most of his writings are exegetical homilies on the Old and New Testaments delivered at Antioch between 386 and 397.[131] He delivered approximately eight hundred discourses with eighteen thousand biblical quotations and knew Scripture by heart; he also tried to live according to the Word and penetrate people's hearts with Scripture in order to transform their lives.

His Old Testament Homilies began in 388 when Chrysostom started the preaching of his sixty-seven homilies on Genesis at the Antioch Church.[132] While always conscious of his pastoral role in caring for people,[133] Chrysostom did not neglect theological exhortation regarding God's sovereign will

127. Chrysostom, *Praise of Saint Paul*, 29.

128. Chrysostom, *Homilies on Second Corinthians* 23 (*NPNF1* 12:383).

129. Ibid., 103–06. See also Chrysostom, *Chrysostom and His Message*, 69–79. Stephen Neil stated that: "Chrysostom, as we have seen, had a special affection for the apostle Paul, whom in some ways he resembled, being small in stature and of fiery speech, and of whom he must often have thought in his own time of exile and suffering."

130. Mitchell, *Heavenly Trumpet*, 5. Mitchell emphasized the importance of Chrysostom's contribution for the understanding of Pauline theology. She writes: "Chrysostom's interpretation and his letters are of monumental importance, both for what it teaches us of trends and ideas in Pauline interpretation in the patristic age."

131. Quasten, *Patrology*, 3:433.

132. Ibid., 3:285.

133. Hill, "Introduction," in *Homilies on Genesis*, 74:11.

Conversation with Chrysostom

for the salvation of people as he preached through Genesis. He focused on the theme of salvation history beginning with Adam, Noah, Abraham, Jacob and the chosen people of Israel. Chrysostom's priority in preaching was to help people through Scripture so they would be enabled to live from God's perspective. Chrysostom most likely delivered his commentary on Isa 1–8 in the year 388.[134] Duane A. Garrett writes, "Although not a series of homilies, it reflects the moral and spiritual concerns of its author."[135] Here, he used an expository method and employed Scripture to interpret the text. Challenging the religious leaders of his time, he also attacked their insensitivity towards their neighbors. Chrysostom wrote:

> Those who do not feed the hungry, but who do not steal others' possessions, while still not letting their possessions to go to the needy, will be sent to the fire of hell. So now they are reproached, not for being greedy or oppressive, but because of they do not extend a helping hand to the needy.[136]

Providing material assistance to the needy was an exhortation he included in nearly all of his sermons. This constant exhortation can also be attributed to the context of the Church of Antioch, where he served until 398.[137] Chrysostom's other commentary on the Old Testament is based on fifty-eight selective Psalms including Pss 4–13, 44–50, 109–18, and 120–50.[138] Similar to his homilies, the Psalms commentary has spiritual characteristics with strong moral tones.[139] Just as in the Genesis homilies, the sin of the first parents was identified as indifference, sloth, neglect, so too in the conduct of spiritual life.[140] Chrysostom's preaching ministry thus provided a significant opportunity for the spiritual renewal of the people. But in his exegesis of Old Testament books, I agree with Chase who concludes Chrysostom was not a Hebrew scholar but rather depended on the

---

134. Baur, *John Chrysostom*, 1:285.

135. Garrett, *Analysis of the Hermeneutics*, 245.

136. Ibid., 56.

137. Chrysostom, *Homilies on Matthew*, 66 (NPNF1 10:407). He writes: "Consider how many widows it succors every day, how many virgins; for indeed the list of them hath already reached unto the number of three thousand."

138. Hill, "Introduction," in *Commentary on the Psalms*, 1:1–3.

139. Ibid., 36. In regard to spirituality, Robert Hill writes: "In general it could be said of his treatment of this great spiritual resource, the Psalms, that, faithful to the principles of Antiochene realism, Chrysostom has his feet on the ground not only in biblical commentary but also in his approach to spirituality."

140. Ibid., 40. *Rathymia* in Greek means "unconcerned, idle, and relax."

Pastoral Leadership

Septuagint version.[141] His lack of Hebrew may have caused him to produce fewer commentaries on the Old Testament than on the New.[142]

Regarding his *New Testament Homilies,* Chrysostom wrote commentaries on all four gospels,[143] although the manuscripts for the Mark and Luke commentaries are not available.[144] Among the New Testament books, Chrysostom wrote homilies on Matthew, John, Romans, 1 and 2 Corinthians, Galatians, Ephesians, Philippians, 1 and 2 Timothy, Titus and Philemon and he preached these homilies at the Antioch Church. The homilies on the Acts of the Apostles, Colossians and Hebrews were written at Constantinople.[145]

In recent years, however, Wendy Mayer has challenged the validity of the date and provenance of Chrysostom's individual homilies on the basis of internal evidence as well as textual and archaeological sources.[146] As far as the churches are concerned, Mayer stated: "At Antioch, we have evidence of only three churches, the Old Church, the Great or Golden Church and the Church of St. Babylas."[147] She also named five different churches that

---

141. *The Septuagint (LXX)* or *Interpretation of the Seventy Men* was the earliest translation of the Old Testament into Greek at Alexandria about 250 BC. The purpose of translation was that the Alexandrian Jews spoke Greek but no longer understood Hebrew. Seventy-two elders, six from each tribe of Israel, were brought to Alexandria from Palestine under the auspices of Ptolemy II Philadelphus (285–46 BC). Pfeiffer, *Introduction to Old Testament,* 104–5. See also Philo, "On the Life of Moses," 493–94. Philo writes, "He, then, being a sovereign of this character, and having conceived a great admiration for and love of the legislation of Moses, conceived the idea of having our laws translated into the Greek language; and immediately he sent out ambassadors to the high-priest and king Judea, for they were the same person."

142. Ibid., 30.

143. Baur, *John Chrysostom,* 1:289. Baur also mentions, "Suidas states in his Lexicon that Chrysostom had spoken of all the four Gospels through homilies. Actually some few manuscripts exist, which contain commentaries on Mark and Luke under the name of Chrysostom. However, these are merely anthologies. As a matter of fact, Chrysostom only explained two Gospels homiletically: Matthew and John."

144. Quasten, *Patrology,* 3:436. Quasten writes, "There are in fact a few manuscripts which contain explanations of Mark and Luke attributed to Chrysostom, but they amount to no more than florilegia. Nobody else ever speaks of works by Chrysostom on those two Gospels."

145. Ibid., 437–50.

146. Mayer, "Extraordinary Preacher," 105–37.

147. Ibid., 126.

Conversation with Chrysostom

Chrysostom preached at in Constantinople: "St. Anastasia, St. Eirene, St. Paul, the Great Church, and the Church of Holy Apostles."[148]

The Commentary on the Gospel of Matthew has been generally accepted as the ninety homilies on Matthew, which were preached during 386–90 at Antioch.[149] It is assumed that Chrysostom used the Syrian text of the New Testament, as Westcott and Hort have shown, because it was the standard text in the Eastern Church around AD 350.[150] In addition to his spiritual and moral exhortations, Chrysostom also did not neglect to correct heretical beliefs, stressing the equality of the Son with the Father in order to refute the Arians but especially the Manicheans,[151] throughout the entire series of his homilies.[152]

The Commentary on the Gospel of John consisted of eighty-eight homilies on the Gospel of John delivered around 391 at the Church of Antioch. Here, the defense of the deity of Christ is particularly evident and was used against the Arians. However, Chrysostom's homilies on the book of John are far more controversial than those on Matthew.[153] Vehemently set against the beliefs of the Arians, Chrysostom was inclined to be polemical, defending Christ's deity and equality with the Father but he never neglected opportunities to preach on, and demand, personal virtue.

---

148. Ibid., 127.

149. Baur, *John Chrysostom*, 1:289. The Oxford edition of the *Homilies of Chrysostom on the Gospel of Matthew* was published in three volumes, respectively in 1843, 44, and 45.

150. Riddle, "St. Chrysostom as an Exegete," in Chrysostom's *Homilies on Matthew* (*NPNF1* 10:xxi).

151. In the latter half of the third century Mani the Persian founded a religion called Manichaeism based on the religious system of Zoroastrian Dualism, opposing the absolute creation of God. They believe in the theory of two eternal principles of good and evil. Chrysostom refuted them by teaching the absolute creation of monotheistic activity of God. He writes: "And why does He not make it of things that are not? Stopping the mouth of Marcion, and of Manichaeus, who alienate His creation from Him, and teaching by His very works, that even all things that are seen are His works and creatures, and signifying that it is Himself who gives fruits." Chrysostom, *Homilies on Matthew* 49 (*NPNF1* 10:5).

152. Baur, *John Chrysostom*, 1:289.

153. Quasten, *Patrology*, 3:439.

Pastoral Leadership

Commentary on Romans[154] was the first Pauline commentary Chrysostom wrote and is also considered the best commentary he produced.[155] Chrysostom had a special affection for the Apostle Paul as evidenced, for example, in his commentary on Rom 9:3 in the sixteenth homily.[156] The eighth and thirty-second homilies point to Antioch as the place of origin and between 381 and 398. Chrysostom clearly defined theological politics in his twenty-third homily on the exegesis of Rom 13:1. Chrysostom believed that Christian theology does not only include the doctrine of God and salvation, but also ethical teaching on how to live a virtuous life.

Homilies on First and Second Corinthians[157] consisted of his forty-four homilies on 1 Corinthians and his thirty homilies on 2 Corinthians written in Antioch[158] during 386–97, most likely after Chrysostom had written his Romans commentary.[159] He eloquently refuted the thinking of unbelieving Greeks and Jews in his exegesis of 1 Cor 1–2.

Commentary on Galatians[160] was written as an ordinary commentary, providing a verse-by-verse explanation. Similar to the homilies of the Gospel of John, Chrysostom persuaded the Galatians to depart from Judaism. For example, he labeled the false teachers by using expressions such as "intoxicated by vain-glory" or "desirous of obtaining for themselves the dignity of teachers."[161] Chrysostom was also indignant against another class of heretics, the Manichees who considered matter intrinsically evil and worshiped the sun and stars.[162] His *Homilies on the Epistle to the Ephesians*[163] in-

---

154. The Greek text of the Romans commentary was first published by Henry Savile (1549–1622) in 1616.

155. Baur, *John Chrysostom*, 1:297–98.

156. Marriott, "Preface to Homilies on Romans," in Chrysostom's *Homilies on Romans* (*NPNF1* 11:331).

157. Young, "First and Second Corinthians," 349–52.

158. In homily twenty-one on First Corinthians, he specifically mentioned the name Antioch, which suggests he wrote this during his ministry there.

159. Baur, *John Chrysostom*, 1:298.

160. Kelly believes that he wrote *Galatians* perhaps in 394. Kelly, *Golden Mouth*, 91. Newman assigned the date earlier than 394. Newman, "Preface," in Chrysostom's *Commentary on the Galatians* (*NFNP1* 13:611–82).

161. Chrysostom, *Commentary on Galatians* (*NPNF1* 13:2).

162. Ibid., 5. Manichaeism was founded by the Syrio-Persian, Mani (AD 216–76) who was raised in a Jewish-Christian sect in south Babylonia. It was regarded as a Christianized form of Zoroastrianism that holds the dualism: light and darkness, good and evil.

163. Quasten, *Patrology*, 3:447.

Conversation with Chrysostom

clude twenty-four homilies probably written in Antioch before 398 because two familiar names, St. Babylas in homily nine[164] and St. Julian in homily twenty-one,[165] are mentioned.[166] However, Wendy Mayer and Pauline Allen have recently challenged this belief and stated that the composition of the homilies on Ephesians occurred in Constantinople.[167] Chrysostom stated in his eleventh homily: "I am ready to retire from my office, and resign it to whomever you may choose. Only let the Church be one."[168] Mayer and Allen have conjectured that the church schism could only have occurred in Constantinople[169]; however, no conclusive evidence exists.[170] During his twelve years of pastoral ministry at the Antioch Church, Chrysostom preached through all thirteen books of the recognized Pauline Epistles except for Colossians and I and II Thessalonians. Expounding Ephesians, he did not neglect ecclesiology[171] or Christian matrimony.[172]

The Homilies of the Philippians[173] numbered fifteen and probably given in Antioch. The fifteenth homily refers much more to the Emperor

164. Chrysostom, *Homilies on Ephesians* 9 (*NPNF*1 13:96). Chrysostom said, "Shall I mention, in passing. A thought, which just at this moment occurs to me? The blessed martyr Babylas was bound, and he too for the very same cause as John also was, because he reproved a king in his transgression." Babylas was Bishop of Antioch when he was martyred in the Decian persecution.

165. Ibid., 13:155. Chrysostom praised Julian in his sermon: "I mean the admirable Julian. This man was a rustic, in humble life, and of humble parentage, and totally uninstructed in all outward accomplishments, but full of unadorned wisdom."

166. Quasten, *Patrology* 3:447.

167. Mayer and Allen, *John Chrysostom*, 59. See also Mayer, "Provenance of the Homilies."

168. Chrysostom, *Homilies on Ephesians* 11 (*NPNF*1 13:108).

169. Mayer and Allen, *John Chrysostom*, 59–60.

170. Mayer, "John Chrysostom and His Audiences," 70–75. Mayer stated that: "Moreover, since Chrysostom preached at Antioch for some twelve years and at Constantinople on and off for six, one would expect that the relationship at each location would not be static, but would alter as different local factors entered into the equation."

171. Regarding the Apostle Paul's teaching on the unity of the church where there is diversity, Chrysostom explained, "The body is composed of members both honorable and dishonorable. Only the greater is not to rise up even against the meanest, nor this latter to envy the other. They do not all indeed contribute the same share, but severally according to the proportion of need." Chrysostom, *Homilies on Ephesians* (*NPNF*1 13:99).

172. Chrysostom clearly understood and taught correctly in regard to the responsibilities of husband and wife respectively. He wrote, "Would not you have your wife obedient unto you, as the Church is to Christ? Take then yourself the same provident care for her, as Christ takes for the Church." Chrysostom, *Homilies on Ephesians* (*NPNF*1 13:144).

173. Baur, *John Chrysostom*, 1:299. It is reasonable to consider Antioch as the place

Pastoral Leadership

Theodosius than Arcadius[174] because Chrysostom was in Constantinople at the time of Arcadius.[175] The seventh homily on Phil 2:5-11 is a very strong defense of the doctrine of the Incarnation, arguing against the heretics of Marcionites,[176] Paul of Samosata,[177] and the Arians.[178] Chrysostom theologically defended Christ's simultaneous divinity and his humanity.

Bernard de Montfaucon[179] provided two reasons why *Homilies on the Epistles to Timothy, Titus, and Philemon* were written in Antioch rather than in Constantinople. First, Chrysostom often speaks of the monks who demonstrated exemplary devotion and discipline as he himself had shown in Antioch. The second reason is that "in homily eight on 2 Tim 3, he seems pretty evidently to allude to the burning of the Temple of Apollo at Daphne. One can hardly doubt the allusion, in reading the full account in the homily on St. Babylas."[180] The mention of Daphne and the cave of Matrona in homily three on Titus also point to the Antioch origin of the homilies because these places are located near the Syrian capital.[181]

---

where he preached these homilies.

174. Theodosius I was the roman Emperor who was born in Spain about 346 and died in 395 before Chrysostom was transferred to Constantinople.

175. Baur, *John Chrysostom*, 1:300. Chrysostom writes: "For he would not have broken out into such vengeance, had he not been deeply affected with that distress." Chrysostom, *Homilies on Philippians* 15 (*NPNF1* 13:254).

176. Schaff, *History of the Christian Church*, 2:482-85. Marcionites are a sect founded by Marcion in AD 144 at Rome. He rejected the writings of the Old Testament as an extreme anti-Jewish. He taught that Christ was not the Son of God of the Jews, but the Son of good God of the ancient covenant. He anticipated the more consistent dualism of Manichaeism. Marcion was the son of a bishop of Sinope in Pontus and was excommunicated by his own father.

177. Ibid., 575-76. Paul of Samosata was a bishop of Antioch from 260. He denied the personality of the Logos and of the Holy Spirit, and regarded them merely as the power of God. He was deposed at the third synod held in Antioch AD 269 or 268.

178. Quasten, *Patrology*. 3:448.

179. Bernard de Montfaucon was a French scholar born in 1655 at the chateau de Soulatge.

180. Marriott, "Preface" in *Homilies on Timothy* (*NPNF1* 13:401).

181. Chrysostom, *Homilies on Timothy* (*NPNF1* 13:529). See also Quasten, *Patrology*, 3:450

Conversation with Chrysostom

398–404 AD (FROM CONSTANTINOPLE TO EXILE)

Chrysostom was writing more prolifically while he was at Antioch from 381 to 398[182]; during this period he produced many important writings including many of the homilies. This productive writing period was partly due to the increased time he had available to prepare these works as compared to his time constrained in Constantinople[183] as well as his distress and humiliation.[184]

Chrysostom began his *Fifty-five Homilies on the Acts of the Apostles*[185] during Easter week of the third year of his residency as Archbishop in Constantinople in AD 400.[186] At the beginning of homily one, Chrysostom explained the purpose of this series: "To many persons this Book is so little known, both it and its author, that they are not even aware there is such a book in existence. For this reason especially I have taken this narrative for my subject."[187] Chrysostom especially emphasized the important value of the book of Acts in that it spoke of the Holy Spirit, Christian wisdom and sound doctrine, and he emphasized that these treasures should not remain hidden.[188] His emphasis on the necessity of expounding Acts also revealed his desire for prayer and for the working of the Holy Ghost in his situation.[189]

Homilies on the Epistle to the Colossians[190] were twelve in number and must have been delivered at Constantinople as homily three states:

> You despise not Me, but the Priesthood; when you see me stripped of this, then despise me; then no more will I endure to impose commands. But so long as we sit upon this throne, so long as we have the first place, we have both the dignity and the power, even though we are unworthy.[191]

---

182. Schaff, "Prolegomena" (*NPNF1* 9:10–12).
183. Socrates, *Ecclesiastical History* (*NPNF1* 2:138–40).
184. Quasten, *Patrology*, 3:429.
185. Marriott, "Preface," in *Homilies on Acts* (*NPNF1* 11:ix).
186. Ibid.
187. Chrysostom, *Homilies on Acts* (*NPNF1* 11:1).
188. Ibid., 1.
189. Quasten, *Patrology*, 3:441.
190. Chrysostom, *Homilies on Colossians* (*NPNF1* 14:181–334).
191. Ibid., (*NPNF1* 13:274). Here "this throne" indicates his patriarchal position at Constantinople so that it is certain these homilies were delivered at Constantinople. See also Quasten, *Patrology*, 3:448.

Pastoral Leadership

Theologically, these homilies have an important value because Chrysostom again defended Christ's deity.[192]

Homilies on the First and Second Epistles to the Thessalonians must also have been delivered in Constantinople. In homily eight of 1 Thessalonians, for example, Chrysostom described the frightening circumstance he faced: "Because while each of you fears for his own soul, I have to answer for this office also in which I preside over you."[193] In homily four of 2 Thessalonians he asks the congregation to offer prayers to overcome their enemies:

> Thus let us make war with our enemies with prayers and supplications. For if thus the ancients made war with men in arms, much more ought we so to make war with men without arms. So Hezekiah triumphed over the Assyrian king, so Moses over Amalek, so Samuel over the men of Ascalon, so Israel over the thirty-two kings.[194]

Homilies on the Epistle to the Hebrews[195] were also delivered in Constantinople in 403–04, as the title states, "Published after his falling asleep, from notes by Constantine, Presbyter of Antioch."[196] These homilies are important for understanding his pastoral ministry and leadership, because they were the fruit of his final ministry before exile. Chrysostom must have realized this was his last opportunity to serve his people in Constantinople, and thus he poured out his spirit and his pastoral theology in these homilies. In regard to their value, P. E. Pusey states:

> One very special value of them lies in the pious fervent exhortation at the end of each, on Penitence, Almsgiving, or whatever St. Chrysostom had at the time chiefly in mind, breathing forth words from a heart, filled with the love of God and that longed for his flock to partake it.[197]

---

192. Chrysostom, *Homilies on Colossians* (*NPNF1* 13:270–71).
193. Chrysostom, *Homilies on First Thessalonians* (*NPNF1* 13:359).
194. Chrysostom, *Homilies on Second Thessalonians* (*NPNF1* 13:391).
195. Quasten, *Patrology*, 3:450.
196. Chrysostom, "Argument and Summary of the Epistle," in *Homilies on Hebrews* (*NPNF1* 14:363). See also Quasten, *Patrology*, 3:450.
197. Pusey, "Preface," in *Homilies on Hebrews* (*NPNF1* 14:338).

Conversation with Chrysostom

LETTERS

Chrysostom wrote approximately 236 letters during his second exile. The most important ones are the two letters he sent to Innocent, Bishop of Rome.[198] The first was written before his second exile in AD 404[199] in which he pleaded for help. He wrote, "I beseech your charity to rouse yourself and have compassion, and do everything so as to put a stop to the mischief at this point."[200] However, the Roman Bishop legally ruled over the case, but as a friend wrote to Chrysostom to console and to encourage him:[201] This correspondence reflects Chrysostom's integrity; as there was no higher authority that he could appeal to he felt he had to submit himself even to an unjust ruler. Chrysostom has left behind the most extensive literary legacy of all the Greek Fathers and he is consequently one of the most widely studied figures of early Christianity.[202] Because of the basic five source materials authored by Socrates, Palladius, Dialogues, Theodoret, George Alexandrinus,[203] Martyrius Antiochenus,[204] and Leo Imperator, historians were able to produce biographical books on Chrysostom. Besides Sir Henry Savile (1549–1622) who published a book on Chrysostom in 1613, August Neander wrote *Life of St. Chrysostom* (1845), translated by J. C. Stapleton, and W. R. W. Stephens published his classic work, entitled *Saint Chrysostom, His Life and Times*, which is a sketch of the church and the empire in the fourth century, published in 1872. Stephens' book is comprehensive and comprises all areas of Chrysostom's life and writings, including his roles as a theologian, interpreter of Scripture, social reformer, as well as a pastor and preacher.[205] After Stephens' work was published, Donald

---

198. Quasten calls Chrysostom's two letters to Innocent the most important ones because in the first letter written from Constantinople in 404 before his second exile he defended his integrity with other forty Bishops who stood by him to the last.

199. Quasten, *Patrology*, 3:469.

200. Chrysostom, "Letter to Innocent" (*NPNF1* 9:310).

201. Stephens, "Introduction," in *Chrysostom with the Bishop of Rome* (NPNF1 9:307).

202. Mayer and Allen, *John Chrysostom*, 1128–50.

203. George Alexandrinus has been identified with the Patriarch George of Alexandria who died about 630. The date of his authorship is probably from 680 to 725. Baur, *John Chrysostom*, 1:xxxiv.

204. Martyrius Antiochenus was the Patriarch Martyrius of Antioch who died 471. He produced the oldest true biography of Chrysostom. He utilized the materials from Palladius and Sozomen. Baur, *John Chrysostom*, 1:xxxii–iii.

205. Ibid., 407.

Pastoral Leadership

Attwater published *St. John Chrysostom: Pastor and Preacher*. Chrysostomus Baur also published a monumental work entitled *Der heilige Johannes Chrysostomus und seine Zeit* in 1929–30 and the English translation was published in 1959. After collecting the available resources and literature on Chrysostom, including most of Chrysostom's writings, Baur wrote "an erudite two-volume commentary" which dominated the field on Chrysostom studies for more than sixty years.[206] In regard to Chrysostom's chronology, Robert Carter and others contributed useful insights.[207] After Baur's comprehensive work on Chrysostom, J. N. D. Kelly published *Golden Mouth: The Story of John Chrysostom—Ascetic, Preacher, Bishop* in 1995. Wendy Mayer reviewed Kelly's work, stating:

> In essence, the value of this book lies in its matter-of-fact drawing together of recent opinion into a fresh, more balanced perspective of this most famous preacher, his life and times. In this alone it displaces Baur as the standard work on the subject.[208]

Kelly produced a monumental resource that included reliable sources and thoughtful selections in order to accurately convey Chrysostom's life, preaching and theology. Recently, Claudia Tiersch published a useful study on Chrysostom's ministry in Constantinople, entitled *Johannes Chrysostomus in Konstantinopel (398–404): Weltsicht und Wirken eines Bischofs in der Hauptstadt des Ostromischen Reiches*.

Exegetical and Homiletic Studies on Chrysostom's Works

In 1887, Frederic Henry Chase published a very important scholarly resource on Chrysostom studies, entitled *Chrysostom, A Study in the History of Biblical Interpretation*. Here Chase dealt with a variety of subjects regarding the understanding of Chrysostom's interpretation of Scripture.[209] Thomas Edward Ameringer explored Chrysostom's style on the Greek rhetoric of his panegyric sermons.[210] In 1970, Frans Van Paverd published *Zur Geschichte Der Messliturgie*. A French scholar, Anne Marie Malingrey, made a significant contribution to Chrysostom studies in the area of criti-

---

206. Kelly, *Golden Mouth*, vii.

207. Carter, "Chrysostom's Early Life," 357–64. See also Ettlinger, "Some Historical Evidence," 373–80.

208. Mayer, Review of *Golden Mouth*, 82.

209. Chase, *Chrysostom: Biblical Interpretation*, xi–xiii.

210. Ameringer, "Study in Greek Rhetoric," 103.

cal text and translations. Blake Goodall also published a noteworthy resource, entitled *The Homilies of St. John Chrysostom on the Letters of St. Paul to Titus and Philemon*. Since Henry Savile's first edition of Chrysostom's works was published in 1612, the writing of manuscripts and textual criticisms has been an enormous task for scholars on Chrysostom studies.[211] In regard to textual criticism, Michel Aubineau published an article on the textual problem of Chrysostom's work. Laurence Brottier also published a work on textual criticism with regard to Chrysostom's sermons on Genesis. Scholars have also devoted much research to exegetical studies of Chrysostom's commentaries. Frans van de Paverd published *St. John Chrysostom, the Homilies on the Statues*, which is a critical and exegetical study of the twenty-two sermons Chrysostom delivered during the season of Lent in 387. Robert Charles Hill published *St. John Chrysostom's Commentary on the Psalms*, which is translated with an introduction. Hill also published an important article entitled *The Spirituality of Chrysostom's Commentary on the Psalms*.[212] Investigating Chrysostom's spirituality through his commentary on the Psalms is a challenging task. Duane A. Garrett also added *An Analysis of the Hermeneutics of John Chrysostom's Commentary on Isaiah 1-8*. Wendy Mayer and Pauline Allen published an important resource on Chrysostom's homilies, entitled *John Chrysostom*. These authors indicated that: "critical assessment of John as preacher, analysis of the character, composition and behavior of his audience, and nuanced discussion of John's involvement in pastoral care, is scarce."[213] Mayer and Allen, therefore, have sought to investigate Chrysostom's unique pastoral effort through his homiletic approach. Reviewing this book, Gerard Ettlinger concludes that:

> This particular volume shows that John Chrysostom's influence did not stem from theology, but from the power of his preaching and pastoral work as a deacon and priest in Antioch and as bishop of Constantinople.[214]

Margaret M. Mitchell also contributed a monumental commentary on Chrysostom's interpretation of the Pauline Epistles through her publication of *The Heavenly Trumpet* in 2002. Through comprehensive

211. Ibid., 2-5.
212. Hill, "Chrysostom's Commentary on the Psalms," 569-79. Hill was convinced that "Chrysostom has a lively sense of his role in providing nourishment for the spiritual lives of his listeners, especially by breaking the bread of the Word to them."
213. Ibid., vii.
214. Ettlinger, Review of *John Chrysostom*, 422-23.

scholarly research on all of Chrysostom's commentaries on the Pauline epistles, Mitchell was able to highlight Chrysostom's remarkable portraits of Paul and establish that Chrysostom had achieved the standard work of patristic hermeneutics on the Apostle Paul.

THEOLOGICAL AND DOCTRINAL STUDIES ON CHRYSOSTOM

In the article entitled "The Future of Chrysostom Studies: Theology and Nachleben," Robert Carter states:

> Studies of Chrysostom's theological thought should be seriously historical and avoid all neo-scholasticism. Since Chrysostom was not a systematic theologian, but a popular preacher, we should not try to tailor his thought to fit some later system.[215]

Melvin E. Lawrenz revealed in greater depth Chrysostom's understanding of Christ's deity in his book *The Christology of John Chrysostom*.[216] Chrysostom was a preacher and pastor rather than a theologian: "All of Chrysostom's theology is exegetical in nature. Recent studies of history of exegesis have aroused interest in the relationship of exegesis and speculative theology."[217] Recent studies on Chrysostom indicate that scholars are more inclined to explore Chrysostom's ethical theology as he was not considered a speculative thinker, but a reformer through pastoral leadership. In his article, Rudolf Brandle developed the concept of the relationship between Chrysostom's faith and work in the light of his ethics. Brandle also published a book, entitled *Johannes Chrysostomus: Bischof, Reformer, Martyr* exploring Chrysostom's life in three sections, namely his time spent in Antioch, Constantinople and in exile. Brandle depicted Chrysostom as a preacher, reformer and martyr who had fulfilled his responsibility, endangering his own life for the sake of his integrity until the very end. Martin Illert attempted to investigate the relationship between Chrysostom and Syrian ascetic theology in his publication, entitled *Johannes Chrysostomus und das antiochenisch-syrische Mönchtum*. Wendy Mayer commented: "Pursuing this path, Illert argues that the construction and evaluation of monasticism in Chrysostom's writings cannot be seen as a reflection of John's own rhetorical, church political and theological agenda."[218]

---

215. Carter, "Future of Chrysostom Studies," 129–41.
216. Lawrenz, *Christology of John Chrysostom*, 178.
217. Ibid., 166.
218. Mayer, Review of *Golden Mouth*, 86–88.

Conversation with Chrysostom

SOCIAL ISSUES

In recent years, we have witnessed a special interest in Chrysostom's writings regarding social issues, as he was a strong advocate for social justice and for the needs of the poor. Dolores Greeley called Chrysostom "one of the strongest and most eloquent spokesmen" for social justice.[219] Adolf Martin Ritter also depicted Chrysostom as an interpreter of Pauline social ethics.[220] Jaroslav Jan Pelikan's book is a comparative study of the divine rhetoric on the ethical issues of Kingdom life. Gus George Christo published Chrysostom's sermons on repentance and almsgiving to demonstrate the importance of Chrysostom's ethical teachings in reference to his ecclesiology.[221] Christo indicated that, "in Chrysostom's writings, repentance is certainly one of the basic foundations of Church membership and practice."[222] The issue of gender was one focal point in the discussion of social problems in Chrysostom's writings. Regarding Chrysostom's view on marriage, Blake Leyerle published *Theatrical Shows and Ascetic Lives*, describing Chrysostom's attack on spiritual marriage. He discussed the phenomenon of the longstanding ascetic practice of spiritual marriage in which a man and a woman live together without consummating their marriage. Leyerle discusses Chrysostom's argument against spiritual marriage on the grounds it is dangerous to those involved and wrote: "John insists that the couples' presentation of holiness is an elaboration and deceptive façade."[223] In regard to James Parkes' charge that Chrysostom was an anti-Semite,[224] Robert L. Wilken has presented a new understanding of Chrysostom's position on Anti-Semitism through analyzing the contemporary social and cultural situation in Antioch.[225] William L. Mullen concluded, "For Chrysostom, the

---

219. Greeley, "Prophet of Social Justice," 1163.

220. Ritter, "Interpreter of Pauline Social Ethics," 183–92. Ritter claimed: "It is certainly true of Chrysostom, at any rate, that all through his years as presbyter in Antioch, the third largest city in the Oikumene, and later as bishop in Constantinople, the imperial capital, he expressed his position on questions of social justice with a constancy, an urgency, and a fearlessness that are hardly matched by any other theologian of the early church, whether orthodox or heretical."

221. Christo, "Introduction," in Chrysostom's *On Repentance and Almsgiving*, xi–xviii. See also Mayer, Review of *Golden Mouth*, 323–24.

222. Christo, "Introduction," in Chrysostom's *On Repentance and Almsgiving*, 96:xv.

223. Ibid., 9.

224. Parkes, *Anti-Semitism*, 63–65. See also Parkes, *Church and the Synagogue*, 79.

225. Wilken, *John Chrysostom and the Jews*, 72–73. Wilken found that Judaizers in Chrysostom's writings were not the Jews, but the Christian leaders who adopted Jewish

church was in a struggle for its very existence, and he was totally committed to ensuring its survival and well being."[226]

Briefly, I want to indicate some current trends in researching Chrysostom's pastoral theology. Almost three decades ago, Robert Carter emphasized the necessity of studying Chrysostom's pastoral theology:

> Chrysostom's fundamental interests were pastoral and moral rather than speculative and systematic. Therefore it has been fashionable for speculative theologians to dismiss Chrysostom as a conventional moralist whose contribution to the history of theology was minimal. Today theology is much more pastorally oriented and concerned with Christian life and action. It is possible, therefore, that theologians may find Chrysostom more relevant to their concerns than they have in the past.[227]

In recent years Wendy Mayer and Pauline Allen have published numerous scholarly works on Chrysostom's preaching from a pastoral perspective. Wendy Mayer has stimulated the academic community of Chrysostom scholars to research the pastoral aspects of Chrysostom's writings. R. A. Krupp published *Shepherding the Flock of God: The Pastoral Theology of John Chrysostom*, which is the first of its kind in labeling the pastoral aspects of Chrysostom's writings as his "pastoral theology." Krupp, however, did not discuss the core content of Chrysostom's pastoral theology, namely, the pastoral care of the congregation. Frances Young also pointed out, "There is no attempt to link together the topics in some kind of overarching pastoral theology."[228] Andrew Purves, in his recent book, *Pastoral Theology in the Classical Tradition*, included a brief section on Chrysostom's pastoral theology extracted from his *On Priesthood*.[229] Aideen M. Hartney's work, *John Chrysostom and the Transformation of the City* depicted Chrysostom as a transformer of the city through his preaching and example. More research on this subject from a wider circle of scholars is urgently needed.

My own research confirms for me the fact that no Chrysostom scholar has published books or articles on the Pastoral Leadership of John

---

customs in the church making endanger of the whole church to become Judaizers so that Chrysostom did not call the Jews Judaizers, but the Jewish and non-Jewish Christians in his congregation.

226. Mullen, "Polemical Sermons," 186.
227. Carter, "Future of Chrysostom Studies," 129.
228. Young, Review of *Shepherding the Flock*, 825–26.
229. Purves, *Pastoral Theology*, 33–54.

Chrysostom and I have not discovered any similar study or research of the subject. *Renouncing the World Yet Leading the Church: The Monk-Bishop in Late Antiquity* by Andrea Sterk does include a sub-section on this aspect but only nineteen pages, entitled "John Chrysostom: The Model of Monk-Bishop in Spite of Himself."[230] As the title suggests, Sterk presents Chrysostom as an ancient model of the Monk-Bishop. This theme really needs to be developed extensively and expanded from a pastoral leadership perspective. The only article I have discovered that touches on Chrysostom's pastoral leadership is a sixteen-page article by Richard Valantasis, entitled "Body, Hierarchy, and Leadership in Chrysostom's *On the Priesthood*." He attempted to discuss the role and function of church leadership from Chrysostom's *On the Priesthood*. The weakness of his subject matter is, however, confined to *On the Priesthood* so that it could not cover Chrysostom's pastoral leadership as a whole. An important aim in this dissertation is, therefore, to identify and explore key principles regarding pastoral leadership from a reasonable sample of Chrysostom's writings so that I can enter into conversation with him with regard to pastoral leadership. To date, Chrysostom scholars have not explored this subject using Chrysostom's *On the Priesthood*, or his commentaries on the Pauline Pastoral Epistles and his New Testament Homilies. While my sample of his writings is limited, I suggest that my sample is adequate in order to initiate a conversation across the centuries with this important fourth-century Christian leader. As I have indicated, Chrysostom was essentially a preacher, pastor and reformer as well as an outstanding, prolific writer and the pre-eminent Doctor of the Church along with Basil the Great, Gregory of Nazianzus, and St. Augustine.

---

230. Sterk, *Renouncing the World*, 141–60.

5

Chrysostom's Pastoral Leadership Principles: On the Priesthood

THE MODEL OF CRITICAL conversation that I outlined early in chapter four presents methodological challenges, particularly because of the enormous gaps as well as similarities that exist when engaging in conversation across the centuries. In adopting Pattinson's suggestion of finding "a way into critical conversation," I am also adapting his recommendation of a "three-way conversation" between one's own assumptions, values, and tradition then secondly those beliefs and practices of Chrysostom within Christian tradition and, thirdly, the particular contemporary situation which is being examined, namely, my pastoral experience at KCPC. This is a necessary task but my focus throughout will be on the key principles of pastoral leadership. Before proceeding to identify Chrysostom's pastoral leadership principles however, I want to discuss briefly some of the gaps that exist between Chrysostom's situation and my own situation in KCPC.

DIFFERENCES BETWEEN THE TWO PASTORAL SITUATIONS

First of all, there is a major difference in ecclesiology with regard to the nature and sacraments of the church. For example, Chrysostom understood the church to be sacramental, episcopal, hierarchical, Trinitarian, and orthodox in terms of adhering to, and promoting, the Nicene and, later, the Chalcedon Creeds. Chrysostom's ecclesiology was essentially Christological and based on the mystical union enjoyed by believers with Christ through the Communion. Unless individuals participate in the "Mysteries,"

Chrysostom's Pastoral Leadership Principles: On the Priesthood

including, for example, the bread and wine of communion, they are unable to become members of the church. There are as many as thirteen references to the church as the body of Christ in his second homily dealing with the Lord's ascension. This corporate, mystic union is integral to the essence of the church.[1] In regard to the interpretation of John 19:34, Chrysostom writes:

> There came forth water and blood. Not without a purpose, or by chance, did those founts Came forth, but because by means of these two together the Church consists. And the initiated know it, being by water indeed regenerate, and nourished by the Blood of Flesh. Hence the Mysteries take their beginning; that when you approach to that awful cup, you may so approach, as drinking the very side.[2]

By contrast, KCPC as a Protestant church and influenced strongly by the sixteenth-century Protestant reformer, John Calvin, emphasizes the spirituality of the church like Chrysostom but members are grafted into the church by the miracle of regeneration and faith in the Lord Jesus. These believers and their children constitute the members of the visible church in which the Word of God is primary as the supreme standard of faith and practice. The preaching of the Word therefore goes before, and gives meaning to, the sacraments; in Holy Communion, the Lord Jesus is present only spiritually and members by faith fellowship with Him. For KCPC, regeneration would not be automatic for children of believers at baptism, however within the covenant God gives warrant for believers to anticipate their regeneration and consequent life of faith in later months and years in fulfillment of divine promises and as a consequence of prayer, bible teaching, godly example and corporate church life and spiritual nurturing. KCPC does, however, put a strong emphasis on the two sacraments of baptism and Holy Communion but without affirming the mechanical and automatic conveyance of grace through these sacraments. In terms of Trinitarian theology, and fidelity to the Nicene as well as the Chalcedon Creeds, KCPC gives unquestioning commitment and, following Calvin, shows considerable respect also for the Patristic writers.

1. Christo, *Church's Identity*, 10. Christo writes: "Thus, the Church is understood both as Christ's Flesh Incarnate and also as the exact same Flesh present in the Mysteries. The Church cannot be understood apart from the Son of God to whom she is indissolubly united. Unless human beings partake of Christ's Flesh through the Mysteries, they cannot become members of the Church."

2. Chrysostom, *Homilies on John* (NPNF1 14:319).

Pastoral Leadership

Secondly, these ecclesiological differences become even more apparent in terms of the various church officers recognized in these two different pastoral situations. At the time of Chrysostom, the religious hierarchy consisted of bishop, priest and deacon. Bishops were sometimes recognized as Patriarchs, Metropolitans, or Archbishops but all were equal in authority, although greater honor was usually given to the Patriarch of Constantinople. The office of deacon was responsible to, and under, that of the priest. In addition to these clerical orders, the early Eastern Orthodox Church also recognized lay orders. For example, Timothy Ware records that in 612 AD, "There were 80 priests, 150 deacons, 40 deaconesses, 70 subdeacons, 160 readers, 25 cantors, and 100 doorkeepers."[3] Gus George Christo refers to Chrysostom's homily eleven, which is a commentary on Ephesians, where he discusses the bishop's central role in keeping Christ's body undivided. Then, he explains that the church as the body and fullness of Christ remains united by the orthodox ordination of clergy, something equally as important as maintaining unity of faith. Regarding the church as the body of Christ, Chrysostom emphasized the unity of the church among the Gentiles and the Jews. He addresses the unity in Christ regarding the Jews and Gentiles that:

> Behold, they are exalted to one and the same dignity, the two are become one, the one coming from a longer, the other from a nearer distance, and the slave becoming more noble than he was before he offended. And break down, he proceeds the middle wall of partition. What the middle wall of partition is, he interprets by saying, the enmity having abolished in His flesh, even the law of commandments contained in ordinances. Some indeed affirm that he means the wall of the Jews against the Greeks, because it did not allow the Jews to hold intercourse with the Greeks.[4]

For Chrysostom, the Church's "fullness" is expressed in each local congregation or church, which is led by a priest under the shepherd care of a bishop.[5] Chrysostom, therefore, understands the bishop's role as being the most important in shepherding believers in the Church. In regard to the bishop's role in the church, R. A. Krupp confirms that: "The bishop was the leader of the church, and as he maintained the unity and discipline of the

---

3. Kallistos, *Orthodox Church*, 265.
4. Chrysostom, *Homilies on Ephesians* (*NPNF*1 13:71).
5. Christo, *Church's Identity*, 50.

Chrysostom's Pastoral Leadership Principles: On the Priesthood

flock he was a figure of Christ the Shepherd."[6] When Bishop Flavian was absent from the Church of Antioch on one occasion, Chrysostom observed:

> What is this I see? The shepherd is not here and still his sheep show a well-disciplined attitude. And this marks the pastoral success and virtue of the shepherd when, whether he is present or away, his flocks display complete earnestness and attention. Dumb sheep must remain in their pens when no one is there to lead them to pasture. If they put their heads out of the fold when no one is tending them, there must be a risk that they may roam far away, because of your well-disciplined attitude, you have met together in your usual pastures.[7]

Here, Chrysostom underlines the importance of the unity and harmony in the pastoral leadership role in the church. He learned the conflicts between the peoples as well as with the clergy about pastoral leadership while under Bishop Flavian in Antioch for twelve years.

By contrast, the KCPC bylaws acknowledge five classes of church officers: 1) teaching elder who is the ordained clergy, the ministerial pastor, 2) ruling elders who are ordained to office and are responsible for governing the church alongside the minister, 3) deacon who is also ordained and serves the congregation under the supervision of the Elders' Session, 4) kawnsa who is an appointed lady by the Elders' Session and elected at the congregational meeting. Having no women as elders or deacons, Korean Presbyterian Churches made a provision for women to exercise an elder's role but only amongst women, 5) Associates included deacons or deaconesses who are appointed by the Elders' Session in order to serve the church. As in the 2008 statistics, KCPC had 20 ruling elders, 68 deacons, 162 kwansa, 512 associate deacons, and 502 associate deaconesses.[8]

Within Presbyterianism, the pastor is usually regarded as being equivalent to an elder so that a "bishop" is understood to be an elder or Presbyter and one of several men exercising authority and leadership within the local congregation. The pastor is called to assume the major responsibility of preaching the Word regularly and shepherding the flock while elders support him in this pastoral and leadership role. Deacons have a more practical role in the local church ranging from administration, maintenance to caring in various practical ways for the membership of the church. In

---

6. Krupp, *Shepherding the Flock of God*, 117.
7. Chrysostom, *Incomprehensible Nature of God*, 51.
8. *2008 KCPC Members Handbook*, 16–46.

Pastoral Leadership

Presbyterian Church Government, deacons are laypersons only and cannot be classified as clergy. In the United Methodist Church of USA, however, there are two classes of deacons; one class of deacon belongs to the order of clergy while the other one is a layperson. According to the Book of Discipline of the United Methodist Church, Section III-311, the Orders of Deacons and Elders are the clergy orders and also there are lay deacons and elders among the lay people separated from the clergy order.[9] The office of deacon affords a good illustration of the similarities and differences between the two church situations. It is not known, for example, the exact number of deacons in either Antioch or Constantinople. Rudolf Brandle states, "In Antioch there were presumably, as in Rome, seven deacons in office."[10] These seven deacons, however, were clergy members. In addition to these seven, there were also lay deacons and deaconesses. George B. Stevens claims, "The number of deacons in the metropolitan Church at Constantinople should be a hundred."[11] R. A. Krupp reminds us that:

> The office of deacon and deaconess were significant elements of the Church's hierarchy in John's era, in part because the Church was greatly involved in social programs in both Antioch and Constantinople. These offices were also stepping-stones for men in the clerical hierarchy. For women, the office of deaconess was an important path of liberation from the roles reserved for them in the family structure of that ear.[12]

What was the function of deacons in Chrysostom's day? Their main duties related to the liturgical service at Holy Communion and calling on the congregation to pray and then recite the Lord's Prayer. In addition, they were responsible for distributing monies from the church to the poor and needy in and outside the church. The difference between that situation in which Chrysostom ministered and my situation in KCPC is interesting and the differences are not too radical. *The Book of Church Order of the Presbyterian Church in America* (PCA) directs that the PCA should not allow deacons to serve at the Lord's Table because they are not classified as clergy, but rather as laity:

---

9. *The Book of Discipline of the United Methodist Church*, 191.
10. Rudolf Brandle, *John Chrysostom*, 19.
11. Stevens, "Revised Notes," in Chrysostom's *Homilies on Acts* (*NPNF*1 11:91).
12. Krupp, *Shepherding the Flock of God*, 126.

Chrysostom's Pastoral Leadership Principles: On the Priesthood

It is the duty of deacons to minister to those who are in need, to the sick, to the friendless, and to any who may be in distress. It is their duty also to develop the grace of liberality in the members of the church, to devise effective methods of collecting the gifts of the people, and to distribute these gifts among the objects to which they are contributed. They shall have the care of the property of the congregation, both real and personal, and shall keep in proper repair the church edifice and other buildings belonging to the congregation. In matters of special importance affecting the property of the church, they cannot take final action without the approval of the Session and consent of the congregation. In the discharge of their duties the deacons are under the supervision and authority of the Session.[13]

Apart from limited liturgical involvement in Chrysostom's situation, the role of deacons in KCPC and Antioch have a number of similarities rather than dissimilarities; for example, they align in their care for the poor and needy in the church, the varied practical ministries, and the general support of the pastoral leadership.

Thirdly, another major difference between the two situations is the relationship between church and state. While the United States Constitution, which was adopted on September 17, 1787, guaranteed religious freedom for all its citizens, there was no formal relationship at all between church and state. Practically, this means that there is no interference in, or control over, the internal affairs of any church denomination by any of the states or federal government.

The situation was entirely different for Chrysostom. In 313 AD, Constantine issued the Edict of Milan, which legalized Christian worship and activities thus brought an end to a long period of persecution of the church by the Roman state. In 323 AD, Constantine became the last powerful ruler of the Roman world but the church was placed to a large extent under the influence of the Roman emperor. This was confirmed with the removal of the capital of the empire from Rome to Constantinople in 330 AD, and secular rulers were acknowledged increasingly to possess supreme authority over the church. This inseparable relation of church and state influenced the appointment of Chrysostom as bishop in Constantinople and also led to his removal and exile. Chrysostom was perhaps unwise in some of his statements and actions that aroused the opposition of the clergy and the Empress. However, the state control over the church was considerable.

13. Gilchrist, *Book of Church*, 9–2

Pastoral Leadership

In my case, not only was KCPC free entirely of government control, but on my retirement from ministry in KCPC, the House of Representatives, as indicated in chapter one, gave a lengthy tribute to me, acknowledging the religious, community, and social work I had been responsible for leading. This was only an acknowledgement on their part of a contribution made to an American immigrant community and does not represent or imply any control whatsoever; the difference, therefore, is significant.

A fourth area of difference between the two situations concerns the training for the ministry/priesthood. As indicated in the previous chapter, Chrysostom studied rhetoric initially under Libanius then philosophy under Andragathius. These men were almost like mentors at the time to their young disciple. Chrysostom then proceeded to the School of Asketerion where Diodore taught; here, he studied the biblical text and followed the Antioch hermeneutical principles for interpreting scripture. Diodore's Asketerion was an ascetic-type school and an earlier equivalent to the type of theological seminary where I studied theology in America and prepared in detail for understanding and teaching the Bible. J. N. D. Kelly acknowledges that:

> (It) is an intriguing question what exactly this Asketerion was, in which upper-class, deeply religious young Christians of Antioch, like John . . . picked up their grounding in ascetic commitment and the understanding of scripture under Diodore's direction. Scholars have often assumed that it must have been a community of monks living together under a rule, but this suggestion must be ruled out.[14]

We cannot be dogmatic concerning the exact nature of Diodore's school but it is a fact that Chrysostom received his main biblical and theological training from Asketerion. Donald Attwater confirms that:

> Diodore, later to be a bishop of Tarsus, exercised a profound influence on Chrysostom. . . . Diodore was a leader of the Antiochene school of exposition, which laid emphasis on the literal and historical meaning of the text of the Bible, against the allegorical and mystical interpretation of Origen and the Alexandrian school. . . . Chrysostom remained faithful to the method of historical exegesis he had learned from his master, and it is exemplified in all his numerous commentaries on Holy Scripture. He is, indeed, by far the

---

14. Kelly, *Golden Mouth*, 19.

Chrysostom's Pastoral Leadership Principles: On the Priesthood

most important and successful exponent of the principles of the exegetical school of Antioch.[15]

Chrysostom's personal journey into the priesthood in Antioch and Constantinople indicates that the important training he received was from personal mentors, like Libanius, Diodore, then Meletius, and Flavius. Therefore, the distinctiveness of the training for becoming a priest was to receive training from a personal mentor rather than being restricted to formal schools. Chrysostom's training was thorough and comprehensive for that period; he became an excellent exponent of the Antiochene approach to Scripture. By contrast, my own training was confined largely to various universities and a theological seminary where I received formal classroom teaching and guidance.

Although these are genuine and even "enormous gaps" between the two situations, nevertheless, I submit that it is legitimate to enter into a critical conversation between Chrysostom and myself in terms of our pastoral leadership principles. There are three reasons that I offer in support of this submission:

First of all, provided we follow Pattinson's general guidance in adopting a "three-way" conversation then this will enable us to be self-critical and also appreciative of Chrysostom's work. Secondly, despite the various "gaps" and differences identified above, I submit that similar pastoral leadership principles can be identified, although they may of necessity be applied somewhat differently because of the different situations.

Thirdly, it is also possible to exaggerate the "gaps" between the situations and overlook the fact that there are some important similarities, which I will describe later in this dissertation. These similarities include the primacy of preaching, spirituality, multi-ethnic congregations, divisions within churches and socio-political factors, opposition and personal criticisms of a leader, and social ministry to the needy then finally mission. These are all aspects that the two situations have in common. In addition, as I have already indicated, Chrysostom was not an academic or even speculative theologian but essentially a preacher, a pastor, and reformer as well as a prolific writer and church leader. I identify myself with Chrysostom in some of these respects. For example, although I have pursued advanced postgraduate studies yet I do not regard myself as an academic theologian but essentially a pastor and preacher who has been committed to the pastorate at KCPC for many years. What impresses me also is the fact that

---

15. Attwater, *Pastor and Preacher*, 25.

Pastoral Leadership

some of our concerns and pastoral leadership principles are shared and also emphasized in our respective situations. These similarities together with an acute awareness of the dissimilarities encourage me to proceed with this critical conversation.

A brief word at this point is necessary concerning the way I intend to use Chrysostom's primary sources. I will largely focus on Chrysostom's *On the Priesthood*, which was his first major writing and written prior to his ordination. Reflecting his experience as a deacon in the church at Antioch, *On the Priesthood* is possibly the most valuable source among all his other writings for understanding his theology of pastoral leadership. Between the time when Chrysostom avoided his ordination in 373 to the year when the treatise was published in 387, he had ample opportunities as a deacon to observe and reflect on the nature and work of the priesthood as well as the needs of the people in general. I will focus on this work with regard to identifying Chrysostom's pastoral leadership principles. I acknowledge that while *On the Priesthood* is one of the outstanding patristic writings on the priesthood, it does not completely reflect Chrysostom's pastoral theology if only for the reason it does not cover the entire period of his pastoral ministry. In addition, the motive for writing *On the Priesthood* was unique and somewhat personal, as Chrysostom himself wrestled with the possibility of being ordained to the priesthood. For this reason, I intend to use a sample of Chrysostom's New Testament Homilies, especially his homilies on the Pastoral Epistles in order to ascertain whether the principles identified in the early writing were retained and developed in these Homilies or were seriously modified. All his Homilies were preached after his ordination while he ministered in Antioch and Constantinople. While I am delimiting my use of Chrysostom's homilies, my rationale is that this is essentially research in pastoral theology rather than in Patristics and that, in addition, my choice of the Homilies on the Pastoral Epistles is appropriate, given my focus on pastoral leadership principles. In order to confirm my findings in *On the Priesthood* and in the homilies on the Pastoral Epistles, I intend to sample a few of the other New Testament homilies in addition. I submit that this sampling is adequate within my narrow focus on pastoral leadership in order for me to identify then describe Chrysostom's major principles for pastoral leadership. I expect that others, if they wish to pursue a more extensive and Patristic examination of these principles, will examine all Chrysostom's homilies and sermons in order to obtain an even more complete and definitive understanding of his pastoral leadership principles.

Chrysostom's Pastoral Leadership Principles: On the Priesthood

ON THE PRIESTHOOD

Chrysostom's *On the Priesthood* is one of the three best known patristic writings in this period. One is Gregory Nazianzus' *Apologetic Composition*, which is usually referred to by its Latin title, *de fuga*. Another one is Pope Gregory the Great's *Book on Pastoral Rule*. Nazianzus, born around 330 AD, eventually became the bishop of Constantinople in 381 and was regarded as one of the outstanding theologians in the Eastern Church. Like Chrysostom, Nazianzus was reluctant to become ordained but his ordination occurred in December 361 but his personal struggles did not end then as he sought to hide for a period in solitude. His *Apologetic Composition* was originally written in 362 but was extensively amplified after 382. "The flight to Pontus" in his Oration 2 is Nazianzius' pastoral theology describing the character and responsibilities of the sacerdotal office on the priesthood.[16] He emphasizes the most important qualifications for being a priest: 1) A priest needs to be free from evil, 2) not only to be free from evil, but eminent in goodness, 3) The priest is a physician of souls, 4) The priest must distribute the Word of God.[17] The pastoral theology of Gregory of Nazianzus is focused on the concept of the pastor as a "Physician of Souls." According to Nazianzus, the pastoral ministry is the salvation and sanctification of a person as Christ commanded Peter in John 21:15.[18] Gregory, the Great (540–604) wrote his *Book on Pastoral Rule* in 590, and it is the most famous of his writings. It was addressed to John, bishop of Ravenna in response to questions from him with regard to the duties and obligations of the clergy. In this work, Gregory explains the difficulties of pastoral duties and the requirements pastors must fulfill. In the second part, he proceeds to discuss the pastor's life and character, providing some practical guidelines. These chapters highlight the need for exemplary character, humility, integrity, and compassion on the part of the pastor. The third part contains forty brief chapters with lessons on preaching. Finally, he urges the preacher to examine himself to avoid becoming proud and that in caring for others he should not neglect his own character. There is no evidence that Gregory was familiar with, or used, Chrysostom's *On the Priesthood* for he was unable to read Greek so he had little, if any, knowledge of Chrysostom's writing. All three treatises, however, have common themes, such as an apology for seeking to avoid entering the priesthood, the holy character of the priest,

16. Quasten, *Patrology*, 3:243.
17. Purves, *Pastoral Theology*, 28–29.
18. Ibid., 17.

Pastoral Leadership

the important ministry of caring for people spiritually, and the importance of preaching. These treatises are also distinctive in dealing with their subject matter and there are similarities in terms of motive, methodology, and literary style.

Turning to Chrysostom's *On the Priesthood* this contains six books that are arranged in logical sequence, each book emphasizing a different aspect of the pastoral ministry.[19] Book one contains a general description of the friendship between Chrysostom and his friend Basil, and the beginning of the apology that Chrysostom made to Basil who was bitter because of Chrysostom's deception regarding ordination. This introductory book does not provide any hint that the deception was constructed as a literary device.[20] In their dialogue, Basil told Chrysostom: "For I entrusted all my interests to your judgment, and always followed it whenever you bid me."[21] Chrysostom responded: "For great is the value of deceit, provided it be not introduced with a mischievous intention."[22] This dialogue indicates that Chrysostom's main objective was not to deceive Basil in order to inflict personal damage, but rather to communicate his pastoral theology through the Pedagogy of the Platonic dialogue.

Book two contains Chrysostom's argument about the nature of the pastoral office as a response to Basil's question regarding Chrysostom's love for Christ. In the priesthood, the latter's ultimate concern was having the greatest possible evidence of love for Christ[23] and he confessed: "I love Him, and shall never cease loving Him; but I fear lest I should provoke Him whom I love."[24] Chrysostom reminded Basil that the character of the priest as a shepherd is of utmost importance in the pastoral ministry.

Book three discusses the dignity and heavenly origin of the priesthood. Chrysostom defended himself by saying he did not decline the priesthood due to pride or vainglory; in fact his treatise powerfully attributes the highest importance to the priesthood so, in one of the most impressive passages, he discourses on the greatness of the priesthood.[25] In Book three, Basil

---

19. Neville, "Introduction," in Chrysostom's, *On the Priesthood* (NPNF1 9:14).
20. Purves, *Pastoral Theology*, 36.
21. Chrysostom, *On the Priesthood* (NPNF1 9:37).
22. Ibid., 38.
23. Ibid., 39.
24. Ibid., 42.
25. Quasten, *Patrology*, 3:460.

Chrysostom's Pastoral Leadership Principles: On the Priesthood

only makes one statement: "Those who know the truth will be surprised,"[26] which becomes Chrysostom's main theme concerning the true nature of the priesthood. I suggest that the purpose of the treatise was to defend his high view of the priesthood and also provide a description of the priest's character. This treatise then reflects on the core concepts that underlie his pastoral leadership theology.

Book four issues the warning of punishment for those who enter, or are forced into, the priesthood without proper qualifications and integrity. Chrysostom also emphasized the priest's duty of preaching and he used the example of the apostle Paul in this respect. Chrysostom attempted to excuse himself from the priesthood because he felt unqualified and unworthy to be ordained and undertake such glorious work.

Book five continues to discuss preaching; Quasten calls this section "a manual for preachers."[27] Public preaching requires a great deal of labor and study; preaching is aimed at pleasing God and thus, "it is especially necessary to be trained to be indifferent to all kinds of praise."[28] Books four and five both emphasize the fact that the pastor's main duty is to preach well-prepared sermons and to please none other than God.

Book six deals with the piety of the priesthood and the severe punishment associated with the priesthood because the priest is accountable to God, not only for his own sins but also for the sins and welfare of others under his care. Chrysostom understood that the pastor is required to preserve his own spiritual and moral purity in order to be an example to the people he served. He stated: "For the soul of the Priest ought to be purer than the very sunbeams, in order that the Holy Spirit may not leave him desolate, in order that he may be able to say, 'Now I live; and yet no longer I, but Christ lives in me.'"[29]

Through his use of Platonic dialogue with his friend Basil, Chrysostom expresses clearly here the core concepts relating to the priesthood, which serve as the foundation of his pastoral leadership teaching in six books on the priesthood. Scholars have only investigated, until recently, the date and circumstances of the composition and purpose of *On the Priesthood*. However, in recent years, patristic scholars have showed interest in Chrysostom's pastoral theology. R.A. Krupp's *Shepherding the Flock of God:*

26. Chrysostom, *On the Priesthood* (NPNF1 9:46).
27. Quasten, *Patrology*, 3:461.
28. Chrysostom, *On the Priesthood* (NPNF1 9:73).
29. Ibid., 75.

Pastoral Leadership

The Pastoral Theology of John Chrysostom, published in 1991, is the first research publication on the subject of Chrysostom's pastoral theology. In this book, he explores seventeen various subjects relating to Chrysostom's life, ministry and thought. For example, the subjects include the context of John's ministry, the desert father, the martyr and the bishop as the father of the people. In 1984, Krupp also published a useful work for Chrysostom researchers entitled *Saint John Chrysostom: A Scripture Index* with a comprehensive compilation of all Chrysostom's writings. Krupp, however, did not cover Chrysostom's pastoral theology in depth, but dealt with it only generally with regard to Chrysostom. He failed to explore Chrysostom's writings on the subject of pastoral theology and pastoral leadership principles in his books. Derek J. Tidball also published a book entitled *Skillful Shepherd: An Introduction to Pastoral Theology* that included a brief section on Chrysostom. Citing Chrysostom's *On the Priesthood*, Tidball writes: "The pastor needed to be unsullied in holiness and possess the virtues of an angel, for there was no way in which his faults could be concealed from the public."[30] As a historical survey to explore the pastoral theology of the post-Constantine period, he deals with Basil of Caesarea (329–79), John Chrysostom (344–407), and Gregory the Great (540–604) then compares briefly their pastoral writings. Tidball's treatment of Chrysostom and *On the Priesthood* is brief and inadequate. Andrew Purves published an excellent review of the patristic writers, including Gregory Nazianzus, John Chrysostom, Gregory the Great in his book, entitled *Pastoral Theology in the Classical Tradition*.[31] Purves wrote an excellent summary of Chrysostom's six books in *On the Priesthood*. He stated, "John, Bishop of Antioch and then of Constantinople, ranks not only as the foremost preacher of the Greek Church, but also as a pastor of the highest reputation."[32] More recently, Andrea Sterk[33] and Aideen Hartney also published their studies on Chrysostom. Hartney concludes:

> In De Sacerdotio we see Chrysostom's discussion of the greater pressures and responsibilities placed on any prelate, since he is responsible not only for his own soul, but for the souls of the

---

30. Tidball, *Skillful Shepherd*, 155.

31. Purves, *Pastoral Theology*, 137.

32. Ibid., 33.

33. Andrea Sterk, *Renouncing the World*, 350. She concluded that John Chrysostom is an ideal model for leadership as monk-bishop. However, she did not explore in depth Chrysostom's pastoral leadership from his *On the Priesthood*.

Chrysostom's Pastoral Leadership Principles: On the Priesthood

multitude, and failure in his duties is judged more harshly than a similar slip by a member of the laity.[34]

Other prominent Chrysostom scholars like Wendy Mayer,[35] Pauline Allen, Margaret Mitchell,[36] and J.N.D. Kelly[37] have contributed helpful, if not outstanding, studies on Chrysostom; however, not one of them has published work on the subject of Chrysostom's pastoral leadership teaching from his *On the Priesthood* or from his other works. It is, therefore, my intention to explore Chrysostom's pastoral leadership from his *On the Priesthood* in this chapter. Wendy Mayer and Pauline Allen stated that the value of studying Chrysostom is in investigating his experiences as a preacher and his involvement in pastoral care at both Antioch and Constantinople.[38]

There are three major categories of principles relating to pastoral leadership in the treatise: namely, the nature of the priesthood, the personal character of the priesthood, and the duty of the priesthood. Several important principles among the three categories include dialogic methodology for communication, the importance of the people themselves, the dignity of the priesthood, the moral character of the priesthood, caring spiritually for the people and also for the needy, and the duty of preaching. These principles need to be explored from a pastoral leadership perspective. The first three pastoral leadership principles belong to the first category, namely, the nature of the priesthood.

The significance of the pastoral leadership principles reflected in Chrysostom's *On the Priesthood* is, first of all, his method of dialogue in communicating which emphasizes the importance of personal relationships. Without genuine love and honesty, dialogue cannot continue and it rather results in dispute and anger. From the beginning to the end of the treatise Chrysostom maintained a dialogue with his friend Basil. Throughout the treatise, Basil addressed questions to Chrysostom as many as fourteen times and he responded to Basil with lengthy explanations with regard

---

34. Ibid., 184.

35. Mayer and Allen, *John Chrysostom*, 3–47. They provided the latest research on Chrysostom studies, particularly on his preaching and pastoral care.

36. On the back cover of Mitchell's, *Heavenly Trumpet*, Mayer comments, "*The Heavenly Trumpet* is a meticulously executed and detailed work full of delightful turns of phrase and elegantly translated passages." However, Mitchell did not publish any study on Chrysostom's pastoral leadership.

37. Kelly's *Golden Mouth* was acclaimed by many scholarly journals. However, Kelly did not explore Chrysostom's pastoral leadership at all.

38. Mayer and Allen, *John Chrysostom*, vii.

to the reason for his deception and also the true nature of the priesthood. Quasten may be correct in pointing out that Chrysostom's main purpose in this treatise was to provide a description of "the greatness and responsibilities of the priesthood"[39] rather than a personal apology to Basil.

Initially, Basil started a complaint against Chrysostom in his questions. In the beginning of their dialogue, Basil accused Chrysostom, stating: "For some accuse you of arrogance, and others of pride."[40] In spite of the latter's earnest apology Basil did not want to listen, but responded: "Nothing of this has any application to me."[41] He disagreed with Chrysostom's proposition that "it is lawful to employ deceit in the pursuit of a good end."[42] During the course of their dialogue, Basil's attitude, however, began to change and he asked Chrysostom sincerely: "Tell me, then, what advantage I have gained by your tact or wisdom, or whatever you call it, that I should be convinced you have not wrought me an injury."[43] The reason for Basil's change of attitude was due to Chrysostom's use of his pastoral leadership principles demonstrated in this dialogue with Basil. He must have felt Chrysostom's genuineness towards him. Noting the contrast between Christians and secular authorities, Chrysostom introduced a significant pastoral principle:

> For Christians above all men are not permitted forcibly to correct the failings of those who sin. Secular judges indeed, when they have captured malefactors under the law, show their authority to be great, and prevent them even against their will from following their own devices: but in our case the wrong-doer must be made better, not by force, but by persuasion.[44]

The principle of personal persuasion by example is the heart of the personal dialogue principle. Chrysostom did not fail to maintain the spirit of respect and honor for his friend Basil who, in turn, was persuaded to understand Chrysostom's view on the priesthood through his friendship and integrity. Chrysostom described the last moments of his personal dialogue with Basil:

---

39. Quasten, *Patrology*, 3:462.
40. Chrysostom, *Priesthood*, 7.
41. Ibid., 11.
42. Ibid., 15.
43. Ibid.
44. Chrysostom, *On the Priesthood* (NPNF1 9:41).

Chrysostom's Pastoral Leadership Principles: On the Priesthood

At this, Basil arose, weeping still more. When I had embraced him and pressed a tender kiss upon his cheek, I led him forth, exhorting him to bear his lot with courage. I said to him: I believe that through Christ, who has called you and set you over his sheep, you will receive such confidence from this ministry that if I am in danger on the last day, you will receive me into your everlasting dwelling.[45]

At last, through this personal dialogue with Basil Chrysostom had succeeded in persuading him to understand his reason for avoiding ordination as well as appreciating the essence of the priesthood. The focus of pastoral ministry is to care for people with sincerity and integrity through the love of Christ.[46] The entire treatise depicts Chrysostom's genuine care for Basil who had been deeply hurt by his earlier action. "Soul care is one way of describing the pastor's entire task."[47] Personal care received through a one-on-one relationship is a fundamental principle in Chrysostom's pastoral leadership theology. The following statement reveals his pastoral conviction regarding personal care: "A priest must be sober and watchful; he must have a thousand eyes, to see in every direction, inasmuch as he lives not for himself alone, but for the whole people."[48]

This is Chrystostom's own understanding of pastoral care and one that he used regularly in his ministry. He also insisted that without true followers no one could claim to be a leader.[49] It is interesting how Basil responded to Chrysostom: "I am neither your enemy nor adversary, nor one of those who strive to injure you. Quite the contrary, I always submitted my interests to your decision; and whatever you advised I was pleased to follow."[50] Clearly, Chrysostom demonstrated his pastoral leadership through his genuine personal care of individuals and this was demonstrated; for example, during the Lent season of the Riot in 387 in Antioch over new taxes imposed on people by the Emperor Theodosius.[51] Amidst their fears, anger and frustration, Chrysostom consoled the people and encouraged them

---

45. Chrysostom, *Priesthood*, 112.
46. Ken Blanchard, "Encourage the Heart," 101–18.
47. Oden, *Pastoral Theology*, 187.
48. Chrysostom, *Priesthood*, 41–42.
49. John Gardner, *On Leadership*, 1.
50. Chrysostom, *Priesthood*, 11.
51. Baur, *His Time*, 1:259–65.

Pastoral Leadership

through his twenty-one homilies *On the Statues*.[52] He also encouraged monks in the nearby mountain to help people in despair. In regard to the monks' participation, Mayer and Allen noted: "Yet they exhibit a profound pastoral concern for the well-being of Antioch's inhabitants. They are prepared to take action in a time of crisis and place their own lives at risk by speaking with boldness to the emperor's representatives."[53]

In his second homily in *On the Statues*, Chrysostom preached when the people of Antioch were frightened in their situation:

> What shall I say, or what shall I speak of? The present season is one for tears, and not for words; for lamentation, not for discourse; for prayer, not for preaching. Such is the magnitude of the deeds daringly done; so incurable is the wound, so deep the blow, even beyond the power of all treatment, and craving assistance from above.[54]

It is uncertain how many years elapsed between Chrysostom writing *On the Priesthood* and his *On the Statues*. He continued, however, to demonstrate the same pastoral care and leadership consistently throughout the years, by means of his preaching and practice. Jay E. Adams, a contemporary pastoral theologian agrees with Chrysostom's concept of personal care in the ministry:

> The overseeing of the flock, as flock (congregation) and as individual sheep, is the fundamental notion in the pastoral work as distinguished from teaching. The work to which the Christian minister is called therefore is essentially pastoral.[55]

The second principle in pastoral leadership that Chrysostom identifies is the importance of understanding people under one's pastoral care. Without realizing this, pastoral ministry cannot be properly carried out. Responding to Basil's question of "What advantage I have gained,"[56] Chrysostom spoke of Christ's last dialogue with Peter before his ascension. "Addressing the leader of the Apostles, Christ said, 'Peter, lovest thou me?'

---

52. Mayer and Allen, *John Chrysostom*, 104–05.

53. Ibid., 104.

54. Chrysostom, *On the Statues* (NPNF1 9:344).

55. Adams, *Shepherding God's Flock*, 9. In regard to pastoral theology Adams explains, "The name pastoral is a uniquely Christian term that expresses a fundamental concept that is deeply embedded in every biblical portrayal of Christian ministry."

56. Chrysostom, *Priesthood*, 15.

Chrysostom's Pastoral Leadership Principles: On the Priesthood

When Peter affirmed his love, Christ added, 'If thou lovest Me, shepherd my sheep.'"[57] Christ asked Peter a commissioning question before Peter was charged with shepherding Christ's sheep. Chrysostom understood that the qualifying question for becoming a shepherd was, "Do you love me?" In his exposition of John 21:15-19, Chrysostom wrote:

> The Master asked the disciple whether he loved him, not in order to ascertain this of him (for how should he be taught who searches the hearts of all?), but in order to show us how close to his heart is the guidance of his flock. This being clear, it must also be plain how great and ineffable is the reward for him who labors among those who are so dear to Christ. When we see anyone taking care of our servants or our flocks, we consider their care of them as a proof of love for ourselves, even though all these things are purchased for money. And he who purchased his flock, not with a price of money, but with the price of his blood—what reward will he give to his shepherds?[58]

A valuable insight in Chrysostom's exposition of this passage is that he understood Christ was not only asking about Peter's love for Christ, but even more about Peter's love for Christ's people for whom he gave his life to redeem them. Unless Peter was aware of how precious they were, he could not shepherd them appropriately. In regard to their value as God's people, Chrysostom continues:

> Why did God not spare his only-begotten son? Why did he deliver him up, the only son he had? It was the divine plan by which he might reconcile to himself those who were his enemies, and make them his own people. Why did he shed his blood? To purchase those sheep which he had entrusted to Peter and to his successors. Rightly, and with reason then, did Christ say, "Who then is the faithful servant and wise, whom the master has set over his household?"[59]

This exposition reaffirmed that Christ wanted Peter's acknowledgement of love primarily for his people's sake, and that it verifies the validity of the shepherd who cares for Christ's people. Through an understanding of the cost of Christ's death for his people, the priest is entrusted with, and enabled to exercise, pastoral leadership. Chrysostom emphatically taught

57. Ibid.
58. Chrysostom, *Priesthood*, 15-16.
59. Ibid., 16.

Pastoral Leadership

the reality of Christ's earthly body as the Church,[60] and believed that Christ blesses and endorses pastoral leadership only to those who know how much Christ loves his people. The logic is that the person who understands the value of Christ's people can honor them genuinely by caring for them. For this reason, he emphasized, "The priesthood is the greatest evidence of love for Christ."[61] Basil, then, asked Chrysostom, "But you yourself, do you not love Christ?" To this Chrysostom replied, "I do love him; and never will I cease loving him. Yet I do fear to offend him whom I love."[62] This is a sincere yet somewhat weak argument for declining ordination. When Christ repeated the same question, Peter did not decline and Basil expected the same response from Chrysostom who in turn added: "I fear lest, having received the flock of Christ in sound and healthy condition, I should harm it by negligence, and draw upon myself the anger of God who so loved the flock as to give himself as the price of its salvation." Having heard this excuse, Basil protested: "You say this in jest." Moreover, Basil could not accept Chrysostom's explanation that "he fled from the priesthood because of his burning love for Christ."[63] Basil, after many doubts, finally accepted Chrysostom's apology.

The third pastoral principle I identify is the dignity of the priesthood. In the process of making his apology to Basil, Chrysostom gave his view of the people of God as well as the shepherd who cares for them. He emphasized the immeasurable value of the Lord's people, and also the highest dignity of the shepherd who is privileged and responsible for caring for his people. Chrysostom claimed: "The office of the priesthood stands preeminent above all others."[64] In regard to his action with regard to ordination, Chrysostom was accused of seeking vainglory. Chrysostom, however, insisted: "If I had been motivated by pride, I ought to have accepted rather than to have declined this office. Why? Because that would have brought me great glory."[65] Chrysostom's moving description of the nature of the priesthood is found in the following statement:

60. Greeley, "Church as Body of Christ," 75. Greely explains that: "Since Christ went through the very experiences which we suffer, he knows our trials not only as God but as man. Most of all, Christ felt the agony of his coming death, yet chose it. He clung to the present life proving that he was not exempt from human feeling."
61. Chrysostom, *Priesthood*, 15.
62. Ibid., 21.
63. Ibid., 23.
64. Ibid., 17.
65. Ibid., 30.

Chrysostom's Pastoral Leadership Principles: On the Priesthood

Though the office of the priesthood is exercised on earth, it ranks, nevertheless, in the order of celestial things—and rightly so. It was neither man nor an angel nor an archangel not any other created power, but the Paraclete himself who established this ministry, and who ordained that men abiding in the flesh should imitate the ministry of the angels. For that reason it behooves the bearer of the priesthood to be as pure as if he stood in the very heavens amidst those power.[66]

According to this description, the effectiveness of pastoral ministry depends on the pastor's own understanding of its nature, namely that the priesthood was ordained by the Holy Spirit, rather than by humans, and its ministry has a heavenly status and significance. No other earthly employment compares with it and thus it requires more commitment and skill than all other occupations. "The priesthood is an august service,"[67] Chrysostom writes. "Who then can despise this most awful mystery, unless he has utterly lost his mind?"[68]

While Chrysostom's description of the honor and dignity of the priesthood compares favorably with other writings,[69] some of his descriptions are questionable. For example, several of his statements raise theological issues, such as: 1) "The spiritual labor and rebirth accomplished through Baptism is entrusted to priests."[70] 2) "But priests are the authors of our birth from God, and of that blessed regeneration which is true freedom, and son-ship through grace."[71] 3) "Our parents begot us to temporal existence; priests beget us to the eternal. The former are unable to ward off from their children the sting of death, nor prevent the attack of disease; yet the latter often save the sick and perishing soul."[72] These statements are controversial and at least imply baptismal regeneration and the indispensability of the priesthood in conveying special life, grace and forgiveness to people. "Not only at the time of our regeneration in Baptism," writes Chrysostom, "but even

---

66. Ibid., 31.
67. Ibid.
68. Ibid., 32.
69. Nazianzus, *Oration II* (*NPNF2* 7:227). Nazianzus' description of the priesthood is not like Chrysostom's, but he made a resolution to submit himself to God: "Here is my obedience, reward it with your blessing. Lead me with your prayers, guide me with your words, establish me with your Spirit."
70. Chrysostom, *Priesthood*, 33.
71. Ibid., 34.
72. Ibid., 34.

Pastoral Leadership

afterward, they have the authority to forgive sins."[73] This reflects again a sacerdotal view of the priesthood. I share Chrysostom's view of the dignity of the Christian ministry but I want to restrict the priest's authority concerning forgiveness to a declarative authority only. However, Chrysostom argued his position on the basis of Matt 16:16–20 in which he understood that Christ entrusted the authority of spiritual regeneration and forgiveness of sins to Peter and his successors:

> Priests have received a power, which God has given neither to angels nor to archangels. It was said to them: "Whatsoever ye shall bind upon earth shall be bound in heaven; and whatsoever ye shall loose, shall be loosed." Temporal rulers have indeed the power of binding; but they can bind only the body. Priests, however, can bind with a bond, which pertains to the soul itself, and transcends the very heavens. Whatever priests do here on earth, God will confirm in heaven, just as the master ratifies the decisions of his servants. Did he not give them all the powers of heaven? "Whose sins ye shall retain, they are retained." What greater power is there than this? The Father has given all the judgment to the Son. And now I see the Son placing all this power in the hands of men.[74]

Chrysostom understood that the authority Jesus received from God had also been entrusted by Jesus to the apostles, including *the* authority to forgive sins and grant eternal life through baptism. Chrysostom may have misunderstood the true intention of our Lord. The gospel does not state that authority be granted to men because, biblically, that belongs to Christ alone. The Reformers did not agree with Chrysostom's interpretation of the apostles' authority.[75] Chrysostom, however, was inclined to regard the priest as the highest representative ordained by God for the salvation of human beings. To support this view Chrysostom introduced the apostle Paul as an example of the greatness of the priesthood:

> No one loved Christ more than Paul did. No one exhibited a greater zeal; no one was found more worthy of grace. Nevertheless, Paul was filled with fear and trembling at the thought of this office and for the sake of those whom he must lead.[76]

73. Ibid., 35.

74. Ibid., 33.

75. Calvin, *Calvin's Commentaries*, 7:338. Calvin understood that it is not ministers who have authority but Christ through the gospel. God alone has authority to grant salvation and ministers only have a declaratory authority.

76. Chrysostom, *Priesthood*, 35. Chrysostom pointed out that Paul, as the apostle of

Chrysostom's Pastoral Leadership Principles: On the Priesthood

If Paul was trembling with fear when he ministered to the people, how much more are we are obligated to reverently serve God's people? Such is Chrysostom's view of the highly privileged position of the priesthood. On the contrary, Martin Luther's doctrine of the priesthood of all believers[77] is based on 1 Peter 2:9, which says, "But you are a chosen race, a royal priesthood, a holy nation, God's own people." Luther interpreted this verse from a biblical perspective:

> Therefore we are willing to let them call themselves priests, for we do not care how they want to be dubbed. No, the question at issue is whether they are called priests in Scripture and whether God calls them priests. Some can be selected from the congregation who are officeholders and servants and are appointed to preach in the congregation and to administer the sacraments. But we are all priests before God if we are Christians. For since we have been laid on the stone who is the Chief Priest before God, we also have everything He has.[78]

More than eleven centuries after the patristic era of Chrysostom, Martin Luther challenged this view of the priesthood. Luther believed in the priesthood of all believers. The fourth-century doctrine of the priesthood did not produce theological disputes; rather, discussion was geared to a theological emphasis on the priesthood. In regard to the priests of Judaism, for example, Chrysostom compared the differences of the two priesthoods: "The priests of Judaism had power to cleanse the body from leprosy. Our priests have received the power not of treating with the leprosy of the body, but with spiritual uncleanness; not of declaring cleansed, but of actually cleansing."[79]

Christ, was in fear of executing his ministry in 2 Cor 11:3. "But I am afraid that just as Eve was deceived by the serpent's cunning, your minds may somehow be led astray from your sincere and pure devotion to Christ."

77. Luther, *Luther's Works*, 35:101. Luther declared the priesthood of all believers. He wrote: "All such, then, wherever they may be, are true priests. They truly observe the mass right and also obtain by it what they desire. For faith must do everything. Faith alone is the true priestly office. It permits no one else to take its place. Therefore all Christian men are priests, all women priestesses, be they young or old, master or servant, mistress or maid, learned or unlearned. Here there is no difference, unless faith be unequal."

78. Luther, *Luther's Works*, 30:63.

79. Chrysostom, *Priesthood*, 34. Chrysostom does not only honor the priests but also warns those who despise the priests with an example from Num 16: "Anyone, therefore, who would despise our priests would be far more detestable than Dathan and his companions, and would deserve an even greater punishment."

Pastoral Leadership

In comparing the body with the spirit, Chrysostom placed the spiritual on a higher level than the physical and thus regarded the priesthood as the highest of all other occupations. This notion challenges priests to take greater responsibility in carrying out their pastoral ministry.

Having considered the significance of the nature of the priesthood in the areas of pastoral care, the enormous value of God's people, and the high dignity of the office and the work of the shepherd, the next category of pastoral leadership principles to be discussed is the personal character of the shepherd. In order to carry out the "the multidimensional nature of pastoral care,"[80] pastors must possess exemplary character.

Once again, Chrysostom introduces Paul's compassionate pastoral heart for the Israelites by citing Rom 9:3, and in defense of his avoidance of ordination Chrysostom confessed he did not possess Paul's godly character:

> Any man who can so speak, any man possessed of such a character that he can offer this prayer, may justly be accused if he flee. But any man who is so far removed from such virtues as I am, should be detested not if he flee, but if he accept this office.[81]

Defending his own sense of unworthiness for the priesthood, Chrysostom emphasized that noble personal character is a necessary criterion for ordination because priests assume responsibility for the precious people of Christ. Chrysostom provided a reason why he declined ordination.[82] "He who enters into the priesthood will have many temptations. To overcome them he must have a very strong character."[83]

He then lists many character traits that unqualified priests may have, including pride, anger, despondency, envy, contention, slander, accusations, lies, hypocrisy, intrigue, and despising. Chrysostom calls these traits "beasts" and stated: "I am unable to escape from the trap. If anyone would entrust me with the priestly office it would be the same as if he were to deliver me up, hands bound behind my back, to be torn to pieces daily by

---

80. Gerkin, *Introduction to Pastoral Care*, 118. A pastor cannot meet the needs of the multidimensional individuals, but he can be an example for them through exemplary character.

81. Chrysostom, *Priesthood*, 36.

82. Chrysostom writes: "If anyone in charge of a merchant vessel carrying a priceless cargo and manned by a full crew of rowers were to place me at the helm and order me to cross the Aegean or Tyrrhenian Sea, I would reply that I did not wish to sink the ship." Ibid.

83. Ibid., 37.

Chrysostom's Pastoral Leadership Principles: On the Priesthood

the beasts dwelling on the rock."[84] Among all these traits he points out that pride is by far the worst; priests are subject to all these weaknesses and their evil consequences, particularly pride.[85] He believed: "It is never possible to hide the faults of priests. Even their slightest imperfections are easily detected."[86]

For this reason he, therefore, "treats character as the crucial question and as the source of the priest's authority."[87] In the process of selecting ecclesiastical officers, Chrysostom had observed that the character of the priest, to him the most crucial requirement, was not usually the determining criterion:

> All those who have the privilege of electing to this honor are split into many factions, and one can never find the council of priests in agreement among themselves as to whom the lot of the episcopacy has fallen. Each stands apart from the others, one voting for this man, another for that. The reason for this divergence of opinion is that they do not all look to the one thing that should be kept in mind—strength of character. Instead, they allege various other qualifications for the honor.[88]

Chrysostom observed many priests who exercised the pastoral ministry in a way contrary to biblical principles. "It is not surprising," writes Rowan Greer, "that the ideal priestly character is defined partly by way of contrast to the actual situation, and we can learn much from the vices the church fathers castigate."[89] Throughout the treatise, Chrysostom demonstrated his own integrity by insisting that personal character should be the first criterion in electing the priest. Discovering over a period of time that ecclesiastical officers often did not carry out their duties according to godly principles, Chrysostom illustrated from his experience that some priests should not have been ordained:

---

84. Ibid.
85. Ibid.
86. Ibid., 44. Again, he argues for his reason to decline the ordination to the priesthood and brings out the character issue: "Seclusion is the veil which hides their shortcomings. When, however, they are brought into public, they are compelled to put aside this garment of seclusion and to lay bare their souls to all through their external actions."
87. Greer, "Reflection on Priestly Authority," 106.
88. Ibid., 47.
89. Greer, "Reflections on Priestly Authority," 107.

Pastoral Leadership

> I knew many men who constantly practiced self-denial, and who became emaciated from fasting—men who, as long as they were allowed to be alone and to look after none but their own concerns, were pleasing God, and who made daily progress in the science of sanctity. But some of these same men, as soon as they were advanced to a public office in which they were obliged to reprove the faults of the people, proved themselves from the outset unfitted for such a task.[90]

On the other hand, these men were appointed to office in good faith and with evidence of godliness and seriousness. Would Chrysostom's observation here be met by a probationary period for such appointees? In regard to his own personal character, Chrysostom argued that he was more like the former category that does well when alone: "Are you not aware that I am successful not by virtue but by a love of retirement?"[91] He was well aware of his own character flaws such as anger and its dangers: "The passion of anger is a kind of pleasure, and it exercises a greater tyranny over the soul than any other pleasure, and it destroys the soul's tranquility."[92] Another sin he pointed out was envy, the root of all sin:

> "If you wish to inquire after the causes of this terrible evil you will find them similar to those already mentioned. They have all one root, and so to speak, one mother—envy. Nevertheless, this envy is manifested not in one form but in many"[93]

Therefore, genuine relationships among God's people and the priestly shepherds are damaged, even destroyed. Chrysostom was a perfectionist who always pursued the highest possible standards. He expressed his ideal of the priest's character as follows:

> He must be dignified, but not haughty; awe-inspiring, but kind; affable in this authority; impartial, but courteous; humble, but not servile; strong, but gentle; and he will then be able easily to cope with all these difficulties. With this full authority he ought to bring forward the man who is qualified, even though all oppose him. With the same power he should reject the unqualified, even though all conspire in his favor. He must keep one thing only

---

90. Chrysostom, *Priesthood*, 47.
91. Ibid., 44.
92. Ibid., 43.
93. Ibid., 49.

Chrysostom's Pastoral Leadership Principles: On the Priesthood

before his eyes—the welfare of the Church; and he must do nothing through enmity or partiality.[94]

Such perfect standards as Chrysostom described here are unattainable in his view; although his dream of obtaining such a perfect character was never realized, he knew that the Messiah possessed the character of the ideal shepherd.[95] This pastoral principle of obtaining a godly character is essential if priests are to carry out their pastoral duties properly. At the end of the treatise, Chrysostom asked Basil if he was persuaded with the reasons he had given for escaping ordination: "Now does it seem to you that I have done well in refusing this ministry?"[96] He added: "He who takes this ministry for his path in life must examine all things well, prior to his setting out."[97]

It is, however, unlikely that Chrysostom could have illustrated all the personal character requirements for the priesthood unless he had personal experience as an ordained priest. Andrea Sterk also noted: "While condemning such abuses and presenting his own defense in his treatise, *On the Priesthood*, John also gives a detailed and eloquent exposition of duties, demands, and dignity of the sacerdotal office."[98] This leads us to conclude that his treatise was his own leadership manual for a successful priesthood acquired through personal experiences.[99]

After discussing the nature and personal character of the priest, Chrysostom finally discusses the duty of the priesthood. While the development of godly character is a prerequisite for a priest in performing his duties, caring for souls[100] is the first priority as holistic pastoral care cannot be achieved without tending to the soul's well being. The priest is the healer of the soul just as the physician is of the body. Chrysostom stated, "The physician came not to condemn you, but to heal you; not to pass you by

---

94. Ibid., 51.
95. Isaiah depicted the character of Messiah in resemblance of Chrysostom's picture in Isa 42:1–4.
96. Chrysostom, *Priesthood*, 51.
97. Ibid., 51.
98. Sterk, *Renouncing the World*, 150.
99. Ibid., 151. Sterk assumed that this treatise was written by a priest: "Since *De Sacerdotio* was written by a priest who also intimately acquainted with monastic life, it is not surprising that ascetic ideals often enter into his discussion of church office."
100. Willard, "Personal Soul Care," 11–19.

Pastoral Leadership

when you were sick, but to deliver you completely from your malady."[101] Basil then responded by saying, "Your words have inspired me with such fear and trembling that I can no longer control myself."[102] Caring for the souls of the flock is a new theme and one that Gregory of Nazianzus had not dealt with.[103]

Next, Chrysostom discusses how the priest should exercise his duty to heal and protect the Lord's people as the physician of the souls. Realizing his inadequate personal character as a spiritual physician, he depicts the sacred soul of the priest, which "should be as a light which shines in the whole world; but my soul, because my conscience is stained with guilt, is engulfed in such darkness that it hides itself and dares not look confidently upon its Master. The Priest is the salt of the earth."[104] As such, "the pastor has need of great prudence—yea, and a thousand eyes, so as to examine the condition of the soul from every aspect."[105] Chrysostom then discusses the work of the priest, namely how he should heal those who were in spiritual ill health[106]; with regard to the spoken word a priest ministers to heal the sick, he writes:

> In the spiritual order, however, it is useless to consider such remedies. Save for good example, there is but one means and cure: the spoken word. This is the sole instrument, the only diet, the finest climate. It takes the place of medication, of cautery, and the knife. If it is necessary to burn or cut, this is the instrument which must be used; and if it fails, all else is useless. By this means we raise up the prostrate soul, and cool the fevered; we cut away its excess and supply its defects; and we do everything else which is required for the health of the soul.[107]

Theologically, Chrysostom attempted to define the spiritual duty of the priesthood not as a political and ecclesiastical officer, but as a heavenly servant curing the sick soul through the ministry of the word. Such a ministry is one of the most important duties in caring for the Lord's sheep. Chrysostom considered it his most crucial responsibility as a priest

---

101. Chrysostom, *Priesthood*, 65.
102. Ibid., 65.
103. Yanney, "Priesthood," 137.
104. Chrysostom, *Priesthood*, 96.
105. Ibid., 20.
106. Chrysostom, *Priesthood*, 70.
107. Ibid., 70.

Chrysostom's Pastoral Leadership Principles: On the Priesthood

throughout his priestly service. Chrysostom challenged his contemporary Episcopal leadership in regard to their priestly practices, ranking the leadership of the priesthood as the highest. It is, therefore, necessary to raise the moral and theological standards for people seeking the priesthood. Richard Valantasis correctly pointed out that: "For Chrysostom there is no question: the core of the leadership of the Church is spiritual, not political, and he dramatically brings the nature and the structure of priest and bishop to a higher theological plane."[108]

Ministry for the soul as belonging to the heavenly realm was a new ontological concept of ministry as Chrysostom described in his treatise. Interpreting the theological concept of the priest's duty, Chrysostom uncovered an opportunity for religious reformation. This theological understanding of the priesthood may have motivated religious reform when he became the Patriarch of Constantinople in 398.[109] Caring for the soul is, however, actually carried out through the Eucharistic ministry by the priest because Chrysostom believed that the salvation of the soul is impossible without the priest's ministry at the Eucharistic service. Purves criticized Chrysostom for replacing "the priesthood of Christ with the priesthood of the pastor/priest,"[110] and one expects Chrysostom's doctrine of salvation through the Eucharistic service administered by the priesthood to be challenged theologically.[111] Chrysostom wrote:

> Inasmuch as no man can enter into the Kingdom of Heaven unless he be born again of water and Spirit, and since unless he eats the flesh of the Lord and drinks his blood he is excluded from eternal life—since, I say, all these things are administered only by those holy hands, the hands of priests, how could any man without those priests either escape the fire of hell or obtain the crown which is intended for him?[112]

---

108. Valantasis, "Body, Hierarchy, and Leadership," 459. Indicating Chrysostom's theological argument for the function and the duty of the priesthood Valantasis pointed out Chrysostom's intention in his treatise that: "The criteria for the episcopacy are too secular for Chrysostom. He wants to develop other criteria because the leadership of the Church was being devalued by the social and political aspects of selection and election of bishops."

109. Baur, *John Chrysostom*, 2:58–69.

110. Purves, *Pastoral Theology*, 47.

111. Barth, *Church Dogmatics*, 3:155.

112. Chrysostom, *Priesthood*, 33.

Pastoral Leadership

W. R. W. Stephens is correct in suggesting, "There are, perhaps, no passages elsewhere in Chrysostom expressed in such a lofty sacerdotal tone."[113] Without receiving the Eucharist at the hands of the priest, Chrysostom believed one is unable to enter heaven and also he perceived: "Priests have received a power which God has given neither to angels nor to archangels."[114] Beside the Eucharist, Chrysostom also claimed: "The spiritual labor and rebirth accomplished through Baptism is entrusted to priests."[115]

Considering the significant duty of caring for Christ's people and the authority entrusted to the priest by God, Chrysostom could not help but take the responsibility of an ordained priest very seriously. Furthermore, he was obligated not only to care for souls spiritually, but also to provide for people's physical needs. During the entire period of his ministry, from 386 to 404, Chrysostom was vigilant in serving the poor. In ministering to the poor, widows, virgins, and strangers,[116] Chrysostom considered that his attitude towards the people was more important than the service itself. He wrote:

> A man who has been given alms in an insulting manner does not appreciate the money, even though the alms were most generous; for the insult which he has received is a blow to him. On the other hand, a man who has been spoken to in kind and gentle words is consoled by what is given to him. He is gladdened and rejoices; and the gift is doubled in value by reason of manner in which it is given.[117]

Chrysostom's consistent ministry for the poor throughout his pastoral ministry as deacon then priest sprung from his theological conviction that the priesthood should imitate the ministry of angels.[118] For this reason,

---

113. Stephens, *His Life and Times*, 49.

114. Chrysostom, *Priesthood*, 32–33.

115. Ibid., 33. Chrysostom regards the priests as higher than any one on earth: "Hence, we should, by rights, regard them as more august than kings and princes, and more venerable than our fathers."

116. Ibid., 54. In the ministry for the needy, Chrysostom suggested careful management not only how to provide the funds, but also the attitude in serving. He writes: "In providing hospitality for strangers and in caring for the sick, think what a great expenditure of money is necessary and how much attention and prudence on the part of those to whom this duty falls."

117. Ibid., 53.

118. Ibid., 31. When Chrysostom placed the priesthood in the order of the celestial things it is certainly a theological conviction concerning the ministry of the priest.

Chrysostom's Pastoral Leadership Principles: On the Priesthood

Chrysostom believed that priests should serve the flock just as the angels are directed by God to minister to people. Chrysostom insisted that mercy ministry belongs to the priest who is ordained to perform celestial works and that the work starts from the heart, which in turn precedes the workings of grace.[119]

Asserting the importance of the inner attitude in performing works of mercy, Chrysostom, however, confessed his weakness again concerning anger[120] and he must have tried hard to overcome this and depended on Basil for help: "But look, my dear friend! Do you wish to bring me closer to the fire, and to arouse the best from his slumber?"[121] If it were not for his anger, his integrity in leadership may have persuaded other priests to his side and he may not have faced exile. On the other hand, Chrysostom was an excellent administrator in ensuring almsgiving for the needy; he provides, for example, directions and guidelines in regard to providing hospitality for strangers, caring for virgins and widows, and visitation for the sick.[122] He upheld the importance of regular or daily visitations, not only for the sick but also for the healthy because all desire to receive pastoral visitation.

Chrysostom indicated that church discipline in pastoral leadership should not be neglected. He asks: "Who can say what sorrow a bishop feels when it is necessary for him to cut anyone off from full communion in the Church?"[123] Even though it is may be necessary to discipline the person who commits sin,[124] he insists that: "the greatest care is to be taken in these matters lest that which is intended to be profitable to a man should really become the occasion of greater harm."[125] Discipline without restoration is unprofitable and results in greater wounds.

Finally, Chrysostom discussed the priest's significant responsibility for preaching and he explored this subject more extensively than any other previous pastoral leadership topic.[126] To illustrate the main purpose

119. Chrysostom, *Priesthood*, 31.
120. Ibid., 43.
121. Ibid., 43.
122. Ibid., 54, 55, 57.
123. Ibid., 58.
124. Ibid., 58. Chrysostom pointed out that the one who discipline the sinner is also responsible for one's recovery. He writes: "The responsibility for whatever sins he may commit after such treatment will be shared by the physician who did not properly lance the wound."
125. Ibid.
126. Chrysostom devoted his discussion on preaching to Books Four and Five. The

Pastoral Leadership

of preaching, Chrysostom referred to a physician's care for the sick body: "Physicians have discovered various medications, different kinds of instruments, and diets suitable for the sick."[127] In the spiritual order, Chrysostom claimed, "There is but one means and method of cure: the spoken word."[128] The purpose of preaching is to cure sick souls through the Word of God and includes unbelievers for their salvation but also believers for their growth in Christlikeness.[129]

Chrysostom valued Scripture highly and, according to W. A. Jurgens, cited Scripture two hundred and eleven times in this treatise and the Apocrypha six times.[130] His citations demonstrate his emphasis on the importance of Scripture. To effectively preach the Word, he emphasized that two elements are indispensable: the Word and deed. He wrote: "Indeed, this is the most perfect end of teaching: to lead one's disciples by word and deed to the blessed life which Christ instituted. It is not sufficient to teach by example alone."[131] He then cited Matt 5:19 to support his pastoral leadership principle that preaching without a Christlike character is ineffective and that preaching the Word should always be accompanied and followed by a godly life. Chrysostom did not advertise his ability to preach eloquently, but freely admitted his weakness in character.[132] After an analysis of Chrysostom's qualifications for being a preacher in this treatise, Lewis Patsavos identified two important features, namely, "humility and fluency in speaking."[133] Character and proficiency in preaching are the fundamental components in Chrysostom's pastoral leadership principles in his treatise.

---

subject was discussed more thoroughly than other subjects.

127. Ibid., 70.

128. Ibid.

129. Stott, *Between Two Worlds*, 147. In a summary of Chrysostom's preaching Stott wrote, "We have two qualities in Chrysostom, which in their combination make him unique—he is a man of the Word and a man of the world. Again as with all effective preachers, his message had both a timeless and a timely element in it."

130. Jurgens, "Notes," in Chrysostom's *Priesthood*, 124–27.

131. Chrysostom, *Priesthood*, 79.

132. Ibid., 65. He argued for his weakness in character and said, "As for me, since I am weak, my security lies in never undertaking the office of the priesthood at all."

133. Patsavos, "Image of the Priest," 68. In regard to Chrysostom's argument for the qualified priest for preaching in this treatise Patsavos writes, "To effectively realize the purpose of his teaching, there are two indispensable qualifications—humility and fluency in speaking—both of which are an advantage to the priest himself as well as his community. The preacher is worthy of his mission only when he possesses both of these qualifications."

Chrysostom's Pastoral Leadership Principles: On the Priesthood

In order to emphasize the importance of character and eloquence in preaching, Chrysostom always presented Paul as a model for pastoral leadership. Regarding Christian character, he thought Paul surpassed all others in his prayer life, love for Christ, miracles, and his spiritual experience.[134] Chrysostom affirmed Paul's eloquence in preaching except for one occasion in 2 Cor 11:6, where "he was unskilled in speech." Paul, however, was not only incomparable in his Christlike character, but he was also an eloquent speaker. In regard to Paul's eloquence, Chrysostom wrote:

> Why did the Lycaconians mistake him for Hermes? The fact that they (Paul and Barnabas) were taken for gods was due indeed to their miracles; but that Paul was thought to be Hermes was due not to his miracles but to his eloquence. How did this blessed man surpass the other Apostles? Why is his name on every tongue throughout the whole world?[135]

Chrysostom insisted that one could not achieve Paul's standard of pastoral leadership without a great deal of labor and study for public preaching. He warned: "If a preacher introduces into his discourse anything which was composed by another, he is reproached more severely than if he had been guilty of stealing money."[136] Chrysostom's axiom on preaching is that "Preaching comes not by nature, but by study"[137] and its goal must be God-centered. He encouraged preachers to focus on God rather than receiving praises from men.[138] Chrysostom concluded his remarks on pastoral preaching, stating that, "this cannot be attained except by two means: indifference to praise, and ability in eloquence,"[139] and "a good leader must be strong in both these qualities."[140] Ideal pastoral leadership, then,

---

134. Chrysostom, *Priesthood*, 74. Chrysostom writes, "All the men together of the present day could not accomplish with endless prayers and tears what was done by means of Paul's aprons." These descriptions of Paul refer to his character imitating Christ.

135. Ibid., 77.

136. Ibid., 81.

137. Ibid., 85.

138. Ibid., 87. Chrysostom's advice on the direction of preaching is a valuable insight. He writes, "Nevertheless, while he composes his sermons to please God alone (this should be the only guide and purpose of his best workmanship—neither praise nor applause), if men praise him he ought not to despise such praise. If, on the other hand, he receives no praise from his listeners, let him neither seek it nor be aggrieved."

139. Ibid., 82.

140. Ibid., 83.

Pastoral Leadership

is achieved through a Christlike character and eloquence in preaching and that through dedicated study of Scripture.

I conclude that Chrysostom's *On the Priesthood* is his most valuable treatise for the purpose of reflecting on, and exploring, his pastoral leadership principles, although the treatise has not been sufficiently explored for this purpose by scholars. Furthermore, I consider the treatise to be more useful than the works of Gregory Nazianzus or Gregory the Great in regard to the study of patristic pastoral leadership. For Chrysostom, the priesthood requires compassionate care for people, a Christlike character, and the eloquent preaching of God's Word through diligent labor. In *On the Priesthood*, Chrysostom expressed the principle of compassionate care for people through his dialogue with Basil; despite the rhetorical and literary nature of the dialogue, it is a personal and helpful exercise in pastoral counseling. In this way he expresses the value of individuals and the importance of relating to others. On the other hand, because of his background—especially his earlier ascetic life—coupled with an intolerant attitude on occasions and a temper, his inter-personal skills tended to be poor, and he did not find it easy to develop and maintain personal relationships. His second pastoral principle relating to the integrity and Christlike character of the priest, received a strong emphasis from Chrysostom, which was retained throughout his ministry. The standard was exceptionally high and to what extent he himself achieved this standard is open to debate. What is certain is that his third principle of diligent preaching of God's Word was achieved and exemplified by Chrysostom throughout his ministry.

# 6

Chrysostom's Pastoral Principles: New Testament Homilies

HAVING OUTLINED THE CONTENT and context of Chrysostom's early major writing, *On the Priesthood*, and having identified major principles in that work relating to pastoral leadership, I want to move forward to sample his New Testament homilies, including those on the Pastoral Epistles that he preached in churches in Antioch and Constantinople. My purpose is to describe and assess these principles, and compare them with those identified in his early treatise.

ANTIOCH

Chrysostom was ordained deacon in Antioch in 381 and five years later was ordained priest, continuing to serve there until he was obliged to move to Constantinople in 398. For seventeen years in Antioch, Chrysostom demonstrated his main pastoral leadership principles of caring for people and preaching the Word of God, as a deacon and an ordained priest. Donald Attwater assumes that Chrysostom was responsible for the collection and distribution of alms during his diaconate ministry.¹ According to homily sixty-six on Matthew, it appears that Chrysostom experienced administrative difficulties because he lacked the necessary skills as well as helpers to oversee and fulfill this huge task of providing relief to the needy folks in the city.² Despite this, Chrysostom served those in need and also continued

---

1. Attwater, *Pastor and Preacher*, 32–33.
2. Chrysostom, Homilies on Matthew 66 (*NPNF*1 10:407). Chrysostom said, "For if

Pastoral Leadership

to preach so that his pastoral ministry in Antioch was well balanced in terms of deed and speech. In this manner, he won over his congregation and earned their respect.³

During his priesthood in Antioch from 386 to 398, Chrysostom preached through the books of Matthew (90 homilies), John (88), Romans (32), First (44) and Second (30) Corinthians, Galatians (6), Ephesians (24), Philippians (15), First (18) and Second (10) Timothy, Titus (6), and Philemon (3), resulting in a total of 366 homilies.⁴ It was in Antioch that Chrysostom laid and clarified the theological and biblical foundation as well as the development of his pastoral leadership principles through his preaching and serving of others. He distinguished himself as a priest who excelled in preaching and ministering to the poor at Antioch. It is clear that Chrysostom would not have been persuaded to relocate from Antioch to Constantinople unless the imperial order had been enforced.⁵ On the emperor's order, the eunuch Eutropius, chief of the royal chamberlains "put him on a public carriage and entrusted him to the care of the eunuch along with the magistrate's guard. In this way he was brought to Constantinople and ordained bishop of the church of Constantinople."⁶ Unwillingly, Chrysostom was transferred to Constantinople, but he had gained the confidence of his Antioch congregation through his ministry there and had a genuinely deep burden for the practical as well as spiritual needs of people in the city. Pauline Allen and Wendy Mayer described the state of Antioch during Chrysostom's ministry:

> By the time John was ordained priest at Antioch the church-administered orphanages, hospitals and perhaps even old people's homes were becoming a familiar part of the urban landscape. At Antioch, a city plagued by the economic effects of seasonal work, periodic drought, and economic strain caused by periodic military activity.⁷

---

both the wealthy, and next to them, were to distribute among themselves those who are in need of bread and raiment, scarcely would one poor person fall to the share of fifty men or even hundred."

3. Palladius, *Life of St. John Chrysostom*, 36.
4. Quasten, *Patrology*.
5. Mayer and Allen, "John Chrysostom," 1134–35, 1128–50.
6. Palladius, *Life of St. John Chrysostom*, 36.
7. Mayer and Allen, *John Chrysostom*, 47.

Chrysostom's Pastoral Principles: New Testament Homilies

In this sociological, economic, and religious environment, Chrysostom tried hard to meet the daily needs of people in the city. His emphasis on mercy ministry in his preaching was forceful. Likewise, most of his writings, based on his preaching, were the product of his years in Antioch and his ministry in serving the needy.

CONSTANTINOPLE

Once he had been consecrated as Patriarch of Constantinople in 398, we would expect Chrysostom to have developed a relationship with other clergy and laity in the city before commencing his major religious reforms. However, Palladius witnessed that Chrysostom, immediately began to reform the religious lifestyle of the clergy, laymen and women, and also the church's finances.[8] "He ordered all unnecessary spending to be stopped at once."[9] Chrysostom started reforming with the right motives and objectives, but his reforms still created problems. His actions drew strong opposition and some people began to plot against him. Sozomen pointed out that: "Immediately upon entering the episcopate, he strove to put an end to the dissension which had arisen concerning Paulinus, between the Western and Egyptian bishops and the bishops of the East; since on this account a general disunion was overpowering the churches in the whole empire."[10] Chrysostom failed to develop good relationships both within the religious community and in the royal court, especially with Emperor Arcadius and Empress Eudoxia. It was thought by some that Chrysostom expressed a disrespectful attitude towards the empire's leaders. Sozomen illustrates, "Addressing himself to the emperor, John exhorted him to maintain the laws which had been established against heretics; and told him that it would be better to be deprived of empire, than to be guilty of impiety by becoming a traitor to the house of God."[11] Chrysostom could have been more polite and respectful in addressing the emperor but "we know, however, that John was not afraid to make his opinion known to the emperor regarding certain decisions."[12] Ultimately, Empress Eudoxia sought to take Chrysostom out of the church in Constantinople.[13]

8. Palladius, *Life of St. John Chrysostom*, 38–40.

9. Ibid., 39.

10. Sozomen, *Ecclesiastical History* (NPNF2 2:400).

11. Ibid., 401.

12. Mayer and Allen, "John Chrysostom," 1134.

13. On account of Severian's deposition by Chrysostom, Socrates writes: "On being

Pastoral Leadership

From the beginning, too, Chrysostom had relational problems with many classes of people, including those in the royal court in Constantinople.[14] In regard to his relationship with Eudoxia, Liebeschuetz points out that:

> A relationship between two extremely strong-willed and at the same time hypersensitive personalities was bound to be difficult. Besides, there was an element of ambiguity in the Empress's position when seen through the eyes of an ascetic. Eudoxia was a committed Christian and her role religious, pious, and charitable. But the symbolic expression of her role was through elaborate dress, jewels, and court ceremony, including a retinue of gorgeously dressed women. In other words, the ceremonial magnification of the Empress could be said to emphasize and develop that worldly and frivolous aspect of female nature that Chrysostom had berated in so many sermons.[15]

The empress and the patriarch were different in lifestyle and attitude concerning their religious practice. Although he always aspired to have a Christlike character, Chrysostom's values and convictions would not permit him to cope with Eudoxia's excesses. From a pastoral leadership perspective, we can suppose that Eudoxia could have been encouraged, and possibly corrected, had Chrysostom exhibited more patience, wisdom, and love. In his *On the Priesthood*, Chrysostom regarded the principle of personal dialogue as an important principle of pastoral leadership, and he applied it rigorously in Antioch. In Constantinople, however, while Chrysostom established a hospital, implemented changes in religious public ceremonies, and reformed church administration, he could not win the affection of the leaders there, whom he challenged to live "according to his understanding of God's demands within this world and its society."[16]

Evaluating Chrysostom's ministries in Constantinople on the basis of the pastoral leadership principles reflected in *On the Priesthood*, he failed due to weaknesses in his own character and responses, rather than in his doctrine. Regarding pastoral leadership, Susan K. Hedahl affirmed that one of the essential tasks in pastoral ministry is listening, which in turn is

---

informed of this, the Empress Eudoxia severely reprimanded John, and ordered that Severian should be immediately recalled from Chalcedon in Bithynia." Socrates, *Ecclesiastical History* (NPNF2 2:146). See also Ibid, 2:405.

14. Socrates, *Ecclesiastical History* (NPNF2 2:146).

15. Liebeschuetz, *Barbarians and Bishops*, 202.

16. Young, "They Speak to Us," 40.

"thoroughly theological in orientation and meaning."[17] If Chrysostom had been more modest in his demands, patient and persistent in persuading others and humble also through listening, Eudoxia and other opponents may have been helped under his leadership.

I have been unable to discover any essential differences in content and emphasis in Chrysostom's preaching in Constantinople from that in Antioch. In Constantinople, from 398 through 407 (including his two exiles), Chrysostom preached homilies on Acts (55), Hebrews (34), Colossians (12), First Thessalonians (11), and Second Thessalonians (5), resulting in a total of 117 homilies. In Antioch, Chrysostom preached at three different churches and concentrated on preaching and ministry to the poor. At Constantinople, however, he preached at five different churches and was occupied with the wider ecclesiastical business so that he could not focus on his preaching as much as he had done in Antioch.[18] Liebeschuetz, however, has pointed out that Chrysostom's homilies at Constantinople "are thoughtful, eloquent, and in many ways of timeless relevance"[19] and he refers to "the passion with which moral commands were expounded as divine commandments."[20] He was more experienced and passionate in Constantinople, preaching with boldness and confidently rebuking his congregation.[21] Instead of focusing on theological issues in his sermons, he dealt more with social and practical issues like poverty and the extravagance and abuses of the rich.[22] Chrysostom suggested that there were 100,000 people in Constantinople and of these, 50,000 were poor; he suggested that if everyone equally shared their wealth, the problem of poverty could be resolved.[23] With this insight in mind, he attempted social reform in order to resolve the poverty problem in the city. His approach was helpful, putting his theology into practice through church reformation.[24] Along the way, in

17. Hedahl, *Listening Ministry*, 15.

18. Mayer, "Extraordinary Preacher, Ordinary Audience," 126–127, 103–137. The three churches at Antioch were the Old Church, the Great or Golden Church, and the Church of St. Byblas. Mayer also outlines the five churches at Constantinople: St. Anastasia, St. Eirene, St Paul, the Great Church, and the Church of the Holy Apostles.

19. Liebeschuetz, *Barbarians and Bishops*, 172.

20. Ibid.

21. Kelly, *Golden Mouth*, 134–35.

22. Ibid., 136.

23. Chrysostom, *Homilies on Acts* 11 (*NPNF*1 11:74).

24. Volf, "Way of Life," 246–47, 245–263. Volf argues that theology is a practical science rather than a theoretical as Thomas Aquinas understood. Volf believes that theology

Pastoral Leadership

Constantinople, Chrysostom sought to theologize social and religious issues while he applied his pastoral principles. He failed, however, to achieve this goal.

FOUR PASTORAL PRINCIPLES

I now proceed to the main part of this chapter, namely, to deal with the major pastoral leadership principles that I have identified in a sample of Chrysostom's New Testament homilies.

1. Almsgiving

The first principle of pastoral leadership in the homilies is caring for people, with significant emphasis on almsgiving. Throughout his priesthood, one of Chrysostom's main priorities in pastoral ministry was addressing the practical needs of the people. He saw almsgiving as an effective way of dealing with poverty and other related needs. While he discussed almsgiving in *On the Priesthood*,[25] he did so more particularly in his homilies on the New Testaments books. For example, "In the ninety sermons on the Gospel of St. Matthew, Chrysostom spoke forty times on almsgiving alone."[26] The New Testament homilies teach that the poor can be served most effectively through almsgiving. In this way, one can fulfill the law of God by caring for neighbors. Chrysostom believed that serving the poor is a prime responsibility for church leaders, as well as Christians generally; in this context he appealed to a major emphasis in his thinking, namely, the imitation of Christ. Interpreting 1 Cor 11:1, for example, Chrysostom wrote:

> "Be ye imitators of me, even as I also am of Christ." This is a rule of the most perfect Christianity, this is a landmark exactly laid down, this is the point that stands highest of all; viz. the seeking those things which are for the common profit: which also Paul himself declared, by adding, "even as I also am of Christ." For nothing can so make a man an imitator of Christ as caring for his neighbors.[27]

---

is more properly described as a practical than as a theoretical science.

25. Chrysostom, *Priesthood*, 53. He instructs, "All contributions should be distributed to the poor immediately. Then the generosity of the faithful may be depended upon as a ready treasury of the church."

26. Baur, *John Chrysostom*, 1:217.

27. Chrysostom, *Homilies on First Corinthians* (NPNF1 12:146).

Chrysostom's Pastoral Principles: New Testament Homilies

To put it more negatively, Chrysostom understood that attempts to imitate Christ are defective if they fail to express practical care for one's neighbors. Examining Chrysostom's fundamental theological emphasis, F. X. Murphy concluded that:

> In substance, the love and care of one's neighbor are based upon the imitation of Christ who gave man both the commandment and a supreme example of charity for all of mankind. This love of neighbor is to be pursued within the Church that is the continuation of the Old Testament dispensation.[28]

Chrysostom was concerned for the poor not only because of the pressing, even appalling, sociological and economic needs of that period but also because of his theological principles. Theologically, I suggest that Chrysostom may have overemphasized the importance of almsgiving, especially in his implication that it is necessary for salvation. But in his exposition of John 2:11, for example, Chrysostom boldly proclaimed that without almsgiving no one can enter the kingdom of God. He wrote: "for it is impossible, it is impossible, though we perform ten thousand other good deeds, to enter the portals of the kingdom without alms-doing."[29] In order to emphasize the significance of almsgiving, Chrysostom here repeats the phrase "it is impossible" twice. He also suggests that the forgiveness of sin was at least partly based on almsgiving: "There is no sin, which alms cannot cleanse, none, which alms cannot quench: all sin is beneath this: it is medicine adapted for every wound."[30] This attaches a more specific aspect to the act and he emphasized that one benefit of almsgiving is the removal of sins: "for them, not one of their sins is forgiven when they receive, but for you, the more part of your offenses is removed."[31] In regard to personal salvation and the Christian life, Chrysostom concluded, "Without the giving of alms one cannot be saved."[32] This theme of salvation linked with the almsgiving is found in his homilies on Philippians, Second Timothy, John, Matthew, Acts, and Second Corinthians. Chrysostom writes, "Hear Daniel, saying, Redeem thy sins by alms-deeds, and thine iniquities by showing mercy to the poor."[33] I question whether alms-deeds have the power to redeem

---

28. Murphy, "Moral Doctrine," 57.
29. Chrysostom, *Homilies on John*, (*NPNF*1 14:83).
30. Chrysostom, *Homilies on Acts* (*NPNF*1 11:166).
31. Chrysostom, *Homilies on Philippians* (*NPNF*1 13:187).
32. Krupp, *Shepherding the Flock of God*, 153.
33. Chrysostom, *Homilies on John* (*NPNF*1 14:29).

Pastoral Leadership

sins, and suggest that they could rather be viewed as evidence that one's sins are forgiven. I agree with Eun Hye Lee, however, that "the redemptive value of almsgiving is a common thread among the early fathers. Clement of Alexandria and Cyprian[34] consider the role of almsgiving in achieving or guaranteeing salvation."[35] In his homily on the book of Matthew, Chrysostom stated, "Let us imitate then this virtue, and most of all his humility and almsgiving, without which one cannot be saved."[36]

Realizing the theological, ethical, as well as practical significance of almsgiving, Chrysostom preached on its spiritual value: "For consider; have you sown almsgiving? The treasures of heaven and eternal glory await thee."[37] He also encouraged his congregation to change their attitudes toward the poor: "When then you see a poor believer, think that you behold an altar: when you see such one beggar, not only insult him not, but even reverence him."[38] Chrysostom also preached seven sermons about Lazarus and the rich man.[39] He stated that "the rich man's chief fault was his failure to give alms; he neglected the duty of helping his neighbor."[40] At the end of his seventh sermon, Chrysostom encouraged the congregation with these words: "I mean the way of virtue, they may be counted worthy of the patriarch's bosom like Lazarus, and in order that all of us together, freed from the fire of hell, may enjoy those ineffable good things which eye has not seen nor ear heard."[41] Along with this encouragement for almsgiving he also stated: "Whenever money is stored up for the poor, that place is inaccessible to the demons; and the money that is collected together for almsgiving fortifies Christian homes more than a shield, spear, weapons, physical power, and multitudes of soldiers."[42]

While he was convinced that almsgiving was the economic solution to the needs of the poor in his society, yet this pastoral care for the poor was the result of his interpretation of specific biblical texts. His preaching of Matt 25:31–41, for example, clearly reflected the significance of ministering

34. Ibid.
35. Lee, "A Glorious Failure," 82–83.
36. Chrysostom, *Homilies on Matthew* (*NPNF1* 10:295).
37. Chrysostom, *Commentary on Galatians* (*NPNF1* 13:45).
38. Chrysostom, *Homilies on Second Corinthians* (*NPNF1* 12:374).
39. Chrysostom, *On Wealth and Poverty*.
40. Roth, "Introduction," in Chrysostom's *On Wealth and Poverty*, 12.
41. Chrysostom, *On Wealth and Poverty*, 140.
42. Chrysostom, *On Repentance and Almsgiving*, 96:141.

Chrysostom's Pastoral Principles: New Testament Homilies

to the poor and the sick as Christ had done.[43] Chrysostom, therefore, sought to encourage the rich to contribute in almsgiving for the poor, and to fund the creation of a ministry for the needy. In regard to his stance on almsgiving, Blake Leyerle concluded:

> Chrysostom's overall message is therefore one that stresses mutuality. The wealthy who were accustomed to showcasing their high status in the marketplace should subordinate themselves in Christian community. They should know at all times their inferiority to the poverty-stricken and indigent in the world. In the eyes of God, which are, after all, the only eyes that truly matter, the poor are the patrons of the rich.[44]

Chrysostom, an idealist in his moral theology, attempted as best as he could to create a well-balanced church community comprised of the wealthy and poor, so he encouraged congregations to unite through almsgiving.[45] F. X. Murphy has pointed out that for Chrysostom, "a fundamental rule of the Christian way of life is service to one's neighbor. God has made all men brothers, so that the interest of one is the interest of all. Hence no one can bring his own affairs into order without providing for the love and salvation of his neighbor."[46] Because of this principle, Chrysostom sought to achieve his goals not only through eloquent homilies on almsgiving, but also by religious reformation and the establishment of institutes for the poor. Later, after being installed as patriarch, Chrysostom proceeded to reform the church's finances in order to save money for the poor. In this context, he abolished the extravagant banquets that had been so numerous under the rule of Bishop Nectarius, considering them to be robbing the temple because church resources were used for such events.[47] Chrysostom's reform extended to the area of holy living beyond matters of church finance.[48] In addition to gambling and immorality, he also prohibited all activities that corrupted behavior and thinking. He attacked centers of immorality that

---

43. Chrysostom, *Homilies on Matthew* (NPNF1 10:476).

44. Leyerle, "John Chrysostom on Almsgiving," 46.

45 Ibid., 46–47. See also Benestad, "Chrysostom on Wealth and Poverty," 201–10. Benestad concluded, "John Chrysostom makes a contribution to the solution of political and social problems by being concerned about people's salvation. Living for the common good is important for salvation, but also contributes to the resolution of political and social problems."

46. Murphy, "Moral Doctrine of St. John Chrysostom," 56.

47. Palladius, *Life of St. John Chrysostom*, 75–77.

48. Chrysostom, *On Wealth and Poverty*, 139.

Pastoral Leadership

he viewed as schools of sensuality, and compared them to the furnace of Babylon.[49] He constantly faced the struggle of mediating between the rich and the poor as he ministered to his congregations in both Antioch and Constantinople. Although the rich wanted to control how the money they donated to the church was spent, Chrysostom's heart was always with the poor.[50] As bishop, Chrysostom established philanthropic houses called "*nosokomeia*," literally, "a place to care for the sick."[51] He also appointed two priests to be hospital directors and hired physicians, cooks, and servants to assist.[52] Palladius described the purpose and work of these hospitals:

> Here again he found an over abundance of funds and he ordered the large portion of them to be shared with the hospital. He built more hospitals. . . . In this way strangers coming from afar to the city and becoming ill could receive proper medical care [most often for what we call epilepsy.[53]

Chrysostom thus invested the Episcopal fund into caring for the physical needs of the sick in innovative ways, and so his financial reformation of the Church was commendable. The *nosokomeia* provided a variety of services for the needy, including foreigners, and exemplified the creative social and spiritual reformation that took place under his service as bishop.[54] Chrysostom's pastoral care for the needy was consistent to the end of his life, not only to his congregation in Constantinople, but also during his last exile. Sozomen testified to Chrysostom's pastoral activity during his second exile, before his death:

> He also administered to the necessities of many who were in want; and by his kind words comforted those who did not stand in need

49. Vandenberghe, *John of the Golden Mouth*, 59.
50. Leyerle, "John Chrysostom on Almsgiving," 45.
51. Miller, "Byzantine Hospitals," 53–63.
52. Ibid., 53. Miller suggested that "Thus, words such as xenon or *nosokomeia* which came to designate hospitals exclusively might have had more general meanings in the formative stages of Byzantine philanthropic institutions."
53. Palladius, *Life of St. John Chrysostom*, 39.
54. Miller, *Birth of the Hospital*, 22. Miller described the various services that the *nosokomeia* provided: "Perhaps each of Chrysostom's *nosokomeia* formed a small complex of different philanthropies, one building serving as a place for the sick and another as a lodge for travelers, just as the twelfth-century pantokrator maintained a xenon to heal the sick of fourth-century Constantinople food, shelter, nursing care, and some access to professional physicians; in other words, they were institutions which come very close to fitting our definition of hospital."

Chrysostom's Pastoral Principles: New Testament Homilies

of money. Hence he was exceedingly beloved not only in Armenia, where he dwelt, but by all the people of the neighboring countries, and the inhabitants of Antioch and of the other parts of Syria, and of Cilicia, who frequently sought his society.[55]

Chrysostomus Baur also stated: "When the priest Domitian complained to him of his need because he could no more support the poor widows and maids committed to his care, Chrysostom begged a certain Valentinian to give him the necessary means to provide them."[56] Caring for the needy through almsgiving was an important strand in Chrysostom's preaching and a major pastoral leadership principle. He believed that caring for one's neighbor was a foundational step in the imitation of Christ. Even though Chrysostom was driven into exile by the combined opposition of Theophilus (the Patriarch of Alexandria) and the Empress Eudoxia, it is unfair to conclude that Chrysostom was a failure in his pastoral ministry. One major line of evidence here is that he faithfully served the people around him to the end, and his care for them was greatly appreciated.[57] Aideen Hartney pointed out that Chrysostom did not achieve the reform in Constantinople that he expected and argued, "Chrysostom misjudged the extent of his influence in Constantinople, for his tremendous zeal did not have the same impact in the capital of the eastern empire as it had in the more provincial Antioch."[58] There is truth in this statement, and the complexities of the church-state relationship were such that any responsible church leader wanting to introduce reforms into the church would have found it difficult to achieve. In some ways, Chrysostom may be regarded as a relative failure in terms of his pastoral leadership in Constantinople, but he remained faithful to his pastoral principles until his death.

2. Leadership through Example

Chrysostom's second pastoral leadership principle is leadership through example. Priesthood is intended to build up a Christlike character through the imitation of Christ. Chrysostom believed that leadership through example is best exemplified by the life of Christ during his earthly ministry.

55. Sozomen, *Ecclesiastical History* (NPNF2 2:417).

56. Baur, *John Chrysostom*, 2:383. During his last exile Chrysostom cared not only the poor but also paid ransom money for the prisoners taken by Isaurians with the money he received from Olympias and other friends..

57. Pelikan, "Introduction," in Chrysostom's *Homilies on Sermon on the Mount*, 6.

58. Hartney, *Transformation of the City*, 30.

Pastoral Leadership

Regarding Paul's statement in 1 Corinthians 11:1, urging others to follow his own personal example, Chrysostom commented, "This is a rule of the most perfect Christianity"[59]; imitating Christ, he believed, is the ultimate goal of the Christian life and could be achieved by imitating Paul: "Any nobility displayed by prophets, or patriarchs, or the just, or the apostles, or martyrs, Paul has in a superabundant degree."[60] Demonstrating his devotion to Paul, Chrysostom preached as many as 250 homilies on all twelve Pauline Epistles and Hebrews.[61] In the introduction to his Romans homilies, Chrysostom testified how much he attempted to imitate Paul:

> As I keep hearing the Epistles of the blessed Paul read, and that twice every week, and often three or four times, whenever we are celebrating the memorials of the holy martyrs, gladly do I enjoy the spiritual trumpet, and get roused and warmed with desire at recognizing the voice so dear to me, and seem to fancy him all but present to my sight, and behold him conversing with me. But I grieve and am pained, that all people do not know this man, as much as they ought to know him.[62]

He desired to imitate Paul by reading Paul's epistles and he taught his congregation to follow Paul's pattern of life. More importantly, Chrysostom believed that "it is possible even thus to imitate Christ. For he who copies the perfect impression of the seal, copies the original model."[63] He perceived that one who imitates Paul should be considered as one imitating Christ, the original model. Acknowledging that it is impossible for anyone to imitate Christ perfectly and fully, Chrysostom accepted that Christians had the ability to imitate Christ, just as Paul urged the Ephesians: "Be ye imitators of God." Believing that Paul was greater than Abel, Noah, Abraham, Isaac, Jacob, Joseph, Job, Moses, David, Elias, John the Baptist, and the angels,[64] Chrysostom advocated that following Paul was the best way to imitate Christ. In one homily he concluded, "How blameworthy we would be, if we should not strive to imitate in particular a man who combined all good qualities in a single person."[65]

---

59. Chrysostom, *Homilies on First Corinthians* (NPNF1 12:146).
60. Ibid., 15–16.
61. Halton, "Introduction," in Chrysostom's *Praise of Saint Paul*, 9–10.
62. Chrysostom, *Homilies on Romans* (NPNF1 11:335).
63. Chrysostom, *Homilies on First Corinthians* (NPNF1 12:24).
64. Chrysostom, *In Praise of Saint Paul*, translated by Thomas Halton, 13–26.
65. Ibid., 25. In comparison with all the spiritual giants Chrysostom claimed Paul's

Chrysostom's Pastoral Principles: New Testament Homilies

There are several reasons why Chrysostom admired Paul. Margaret Mitchell reminds us, for example, that Chrysostom received his early Christian education under Diodore of Tarsus, who is known to have written commentaries on the Pauline letters. Again, the Apostle Paul was also regarded as a local hero in Antioch, even during Chrysostom's life; his early experiences also in monasticism most likely became the seedbed of his lifelong devotion to Paul.[66] Moreover, Mitchell added, "When he lived a solitary monastic life in a cave for two years, devoting most of that time to memorizing the New Testament, Chrysostom inscribed on his brain a lot of Paul."[67] From his extensive study of Scripture, Chrysostom believed that Paul was the best example for Christians to follow; he was a dominant character in the New Testament who aspired to imitate Christ more than anyone else. "Therefore Chrysostom can exhort his audience to emulate Paul, for Paul was human just as they were."[68] Another reason for admiring Paul arises from his conviction that the most important qualification in pastoral leadership is to have a Christlike character, for it is one's character that challenges and persuades the congregations to follow Christ. In another homily, entitled "St. Paul, outstanding example of the possibilities of human nature for virtue," Chrysostom praised Paul:

> St. Paul was the noblest of men and the most outstanding example of the nobility of human nature and of its possibilities for virtue. By speaking up for the Master and exhorting us to virtue he completely refutes those who find fault with human nature, seals the lips of those who make slanderous charges, and shows that little divides angels from men if they are willing to perfect themselves. Paul's nature was no different from ours. His soul was no different. He was inhabitant of no different world.[69]

Chrysostom urged his congregation "not merely to admire but to emulate this archetype of virtue. That way we will be able to share his crown."[70] Paul's final testimony in 2 Tim 4:6–8, in which Paul shares his achievement with other believers, only added to Chrysostom's admiration

---

superiority to them all. If the angels constitute the greatness for their absolute obedience, he said, "But Paul's obedience cannot be matched even by countless incorporeal beings."

66. Mitchell, *Heavenly Trumpet*, 67.
67. Ibid.
68. Ibid., 51.
69. Chrysostom, *Praise of Saint Paul*, 29.
70. Ibid., 36.

Pastoral Leadership

for him. Paul's emphasis on Christian virtues points to the balance between his deeds and eloquent preaching. Furthermore, Chrysostom called Paul "A Standard-Bearer of Christ."[71] When royal standards were carried in a procession the whole city turned out to watch. Similarly, Chrysostom presented Paul as an example: "Paul carried this cross not just for himself, but to teach all to do likewise. Therefore he said: Be imitators of me, after the pattern you have in us (Phil 3:17)."[72] In carrying Christ's cross, Paul became an example for Chrysostom and also for the whole world. Chrysostom was also impressed by the fact that Paul began to imitate Christ immediately from his conversion.[73] Realizing the significance of Paul's example, Chrysostom sought to follow him, urging others to do the same. In the homily entitled "Paul, A Standard-Bearer of Christ" Chrysostom wrote: "You see, then, that all are standard-bearers of Christ, and that each carries His name before nations and kings."[74] Chrysostom explained that spiritual power to imitate Christ comes from two sources: partly from God and partly from oneself. He illustrated this statement by referring to Paul's example. If Paul was able to imitate Christ, Chrysostom believed that others could do the same since Paul was also only a man.[75] This is Chrysostom's persistent argument in leading his congregations to follow Paul's example. As illustrated in Phil 1:14, men proclaimed the gospel with confidence because of Paul's example.[76] Elizabeth Castelli, commenting on Chrysostom's persuasion of his congregations to imitate Paul in her study of the Pauline passages in 1 Thess 1:6–11, 2:14; Phil 3:17; 1 Cor 4:16, 11:1; and Gal 4:12, writes:

> His use of the notion of mimesis, with all of its nuances, reinforces both Paul's own privileged position and new power relations of the early Christian communities as somehow "natural." That is to say, the hierarchy of power is in tune with a much larger and more self-evident structure, which incorporates both the earthly community and divine order. Participating positively in the mimetic

---

71. Ibid., 103.
72. Ibid., 106.
73. Mitchell, *Heavenly Trumpet*, 264.
74. Chrysostom, *Praise of Saint Paul*, 107.
75. Ibid., 108–09. Chrysostom explains the possibility of following Paul's Christian life: "If you were to say how is it possible to imitate such people, hear what he says: Be imitators of me as I am of Christ (1 Cor 11:1). He imitated Christ. Will you not imitate your fellow slave? He emulated his Master. Will you not emulate your fellow servant? What excuse can you make for yourself?"
76. Ibid., 113.

Chrysostom's Pastoral Principles: New Testament Homilies

relationship with Paul, the early communities are to be rewarded with salvation. Resisting the mimetic relationship, by contrast, has dire consequences.[77]

Castelli's study on Paul's imitation theory reinforces Chrysostom's pastoral leadership principles, in which he exhorts others to follow Paul's example in following Christ. In regard to Paul's pastoral vision, Castelli added, "Christians are Christians insofar as they strive for the privileged goal of sameness. Christians distinguish themselves from those who are not Christians, who are not saved, precisely in this drive for sameness."[78] When Chrysostom attempted to apply Paul's exemplar theory to his own pastoral leadership, he mainly focused on Paul's exemplary life, rather than on his theology. In one of his homilies on 2 Timothy, Chrysostom expounds on 2 Tim 2:1–7, focusing on the faithful men whom Paul encouraged Timothy to train as godly, reliable disciples. Interpreting this passage, Chrysostom applied his exemplar principle to his preaching: "But let us, my beloved children, be imitators of Paul, not in his faith only, but in his life, that we may attain to the heavenly glory, and trample upon that glory that is here."[79] Chrysostom considered practice more important than theory, especially the imitation of Christ which is the ultimate goal, and achievable through Paul's example which may involve following Paul in his suffering and also in transforming one's mind to live a new life. On Gal 4:12, where Paul urged the Jewish Christians, "Become like me, for I became like you," Chrysostom states: "he [Paul] brings his own example forward, to induce them thereby to abandon their old customs."[80] Chrysostom learned from Paul's teaching and example, therefore, that a pastor's character is very important and the Pastoral Epistles provided a strong biblical basis for Chrysostom's instructions regarding his pastoral leadership principles. In his introduction to his homilies on 1 Timothy, Chrysostom pointed out that Paul considered Timothy's personal character to be an important qualification for his ordination:

---

77. Castelli, *Imitating Paul*, 116. The word "mimetic" refers to a Greek word (*mimeomai*) for imitating.

78. Ibid., 117. This study provided a theoretical basis for the effectiveness of the imitation in the pastoral leadership as Chrysostom practiced in his ministry. Castelli witnessed, "Furthermore, the privileged position of the model in the mimetic relationship has far-reaching implications for the nature of early Christian power relations."

79. Chrysostom, *Homilies on 2 Timothy* (*NPNF1* 13:491).

80. Chrysostom, *Homilies on Galatians* (*NPNF1* 13:31).

Pastoral Leadership

> The affection of Paul for him is a sufficient evidence of his character. For he elsewhere says of him, "Ye know the proof of him, that as a son with a father, he hath served with me in the Gospel." (Phil 2:22) And to the Corinthians again he writes: "I have sent unto you Timothy, who is my beloved son, and faithful in the Lord" (1 Cor 4:17). And again: "Let no man despise him for he works the work of the Lord, as I also do" (1 Cor 16:10, 11).[81]

Chrysostom believed that the reason why the council of elders entrusted pastoral duties to Timothy was because of his godly character, not just his gifts. Chrysostom noted: "For so preeminent in virtue was Timothy, that his youth was no impediment to his promotion."[82] Throughout the Pastorals, Paul emphasized the importance of a pastor's character so he encouraged Timothy to continue developing a godly character, even after his ordination so he could be a role model for others. Expounding 1 Tim 4:12, Chrysostom wrote: "In all things showing thyself an example of good works: that is, be thyself a pattern of Christian life, as a model set before others, as a living law, as a rule and standard of good living, for such ought a teacher to be."[83] He pointed out that at the center of Paul's pastoral leadership was personal character, which needs to be constantly cultivated in order to be a role model. Chrysostom observed: "Paul gives him counsel concerning the same things, thus showing that a teacher ought above all things to be attentive to these points."[84] Concerning Paul's guidelines for church elders and deacons in 1 Tim 3:1–13, Chrysostom encouraged his congregation to follow Paul's admonition: "For he who bears rule should be brighter than any luminary; his life should be unspotted, so that all should look up to him, and make his life model of their own."[85] The ultimate goal of Paul's pastoral leadership was to produce disciples who would fulfill Christ's mission. In 2 Tim 2:1–2, Paul urged Timothy to make disciples; correctly understanding Paul's methodology of disciple making, Chrysostom told his congregation: "If you are a son, he means, imitate thy father."[86] His implication is that Paul

---

81. Chrysostom, *Homilies on 2 Timothy* (*NPNF*1 13:407).

82. Ibid.

83. Ibid., 449. Without godly character one cannot be a pattern or model for other people. Chrysostom interpreted that "In word," that he may speak with facility, "in conversation, in charity, in faith, in "true" purity, in temperance."

84. Ibid.

85. Ibid., 438

86. Ibid., 488.

Chrysostom's Pastoral Principles: New Testament Homilies

is asking Timothy to follow his footsteps so that Timothy also becomes like Paul, his spiritual father, in his own disciple-making ministry.

Chrysostom wanted the entire congregation to pursue this imitation principle: "But let us, my beloved children, be imitators of Paul, not in his faith only, but in his life, that we may attain to heavenly glory, and trample upon that glory that is here."[87] Realizing that imitating Paul's example was ultimately following Christ's example, Chrysostom wanted to lead his congregation in achieving Christian ownership, as he ministered to the church. In his *On the Priesthood*, Chrysostom had insisted that: "You behold not only the marvelous, but that which surpasses all admiration. Here stands the priest bringing down not fire, but the Holy Spirit."[88] Here, he teaches that the priest maintains direct contact with God through prayer and thereby receives divine power for ministry; he insisted that the source of this divine power is the Holy Spirit, by whom God prophesied through the prophets.[89] According to these prophesies, such as those from Isaiah and Joel, the whole world would receive this Spirit, and Chrysostom insists that for "the Spirit who moves the mind, there is no obstacle; instead, just as a flood of water moves forward under the impulse of a mighty torrent, so too the grace of the Spirit moves forward with great speed, carrying everything in its path with utter force."[90]

Interpreting Psalm 8, Chrysostom also realized that marvelous things occur through the mighty name of God and his Spirit: "Through this name, in fact, death was dissolved, demons imprisoned in bonds, heaven opened, gates of paradise thrown wide, the Spirit sent down, slaves made free, enemies become sons, strangers become heirs."[91] These wonderful things take place when we receive the grace of the Spirit and the power of his anointing.[92] The Holy Spirit, who is essential for living the Christian life, is

---

87. Ibid., 491. Imitating Paul as disciples of Christ, Chrysostom continued to tell his congregation: "Let us despise visible things, that we may obtain heavenly things, or rather may through these obtain the others, but let it be our aim preeminently to obtain those, of which God grant that we may be all accounted worthy, through the grace and loving kindness."

88. Chrysostom, *Priesthood*, 31.

89. Chrysostom, *Commentary on the Psalms*, 1:261. Chrysostom writes: "Upon him will rest a Spirit of wisdom and understanding, a Spirit of counsel and strength, a Spirit of knowledge and piety. A Spirit of fear of God will fill him."

90. Ibid., 260.

91. Chrysostom, *Spiritual Gems*, 25.

92. Ibid., 163.

Pastoral Leadership

prominent in Chrysostom's *Baptismal Instructions*, which he taught during his pastoral ministry in Antioch.[93] The twelve instructions for baptismal candidates reflect Chrysostom's emphasis on conversion and spiritual maturity in the Spirit. In the fourth instruction, Chrysostom urged candidates to be eager to do nothing which grieved the Holy Spirit,[94] and in the eighth instruction he also encouraged them, saying: "If we give priority to the spiritual, we shall not have trouble with material things."[95] He understood that the Holy Spirit is the life-giving fountain for glory, honor, and power.[96] In his New Testament homilies, Chrysostom preached to his congregations on the significance of the Holy Spirit's ministry in a Christian's life.[97] Realizing the indispensable ministry of the Holy Spirit, spirituality became a main focus of Chrysostom's pastoral leadership.[98] To achieve this objective, Chrysostom emphasized the priority of prayer:

> Prayer is the fortress of the faithful, prayer is our invincible weapon, prayer is the cleansing of our souls, prayer is the ransom for our sins, prayer is the foundation and source of countless blessings. For Prayer is nothing more than conversation with God and association with the Master of all. What could be more blessed than a man who is deemed worthy of constant association with the Master?[99]

---

93. Harkins, "Instruction," in Chrysostom's *Baptismal Instructions*, 15-17, 3-19. This can be dated about 390 in Antioch. Harkins writes, "The data of internal criticism are scarcely favorable to the other years at Constantinople, because in no place does Chrysostom speak as a bishop."

94. Ibid., 75.

95. Ibid., 127.

96. Ibid., 65.

97. Chrysostom, *Homilies on John* (*NPNF2* 14:274). Chrysostom emphasized the importance of the ministry of the Holy Spirit for the spiritual life of Christians in all of his homilies of the New Testament. Introducing the Holy Spirit, Chrysostom explained, "He will not be with you as I have been, but will dwell in your very souls." Chrysostom explained the ministry of the Holy Spirit in many different ways; revealing Christ as Lord (1 Cor 12: 3), granting power (Acts 1: 8), and distributing the spiritual gifts (1 Cor 12: 4). He tried to convince people that the Christian life is impossible without the ministry of the Holy Spirit.

98. Chrysostom, *Baptismal Instruction*, 182. At the conclusion of the twelfth instruction, he urged them to win the spiritual battle: "But earthly kings recruit soldiers because of the service they will give. They lead their troops into war against a visible foe; He leads His troop into a spiritual battle."

99. Ibid., 115. See also Chrysostom, *Incomprehensible Nature of God*, 163.

Chrysostom's Pastoral Principles: New Testament Homilies

If spirituality is related to power in a Christian's life, prayer is the channel through which that power is supplied from the fountain of the Holy Spirit. Chrysostom, therefore, maintained his prayer life as a priority in his pastoral ministry. To the congregations in Thessalonica, he wrote: "I make my prayer above all other things for your health both in soul and in body. For there is no other prayer so becoming to a priest, as to draw nigh to God and entreat Him for the good of the people, before his own."[100]

On the other hand, Chrysostom tried to avoid vainglory as he thought it was the cause of all evils.[101] In the fifth instruction of his *Baptismal Instruction*, Chrysostom insisted that vainglory is more deadly than drunkenness.[102] He urged his congregations to learn and develop the humility of Christ in order to avoid vainglory and in this way preserve unity in the church.[103] In the priesthood, Christian spirituality is, therefore, an integral part of Christian maturity in the imitation of Christ and is required to lead one's congregation by example. Once again, for Chrysostom, the ministry of the Holy Spirit, prayer, and spiritual maturity are located only within the context of moral integrity on the part of the priest and individual Christians. Integrity of character is a necessity for all those in pastoral leadership.

3. Leadership Care through Preaching

Chrysostom's third pastoral leadership principle reflected in his homilies is caring for people through preaching. This was an integral part of his pastoral ministry and the most effective means of caring for his congregation. Chrysostom's homilies are, first of all, to be classified as pastoral preaching.[104] Labeling Chrysostom as a pastor, Robert Hill rightly points, "Homilists, however, generally also pastors, as Chrysostom was, have responsibilities to meet. It was because of his pastoral priorities that he engaged in a lifelong program of preaching."[105] Along with caring for people and leadership by example, his preaching ministry was the central focus of his leadership, reflected not only in his *On the Priesthood*, but also in all his homilies preached in Antioch and Constantinople.

---

100. Chrysostom, *Homilies on 2 Thessalonians* (NPNF1 13:391).
101. Chrysostom, *Homilies on Philippians* (NPNF1 13:203).
102. Chrysostom, *Baptismal Instructions*, 82.
103. Chrysostom, *Homilies on Philippians* (NPNF1 13:203).
104. Long, *Witness of Preaching*, 31–32.
105. Hill, "Preacher on the Old Testament," 280.

Pastoral Leadership

The first characteristic of his preaching is that it was *pastoral*. Chrysostom's constant desire was to lead his congregation to spiritual maturity through his preaching. He viewed the church of God as a house of spiritual surgery that heals all wounds in the Word through which the Holy Spirit speaks.[106] Johannes Quasten correctly points out, "In his sermons Chrysostom appears as the real physician of souls who diagnoses with unerring instinct their maladies and shows a sympathetic understanding of human frailty."[107] During the Riot of 387 in Antioch, the people's responses to Chrysostom's twenty-one homilies, *On the Statues*, demonstrated that his preaching was a major source of encouragement and healing.[108] Duane A. Garrett also judges that "His twenty-one messages, called *De Statuis* because of the incident of the statues, are testimonies to his eloquence and his pastoral heart."[109] Chrysostom, however, ascribed the successful reconciliation and blessings to God, not to himself, and stated: "And let us never fail to give God thanks continually for all these things."[110] According to Chrysostom, preaching heals wounded hearts:

> If we train by words the animals which we have, and so tame them, how much more shall we effect this with men by this spiritual teaching, when there is a wide difference between the remedy in each case, and the subject healed as well. Let him come continually to this house of healing, let him hear at all times the laws of the Spirit, and on retiring home let him write down in his mind the things which he heard.[111]

Believing the church to be the house of healing, Chrysostom felt that the ministry of God's Word was the means by which God brought healing and maturity as well as other blessings to his people. A second characteristic of his preaching is that it was *expository*, as his homilies illustrate. Johannes Quasten correctly classified all of Chrysostom's sermons as exegetical homilies on the books of the Old and New Testaments delivered at Antioch between 386 and 397.[112] Chrysostom was faithful in interpreting the biblical text and "the depth of his thought and the soundness of his

---

106. Chrysostom, *Homilies on John* (NPNF1 14:9).
107. Quasten, *Patrology*, 3:433.
108. Stephens, *His Life and Times*, 161
109. Garrett, *Analysis of the Hermeneutics*, 29.
110. Chrysostom, *On the Statute* (NPNF1 9:489).
111. Chrysostom, *Homilies on John* (NPNF1 14:10).
112. Quasten, *Patrology*, 3:433.

Chrysostom's Pastoral Principles: New Testament Homilies

masterful exposition are unique and attract even modern readers."[113] A. M. Malingrey claims that Chrysostom is "the most illustrious representative of the school of Antioch, whose exegesis is based on minute explanation of the texts."[114] Even though he was not skilled in Hebrew and Aramaic, he had a profound knowledge of the Scriptures and his congregations received considerable help from his exegesis.[115] According to Chrysostom, the Scriptures "are given by inspiration of God; therefore, he means do not doubt."[116] The Scriptures are infallible and most profitable for instruction regarding morality. He affirmed: "For the Scriptures suggest to us what is to be done, and what is not to be done."[117] For this reason, he was persuaded that his duty was to expound Scripture to the congregations as God's Word and admonition them:

> "For all these things," says the Apostle, "were written for our admonition to them" (1 Cor 11). If then Scripture in all its discoursing is for our admonition, let us attend to it as we ought. Why do we deceive ourselves in vain? I fear it may be said of us also that "our days have fallen short in vanity, and our years with haste" (Ps 33).[118]

Following Paul's admonition regarding the Scriptures, Chrysostom was persuaded that exegetical preaching was the most efficient way to guide his congregations to conform more closely to God's holy character and, more importantly, how to gain eternal life, which he felt was the ultimate goal of Scripture.[119] Chrysostom argued that even in the secular world the fear of the law restrains people from wicked deeds. If true, he asks, "How much more should the remembrance of things future, the vengeance that is immortal, the punishment that is everlasting? Whence then can we

---

113. Ibid., 433.
114. Malingrey, "John Chrysostom," 441.
115. Hill, "Preacher on the Old Testament," 269.
116. Chrysostom, *Homilies on 2 Timothy* (NPNF1 13:510).
117. Ibid., 508.
118. Chrysostom, *Homilies on Acts* (NPNF1 11:182).
119. Chrysostom, *Homilies on 2 Corinthians* (NPNF1 12:346). In regard to the priority of the Scripture he urged, "Wherefore I exhort and entreat you all, disregard what this man and that man thinks about these things, and inquire from the Scriptures all these things; and having learnt what are the true riches, let us pursue after them that we may obtain also the eternal good things."

Pastoral Leadership

constantly have this fear? If we continually hearken to the Scriptures."[120] For this reason, he cited many scriptural verses in his homilies to emphasize the importance of Scripture and to aid his congregations in the understanding of biblical truth. For example, he quoted over five hundred Scripture verses in his twenty-one homilies *On the Statues*.[121] He asserted, "This is the cause of all evils, not knowing the Scriptures. We go into battle without arms, and how ought we to come off safe."[122] Chrysostom insisted on the necessity of the knowledge of Scripture as one of the requirements for receiving salvation:

> The precious blood of Christ, if it be received with full assurance, (or this will have power to extinguish every disease); and together with this the divine Scriptures carefully heard, and almsgiving added to our hearing; for by means of all these things we shall be enabled to mortify the affections that mar our soul. And then only shall we live; for now surely we are in no better state than the dead.[123]

The ultimate goal of pastoral ministry is to bring people to salvation and to help them imitate Christ but this is achieved, Chrysostom believed, through expository preaching of Scripture. Consistent with Rom 10:14–15, Chrysostom agreed that hearing God's Word is essential: "For the hearing is by 'the Word of God.' And this is a higher thing than miracles."[124] Therefore, in his pastoral leadership principles the priority for Chrysostom was his expository preaching ministry. As we saw in the previous chapter, Johannes Quasten's classification of Chrysostom's sermons into six groups is based on a broad definition of a "sermon" because moral, liturgical feasts and panegyric sermons were not preached from specific scriptural texts. The value of most of his homilies is that he preached verse by verse from the chapters of the Bible from the beginning to the end without exception.

Evaluating Chrysostom's homilies from a homiletic perspective, there are weaknesses, as John Ker indicates:

> The weakest side of Chrysostom is the want of Scriptural instruction in his sermons or homilies. He takes a portion of the Bible, says something about it, and then leaves it for digressions which,

---

120. Chrysostom, *Homilies on 2 Thessalonians* (NPNF1 12:382).
121. Womack, "Life and Preaching of Chrysostom," 161.
122. Chrysostom, *Homilies on Colossians* (NPNF1 13:301).
123. Chrysostom, *Homilies on Matthew* (NPNF1 10:28).
124. Chrysostom, *Homilies on Romans*, 479.

Chrysostom's Pastoral Principles: New Testament Homilies

though interesting and eloquent, fail to bring out the depth and power of the Word of God in its bearing on the heart and conscience. This, again, was the fault of the time and school, rather than of the man.[125]

In other words, his exegesis of the text and exposition of the text were not sustained in terms of thoroughness, coherence, and depth throughout the sermons and, consequently, the impact of the Word on hearers was weakened somewhat. Ker's evaluation is valid especially in terms of the main theme and logical development of each homily.[126] Chrysostom, for example, preached on Phil 2:5–8 where the central theme is humility.[127] In his homily, after introducing Christ's example and exhortation with regard to humility, Chrysostom digressed to talk about heresies relating to Arius, Paul of Samosata, Marcellus, Sabellius, and Photinus. Chrysostom, then returned to Paul's theme of Christ's humility in assuming the form of a servant before introducing a vineyard song from Isa 5:1–6, and the disciple Judas who betrayed Christ to his enemies. Chrysostom concluded his sermon with a warning about the Day of the Lord in 1 Cor 3:13. While this latter verse speaks of Christ's judgment of believers, Chrysostom applies it to those who did not achieve their final goals for him.[128] Another example is Chrysostom's homily on John 4:21–27. He begins by pictorially describing the concept of faith:

> Everywhere, beloved, we have need of faith, faith the mother of blessings, the medicine of salvation; and without this it is impossible to possess any one of the great doctrines. Without this, men are like to those who attempt to cross the open sea without a ship.[129]

Chrysostom then speaks of the relationship and struggles historically between Samaritans and Jews before continuing to expound verses 23–27 consecutively. His exposition of each verse is helpful, but in terms of theme and logical sequence, it does not fit the pattern of modern homiletics

---

125. Ker, *History of Preaching*, 69.

126. Buttrick, *Homiletic*, 23. He writes, "Sermons involve an ordered sequence—they are not glossolalia. Sermons are a movement of language from one idea to another, each idea being shaped in a bundle of words. Thus, when we preach we speak in formed modules of language arranged in some patterned sequence. These modules of language we will call 'move.'"

127. Chrysostom, *Homilies on Philippians* (NPNF1 13:206–09).

128. Ibid., 206–12.

129. Chrysostom, *Homilies on John* (NPNF1 14:115).

Pastoral Leadership

because Chrysostom's exposition followed, as we should expect, the hermeneutical model of the Antioch School.[130] He seldom restricted himself to a rigidly thematic treatment in his sermons[131] and "was conscious of the thematic and logically built up development of a single principal thought in a sermon, and, purposely turning aside, avoided it."[132] Despite his distinctive style, Chrysostom communicated God's Word to his congregations effectively and eloquently. He knew his listeners and identified with them. As Baur observed, Chrysostom was sensitive to his congregation's spiritual need: "With him the thought stood higher than the word, the content was more to him than the form, and his particular aim was the spiritual and religious needs of his listeners."[133] For this reason, his homilies were well received by his listeners. His twenty-one homilies *On the Statues* demonstrate Chrysostom's personal character, and also the fact that he deeply cared for his congregations. Quasten commented, "Chrysostom proved himself a real guide and father of his fold in this crisis and his sense of responsibility is as admirable as his profound sympathy and passionate sincerity."[134] Chrysostom also demonstrated effective communication skills while delivering his homilies.[135]

---

130. Greidanus, *Preaching Christ*, 96. In contrast to the allegorical interpretation of the Alexandrian School led by Aristobulus, Philo, and Origen, Chrysostom adopted a literal interpretation which is the hermeneutical model of Antioch School. Chrysostom interpreted the Old Testament type as a fulfillment in the New Testament reality when John the Baptist calls Christ "the Lamb of God" in John 1:28–29. The Lamb of Moses at the Passover did not at once the sin of any one, but this Lamb, the Christ, took away sin of the world. See also Nassif, "Antiochene Theoria," 56. Chrysostom says, "Where the type is, there He puts the truth." Therefore, the Antiochene hermeneutics emphasizes literal interpretation with historical meaning.

131. Baur, *John Chrysostom*, 1:221.

132. Ibid., 213.

133. Ibid., 218.

134. Quasten, *Patrology*, 3:457–58.

135. Pelikan, *Divine Rhetoric*, 73. Pelikan states, "The homilies of Chrysostom are probably the only ones from the whole of Greek antiquity which at least in part are still readable today as Christian sermons. They reflect something of the authentic life of the New Testament, just because they are so ethical, so simple, and so clear-headed." For example, when the people of Antioch were so frightened at the time of Riot in 387, the good news came to them that the Emperor's pardon was granted. Chrysostom addressed that "when we were sad, He consoled us, let us give thanks to Him now that we are joyful. In our agony He comforted us, and did not forsake us." By repeating simple and short sentences he communicated the message without any complication.

Chrysostom's Pastoral Principles: New Testament Homilies

The third characteristic of Chrysostom's preaching was its *rhetorical nature*.[136] This element contributes to the effectiveness in communicating his message, and helped to capture the attention of hearers. Philip Kern explains that rhetoric is persuasion—i.e., effective communication, summed up as "strategy." To speak only in terms of discourse is to impose unnecessary restrictions on the discussion, since a painting or a sculpture can have rhetorical force, that is, it may be effective.[137] Having been trained by the most celebrated pagan teacher in rhetoric, Chrysostom became the master's most brilliant student.[138] Concerning Chrysostom's effective usage of the rhetorical question in his *On the Priesthood*, William Maat stated:

> A question that is asked for effect rather than to obtain information is known as a rhetorical question. The effect attained by these questions is the arousing of such feelings as sorrow, admiration, indignation, and contempt. In its cumulative form the rhetorical question adds emphasis and liveliness to the discourse.[139]

Maat also demonstrated how Chrysostom adopted the rhetorical figures of redundancy, repetition, sound, dramatic vivacity, and argumentation in order to create liveliness for more effective communication.[140] He

---

136. Ibid. Chrysostom's rhetorical expressions are found by repetition and redundancy, particularly in his *On the Priesthood*. For example, Chrysostom expressed his frustration at hearing of his appointment for priesthood by repetition of the words. He said, "The rumor was that we were to be promoted to the dignity of priesthood. For my part, as soon as I heard this story, I was overcome with fear and bewilderment: with fear, that I should be seized against my will, and with bewilderment, as I tried again and again to guess what had induced the men concerned to form such a plan for me." *On the Priesthood*, 1:5. Chrysostom repeated the same word within a same clause for emphasis and also for intense and passionate feeling. Maat, "Rhetorical Study," 9. Another example is also found in his *On the Priesthood*. Concerning the difficulty of pastoral care he said: "His fight is not with wolves; his fear is not of robbers; his care is not to protect the flock from pestilence. Well then, against whom is the war? With whom is the battle?" *On the Priesthood*, 2:2.

137. Kern, *Rhetoric and Galatians: Assessing an approach to Paul's epistle*, 7.

138. Attwater, *Pastor and Preacher*, 20. Wilken, *Chrysostom and the Jews*, 5–6.

139. Maat, "Rhetorical Study," 32.

140. Ibid., 1–81. Maat also concluded that rhetorical devices are not only evident in *De Sacerdotio*, but also in *On the Statues*. Maat writes, "It is evident that Chrysostom was a serious man with a serious message. In order to convey this message most successfully he had to make use of the means at his disposal. These means happened to be the Sophistic rhetoric that he had acquired under Libanius; he mastered it and used it to attain his high purpose." For example, Chrysostom demonstrated his rhetorical skill in his *On the Priesthood* when he described the qualification for priesthood. He writes, "A priest ought

Pastoral Leadership

used "the devices of the Sophistic rhetors moderately enough to derive the full benefit from them."[141] In composing portraits of Paul in particular, Margaret Mitchell pointed out that Chrysostom employed the standard rhetorical techniques of his day in various ways for assorted purposes.[142] In spite of the internal evidence of rhetorical usage in his writings, early scholars like H. Hubbell failed to recognize Chrysostom's rhetoric influence due to the negative attitude of Chrysostom regarding the Sophistic rhetoric.[143] Contemporary scholars, however, such as Robert Wilken, Margaret Mitchell, Philip Kern, Janet Fairweather, Malcolm Heath, and Jaroslav Pelikan, have recognized the rhetoric elements in Chrysostom's homilies, particularly in those on Galatians. Pelikan concluded by describing "Chrysostom and Christian rhetoric":

> It is impossible to read the homilies of Chrysostom on the Sermon without being constantly reminded that he was not only a Christian priest but, a Greek orator. Both the exegetical tradition of Antioch and the rhetorical tradition of Antioch helped to shape his composition.[144]

I agree with Lauri Thuren's conclusion that "The training [rhetoric] enabled Chrysostom to identify and interpret rhetorical devices and tactics in the text."[145] In terms of pastoral leadership, his Christian rhetoric provided Chrysostom with an effective platform for communicating to, and for caring for, his congregations.

The fourth characteristic of Chrysostom's preaching is his *emphasis on Christ*. For example, in his homilies on First Timothy, Christ was mentioned sixteen times in homily one, thirteen times in homily two, forty-seven times in homily three, and thirty-six times in homily four, thus demonstrating Chrysostom's prime focus on Christ. He preached eighty-eight homilies on the Gospel of John, as well as three different homilies on

---

to be sober minded, and penetrating in discernment, and possessed of innumerable eyes in every direction, as one who lives not for himself alone but for so great multitude." Another example for his rhetoric expression is found in the statement that, "The rich man is not one who is in possession of much, but one who gives much."

141. Ibid., 81.
142. Mitchell, *Heavenly Trumpet*, 22.
143. Hubbell, "Chrysostom and Rhetoric," 262–67.
144. Ibid., 76–77.
145. Thuren, "Rhetorical Critic," 213.

Chrysostom's Pastoral Principles: New Testament Homilies

John 1:1; this also highlights the centrality of Christ in his homilies.[146] In introducing his first homily on the Gospel of John, Chrysostom describes the beauty of Christ:

> By this Apostle stand the powers from above, marveling at the beauty of his soul, and his understanding, and the bloom of that virtue by which he drew unto him Christ Himself, and obtained the grace of the Spirit. For he hath made ready his soul, as some well-fashioned and jeweled lyre with strings of gold and yielded it for the utterance of something great and sublime to the Spirit.[147]

Considering the Apostle's description of Christ, Chrysostom emphasized Christ's reality in human form and presented him with personality, and as the center of the Christian life.[148] This theme is not simply a theological explanation of his Christology; it is also practically applied to all aspects of the Christian life. Chrysostom's intention was, therefore, to impact the lives of people through preaching Christ. He identified the gospel with the living Christ himself who is the essence of the gospel.[149] Expounding 1 Cor 3:11, Chrysostom emphasized and interpreted the text in terms of spiritual union between Christ and believers:

> Upon this then let us build, and as a foundation let us cleave to it, as a branch to a vine; and let there be no interval between us and Christ. For if there be any interval, immediately we perish. For the branch, by its adherence, draws in the fatness, and the building stands because it is cemented together. Since, if it stands apart it perishes, having nothing whereon to support itself. Let us not then merely keep hold of Christ, but let us be cemented to Him, for if we stand apart, we perish.[150]

Chrysostom understood that this intimate unity between Christ and Christians was inseparable and also a constant source of life so that the Christian's life is completely dependent on Christ. Theologically, in Christ's divine person is the union of his divine and human natures; concerning

---

146. Chrysostom, *Homilies on First Timothy* (NPNF1 13:408–23).

147. Chrysostom, *Homilies on John* (NPNF1 14:2).

148. Ibid., 14:1–2. Concerning the human character of Christ, Chrysostom explains: "Now will he appear before us, not acting a part (for with him there is nothing counterfeit, nor fiction, nor fable), but with unmasked head he proclaims to us the truth unmasked; not making the audience believe him other than he is by carriage, by look, by voice."

149. Stylianopoulos, *Way of Christ*, 17.

150. Chrysostom, *Homilies on First Corinthians* (NPNF1 12:47).

this hypostatic union, Chrysostom stated, "He took, He became."[151] On the basis of this theological interpretation of Christ's humanity, Chrysostom urged his congregation to imitate Christ. It is understandable for these reasons that it became the central theme in his homilies.[152] Concerning Paul's experience regarding the wisdom of philosophers in Athens, Chrysostom emphasized the significance of the Christo-centric message:

> They indeed have ten thousand things to say, and concerning ten thousand things they speak, winding out long courses of words, framing arguments and syllogisms, compounding sophisms without end. But I came unto you saying no other thing than "Christ was crucified," and all of them I outstripped: which is a sign such as no words can express of the power of Him I preach.[153]

Chrysostom was determined to preach Christ-centered homilies. His preaching, therefore, was pastoral, expository, rhetorical, and Christ-centered; these four characteristics are the dominant features of Chrysostom's preaching.

4. Cross-Cultural Mission

The fourth pastoral leadership principle I discern in Chrysostom's homilies is that of cross-cultural mission; interestingly, this was not mentioned in his *On the Priesthood*. Chrysostom positively encouraged missionary outreach during his pastoral ministry and even in his exile. More importantly, Chrysostom understood that one of the most valuable aspects of Paul's example was his witnessing to the gospel wherever he went. From Acts 20:26, Chrysostom urged his congregations, "Think not that these words are spoken to us only: for indeed this speech is addressed to you also, that ye should attend to the things spoken, that ye should not start away from

---

151. Chrysostom, *Homilies on Philippians* (NPNF1 13:215).

152. Chrysostom, *Homilies on John* (NPNF1 14:176). Chrysostom writes: "The things done by Christ after the manner of men, are not so done only to establish the Incarnation, but also educate us for virtue." John Calvin also stated that: "There is no having knowledge of God without Christ, and that, consequently, from the beginning of the world Christ was held forth to all the elect as the object of their faith and confidence." *Institutes*, 2:6, 4:297–98. Bryan Chapell also emphasized, "Theocentric preaching is Christ-centered preaching. Focus on God's redemptive activity sets the stage for Christ's work, alerts the human heart to its necessity, and/or exposes the divine nature. When we see God at work, Christ's ministry inevitably comes into view." *Christ-Centered Preaching*, 296.

153. Chrysostom, *Homilies on First Corinthians* (NPNF1 12:29).

Chrysostom's Pastoral Principles: New Testament Homilies

the hearing."[154] He had understood that Paul's utmost concern was for the salvation of others. Concerning Paul's aspiration for winning people to Christ, Chrysostom stated: "He was a man of many parts and many facets. I do not mean that he was acting. God forbid! But he became all things to all men, whatever was demanded by the needs of the Gospel and salvation of mankind. In this he imitated his Master."[155] From Paul's example ("I do all things for the gospel's sake." 1 Cor 9:23)[156] and other Scriptures, he understood that part of the church's ultimate goal is world mission, for Christ promised to build his church:

> For the Father gave to Peter the revelation of the Son; but the Son gave him to sow that of the Father and that of Himself in every part of the world; and to a mortal man He entrusted the authority over all things in Heaven, giving him the keys; who extended the church to every part of the world, and declared it to be stronger than heaven.[157]

Without questioning Chrysostom's interpretation of Matt 16:18-19 here, Chrysostom is right in including a reference in it to world mission strategy for the church because Christ instituted his church in order to fulfill his worldwide redemptive purpose. Chrysostom's vision of world missions originated in Christ's teachings and also in Old Testament prophecies from Isaiah and other Old Testament books. In regard to the mission of the apostles, which had been predicted in the Old Testament, Chrysostom wrote:

> After these events, he would send forth his apostles, as Isaiah had foretold. "How beautiful are the feet of those who preach the gospel of peace, of those who bring glad tidings of good things," he said. Look what parts of the body he praised. He lauded their feet, which took them everywhere they went. Furthermore, David showed the manner and source of their strength and success when

---

154. Chrysostom, *Homilies on Acts* (NPNF1 11:271).
155. Chrysostom, *In Praise of Saint Paul*, 78.
156. Chrysostom, *Homilies on First Corinthians* (NPNF1 12:129).
157. Chrysostom, *Homilies on Matthew* (NPNF1 10:334). In order to support his interpretation from the world mission perspective on the passage Matt16: 16–20, Chrysostom added that: "For heaven and earth shall pass away, but my word shall not pass away. How then is He less, who has given such gifts, has effected such things? And these things I say, not dividing the works of Father and Son."

Pastoral Leadership

he said: "The Lord shall give the word to them who preach the good tidings with great power."[158]

He interpreted the prophecies of Isa 52:7 and Ps 68:11 from a worldwide missionary perspective but realized, however, that the gospel provided a new and richer perspective on missions as commissioned by Christ (Acts 1:8, John 20:21). Expounding this latter verse, Chrysostom understood that Jesus here gave them divine authority as well as power to fulfill his worldwide mission.[159] His interpretation of Matt 24:14 demonstrated the fact that Christ's Great Commission influenced his pastoral ministry and leadership. In regard to Stephen's martyrdom recounted in Acts 7:54–60, Chrysostom preached on the great value of winning people to Christ:

> Suppose an Emperor had ordered thee to build a house that he might lodge there, would not thou have done everything to please him? And here now it is a palace of Christ, the Church which thou build. Look not at the cost, but calculate the profit. Thy people yonder cultivate thy field: cultivate thou their souls. They bring to thee thy fruits and raise thou them heaven.[160]

Chrysostom's passion for mission was deeply rooted in his conviction that saving people is the most important thing in the world and needs to be accomplished at any cost. He pointed out that the Antioch church would not have existed but for persecution that turned out to be a great benefit to the people.[161] The fact that from Jerusalem, Christianity spread throughout the world, Chrysostom describes as God's "providential management," initiated by the Holy Spirit: "for they were not only ordained by the Spirit, but sent forth by Him."[162] Chrysostom became even more mission-minded as he preached his fifty-five homilies on Acts in Constantinople,[163] attempting to use his pastoral leadership to contribute to Christ's ultimate goal of the church, namely world mission. Many contemporary theologians agree with Chrysostom regarding the church's mission. Jurgend Moltmann, for example, emphasized that: "it is the mission of the Son and the Spirit

---

158. Chrysostom, *Apologist*, 73:210.

159. Chrysostom, *Homilies on John* (*NPNF2* 14:325).

160. Chrysostom, *Homilies on Acts* (*NPNF1* 11:118).

161. Ibid., 162.

162. Ibid., 178.

163. Quasten, *Patrology*, 3:440–42. Quasten stated that Chrysostom himself dates these fifty-five homilies as delivered at Constantinople.

Chrysostom's Pastoral Principles: New Testament Homilies

through the Father that includes the church."[164] The church is participating, and has historically participated, in the work of Christ's mission, so Moltmann calls the church "the Missionary Church," a theological concept that comes from the theology of missions.[165] Although expressed differently, Chrysostom—even during the early fourth century—understood this principle and preached the church's responsibility for world mission.

Church historians who were contemporary with Chrysostom—like Palladius, Socrates, and Sozomen—did not comment on Chrysostom's missionary activity. However, Theodoret did so, and recorded details of Chrysostom's missionary work.[166] Unfortunately, there is no historical information available with regard to Chrysostom's own missionary activities during his pastoral ministry at the Antioch Church.[167] This may be due, in part, to his heavy involvement in administering the almsgiving ministry and also preparing his weekly homilies. After moving to Constantinople, Chrysostom was even more aware of the varied needs related to world mission, from religious, political, social, and racial perspectives.[168] Baur pointed out that as Bishop of Constantinople he had considerable compassion and reached out to evangelize unbelievers, especially those in Phoenicia, Scythia, and Syria.[169] With regard to Chrysostom's missionary activity to Scythians, Theodoret (393–457), a church historian and Bishop of Cyrus, testified that:

> Perceiving that the Scythian multitudes had been entrapped in the perfidious snares of Arianism, John made every effort to liberate them. He selected some persons who were acquainted with their

164. Moltmann, *Church in the Power of the Spirit*, 64.

165. Ibid., 7.

166. Sozomen, *Ecclesiastical History* (NPNF2 2:370). Even though Sozomen did not mention John Chrysostom specifically in regard to foreign mission however, he reported the mission activities of the monks. He states: "Although Coele-Syria and Upper Syria, with the exception of the city of Antioch, was slowly converted to Christianity, it was not lacking in ecclesiastical philosophers, whose conduct appeared the more heroic from their having to encounter the enmity and hatred of the inhabitants of the place." See also Voobus, *History of Asceticism*, 2:342–43. Concerning the role of Monasticism in the missions in Syria and Mesopotamia Voobus wrote, "Sozomen brings up the matter of the significance of Monasticism in the process of Christianization. He mentions a number of such monks who were instrumental in winning the Syrians to the Christian religion." See also Theodoret, *History of the Church*, 5:28–31.

167. Baur, *John Chrysostom*, 2:387.

168. Liebeschuetz, *Barbarians and Bishops*, 166–71.

169. Baur, *John Chrysostom* 2:387.

Pastoral Leadership

language, and after having had them ordained, some as presbyters, others as deacons, and the rest as readers of the Scriptures, he assigned a church to them, and many were, by their instrumentality, reclaimed from error. He frequently visited this church himself, and addressed the people by the aid of an interpreter: and he exhorted all who were endowed with requisite powers of mind to engage in the same service. By these means he delivered many of the inhabitants of the city from the snares in which they had been entangled, and convinced them of the apostolic doctrines.[170]

Theodoret's testimony is significant. Chrysostom was aware of this spiritual need and the influence of Arianism on the people and felt he should liberate them. Those appointed as missionaries to the Goths needed first to be fluent in their language; only later were they trained and ordained. He also visited missionaries and their people himself, fulfilling a strategic supportive, pastoral role. His mission strategy was thoroughly pastoral in nature as he reached out to the Scythians who originally came from central Asia and founded an empire in the area north of the Black Sea.[171] Tamara Talbot Rice noted that the tribes of the Scythians and kindred nomads occupied the plains from Podolia on the western fringe of European Russia to the borders of China during the first millennium.[172] Aware that they apostatized under Arian influence but desired to hear the good news of Christ, Chrysostom sought to rescue them from their error. He evangelized them by applying principles that are still contemporary in the way he selected leaders and provided training, ordination, and commissioning of the missionaries.[173] This was visionary and fruitful work. Chrysostom was also interested in the Arian or pagan Germans, who were mainly represented by the Goths.[174] He was not only a patriarch for congregations in Constantinople, but also for the Gothic church in Crimea, so he persisted in trying to convert unbelievers in that region. He visited the Crimean Goths to preach the gospel to them through an interpreter.[175] Since the time Chrysostom

---

170. Theodoret, *History of the Church*, 236. Theodoret described that upon hearing the Scythians' thirsty for the water of salvation, no one went to teach them the word of God. Chrysostom sought out men and sent them to these people.

171. The Scythians were a people who moved from central Asia to southern Russia, around Black sea, during the eighth and seventh centuries BC.

172. Rice, *Scythians*, 33.

173. Liebeschuetz, *Barbarians and Bishop*, 170.

174. Baur, *John Chrysostom*, 2:387.

175. Vasiliev, *Goths in the Crimea*, 32–33.

Chrysostom's Pastoral Principles: New Testament Homilies

had become Patriarch of Constantinople in 398, the number of Goths coming from Germany appears to have increased in Constantinople[176] because the Huns had driven them from their settlements.[177] Anderson Scott points out that Chrysostom was especially interested in converting the Goths from paganism to Christianity.[178] According to Baur, Chrysostom designated the Church of St. Paul in the city for them to hold regular worship services in their own language. He even attended their liturgy and delivered a convicting sermon to them. Chrysostom, therefore, became the founder of the German national church in Constantinople.[179] Sozomen also witnessed that even during an uprising of Goths, led by Gainas who had achieved military leadership from the lowest ranks of the army, Chrysostom continued to evangelize them.[180] Liebeschuetz assumed that while Gainas and his army were stationed in Constantinople, Chrysostom's influence in that city allowed him to pursue missionary work among those Goths living along the Danube. In addition, Chrysostom's unique mission policy was to turn these new groups of believers into independent churches.[181] Chrysostom's initial bold confrontation with Gainas, commander of the Gothian troops, opened up an opportunity for mission. Theodoret reports:

> Sometime after, Gainas carried his long-formed project of usurpation into execution; he collected some troops in Thrace, and raised the standard revolt. When this intelligence was announced, all the people, both rulers and subjects, were filled with alarm. There was no one who would venture to take up arms against him, neither would any one undertake to go on an embassy to him, so greatly was the power of barbarian feared by all. All the people at this juncture persuaded this great man [Chrysostom], he being the only one among them who was not intimidated, to go on an embassy to Gainas.[182]

---

176. Heather and Matthews, *Goths in the Fourth Century*, 2.

177. Baur, *John Chrysostom*, 2:48–49. The Huns were a tribe known as the Xiongnnu and existed in western China at the time of Han Dynasty (200 BC). By about 420 AD however, a Hunnic Confederacy had been established and enriched by plunder and tribute.

178. Scott, *Ulfilas Apostle of Goths*, 152–53. Chrysostom endeavored to prevent the Goths from embracing Arianism.

179. Baur, *John Chrysostom*, 2:77.

180. Sozomen, *Ecclesiastical History* (*NPNF2* 2:402).

181. Liebeschuetz, *Barbarians and Bishops*, 190.

182. Theodoret, *Ecclesiastical History*, 238.

Pastoral Leadership

In attempting to meet Gainas, Chrysostom was prepared to risk his own life, especially in order to convert unbelievers. Hearing of Chrysostom's intention to meet him, Gainas joyfully traveled a distance to meet Chrysostom because Gainas remembered well his fidelity.[183] In regard to Chrysostom's missionary concern, Sozomen wrote:

> John governed the Church of Constantinople with exemplary prudence, and induced many of the pagans and of the heretics to unite themselves with him. Crowds of people daily resorted to him; some for the purpose of being edified by listening to his discourses, and others with intention of tempting him. He, however, pleased and attracted all classes, and led them to embrace the same religious sentiments as himself.[184]

This statement makes it clear that Chrysostom's pastoral leadership included a focus on missionary activity, and one that was without any racial prejudice. When he was in Antioch, his influence was limited to local churches whereas in Constantinople he had more opportunities to reach out to other ethnic groups beyond his own immediate boundaries. Concerning the Jews, Chrysostom did not extend as great an effort to convert them to Christianity as he had for unbelievers in the surrounding nations, even though Jews were influential in Antioch.[185] Robert Wilken has pointed out, "Judaism had continued to be a rival to Christianity throughout the fourth century. Judaizing Christians were a source of embarrassment and concern to Christian leaders, especially in Syria and Palestine."[186] Chrysostom, however, asserted that his purpose was to teach and "cure those who are sick with the Judaizing disease."[187] He taught that it was the responsibility of individual Christians to win the Jews and stated: "through a life of good works we may become the occasion of instruction for them."[188] Chrysostom, therefore, encouraged his congregations to continue their evangelistic outreach towards Jews and Gentile unbelievers so that they also could become imitators of Christ.[189] During his first exile (403), Chrysos-

---

183. Ibid., 239.

184. Sozomen, *Ecclesiastical History* (NPNF2 2:402).

185. Harkins, "Introduction," in Chrysostom's "Discourses Against Judaizing Christians," Vol. 68:xxvi. See also Maxwell, "Preaching to the Converted," 148–50.

186. Wilken, *John Chrysostom and the Jews*, xvi–xvii.

187. Chrysostom, *Discourses against Judaizing Christians*, 68:4.

188. Ibid., 398.

189. Chrysostom, *Homilies on Matthew* (NPNF2 10:212).

Chrysostom's Pastoral Principles: New Testament Homilies

tom continued his interest in mission, particularly in Phoenician missions that Baur confirms[190] and his missionary activity continued even during his final exile from 404 to 407.

Exploring Chrysostom's pastoral leadership principles as reflected in his homilies, I have discovered that his pastoral leadership principles were substantially developed from his treatise, *On the Priesthood*. In the latter, Chrysostom emphasized the importance of Christ's people and personal dialogue in caring for them while in his homilies he claimed that almsgiving is of considerable importance in Christian practice and serves to demonstrate one's faith in action. Almsgiving and care for others were consistently dominant themes throughout his homilies, as Chrysostom perceived these to be among the fundamental requirements for the imitation of Christ in discipleship.[191] This indicates that Chrysostom's leadership principles advanced from theory to practice as a result of his pastoral experience in Antioch and then Constantinople. Regarding the integrity of the priesthood, Chrysostom's ideal was to imitate Paul as an example because he believed it was a means of achieving the imitation of Christ. With this conviction Chrysostom preached on all thirteen Pauline Epistles as well as Matthew, John, Acts, and Hebrews. On the other hand, both his *On the Priesthood* and his homilies emphasized the significance of preaching, but from different perspectives. In the former he focused more on the attitude and preparation of the preacher while in his homilies Chrysostom developed his pastoral care of people through his preaching, which was pastoral, exegetical, rhetorical, and Christ-centered. Even though his pastoral leadership principles in his homilies were more advanced and detailed than in *On the Priesthood*, they have three principles in common: caring for people, the moral integrity of the priesthood, and preaching. Cross-cultural mission was not referred to in *On the Priesthood*. However, not only did he teach cross-cultural mission as an important pastoral leadership principle in his homilies, he also practiced this principle in his own life.

I have now identified four pastoral leadership principles from a sample of Chrysostom's New Testament homilies: namely, caring for people particularly through almsgiving, the priest's godly character and integrity, preaching the Word, and, finally, cross-cultural mission. These four principles, from the period between 386 until his death, are extremely significant

---

190. Baur, *John Chrysostom*, 2:388. Phoenicia was an ancient name given to a region corresponding to modern Lebanon, Syria and Israel. Its history may go back to 3000 BC.

191. Chrysostom, *Homilies on First Corinthians* (NPNF1 11:146).

Pastoral Leadership

for understanding and appreciating Chrysostom's ministry and I will refer in the next chapter to their relevance for contemporary church leadership.

IMITATING CHRIST

However, before leaving these four pastoral leadership principles, it is necessary to underline the fact that the concept of the imitation of Christ underlies all four principles. For example, it underlies the responsibility to serve the poor. Love and care for one's neighbor is based on the imitation of Christ, for he not only issued the command but also provided the supreme example for us. This latter fact underlies the principle concerning the godly character of the priest who must imitate the example of Christ, albeit through the role model of the Apostle Paul. Preaching the Word, too, must be Christ-centered and contribute to the spiritual maturity of the church, not only in terms of theological understanding but also in loving obedience and action. The final principle of cross-cultural mission also reflects the commission of Christ to the church but also the love and concern of Christ for sinners worldwide, which is illustrated further by the passionate example of the Apostle Paul. Wherever one looks, therefore, in his New Testament homilies, one finds this common thread running throughout his teaching, namely, the imitation of Christ.

Imitation of Christ: Its Biblical Basis

It is appropriate then at this point to pause in order to open up a little further Chrysostom's understanding of the imitation of Christ. Biblically, Chrysostom used a significant number of New Testament texts as the basis for his understanding and use of this concept. In grappling with Chrysostom's teaching and the use of Scripture, one must emphasize that Christ is the prime example to be imitated and that it is the incarnation of Christ which makes it possible for imitation to take place because Christ took the form of man, thus providing a concrete example for his people. Chrysostom believed that the incarnation revealed not only the person of the Godhead in the Holy Trinity but also provided humanity with the pattern and the ability to imitate Christ. For example, the night before Christ was crucified, he said to his disciples after washing their feet, "I have set you an example that you should do as I have done for you" (John 13:15). Chrysostom discussed the word, "example," in this context stating, "He writes this law not merely for the washing of the feet, but also in all the other acts that He manifested towards us." The main purpose of Christ's action was to encourage people to practice his teaching and example. And Chrysostom confidently preached to his congregation that they could imitate Christ in showing forgiveness and mercy to others, just as Christ did to those who crucified him. In a homily on Acts, Chrysostom declared:

> This is the dignity of Christ's disciples. Those crucified Him, when He had come for the very purpose of doing them good; His disciple they scourged; and after all this, He admits them to the same honor with His disciples, making them equally partakers of His gifts. I beseech you, let us be imitators of Christ: in this regard it is possible to imitate Him: this makes a man like unto God: this is more than human. Let us hold fast to Mercy.[192]

Chrysostom believed that the example of Christ is firmly fixed as an unmovable standard for imitation by the church. As far as imitation is concerned, Chrysostom also presented the idea of kinship between a father and his children as an analogy to the relationship between God and believers. Paul wrote, "Be imitators of God, therefore, as dearly loved children" (Eph 5:1). Here Paul emphasizes the practice of forgiveness and in this respect imitating God. Chrysostom, in a homily on Ephesians, urged his congregation to forgive others' trespasses: "Forgive another, and thou art 'imitating God,' thou art made like unto God. It is more our duty to forgive trespasses than debts of money; for if thou forgive debts, thou hast not 'imitated God'; whereas if thou shalt forgive trespasses, thou are imitating God."[193] He believed that one could be called an imitator of God only when one forgives the trespasses of others: "If you forgive trespasses, you are imitating God"[194] because forgiveness is the manifestation of the love of God. Chrysostom did not consider simply forgiving debts of money as expressing the imitation of God. To practice the highest moral virtue of God one must imitate Christ's forgiveness, as Christ revealed God's love by forgiving those who crucified him. Christians give evidence that they are children of God by practicing his forgiving love: "Since not all children imitate their fathers, but those which are beloved."[195]

At the heart of Chrysostom's concept of the imitation of Christ is his employment of the Pauline teaching. I suggested earlier some reasons

192. Chrysostom, *Homilies on Acts* (*NPNF*1 11:92).
193. Chrysostom, *Homilies on Ephesians* (*NPNF*1 13:129).
194. Migne, *Patrologia Graeca*, 62:117.
195. Chrysostom, *Homilies on Ephesians* (*NPNF*1 13:129).

Pastoral Leadership

why he had chosen Paul to be his role model, but here we need to note the specific Pauline statements which were so important for Chrysostom in forming his interpretation of Paul's approach to the imitation of Christ. In this respect, there were a number of key Pauline texts that he used. One such text was 1 Cor 11:1, which reads, "Follow my example, as I follow the example of Christ." One major reason why Chrysostom admired Paul more than anyone else is that after meeting Christ, Paul used his entire life to benefit others. Chrysostom preached, "For no virtuous action can be very exalted, when it does not distribute its benefit to others also."[196] Paul always set the needs of others before his own and his ministry too was centered on winning others to Christ. Chrysostom had the conviction that he could achieve his goal of imitating Christ by following Paul's example. Margaret Mitchell helpfully observes:

> Paul, "the perfect copy of Christ," served for John [Chrysostom] as the archetypal image for those who follow because, having been a human being, Paul could be set forth as an imitable example, even more so than Christ. While Christ is the master, Paul is a "fellow slave" to the rest of humanity. That is why, though he rose to almost unimaginable heights in his praise of Paul, Chrysostom's Pauline portraits ultimately did not eclipse Christ.[197]

This latter point was profoundly true. Another Pauline text that he used was 1 Cor 9:19, which says, "Though I am free and belonging to no man, I make myself a slave to everyone, to win as many as possible." Chrysostom admired Paul because of his unselfish zeal in seeking to fulfill the commandments of Christ. He wrote, "Thus doing as he did all things of free choice and zeal and love to Christ, he had an insatiable desire for the salvation of mankind. Wherefore also he used to overpass by a very great deal the lines marked out, in every way springing higher than the very heaven."[198] Such a text for Chrysostom provided firm evidence for him that Paul actually did imitate Christ. Surprised at Paul's courage and determination to be a witness for Christ so soon after his conversion, Chrysostom expounded these verses, stating:

> See how many [witnesses] he is confessed to have been of the number of the enemies! But Paul not only was not confounded by these things, nor hid his face for shame, but "increased the more

---

196. Chrysostom, *Homilies on First Corinthians* (NPNF1 12:146).
197. Mitchell, *Heavenly Trumpet*, 396.
198. Chrysostom, *Homilies on First Corinthians* (NPNF1 12:128).

Chrysostom's Pastoral Principles: New Testament Homilies

in strength, and confounded the Jews," i.e., put them to silence, left them nothing to say for themselves, "providing, that this is very Christ." "Teaching," it says: for this man was a teacher.[199]

Another Pauline text that Chrysostom used was Phil 3:17: "Be imitators of me, after the pattern you have in us." Chrysostom comments on these words, "The Apostles, therefore, were a type, and kept throughout a certain archetypal model. Consider how entirely accurate their life was, so that they are proposed as an archetype and example, and a living law."[200] The idea of imitating a teacher had precedent in Paul's Jewish heritage, writes Gordon Fee, "where a pupil learned not simply by receiving instruction but by 'putting into practice' the example of the teacher; the one who 'imitates' thus internalizes and lives out the model presented by teacher."[201] In the following verses (3:18) Paul warns others against succumbing to worldly pleasures and neglecting their eternal hope in Christ, so he reminds the Philippians of "suffering for the sake of Christ and the gospel, and behavior that conforms to the gospel."[202] His intention in urging them to imitate him was not to "say that he is better than anyone else. In calling for imitation, it is not for people to emulate his privileges, achievements or advantages, but rather his self-denying, self-giving acts (1 Cor 11:1), his willingness to suffer for the sake of."[203]

Chrysostom was grieved to see the archetypal image of Christ disappearing in his generation:

> Among all these myriads, there are not to be found one hundred likely to be saved: nay, even as to these I question it. For think, what wickedness there is in the young, what supine in the aged! None makes it his duty to look after his own boy; none is moved by anything to be seen in his elder, to be emulous of imitating such a one. The patterns are defaced, and therefore it is that neither do the young become admirable in conduct.[204]

He urgently pleaded for his generation to recover the moral standard so that an example could be reestablished. Learning by imitation, Margaret Mitchell confirms, is the ancient ethical and pedagogical theory, which held

199. Chrysostom, *Homilies on Acts* (*NPNF*1 11:132).
200. Chrysostom, *Homilies on Philippians* 12 (*NPNF*1 13:240).
201. Fee, *Paul's Letter to the Philippians*, 363–64.
202. Ibid., 364.
203. Hawthorne, *Philippians*, 43:159.
204. Chrysostom, *Homilies on Acts* 24 (*NPNF*1 11:160).

Pastoral Leadership

that learning takes place by imitation of exemplary figures. This tradition, a mainstay of Christian thought from the earliest period of Paul himself, engenders in Chrysostom the powerful sense that Paul the apostle is a supreme example of lived virtue who is to be imitated.[205]

On the other hand, in view of Phil 3:13, which states, "Forgetting what is behind," Paul urged the Philippians to reject confidence in their own merits and look only to Christ in faith, realizing their imperfection yet struggling toward the goal that is Christ.[206] The text of 1 Cor 4:16 was also emphasized by Chrysostom: "Therefore I urge you to imitate me." Here, Chrysostom added the phrase, "as I am also of Christ," according to the Vulgate version.[207] The life of an apostle is a reflection of the crucified Christ so there is no reason why Christians should not imitate Christ directly; but the Corinthians knew much about the life and behavior of Christ through the pattern of Paul's life, which provided such an excellent and immediate example of Christ. Chrysostom expounded on 1 Cor 4:16, stating:

> How great is our teacher's boldness of speech! How highly finished the image, when he can even exhort others hereunto! Not that in self-exaltation he does so, but implying that virtue is an easy thing. As if he had said, "Tell me not, 'I am not able to imitate thee. Thou art a Teacher, and a great one.' For the difference between me and you is not so great as between Christ and me: and yet I have imitated Him."[208]

Chrysostom believed that a man could achieve imitation through steady repetition. "For this imitation needs not time and art, but a steady purpose alone."[209] He argued for the possibility of our imitation of Christ through the analogy of painting: "Thus if we go into the study of a painter, we shall not be able to copy the portrait, though we see it ten thousand times."[210] Only through repetition can imitation be achieved. Paul was deeply concerned about severe divisions within the church, immorality in marriage, and spiritual disorder in church practice. For this reason he wrote, "I am sending to you Timothy, my son whom I love, who is faithful in the Lord. He will remind you of my way of life in Christ Jesus" (1 Cor

---

205. Mitchell, *Heavenly Trumpet*, 49.
206. De Boer, *Imitation of Paul*, 174.
207. Chrysostom, *Homilies on First Corinthians* 13 (NPNF1 12:74).
208. Ibid.
209. Ibid.
210. Ibid.

Chrysostom's Pastoral Principles: New Testament Homilies

4:17). Chrysostom believed that Paul did not send Timothy as a commander or teacher, but as a reminder in order not to offend the Corinthians. Paul took great pains in choosing Timothy, who was faithful in the Lord; his desire was that Timothy should demonstrate a Christlike character to the Corinthians as an imitator of Christ and Paul.[211]

Another Pauline text which was important for Chrysostom was 1 Thess 1:6, where Paul applied the imitation of Christ principle in the context of their afflictions. "You became imitators of us and of the Lord; in spite of severe suffering, you welcomed the message with the joy given by the Holy Spirit." In spite of severe sufferings, they followed the apostles' example by enduring persecution for the gospel's sake and also by sharing the gospel with others.[212] In the process of receiving the word of God, the Thessalonians experienced much affliction and suffered the cost of imitating the Apostle Paul and Christ. Willis Peter De Boer concludes it probable that the Thessalonians were imitating Judean Christians deliberately but were now finding it difficult to cope with continuing persecution and suffering.[213] And yet they continued to give evidence of being imitators of Paul and the Lord, through their perseverance under persecution and sufferings, and in doing so, became an example to believers throughout Macedonia and Achaia (1 Thess 1:7). Chrysostom also pointed out that the Thessalonians joyfully endured much affliction for Christ but in the Spirit's power, following Christ's example wherein he emptied himself for our sake. Chrysostom does not emphasize the theological content or nature of their faith, but rather the fruit of their faith. Similarly, Chrysostom draws attention to Gal 4:12, where Paul also exhorts believers, "I plead with you brothers, become like me." Paul's ultimate ministry goal was to bring the Galatians to the point of possessing a Christlike character and this goal resulted from his knowledge that the ultimate planter was the Holy Spirit, not himself. Just as in Jesus' life everything and every moment were under the control, and within the will, of God, so Chrysostom underlines the rebuke given to the Thessalonians by the Apostle in regard to their disorderly behavior and their idle lifestyle in homily five of Second Thessalonians.[214] Chrysostom reminded believers of the importance of the wise use of time:

---

211. Ibid., 78.
212. Bruce, *1 & 2 Thessalonians*, 45:15.
213. De Boer, *Imitation of Paul*, 106–07.
214. Chrysostom, *Homilies on Second Thessalonians* 5 (NPNF1 13:394).

Pastoral Leadership

> The time is not yours. At the present ye are strangers, and sojourners, and foreigners, and aliens; seek not honors, seek not glory, seek not authority, nor revenge; bear all things, and in this way, 'redeem the time.'[215]

To those who truthfully desire to imitate Christ, Chrysostom advised that it is absolutely necessary to effectively manage one's time and prioritize on activities in one's life.[216]

Paul's goal in imitating Christ was to present himself as an example of a Christlike character. It is not surprising then that Chrysostom drew attention also to 1 Tim 1:16, where Paul wrote, "But for that very reason I was shown mercy so that in me, the worst of sinners, Christ Jesus might display his unlimited patience as an example for those who would believe on him and receive eternal life." Clearly, "Christ's purpose was that Paul should be an example of the application of Christ's redemption."[217] Here the Greek word for example means an "example, rather in the sense prototype."[218] Paul was convinced that Christ had ordained him to be a prototype for those who would believe in Christ and receive eternal life through the mercy of God. It was Christ's intention to use Paul as such an example. Chrysostom also praised Paul's humble attitude and stated:

> See how he further humbles and depreciates himself, by naming a fresh and less creditable reason. For that he obtained mercy on account of his ignorance, does not so much imply that he who obtained mercy was a sinner, or under deep condemnation; but to say that he obtained mercy in order that no sinner hereafter might despair of finding mercy, but that each might feel sure of obtaining the like favor, this is an excess of humiliation, such that even in calling himself the chief of sinners.[219]

Chrysostom described Paul's attitude here as "an excess of humiliation," an indication that the Lord planned to use him to demonstrate Christ's humility, as it is Christ's prime characteristic. Second Timothy 1:13

---

215. Chrysostom, *Homilies on Ephesians* 19 (NPNF1 13:137).

216. Covey, *7 Habits*, 146. Stephen Covey describes seven principles of highly effective people, which are: 1) be proactive, 2) begin with the end in mind, 3) put first things first, 4) think win/win, 5) seek first to understand, then to be understood, 6) synergize, 7) sharpen the saw.

217. Knight, *Commentary on the Pastoral Epistles*, 102.

218. Arndt and Gingrich, *Greek-English Lexicon*, 856.

219. Chrysostom, *Homilies on First Timothy* 4 (NPNF1 13:420).

Chrysostom's Pastoral Principles: New Testament Homilies

was another Pauline text that Chrysostom used for his emphasis on the imitation of Christ, where Paul presents himself as the pattern of sound doctrine for others to follow.[220] Chrysostom states, "After the manner of artists, I have impressed on thee the image of virtue, fixing in thy soul a sort of rule, and model, and outline of all things pleasing to God."[221] Concerning the message of Acts 20:35, where Paul claims "In all things I gave an example," Chrysostom comments, "Observe him employed in work, and not simply that, but toiling. 'These hands have ministered unto my necessities, and to them that were with me.'"[222] Paul tried to imitate every aspect of Christ in his human nature so that he could present himself as an example for others to follow. There is no question that Chrysostom loved and respected Paul the most because he believed that Paul imitated Christ in an outstanding manner, as stated in 1 Cor 11:1. Chrysostom not only preached on all the Pauline epistles, as we previously noted but he also expounded all the passages in the Pauline corpus referring to the imitation of Christ, which I have now identified, including the statement "I die daily." Referring to this text from 1 Cor 15:31, Chrysostom indicated that Paul was able to die daily "by his readiness and preparation for that event."[223] He had identified the key Pauline texts on this subject and applied them; Paul was for him the ultimate model concerning the imitation of Christ. For Chrysostom, imitating Christ is the highest achievement of Christian ethics and human morality.

Imitation of Christ: Its Theological Basis

It is now necessary to explore theologically what the imitation of Christ meant for Chrysostom. His expository preaching on the character of Jesus and the imitation of him in the Pauline Epistles, the Gospels of John and Matthew, Acts, and Hebrews, gave special attention to the concept of *kenosis*, drawing particular insight from Phil 2:5–11, which, I suggest, provided his major theological basis for the imitation of Christ. The concept of *kenosis* is at the heart of Pauline Christology with regard to the incarnation of Christ and Chrysostom recognized this and the importance of the

---

220. Kelly, *Pastoral Epistle*, 166. The Greek word *hupotutosis* (model) denotes "an outline sketch or ground-plan used by an artist or in literature, a rough draft forming the basis of a fuller exposition."

221. Chrysostom, *Homilies on Second Timothy* 3 (NPNF1 13:484).

222. Chrysostom, *Homilies on Acts* 45 (NPNF1 11:273).

223. Chrysostom, *Homilies on First Corinthians* 40 (NPNF1 12:246).

Pastoral Leadership

Phil 2:5–11 passage as being integral to appreciating Christ's humility. G. F. Hawthorne confirms this fact:

> The Christ-hymn (vv 6–11) presents Jesus as the supreme example of the humble, self-sacrifice, self-denying, self-giving service that Paul has just been urging the Philippians to practice in their relations one toward another (vv 1–4).[224]

The Greek word *kenosis* is a feminine noun, meaning "emptying, or depletion,"[225] but the verb form *kenou* is often used with the meaning of "to make empty, to deprive of content or possession, mostly with a genitive of objective."[226] When the verb *kenou* was used in the New Testament, particularly in Phil 2:7, "what is meant is that the heavenly Christ did not selfishly exploit His divine form and mode of being, but by His own decision emptied Himself of it or laid it by, taking the form of a servant by becoming man."[227] Since Phil 2:5–11 provides one of the most thorough theological explanations of the incarnation of Christ, Chrysostom wrote an extensive theological interpretation of this passage.[228] Verse 5 states, "Your attitude should be the same as that of Christ Jesus."[229] The ultimate goal of the imitation of Christ is transformation of the whole person, thus Paul urged the Philippians to have a newness of mind like Christ, especially in the light of the interpersonal disputes within the church. In his understanding of *kenosis* in Phil 2:5–11, Chrysostom identifies three interrelated and foundational strands of teaching, which he proceeds to explain and apply; condescension, humility, and obedience. I now want to outline and analyze these in turn.

1. Condescension

While the humility of Christ is an integral part of kenosis in Chrysostom's Christology, the concept of *sunkatabasis* also provides the principal means of the realization of *kenosis* in the incarnation of Christ. The Greek word *sunkatabasis* is a feminine noun describing "condescension to the level of

---

224. Chrysostom, *Homilies on Philippians* (*NPNF*1 13:206–18).
225. Liddle et al., *Greek-English Lexicon*, 939.
226. Kittel et al., *Theological Dictionary*, 3:661.
227. Ibid. The best commentary on this concept *kenosis* is found from 2 Cor 8:9.
228. O'Brien, *Epistle to the Philippians*, 186–87.
229. Thomas a Kempis' *The Imitation of Christ* is a classic on the subject of the imitation of Christ. His whole idea of following Jesus is humble obedience after the example of Jesus Christ.

Chrysostom's Pastoral Principles: New Testament Homilies

an audience."[230] The verbal form *sunkatabaio* is interpreted as to "go or come down with someone, go down together, or come down to one's aid."[231] As the Greek meaning of the word conveys the concept of humility with regard to Christ's incarnation, *sunkatabasis* highlights Christ's condescension, which is God's chosen means of revealing himself.

A biblical illustration of condescension is found in Acts 25:5, when the Roman governor Festus said, "let the men of authority among you go down with me," where the Greek suggests that Festus, in a high government position, was going with others to see Paul who was a mere prisoner. The Greek word *sunkatabasis/sunkatabaio* appears approximately 450 times in Chrysostom's works, demonstrating its importance in his Christology.[232] The main use of *sunkatabasis* in Chrysostom's writings was to portray the humility of Christ; for example, he believed that Christ demonstrated humility through prayer so "Christ prayed out of condescension."[233] Although he had equality with God, Christ prayed to God the Father with a humble attitude to ask for power in performing miracles during his earthly ministry.[234] Regarding Christ's humility, Chrysostom stated: "When he spoke in a lowly and humble fashion, he spoke as God made flesh and in a spirit of condescension and accommodation because the understanding of his hearers was weak."[235] The true humility of Christ is seen in his attitude of wanting to identify himself with humans, as demonstrated in John 1:14 "And the Word became flesh and dwelt among us." Chrysostom expounded this verse in his understanding of Christ's humility and *sunkatabasis* as he wrote: "Wherefore He tabernacled among us, that we might be able with much fearlessness to approach Him, speak to, and converse with Him."[236] His understanding of the incarnation can be described as the realization of *kenosis* through *sunkatabasis*. Expounding on Heb 4:15 "One who in every respect has been tempted as we are, yet without sin," Chrysostom interpreted the High Priest's divine condescension as evidence of his humble attitude, and remarked, "Seest thou that [for Him] to be made High Priest, is

---

230. Liddell et al., *Greek-English Lexicon*, 1662.

231. Ibid.

232. Rylaarsdam, "Adaptability of Divine Pedagogy," 20.

233. Chrysostom, *Incomprehensible Nature of God*, 72:30.

234. There are many examples of prayer of Christ requesting miracles before the people in the gospels: for example, John 6:11, 11:40–44, Matt 26: 39

235. Chrysostom, *Incomprehensible Nature of God*, 72:34.

236. Chrysostom, *Homilies on John* 12 (NPNF1 14:40).

Pastoral Leadership

not of nature, but of grace and condescension and humiliation?"[237] Chrysostom viewed the incarnation as a measure of divine grace, condescension, and humility.[238]

In addition to providing an understanding of condescension as a means of humility for Christ, it also provided Chrysostom a revelatory channel for communicating divine truth. The phrase in John 1:14, "The Word became flesh," is a divine principle of the revelation of Christ through whom God spoke. Chrysostom also believed that the visible appearance of the resurrected Christ in the form of a normal but glorified physical body was a special act of his condescension that Christ performed in order to reveal an important message. His condescension was also evidenced during the three years of his ministry. For example, in John 3:1–15, with regard to the conversation between Nicodemus and Jesus on spiritual rebirth, Chrysostom exclaimed, "Observe His exceeding condescension."[239] This was characteristic of Christ's entire life and ministry.

2. Humility

The second strand, however, concerning humility, received the greatest attention from Chrysostom in understanding the *kenosis* of Christ. Expounding on Phil 2:5–11, a crucial passage in Christology, Chrysostom explored the concept of *sunkatabasis* as the means of *kenosis* that Christ employed when he, the Word, took flesh. The condescension, however, cannot stand alone without humility because "Christ took flesh upon himself because of his humility."[240] At the center of Christ's incarnation, as we have seen, is Christ's humility, which is realized through his condescension. In regard to the interrelationship of condescension and humility in Chrysostom's Christology, Melvin E. Lawrenz rightly concluded:

> Condescension is thus a key to interpreting Christological passages in Chrysostom. He uses it to describe a mode by which the

---

237. Chrysostom, *Homilies on Hebrews* 7 (*NPNF*1 14:400).

238. Chrysostom, *Homilies on John* 53 (*NPNF*1 14:192). Chrysostom tried to show how Christ condescended himself to the level of the audiences in order to fully communicate. When Christ spoke the Jews in John 5:24–29, Chrysostom also explains Christ's condescending attitude: "Since then He had said that all the world should render account to Him, and that all at His voice should rise again, a thing new and strange and even now disbelieved by many who seem to have believed, not to say by the Jews at that time, hear how He goeth to prove it, again condescending to the infirmity of His hearers."

239. Ibid., 84.

240. Chrysostom, *Incomprehensible Nature of God*, 72:262.

divine Christ takes human roles for two main reasons: either to provide a revelation of deity in veiled form because of human inability to look upon pure deity; or to provide a model of human behavior.[241]

The two elements of condescension and Christ's humility are inseparable and also complementary. The Greek word *tapeino* ("humility") appeared 1,132 times in Chrysostom's writings, demonstrating its importance in his Christology. Christ's humility in the incarnation should be theologically interpreted in terms of the mind of Christ.[242] Etymologically, the original meaning of the word is "lowly, insignificant, weak, or poor in terms of the position a person occupies." It can also express the lowly status that individuals may find themselves acquiring for some reason.[243] This Greek word, then, is well fitted to describe the incarnation of Christ because it includes the notion of transformation of status from the highest to the lowest position. Contextually, Chrysostom's interpretation of the Phil 2 passage is governed also by the fact that Paul was urging the Philippians to imitate Christ's humility in order to recover unity within the church. Thus, he reinforced Christ's humility, citing 2 Cor 8:9 in support.[244] In regard to strife in the church, such as that referred to in Phil 2:1–4, Chrysostom reminded his people of Paul's command for unity and humility: "Not simply humility, but intense humility. As in the case of bodily substances, that which is 'broken' will not rise against that which is 'solid.'"[245] Expounding on Phil 2:2, Chrysostom indicated that this unity could only be achieved through imitating and developing the mind of Christ:

> "Of one accord," he adds, that is appropriating with one soul, the bodies of all, not in substance, for that is impossible, but in purpose and intention. Let all things proceed as from one soul. What means "of one accord"? He shows when he says "of one mind." Let your mind be one, as if from one soul.[246]

---

241. Lawrenz, *Christology of John Chrysostom*, 145.
242. "For I am meek and humble in heart" (Matt 11:29).
243. Kittel et al., *Theological Dictionary*, 8:1–3.
244. Chrysostom, *Homilies on Philippians* 6 (*NPNF*1 13:206).
245. Ibid., 13:204. Chrysostom rebuked severely the haughty people and said, "Are you high minded, O man? And why? Tell me what is the gain? Whence are you high minded against those of your own kind? Do not you share the same nature? The same life? Have not you received like honor from God? But you are wise?"
246. Chrysostom, *Homilies on Philippians* 5 (*NPNF*1 13:203).

He indicates that here it is possible for people to have the same mind as Christ, which Chrysostom called "true wisdom."[247] "But in lowliness of mind, each counting other better than himself"[248] is the true practice of humility. In order to practice such humility, Paul first urged the Philippians to have the mind of Christ: "Have this mind among yourselves, which is yours in Christ Jesus" (Phil 2:5). In the Greek, Paul employed the present imperative verb, expressing repeated action. One immediate area of application for Chrysostom was with regard to the Arian controversy, as he strongly rebuked the Arians for denying the deity of Christ. Christ would not be able to demonstrate humility if he was not coequal and coeternal with the Father. Chrysostom writes:

> Arius confesses indeed the Son, but only in word; he says that He is a creature, and much inferior to the Father. And others say that He has not a soul. Seest thou the chariots standing? See then their fall, how he overthrows them all together, and with a single stroke. How? "Have the same mind in you," he says, "which was in Christ Jesus, who being in the form of God, counted it not a prize to be on an equality with God."[249]

He reminded the Arians of the two distinct natures of Christ, such that one practical example of his humility was demonstrated by washing the disciples' feet even though he was their Master. "The greater person subjected Himself to the lesser."[250] He also defended Christ's divinity by claiming that Christ, in his humility, was God incarnate in the form of man, appealing to the statement in verse six: "who, although He existed in the form of God, did not regard equality with God a thing to be grasped." For Chrysostom, Christ's divine nature did not change from one state to another: "If there is really only one determining nature in the incarnate Christ, then that divine and unchangeable nature remains unmixed."[251] However, the only difference was Christ's attitude:

247. Ibid.

248. Ibid. Chrysostom cited extensive illustrations of humility to emphasize its importance. He related the stories of Joseph and Daniel from the point of their humility.

249. Chrysostom, *Homilies on Philippians* 6 (*NPNF*1 13:207).

250. Ibid., 13:208. Chrysostom explained why the Arians' view on the divinity of Christ is wrong in regard to the humility of Christ: "Now if the Son were inferior, this were not a sufficient example to lead us to humility. And why? Because it is not humility, for the lesser not to rise against the greater, not to snatch at rule, and to be 'obedient unto death.'"

251. Lawrenz, *Christology of John Chrysostom*, 108. Lawrenz explained that there is

Chrysostom's Pastoral Principles: New Testament Homilies

The Word who was God did not degenerate into man, nor was His substance changed, but he appeared as a man; not to delude us with a phantom, but to instruct us in humility. When therefore he says, "as a man," this is what He means; since he calls Him a man elsewhere also, when he says, "there is one God, one Mediator also between God and men, Himself man, Christ Jesus" (1 Tim 5).[252]

In his preaching, Chrysostom's Christology clearly distinguishes between Christ's divinity and humanity. He continued, "Here concerning His divinity, we no longer find 'He became,' 'He took,' but 'He emptied Himself, taking the form of servant, being made in the likeness of men'; here concerning his humanity we find the phrase 'He took, He became.'"[253]

Chrysostom explained that: "[Christ] was made Flesh, not by changing His Essence to flesh, but by taking flesh to Himself, His Essence remained untouched."[254] He emphasized the fact that Christ's incarnation was not imposed on him by someone else, but was voluntary. He employed the phrase "no longer He became, but He took," to describe this idea.[255] The incarnation of Christ is, therefore, a self-explanatory historical event that came about by his own volition because of his humility. In defending Christ's humility and divinity, Chrysostom also argued, "If He being a man washed man, He emptied not, He humbled not Himself. That God should become man is great, unspeakable, inexpressible humility."[256] It should be noted, however, that Christ's humility was most evident in his obedience to God and I refer to this strand of teaching later.[257] But Paul's intent in this

---

no difference in essence between the pre-incarnate Christ and the incarnate Christ in Chrysostom's Christology. "When pure divinity and real humanity come together in the incarnation, humankind is afforded the vehicle for its salvation. A real union has occurred, and a permanent one."

252. Chrysostom, *Homilies on Philippians* 7 (*NPNF*1 13:214).

253. Chrysostom, *Homilies on Philippians* 7 (*NPNF*1 13:215).

254. Chrysostom, *Homilies on John* 11 (*NPNF*1 14:39). For unchanging nature of Christ Chrysostom quoted Ps 102:27, which reads, "Wherefore the prophet says, 'They shall wax old as does a garment, and as a vesture shall Thou roll them up, and they shall be changed; but Thou are the same, and Thy years shall not fail. For that Essence is superior to all change."

255. Migne, *Patrologia Graeca*, 62:232.

256. Chrysostom, *Homilies on Philippians* 7 (*NPNF*1 13:214). Chrysostom added a question: "But what humility is there in that one, who was a man, should do the work of men?" Chrysostom did have a clear distinction between the biblical concept of the humility Christ in his incarnation and the Arians claim on the humanity of Christ.

257. Ibid., 13:215. Chrysostom said: "He is a true son, in honoring His Father more

Pastoral Leadership

Christological hymn was not to demonstrate kenotic theology or Adamic Christology, but rather to provide an example of humility for the church in order to promote unity. In regard to the core motif of this passage, Chrysostom asked, "What does Paul wish to establish by this example? Surely, to lead the Philippians to humility."[258] Upholding Christ's humility, Chrysostom stated that, "He who is lowly minded, when he has it in his power to be high minded, is humble."[259]

While Christ's humility is something to be imitated in the Christian life, there is also a strong soteriological aspect to Christ's incarnation[260] that ultimately brought salvation through the cross. This soteriological aspect of Christ's incarnation is based on the presupposition of the humility of Christ. In regard to the nature of Christ's incarnation and his humility, Chrysostom wrote, partly with reference to the Arians:

> Therefore, if Christ allowed himself to put on flesh because he was inferior to the Father in nature, what was done would not be an act of humility. Then it would have been idle and necessary for Paul to bring this in when he was exhorting his disciples to be humble. For it is an act of humility when an equal obeys an equal. And Paul himself pointed this out when he said: "who being in the form of God, did not think it robbery to be equal to God, but he emptied himself taking the nature of a servant."[261]

God's plan of salvation could not be achieved without such humility on the part of Christ as mediator: If God's eternal plan of salvation was realized through Christ's humility in his incarnation, then blessings must have also been bestowed on people through Christ's personal humility. From 2 Cor 8:9, for example, Chrysostom added: "He [Christ] emptied Himself of His glory that ye, not through His riches but through His poverty, might be rich."[262] For Chrysostom, the value of Christ's humility was inestimable in terms of blessing for people:

than all besides. No one has thus honored God. As was His height, such was the correspondent humiliation that He underwent. As He is greater than all, and no one is equal to Him, so in honoring His Father, He surpassed all, not by necessity, nor unwillingly, but this too is part of His excellence."

258. Chrysostom, *Homilies on Philippians* 6 (NPNF1 13:208).

259. Ibid., 208.

260. Lawrenz, *Christology of John Chrysostom*, 146–47.

261. Chrysostom, *Incomprehensible Nature of God*, 72:264.

262. Chrysostom, *Homilies on Second Corinthians* 17 (NPNF1 12:360). Chrysostom earnestly made his thanksgiving to the Lord, saying, "For He had not become poor, thou

Before he humbled himself, only the angels knew him. After he humbled himself, all human nature knew him. You see how his humbling of himself did not make him have less but produced countless profits, countless deeds of virtue, and made his glory shine forth with greater brightness. God wants for nothing and has need of nothing. Yet, when he humbled himself, he produced such great good, increased his household, and extended his kingdom.[263]

Chrysostom understood that the act of humility honors God, and in turn God also honors those who humble themselves before him. The incarnation is a clear demonstration of Christ's humility before God, and God also exalted Christ to the highest place. Therefore, Chrysostom urged his congregation to be humble, saying, "Why, then, are you afraid that you will become less if you humble yourself? If you do humble yourself, you will become more exalted, you will be great, you will be illustrious, you will be renowned on every side."[264]

In Phil 2:9–11, the Apostle Paul described Christ's exaltation that would occur as a result of his humility. Verse nine states, "Therefore God has highly exalted him."[265] Christ was exalted by God and restored to his original state because of his obedient humility: "He [Christ] was obedient to the uttermost, wherefore He received the honor which is on high, He became a servant, wherefore He is the Lord of all, both of Angels, and of all other."[266]

He illustrated the consequences of both pride and humility, encouraging his congregation to follow the example of Christ's humility:

> Satan was an angel, he exalted himself. What then? Was he not humbled beyond all other? Has he not the earth as his place? Is he not condemned and accused by all? Paul was a man, and humbled himself. What then? Is he not admired? Is he not praised? Is he not lauded? Is he not the friend of Christ? Wrought he not greater things than Christ?[267]

---

wouldest not have become rich."

263. Chrysostom, *Incomprehensible Nature of God*, 231

264. Ibid.

265. Bock, *Jesus According to Scripture*, 295. Bock compared the differences of the attitudes of the Pharisees and the Publicans. God rejects the proud and exalts the humble (James 4:6–10, 1 Pet 5:5).

266. Chrysostom, *Homilies on Philippians* 7 (*NPNF*1 13:216).

267. Ibid., 216.

Pastoral Leadership

Chrysostom observed that throughout biblical history, God has condemned the proud, but praised the humble, so he encouraged the practice of Christ's humility: "He that is exalted by himself is not exalted by others. He who is humbled by himself is not humbled by others. Haughtiness is a great evil, it is better to be a fool than haughty."[268] We now turn to a third strand in Chrysostom's understanding of the *kenosis* of Christ, namely obedience.

3. Obedience

Christ's humility led him to be obedient even to death on the cross. Chrysostom described Christ's surrender at Gethsemane as a mark of his obedience to God and stated, "See by how many things He shows the reality of the incarnation: by what He speaks, by what He suffers."[269] The ultimate goal of humility should be complete surrender and obedience to God's will. Christ's obedience on the cross led him to pronounce, "It is finished" (John 19:30). Philippians 2:8, therefore, includes the words: "[Christ] humbled himself and became obedient unto death, even death on a cross." Chrysostom commented: "[Christ] was obedient to the uttermost, wherefore He received the honor which is on high."[270] Chrysostom believed that assuming the form of a servant captures the true essence of Christ; that even when he became a servant, there was no change to his original divine being. In order to convince others of Christ's voluntary obedience and humility, and unchangeable nature, Chrysostom expounded the phrase "the form of a servant":

> I said that the "form of a servant" was a true form, and nothing less. Therefore "the form of God" also is perfect, and no less. Why says he not, "being made in the form of God," but "being in the form of God"? This is the same as the saying, "I am that I am" (Exod 14). "Form" implies unchangeableness, so far as it is form. It is not possible that things of one substance should have the form of another, as no man has the form of an angel, neither has a beast the form of a man. How then should the Son?[271]

The other notion of *kenosis* in Chrysostom's writings is *diakonos*; the Greek word appears 1,430 times. In his theology of *kenosis*, Chrysostom's

268. Ibid., 217.
269. Chrysostom, *Homilies on Matthew* 83 (*NPNF*1 10:497).
270. Chrysostom, *Homilies on Philippians* 7 (*NPNF*1 13:216).
271. Chrysostom, *Homilies on Philippians* 6 (*NPNF*1 13:209).

Chrysostom's Pastoral Principles: New Testament Homilies

ultimate goal is to imitate the example of Christ's service out of a heart of humility. The primary objective of Christ's humility is to serve; servanthood is the essential characteristic of the Messiah as prophesized through Isaiah.[272] In his exposition of Matt 20:28, Chrysostom interpreted Christ's servanthood in the context of humility:

> Be not then afraid, as though thine honour were plucked down. For how much so ever thou humblest thyself, thou canst not descend so much as thy Lord. And yet His descent hath made His own glory shine forth. For before He has made man, He was known amongst angels only; but after He was made man and was crucified, so far from lessening that glory, He acquired other besides, even that from the knowledge of the world.[273]

When Christ said: "Even as the Son of man came not to be served but to serve, and to give His life a ransom for many" (Matt 20:28), he was not only presenting himself as the Passover Lamb, but also as the greatest example of humility. Chrysostom even dared to exalt humility as a channel to gain salvation by stating, "This [humility] is the door of the kingdom,"[274] because Christ said, "I tell you the truth, unless you change and become like little children, you will never enter the kingdom of heaven" (Matt 18:3). Chrysostom believed that the servanthood of Christ is the outcome of his humility. "[Christ] became a man, he took upon himself the form of a servant."[275] When Paul wrote that Christ took "the form of a servant" in Phil 2:7, he described Christ's humility and recalled the prophetic words of Isa 53:11, "by his knowledge my righteous servant will justify many." Chrysostom interpreted Christ's mission in Isa 53:11 as "the righteous one who has served many well."[276] The Messiah accomplished the mission of salvation by sacrificially serving sinners. Chrysostom added that the service of Christ

---

272. Delitzsch, *Prophecies of Isaiah*, 2:174-75. Delitzsch identified the personification of the Servant figure in Isaiah as a specific individual. He writes: "But the servant of Jehovah who is presented to us here is distinct from Israel, and has so strong an individuality and such marked personal features, that the expression cannot possibly be merely a personified collective." What he means is that the description of the servant of the Lord in Isa 42-54 is no other than the Messiah.

273. Chrysostom, *Homilies on Matthew* 65 (*NPNF*1 10:401). Matt 20:17-28 is the most important Christological passage in regard to Christ's incarnation and servant leadership, which is instructed by Christ on the way to Jerusalem.

274. Ibid., 10:402.

275. Chrysostom, *Incomprehensible Nature of God*, 171.

276. Chrysostom, *Apologist*, 73:207.

Pastoral Leadership

was to give his life as a ransom even for enemies.[277] Paul wrote, "Christ became a servant to the circumcised to show God's truthfulness" (Rom 15:8), for it is impossible to serve without condescension and humility. The discipleship of Christ consists of following the crucified Christ. Richard Hays rightly described: "The norm for discipleship is defined by the cross. Jesus' own obedience, interpreted as servanthood (Mark 10:45), is the singular pattern for faithfulness."[278]

To those about to be baptized and to the newly baptized, Chrysostom, as Archbishop of Constantinople, provided "baptismal instructions"[279] to aid them in their understanding of union with Christ through baptism. Regarding the tenth instruction, Chrysostom asked, "Why did Christ spend three days in the tomb? Surely He who could make His servant arise in an instant of time was all the more able to raise up Himself."[280]

Chrysostom professed that Christ is the true servant of God who came to serve God's purpose, suffering and experiencing three days in the tomb in order to prove the certainty of his death. Paul also wrote, "For I tell you that Christ has become a servant of the Jews on behalf of God's truth, to confirm the promises made to the patriarchs." In Rom 15:8, Chrysostom interpreted the ministry of Christ in terms of sacrifice and obedience:

> When then he calls Him "a Minister of the circumcision," he means this, that by having come and fulfilled the Law, and been circumcised, and born of the seed of Abraham, He undid the curse, stayed the anger of God, made also those that were to receive the promises fit for them, as being once for all freed from their alienation.[281]

Christ condescended to become man to bear the curse for God's chosen people. He demonstrated the concept of *kenosis* through his humble service so that the love of God may be manifested. Believing Christ voluntarily took upon himself the burden of sinners, Chrysostom commented on Rom 15:3, "[Christ] has the power not to have been reproached, power not to have suffered what He did suffer, had He been minded to look to His own things. But yet He was not so minded."[282]

277. Chrysostom, *Homilies on Matthew* 65 (*NPNF*1 10:401).
278. Hays, *Moral Vision*, 84.
279. Chrysostom, *Baptismal Instructions*, 23.
280. Ibid., 152.
281. Chrysostom, *Homilies on Romans* 28 (*NPNF*1 11:538–39).
282. Chrysostom, *Homilies on Romans* 27 (*NPNF*1 11:536).

Chrysostom's Pastoral Principles: New Testament Homilies

We have now identified and outlined the three main strands in Chrysostom's understanding of the *kenosis* of Christ, namely, condescension, humility, and obedience. But inevitably, this emphasis on imitating Christ through the *kenosis* principle involves carrying the cross, which symbolizes suffering for Christ. Therefore, Christian martyrdom is the final step in discipleship. *Kenosis* starts with humility, but ends with martyrdom. In Matt 10:38, Christ taught that imitation is a continuous process of following him until it is consummated by martyrdom. In expounding this passage, Chrysostom wrote:

> Therefore He [Christ] said not, "Let him renounce himself unto death," but, "Let him take up his cross;" setting forth the reproachful death; and that not once, nor twice, but throughout all life one ought so to do. "Yea," said He, "bear about this death continually, and day by day be ready for slaughter."[283]

In Luke 9:23, the word "daily" signifies the continual process of carrying the cross of Christ; it is only possible to carry the cross when the spirit of humility is at work in a person during the entire process of imitating Christ. In agreement with Paul's confession in Phil 1:21, "For to me to live is Christ, and to die is gain," Chrysostom wrote, "But as long as Christ is with me, even though death overtake me, still I live, and in this present life, not this, but Christ is my life."[284] Chrysostom's inner desire for martyrdom for the cause of Christ was revealed when he expounded Paul's farewell passage in 2 Tim 4:7–8:

> Indeed the whole Epistle is full of consolation, and is a sort of Testament. "I have fought the good fight, I have finished my course, I have kept my faith." "A good fight," he says, therefore do thou engage in it. But is that a good fight, where there are imprisonment, chains, and death? Yea, he says, for it is fought in the cause of Christ, and great crowns are won in it. "The good fight!" There is no worthier than this contest. This crown is without end. . . . Henceforth we ought to rejoice. For I am entering on my rest, I am leaving the race. Thou hast heard that "It is better to depart and to be with Christ." I have finished "the course."[285]

Chrysostom's conviction regarding martyrdom for Christ was further illustrated by his response to Paul's words in Rom 14:8: "For we do not die

283. Chrysostom, *Homilies on Matthew* 55 (*NPNF*1 10:340).
284. Chrysostom, *Homilies on Philippians* 3 (*NPNF*1 13:195).
285. Chrysostom, *Homilies on Second Timothy* 9 (*NPNF*1 13:511).

Pastoral Leadership

to ourselves alone, but to our Master also, if we do die. But by death here he means that from the faith."[286] For Chrysostom, Christian martyrdom is the final stage in the process of the imitation of Christ. "All deaths are not alike; His death seemed to be the most ignominious of all, to be full of shame, to be accursed."[287] Realizing the nature of the death of Christ in his indescribable suffering and insult on the cross, Chrysostom praised the glory that Christ received through his obedience in humility, saying, "This glory then is above all glory, and this glory in short that all worship Him!"[288] In regard to the relationship between martyrdom and humility, Chrysostom stated, "Martyrs should suffer their death in humility, for without humility, they would not be imitating Christ's death."[289] Gus George Christo confirms this view of martyrdom and its inseparable link with humility:

> Chrysostom states that it has been prepared for the humble who follow their Lord seek the extreme last position among others; consider yourself, the meanest or worthless of all people, totally humble and totally insignificant, coming after all others. It is only the virtue of humility (in connection with martyrdom) that can grant this honor. Furthermore, Chrysostom says that one must allow oneself to become the most insignificant of all people, be slaughtered, and be exposed to dangers in order to achieve the highest honor.[290]

In expounding on Acts 20:24, Chrysostom's intention was to remind the church elders at Ephesus that martyrdom for Christ is the most noble, glorious act of faith in response to God's grace.[291]

Chrysostom died in exile at Comana on September 14, 407; his death was considered to be martyrdom because he was persecuted for unjustifiable reasons. "It was the almost unanimous conviction of his contemporaries that Chrysostom was a martyr. Palladius, in his Dialog, emphasized not less than five times that his opponents had had the purpose of killing

---

286. Chrysostom, *Homilies on Romans* 25 (*NPNF*1 11:524).
287. Chrysostom, *Homilies on Philippians* 7 (*NPNF*1 13:215).
288. Ibid.
289. Christo, *Martyrdom According to John Chrysostom*, 47.
290. Ibid., 49. Christo continued to state that "In the final analysis, then, the martyr is, for Chrysostom, one who humble himself to such an extent that he imitates exactly Christ's death. It is only in this state of extreme humility that one is, at the same time, the last and most despised of men and the first in the kingdom of Heaven."
291. Chrysostom, *Homilies on Acts* 44 (*NPNF*1 11:270).

Chrysostom's Pastoral Principles: New Testament Homilies

Chrysostom."[292] Chrysostom's martyrdom was not only due to an unjust deposition by the Empress Eudoxia, but also to his strong theological conviction that the true disciple of Christ should carry the cross of Christ continually to the end. Chrysostom understood Matt 16:24 to mean that one must "bear about this death continually, and day by day be ready for slaughter."[293] In the context of 1 Cor 15:31, Chrysostom remarked, "But how does he die daily? By his readiness and preparation for that event."[294] Chrysostom viewed his own martyrdom, then as the final act in his lifelong attempt to imitate Christ. Christo reminds us:

> Chrysostom advises that, just as people decorate their homes, so man should decorate his soul with icons of the martyrs' toils, labors, and tortures. This type of icon is not painted by material means, but by man's readiness and noble and vigilant reasoning.[295]

Having now identified and discussed Chrysostom's four pastoral leadership principles in this chapter, and having drawn attention to his important *kenosis* teaching that underlies his emphasis on the imitation of Christ, I want to turn, in my next and final chapter, to a comparative evaluation of these pastoral leadership principles, which, I suggest, are common to both Chrysostom's ministry and my own ministry in Washington D.C.

---

292. Baur, *John Chrysostom*, 2:432. In regard to the validity of the martyrdom of Chrysostom, Baur stated, "John Chrysostom, the shining star of the Church, the teacher of the whole world—was he not condemned to exile on account of his heroic virtue, and did not endure many trials, even unto death? Shall we then deny to him the honor and reward of a martyr, because he was not attacked on account of the faith? No, no reasonable person will do that; only a fool could think so."

293. Chrysostom, *Homilies on Matthew* 55 (*NPNF*1 10:340).

294. Chrysostom, *Homilies on First Corinthians* 40 (*NPNF*1 12:246).

295. Christo, *Martyrdom According to John Chrysostom*, 190.

7

Conclusion

IN THIS CHAPTER, I intend to more critically compare and assess the pastoral leadership principles that I have identified and described in both my own ministry in KCPC and that of John Chrysostom. Some comparisons have been made earlier, especially when considering the "gaps" which exist between the two pastoral situations; these gaps are historical, geographical, cultural and linguistic. However, there is now the need to pursue and evaluate this comparison in a more sustained manner and self-critically as well. Secondly, I would like briefly to suggest ways in which this research may be useful in the field of pastoral theology, both academically and also in practical church ministry leadership, whatever the denomination or church affiliation may be. First of all, and in more detail, I turn to a more detailed comparison and evaluation of the two ministries described in this research, namely, my ministry in KCPC and that of Chrysostom in Antioch and Constantinople.

CRITICAL COMPARISON

In turning to a more detailed, sustained comparison and evaluation of the pastoral leadership principles in two diverse situations, I need to make some introductory observations.

First, the four pastoral leadership principles, which I identified early in my ministry, all developed and found greater application as the church at KCPC grew but also went through two major crises where serious divisions occurred. Interestingly, similar principles adopted by Chrysostom also developed over a period of time during his ministry. For example, I identified

Conclusion

three major pastoral leadership principles in his *On the Priesthood*; the one principle that was lacking there was that of cross-cultural mission. Although there was development of application and greater emphasis on certain aspects of a principle in his New Testament Homilies, the principles themselves were essentially the same. It was in Antioch and Constantinople that Chrysostom added his fourth principle related to mission. Clearly, both of us developed and sharpened our principles in different ways as we were engaged in pastoral ministry. This aspect is encouraging for me, as I have certainly wrestled with such principles over a long period of time, especially in the earlier years of my ministry.

Second, I have endeavored to establish that the principles as expressed by Chrysostom and myself are essentially the same, though at times expressed and argued differently. For example, in the case of almsgiving and general care for the poor, there is a strong similarity between the principles used in these two pastoral situations. However, the different historical situations in which both of us ministered necessitated a rather different emphasis and application of those principles and I acknowledge these differences.

Thirdly, in terms of temperament and personality, I differ considerably from Chrysostom. While Chrysostom was more outspoken, determined, and stubborn, he also had a capacity on occasions for losing his temper and being angry with those who opposed him, despite his emphasis on the imitation of Christ. He also appears to have been extremely stubborn on occasion when he could disregard the views of others. One wonders whether he lacked wisdom at times, especially when he appeared to adopt a more confrontational approach, particularly in relation to the clergy, the rich, as well as the Emperor and Empress in Constantinople. In the latter relationship, with more wisdom he may have avoided his premature death, but this is somewhat speculative. By contrast, I have not been confrontational in any way in my KCPC ministry, although I have endeavored to stand up for major principles and to commend as well as introduce them, despite opposition on occasions. My own personality is more docile and gracious, as I endeavored to be a peacemaker while at the same time prayerfully allowing God to guide and rule in what were distressing pastoral situations. I am not being critical of Chrysostom, and I am certainly not boasting of a superior attitude on my part but merely acknowledging these personal differences that have impacted the nature of our pastoral work and leadership.

My respect for Chrysostom has not diminished, despite these rather personal characteristics that were evident in his life and ministry.

Pastoral Leadership

Furthermore, I do not suggest that our respective ministries can be interpreted and explained in these purely personal and psychological ways. Our respective personalities conveyed our principles in distinctive ways in very different situations. I acknowledge that if I had been in Chrysostom's situation, my temperament and application of the principles may not have been suitable or effective and that it needed a stronger person who was more prepared for confrontation. In addition, Chrysostom's confrontational approach would have been more acceptable and possibly necessary. My reference, therefore, to different personalities and temperaments on our part is not intended to be reductionist in any way; however, I insist that such factors do affect the way we have applied and taught our pastoral leadership principles.

I now want to look by way of critical comparison at the four pastoral leadership principles that I have identified in Chrysostom's *On the Priesthood* and in a sample of his New Testament Homilies and also in my own ministry at KCPC.

CARING FOR PEOPLE

I share the concern of Chrysostom to express a holistic care for people in one's church and also in the wider community but we have expressed the principle in different ways because of the different social and political situations that prevailed. Both of us, however, understood the term pastoral care comprehensively to include the material and spiritual needs of the people; even though the focus was initially on the congregations, this care was extended more widely to the communities in which we served. The relational aspect of caring and the fact it is focused on people's needs underlies the application of this principle.

The different social and political factors that prevailed in these two pastoral situations resulted in much more pressure being placed on Chrysostom, for example, in providing for the poor and sick people in his community. There was no alternative help available and no direct government help given to poor families. At least in my ministry of care, there were varieties of assistances from local and federal governments, even with regard to transport in enabling older residents to benefit from our church's social facilities. From this perspective, I understand and respect the emphasis that Chrysostom placed on almsgiving as a means of providing for the poor. He rated such almsgiving highly as it was an effective and the only viable way of raising money at the time to meet the needs of the poor. That fact

Conclusion

enables me to appreciate the increasing attention he gave to almsgiving in his homilies for not only was it effective, but for Chrysostom it was a biblical practice and an expression of love for one's neighbor which the Law of God commanded. Through such almsgiving he could supply the needs of about three thousand poor people in Antioch who depended on him and the church for practical assistance. This was a huge burden that he carried as he endeavored to express the love of God and of the church to others in such practical ways. The provision of hospitals by Chrysostom, too, came within this provision at a later date in an attempt to heal and relieve the sick. No wonder, then, that he exposed the rich residents, especially in Constantinople, for their selfishness and luxurious life-styles and their abysmal failure to love their poor neighbors. As patriarch, he also ordered the end of the misuse of church funds by the clergy to support their indulgence in feasting and luxurious living. These were the legitimate means available to Chrysostom to raise and preserve monies for the caring of needy folk; his teaching emphasized obedience but also the imitation of Christ and the Pauline care for the needy brethren in expressing neighborly love.

In my own situation in Washington, I deliberately developed ways of meeting the practical needs of my people as outlined in chapters two and three; some examples included the Central Senior Centre and the Mutual Aid Association, which were extremely helpful to people and greatly appreciated by them. They were examples of holistic care. Like Chrysostom, I encouraged my congregation to give generously and sacrificially to support the church and to meet these practical projects. Unlike the great Chrysostom, however, I was not so pointed and aggressive in addressing the rich in my congregation but quietly taught the Scripture and provided biblical reasons and motivation for such pastoral care and giving. I found this to be effective in my own situation but then I did not have the necessity of providing hospitals for the sick or meeting the desperate food needs of thousands of local people. In a situation where Chrysostom was faced with so many hungry, suffering, and needy people, I think he dealt with the pressure remarkably well.

My ministry concentrated almost exclusively on one people group, namely immigrant Koreans in America who had their distinctive needs in terms of identity, adjustment, integration, and direction. My pastoral situation eventually became more complicated with second and third generation Korean-Americans because of linguistic, cultural, and identity questions but this does not alter the fact that my church was almost exclusively concerned with Korean immigrants in America and also Koreans who were studying or working temporarily there. Currently, about 2.5 million Korean Americans are living in the United States. It was necessary for the church to develop English-language services and the translation of Korean language preaching in two of the main Sunday services. On occasions, I was invited to preach in English at the Mongolian Church in Washington D.C. with the aid of a Mongolian translator.

By contrast, both in Antioch, but especially in Constantinople, Chrysostom was dealing with multi-racial congregations, which added to the demands of pastoral care. For example, in Antioch approximately half of the 200,000 inhabitants were Christians but his congregations would have been very mixed in terms of status in society. Alongside the rich and the middle class were the artisans, laborers, slaves, and farmers. In Antioch, too, there were several ethnic and language groups, including Syriac speaking laypeople and ascetics who particularly visited the city on the occasion of religious festivals.[1] In Constantinople, by contrast, there was quite a significant number of Gothic speaking people, due largely to their inclusion in the armed forces. For this reason, while Chrysostom would preach in Greek in Constantinople, the lessons were often read in Gothic and a presbyter would give a homily in Gothic. Chrysostom was a man who respected the cultural and linguistic differences within his congregations and he adapted wisely in meeting their distinctive needs. He was not by any means a narrow, exclusive nationalist. However, whether multi-racial or not, the pastoral care principle still applied in these situations. Such care was not confined to social, humanitarian needs but, in addition, provided for the spiritual instruction and care of the people.

For this reason, both Chrysostom and myself engaged in preaching as a primary way of caring for people. To supplement this ministry, I developed Home Visitation Ministry, as well as what Schwarz has called "holistic small groups"[2] or cells. While there is no evidence of Chrysostom using this approach, one of my aims in providing such intimate pastoral oversight was also to strengthen the unity of the church. At this point, Denham Grierson speaks of a "consensus" within a church context; however, for Grierson, this "consensus" is only partly formed initially by a confession of faith commonly adhered to by the church member as there are variations occurring within, and between, congregations which are also significant

---

1. Stephens, *Saint Chrysostom*, 93.
2. Schwarz, *Natural Church Development*, 32–33.

Conclusion

and formative. Such variations include factors such as leadership patterns and changes in leadership, openness to change and innovation, the nature and style of church life and witness. When conflict arises, as it did in my own church situation, this can be useful as conflict can provide opportunities for change and a greater recognition of what is viewed as being essential and unchanging by that congregation. Grierson is correct in asserting that "much that is now consensual had a painful birth" but then the responsibility of appropriate pastoral leadership in such a situation is critical[3] and I found this to be so in my pastoral situation. To provide appropriate spiritual and ethical instruction for my congregation, in addition to my own preaching I established cell groups, a Home Visitation Ministry, biblical counseling and a range of other aspects of teaching which served to nourish and instruct members of my congregation. In this context, Jackson W. Carroll refers to "community formation," that is, a sense of belonging that develops amongst the people within the congregation where mutual support and sharing occur, which contributes significantly to the shaping of that congregation as a community. This, remarks Carroll, is a primary task, not an option.[4] That shaping of the congregation can be encouraged further and sustained by the ministry of the Word, the observance of the sacraments, prayer and visitation. Again, this is something that Chrysostom was committed to with his strong emphasis on preaching, the sacraments, prayer, spirituality, and an all-embracing congregational care for his people. Both of us encouraged the emergence, fostering, and dynamics of care arising from within the entire congregation. In this respect, the expression of care did not depend solely on the clergy/deacons but on all the members within the congregation.

In expressing this care, one has discovered what Brynolf Lyon has referred to as the "otherness"[5] within congregational life in which one recognizes, for example, the presence of immigrants, the poor, the sick, the elderly, and any who are disorientated for varied reasons. Now such "otherness" is shaped by factors such as the state, society, family life, gender, age, race, and even culture. Pastoral care, therefore, is the response, not only of church leaders, but also of the whole Christian community to the situations of those in need within the church. This largely explains, especially in Constantinople, Chrysostom's appeals to, and warnings against, the rich in the

---

3. Grierson, *Transforming a People of God*, 80.
4. Carroll, "Leadership," in *Studying Congregations*, 173.
5. Lyon, "Relevance of Congregational Studies," 263.

Pastoral Leadership

churches to assume responsibility for giving generously in order to meet the challenge of this "otherness" within the church and society. In this respect, Chrysostom was faced with a huge task and one in which he showed leadership and courage as he taught, encouraged and appealed to the rich to be generous in their alms-giving. The effect of such pastoral care and leadership, which caters for the spiritual and practical needs of the people, will be a greater sense of unity on the part of those within the church.

Here, there are differences between my own situation and that of Chrysostom. For example, divisions in KCPC on two major occasions led to the withdrawal of numerous members and officers of the church; these divisions were traumatic for people, especially those remaining within the church and there was consequently an inevitable feeling of insecurity, a search for identity, a mistrust of leaders as well as a fear that such divisions would be repeated. However, for Chrysostom the unity of the state church was acknowledged widely within and outside the church. Within Constantinople, for example, there were also many churches under his care; each church had a diaconate structure with many deacons in each congregation in addition to the clergy themselves. The church structure there, including its hierarchy of bishop or patriarch, and its inseparable links to the state through the Emperor ensuring uniformity, all functioned to enforce the unity of the church, despite the number of different congregations. Inevitably, there were tensions and one of the most difficult areas for Chrysostom to deal with, in addition to his relationship to the emperor and empress, was the relationship between the rich and the poor in his churches. I respect the way in which he dealt with this tension and obtained adequate money through almsgiving to meet the daily needs of the sick and the poor.

Despite, therefore, dissimilarities between our two pastoral situations, I submit that the pastoral leadership principle of pastoral care that we forged and expressed was similar and had almost identical biblical support in terms of loving one's neighbor, obeying the command of Christ as well as imitating Christ in his concern and love for others.

PASTORAL CHARACTERS: INTEGRITY AND HUMILITY

From the beginning, as he wrote in *On the Priesthood* prior to his ordination, Chrysostom strongly emphasized the moral character, integrity, and spirituality of the priest who must have a Christlike character. He enforced this even more strongly, as we have seen, in his New Testament homilies with particular emphases on the imitation of Christ plus the apostolic model

Conclusion

of Paul's exemplary life, which all the clergy should follow. The latter, as we saw, is a further help to us; it is also a concession in that Paul was just an ordinary man. His example can assist us in approximating to the imitation of Christ. The standard set for church leaders by Scripture, then, is extremely high. Chrysostom, aware of this fact, underlines various strands of biblical teaching in order to highlight and apply his pastoral leadership principle. Church leaders, in other words, should lead in terms of the teaching of the Word but also lead in the examples they set for their churches in daily living. Clearly, this principle was at the heart of Chrysostom's understanding of the clergy and it partly accounts for the sharp, intolerant attitude on his part towards other clergy who lived sensual, immoral lives.

In my own context, through the example of my own father and church minister in Korea, I came to see that commitment to Christ and a call to the ministry of the Word demanded complete integrity on my part and a resolve to become as Christlike as possible. That has been a governing principle for me over many years now in my personal, family, and church life. This principle has been enforced for me in numerous ways. For example, charges brought against my predecessor in KCPC concerning his integrity and lifestyle divided the church and brought many church members to a distressed state. I recognized again how important was my consistent life before the people. Later, when the church divided again in 1981, and when false charges were brought against me and others, I resolved to respond in as Christlike manner as possible. Furthermore, I know that my integrity has enabled the people to trust me and consequently the church grew considerably in the context of loving, godly, and wise biblical leadership. I am not boasting but rather indicating the importance of this pastoral principle of integrity in my life and ministry. Another way in which the principle has been enforced for me was through the study of Scripture in which I saw clearly, just like Chrysostom, the emphasis there on the imitation of Christ and the model of Paul's own life and leadership of the churches. Here, I found considerable encouragement and instruction. I agree fully with Blackaby, Croft, and Dorr that integrity is of primary importance in the Christian ministry today and that at the heart of this is humility and servant leadership with the example of Christ and the model of the apostle Paul in Phil 2:5-8 serving as necessary standards for me. Furthermore, regular examples in the United States of corruption and immorality on the part of well-known preachers and TV evangelists has only re-enforced my

Pastoral Leadership

personal determination to strive for integrity and Christlikeness in my life and ministry.

The context in which I expressed this principle of integrity and spirituality has been varied and multi-faceted. For example, amongst my own Korean people, there is a growing lack of respect for leaders, partly due to their corruption. This is also reflected in Korean churches where personal ambition and the pursuit of power often result in many church divisions. Relationships between a church minister and his predecessor can often be problematic resulting in further division or discord. Or there can be the brevity of pastoral ministries by Korean pastors, which in turn affects qualitative and quantitative church growth. Exercising servant leadership and modeling Christ in terms of integrity, obedience, and compassion has been an enormous challenge within the Korean church context. But the theological undergirding which Chrysostom provides for the imitation of Christ impressed and encouraged me enormously in seeking to a pastor of integrity. I also agree with Chrysostom's spirituality aspect, particularly his emphasis on prayer, the love of pastoral leaders for their people, the importance of the Word, and sacraments. On this pastoral leadership principle, I find myself in full agreement with Chrysostom and we have both endeavored to express the same principles of Christlikeness, integrity, spirituality, and servant leadership in our respective ministries.

BIBLICAL PREACHING

For Chrysostom and myself, the preaching of the Word of God was central in our ministries; as such, it was viewed as the principal way of nurturing the faith and piety of the congregations as well as the means of introducing individuals outside the church to faith in Jesus Christ and to membership of the body of Christ. I have demonstrated already in earlier chapters how this principle of pastoral leadership was expressed in the different situations so there is little need for me to discuss the principle in detail here except to draw attention to several related matters where differences between us do emerge.

For example, if preaching is so central to the ministry and the well-being of the churches, then the training of preachers is of critical importance. Here some differences emerge because my own training was institutional in terms of a college, a seminary and a university, the latter especially for postgraduate studies in order to deepen my knowledge of the Scripture and also develop my skills in the biblical languages. In these ways, I was

Conclusion

equipped in reasonably competent ways to preach the Word and to sustain a preaching ministry in the church over a long period. The Presbyterian Church of America requires four years of college education, followed by three years of theological training in a seminary with a view of becoming a master of divinity (MDiv). In addition to this long period of training, candidates for ordination are required to take written examination. The *PCA Book of Church Order* specifies the areas that are examined prior to ordination: personal character and family management, Greek and Hebrew languages, Bible content, systematic theology, the sacraments, church history, the history of the Presbyterian Church of America, and the Principles and Rules of the Government and Discipline of the Church which relate, of course, to Presbyterian Church polity. I am glad for that training; although it was demanding, lengthy, and costly, my ministry has benefited from that training. In particular, I have been able to employ Hebrew and Greek in the preparation of sermons and Bible studies, which has enriched my understanding of the biblical text and provided more satisfying content for the congregation. While individuals in these different institutions have exercised an influence on me, my training was institutionally based as of necessity so that my Presbyterian denomination was able to recognize that training as being adequate for one of its ministers.

By contrast, the formal training for the priesthood had not been settled in any uniform way in the fourth century. In keeping with the custom and culture of that period, Chrysostom was trained by individuals like Libanus for rhetoric, then philosophy under Andragathius before coming under the mentoring of Meletius, the archbishop of Antioch. Diodorus, the founder of a theological school in Antioch, also influenced Chrysostom profoundly as he encouraged his student to focus more on biblical studies. But here, he imbibed a significant monastic sympathy for the ascetic life. Under another teacher, Syrus, an aged Syrian ascetic, Chrysostom strove to develop self-discipline and an austere lifestyle for a period of four years. This period impaired his health as he fasted often, lived in primitive, solitary conditions in a cave for two years while he studied and memorized the Bible. Such training was long, formative, and broad as well as practical in terms of oratory and learning to develop his spirituality. I cannot but conclude that the latter period of training only heightened his sense of disgust when he met priests and others who were sensual and careless with regard to their spiritual development and ministries. The training was extensive

Pastoral Leadership

and served to equip Chrysostom for his effective ministry in Antioch and Constantinople.

Another difference between us in our preaching relates to the degree of exposition offered in our messages. I endeavored to open up the biblical texts carefully, establishing the context, explaining the words used and the principles being taught in that text or section of Scripture. My failures were many in this respect but at least I endeavored to be as thoroughly biblical and expository as possible so that the congregation felt the challenge of the biblical text and its relevance for them. Chrysostom did this too but my reading of his homilies suggests that this was more variable. As he lacked any facility in the Hebrew language, this led to a greater concentration on the New Testament for exposition. Chrysostom also appears eager to move from the text at times to application, especially when encouraging almsgiving or warning against heresies like Arianism. However, the expository element was there and possibly he was superior to me in the whole area of the application of the Word to his contemporary situation. In some of his sermons, Chrysostom did not attempt to be expository as he dealt with pastoral issues like forgiveness and schism.

Another difference between us in terms of preaching is in terms of oratory. Here Chrysostom excelled and had a wide and deserved reputation for his eloquence and gifts in public speaking. There were few who equaled him in this respect and people from different perspectives and situations acknowledged his outstanding oratorical gifts. For this reason, I cannot compare myself with Chrysostom at all. While I am comfortable in public speaking and preaching, I would not claim to have his eloquence and reputation as a preacher. While there are these differences, I admire the way in which Chrysostom viewed preaching in such a balanced manner in terms of being pastoral, expository, rhetorical and Christological. I endeavored to adopt this approach but less successfully than Chrysostom and yet preaching needs to have these four aspects in order to feed and challenge the church in its life and witness.

CROSS-CULTURAL MISSIONS

This is the only one of the four pastoral leadership principles that is not found in Chrysostom's *On the Priesthood* and which gradually emerged during his ministry in Antioch but more especially in Constantinople. Although it was a somewhat new principle emerging in his homilies and later

Conclusion

ministry, cross-cultural missions was nevertheless an extremely important principle for Chrysostom.

As we saw in the last chapter, Chrysostom was aware of the way in which the church in Jerusalem (Acts 8) had been persecuted, thus making it necessary for many believers to move to other regions, including Antioch. This fact meant a great deal to Chrysostom, namely that mission had been undertaken in the city of Antioch and had resulted in a strong church there. Strangely, we have no historical evidence of Chrysostom's missionary activity in Antioch. Possibly this was due to disinterestedness on the part of historians during and after that period but another plausible reason may be that he was completely absorbed with his preaching ministry and the preparation of his homilies and overseeing the almsgiving ministry to the poor. What is clear is that when he moved to Constantinople as a bishop, he was well aware of the challenge to reach unbelievers of different cultures and languages with the Christian gospel. In fact, it is impressive what he did in this respect and what he achieved. For example, there were immigrants living in his city and for the Germans there he even founded a German national church. Further afield, in areas like Phoenicia, Scythia, and Syria, Chrysostom was concerned for unbelievers as well as for those who had apostatized under Arian influence.

There are five observations I want to make on Chrysostom's fourth pastoral leadership principle with regard to cross-cultural mission. First, he was concerned not only for unbelievers in other areas but also for people there who had apostatized due to Arianism. This was a matter of deep concern to him as he endeavored to safeguard the Trinitarian and strongly Christological character of the Christian faith embraced by the church. Secondly, in recognizing the extensive influence of Arianism, he identified the need for missionaries to be sent to the Goths but such men required language study and training in order to make them effective in their ministries. This was a visionary approach that I greatly admire and Chrysostom took active steps to provide such training. Thirdly, he was also pastoral in that he visited these missionaries when he was able in order to encourage and support them in their work. This aspect of pastoral support for cross-cultural workers is recognized today as being a necessary and wise provision but across the centuries in Chrysostom's day this was radical and effective. Fourthly, it is significant that he was able to maintain a wise balance in maintaining his pastoral leadership principles in Constantinople, despite all the pressures which were upon him and he maintained his local

Pastoral Leadership

ministry and care for the people with a wide vision for the progress of the church in other regions. Fifthly, while there is controversy and misunderstanding concerning Chrysostom's attitude towards the Jews, I am inclined to be kind to him. For one reason, he was fearful of the Judaizing influence on some of the churches on the part of Jews who claimed to be Christians. Possibly he did not express himself well or adequately on this. In addition, balancing his concern for the various Gentile areas and hard-pressed by the subtle influences of Arianism penetrating some of the churches, I can understand that Jewish evangelism may not have had the same priority for him. For these reasons, I find this fourth principle as articulated and expressed in action by Chrysostom to be remarkable for its breadth of vision and concern.

As I turn to my own adoption of this fourth principle and its implementation, I feel that I have done so little compared with Chrysostom. In addition to encouraging personal evangelism locally, I encouraged KCPC to establish a mission agency called the Central Missionary Fellowship; consequently, the church has commissioned several career missionary families and a few short-term workers to seven different countries. In addition, many summer mission teams have been sent out and in 2000. I encouraged the church to found SEED International as an interdenominational mission agency that other churches could also use alongside KCPC. This cross-cultural mission now has eighty missionary families who live and work in thirty-one countries overseas. While other things are also being done in this respect, I feel that in his own situation that Chrysostom's implementation of this principle was far more radical, effective and innovative.

Having now compared somewhat critically these four pastoral leadership principles in two entirely different church situations, I submit that there is substantial agreement between Chrysostom and myself on these principles, while still allowing for differences in terms of implementation and emphases, some of which I have identified above. I leave these principles as practiced and expounded by Chrysostom with increased respect for him and a desire to share some of the findings of this research with others.

POSSIBLE USEFULNESS OF THIS RESEARCH

Having now achieved my aims in providing a case study of my pastoral ministry at KCPC, then identifying key pastoral leadership principles governing my ministry, I entered into conversation with John Chrysostom across the centuries in order to explore his pastoral theology, especially any

Conclusion

pastoral leadership principles that may have regulated his ministry in Antioch and Constantinople. My study of his *On the Priesthood* and a sample of his New Testament homilies revealed that there were four pastoral principles that corresponded closely to my own, albeit expressed differently in some ways and with different emphases in places. However, despite the dissimilarities, I have argued that the similarities between our principles are striking. I acknowledge that more work needs to be done with regard to Chrysostom in terms of more detailed and a more comprehensive analysis of all his homilies and sermons but I submit that my sample has given me a fair and accurate picture of his pastoral theology and of some of the key principles which governed his ministry throughout his time in Antioch and Constantinople. In closing, I would like to suggest ways in which this research can be useful in the future.

Church Clergies and Presbyters

My research is extremely relevant for the clergy and reinforces much of what has been said in recent pastoral theology. I suggest there are five pressing areas where my research can be helpful with regard to church leaders:

1. Areas of Moral Integrity and Spirituality

I am persuaded from my own experience of ministry and what I have observed in other churches that a warm, gracious spirituality that is rooted in a deep trust in God is an essential prerequisite for any shepherd to God's people. Declining moral standards in society, coupled with secularization and the postmodern denial of objective truth as well as absolute standards have undermined the lifestyle of some clergy and this has brought considerable discredit on the churches and the way that society perceives the church in general. I struggle with this problem and I wonder how integrity and holiness can be fostered and maintained. At the basic level, it is the means of grace provided in and by the church, such as the Word preached and taught, the sacraments, prayer, and fellowship, which should, under God, be encouraging and sustaining individual church members in their desire to be more Christlike. Personal mentoring is also necessary, as well as the provision of good, exemplary models of contemporary Christians who consistently live out their faith in the pressures of family and social life. I have no easy answers and I continue to wrestle with this issue but I cannot but feel that the example of Chrysostom and of that of my own ministry can be useful supplements in this respect.

Pastoral Leadership

Spirituality is essential for pastoral leaders, specifically one that is rooted in the Word of God and dynamically related to the Holy Spirit. This balance between the Word and Spirit that is expressed in holy living is an essential feature in my Reformed tradition. On this principle, experience is not exalted over and above objective truth so there is no excessive and wild emotionalism being encouraged. On the other hand, the priority of the Word must not result in a mere intellectualism that despises the experimental. Rather, this formula is a necessary one, and I would like my research to be shared with clergy more widely in order for these matters to be considered even more seriously.

2. The Need for Clergy to Understand their Congregation

In this respect, John Patton alerts us to the fact that a central part of the ministry of pastoral care today is discerning the contexts most relevant for understanding a pastoral situation. Multiple contexts to be considered include the whole situation, the background, and the environment but Patton reminds us that the context most influential for pastoral theology in the United States have been race, culture, gender, and power.[6] His reference to "multiple contexts" is pregnant with meaning and warns us that there is need to look in greater depth at our church congregations in order to appreciate the range of factors that influence our people. Jackson Carroll reinforces the point, namely, that each congregation develops its own identity and is shaped by its heritage, context and the varied characteristics of its members. Similarly, Denham Grierson poses the theological question: "what forms, shapes, and sustains a faith community?" He, too, emphasizes the time and location, language, ways in which intimacy is expressed among the people and then the existence of a consensus regarding what is affirmed but also the circumstances in which the congregation struggles to know itself.[7] In these respects, my research may alert some clergy to reflect in greater depth on these "multiple contexts" of their congregations and which in turn may foster more appropriate pastoral care for the people.

3. Pastoral and Spiritual Care

Each congregation, whatever its denomination, is a corporate body with numerous and varied tasks committed to it by God. Encouraging a people

---

6. Patton, "Modern Pastoral Theology," in Woodward and Pattison's *Blackwell Reader*, 55.

7. Grierson, *Transforming a People of God*, 11.

Conclusion

to trust God, to experience God in his grace and power, then to please God in their private, family, and corporate life together needs to be a priority. At the same time, however, the congregation needs to learn to live as a family and to be relational or people centered in their dealings with one another. This is an aspect that needs always to be developed and strengthened. In addition to this, there are the challenges of poverty, hunger, injustice, racial hatred, domestic violence, and drug abuse that cry out for the compassion and help of the church. There is a tension here in maintaining a biblical balance for a congregation and maintaining priorities. My research can point to ways in which Chrysostom endeavored to secure this balance and hopefully my own experience at KCPC can be suggestive in working this tension out in a contemporary situation. The contemporary challenge is to maintain excellent spiritual care for the congregation through the ministry of the Word, the sacraments, prayer, fellowship, and visitation while still mobilizing the congregation as a body to care for others. There are theological questions, too, which need to be addressed, especially concerning the precise relationship between the gospel itself and social work. These questions, while they are outside the scope of this dissertation, require careful reflection.

4. Pastoral Training

This is an area where, I believe, my research can be helpful in stimulating those who are responsible for preparing and revising training programs for clergy and missionary personnel. A considerable part of the training provided today can be intellectual and theological but often with limited practical experience of ministry. What may be lacking or weak in some programs is the emphasis on godly character, spirituality, and a genuine caring compassion for people, both in the congregation and in the wider community. Consequently, younger clergy or missionaries may emerge from colleges and seminaries with little interest in people and few interpersonal skills so that they are unable to care for others in genuine and fruitful ways. There is also a tendency to spend all one's time studying for preaching or engaging in the minimum amount possible of pastoral visitation and care or concentrating on administration rather than on the people themselves. Possibly this research and reflection on key pastoral leadership principles can be adapted by one or more of the seminaries to develop an additional track for pastoral leadership training, which will address some

Pastoral Leadership

of the inherent weaknesses current in clergy practice with regard to integrity, spirituality, and fostering greater care for those in the congregation.

The research can be particularly helpful also in strengthening the training for mission personnel. Prior to my retirement, I established the Imitating Christ Missionary Training School (ICMS) in order to provide a basic missionary candidates training program for individuals intending to join SEED International as career missionaries. This training program provides five weeks of training and the curriculum has included basic orientation, meditation on the Word, discipleship training, character of Christ, practical aspects of the missionary's life, the practice of prayer and the ministry of the Holy Spirit, intercessory prayer, the nature and enjoyment of personal union with Christ, team ministry, pastoral leadership, and an introduction to the mission statement and core values of SEED International. Clearly, this curriculum is extremely practical as it is intended to prepare candidates more adequately for their future ministries. However, my ultimate intent is to strengthen the importance of godly character, integrity, Christlikeness, and servant leadership. In this way, the principles identified and discussed in this research are being applied in a contemporary situation to missionary candidates.

5. Conflict Management.

Having experienced the trauma and effects of two major divisions in KCPC and, in addition, having witnessed similar and more frequent divisions in other Korean-American churches, I suggest that this research may be helpful both to clergy and church members in responding appropriately to conflict and unrest in their local churches. Here again, the ingredients of integrity, spirituality, humility, and genuine care for the people are necessary in any approach if conflict management is to be even partly successful. Again, a deeper understanding of the "multiple contexts" within the local church can be helpful in identifying those factors that may be contributing to the conflict. I submit that my own case study regarding KCPC and my reflection on Chrysostom's relationship to his own congregations can be fruitful for clergy in approaching and understanding situations of possible or actual conflict.

Conclusion

CHURCH CONGREGATIONS

Considering Potential Pastors and Leaders

There may be ways in which this research can assist congregations in their reflection concerning the kind of pastor and leaders they need in their churches. From my own case study and the principles I have identified in Chrysostom's ministry, members of church congregations may receive insights into leadership qualities and ways in which pastors can work effectively with their congregations in a united and dynamic way to bring the church to greater spiritual maturity.

From this research I suggest the need for a pastor and those leading alongside to be well-grounded in the Scripture, to be committed to preaching and communicating the Word effectively, interested and concerned for people within the church, a motivator who has vision and wisdom yet who can be deeply respected for their integrity and spirituality. Too often, the choice of church leaders can be made on the basis of mere personality, eloquence, organization, academic qualifications, or even age but without an awareness of the essential qualities that are needed in such leaders.

In this respect, I would encourage congregations not to entertain the possibility of a pastor's relative—such as a son or a nephew—being appointed as a successor when the pastor retires or moves away. Similarly, I suggest to congregations that they can contribute significantly by demanding greater evidence of a servant-type role for their pastor so that the current tendency within Korean Presbyterian churches of treating the pastor as a powerful, unrivalled dictatorship can be weakened and corrected. If the last two suggestions are adopted, then a congregation may well avoid potential conflict and disillusionment.

A Self-Critical Approach

Recent congregational studies over the last two to three decades have been most useful in exposing and discussing the complexities that exist within each congregation and the "multiple contexts" that normally prevail. I have already hinted at some of these "multiple contexts" in this dissertation but a congregation can often be oblivious of these different contexts and influences with the result that a superficial understanding of that congregation may prevail amongst the members. For this reason I would like to use and adapt parts of this research in order to encourage and stimulate congregations to be more self-critical and objective in reassessing the qualitative life

Pastoral Leadership

of their church. The purpose would not be to lay the blame on the shoulders of church leaders, necessarily, but to attempt to achieve mutual understanding of their situations in order to promote unity, fellowship, compassion, and prayerful support for the leaders. I believe this could be a useful contribution, if it is done sensitively and in a supportive manner. There are various ways of achieving this and I may need assistance in determining the best approach. I encourage church members to become historians and sociologists as well as theologians by working through a questionnaire or a worksheet where direction and assistance are given to them in order to stimulate their own reflection on the nature, history, location, mix, and life of their own congregation. This could be useful and beneficial in so many ways.

Encouraging Qualitative Church Growth

There are areas of application of the four pastoral leadership principles identified in this dissertation that, I suggest, can be incorporated into a teaching manual for the benefit of church members. One of my particular concerns is in the area of spirituality and integrity, which are foundational to any church in its life and witness. While respecting the calling of the clergy, too sharp a distinction between clergy and laity can serve to disengage the laity from their responsibilities and privileges within the body of Christ. One troubling aspect is the perspective that prayer and integrity are only to be expected from the professional leaders or that evangelism and pastoral care are the exclusive duties of the clergy rather than the responsibility of the entire congregation. Under some models of leadership, this tendency can be more exaggerated but my appeal is that whatever model is used with regard to church leadership, my four leadership principles can unify congregations and bring about a vibrant and growing church in a locality. Therefore, I view integrity of character and spirituality in terms of prayer and a vital, genuine trust in God, and experience of his grace to be features that ought to permeate the entire congregation. This manual, then, seeks to pick up some of these areas of application in an encouraging, not a condemnatory, manner and gently move members of the congregation into greater spiritual maturity. In that process I anticipate that church members will gain more insight into the pressures on their church leaders and also areas where they can relieve, support, and enhance their work. Preferably, I will use such a manual in smaller groups, such as in a cell group, where

Conclusion

individuals are free to explore these aspects and learn themselves. I suggest that this method may be more effective and fruitful long-term.

In these preceding ways, it is hoped that this research can feed into pastoral theology, but more especially into theological training for the ordained ministry as well as encouraging local congregations to reflect creatively concerning themselves and their corporate life and witness as churches. This may be overly optimistic on my part, but I want to share with these churches and seminaries the benefits I have gained from this conversation—if Patristic scholars devote more attention to Chrysostom's pastoral theology in the future, then I will be delighted.

Bibliography

Abramowski, Rudolf. "Der theologische Nachlass des Diodor von Tarsus." *Zeitschrift fur Die Neutestamentliche Wissenschaft* 42 (1949) 30–31.
Adams, Jay E. *Shepherding God's Flock*. Grand Rapids: Zondervan, 1974.
Aldama, J. A. *Repertorium Pseudochrysostomicum*. Paris: Editions du Centre National de la Recherche Scientifique, 1965.
Ameringer, Thomas Edward. "The Stylistic Influence of the Second Sophistic on the Panegyrical Sermons of St. John Chrysostom: a Study in Greek Rhetoric." PhD diss., Catholic University of America, 1921.
Ammerman, Nancy et al., eds. *Studying Congregations: A New Handbook*. Nashville: Abingdon, 1998.
Anderson, Glausha. *The Element of Chrysostom's Power as a Preacher*. Chicago: University of Chicago Press, 1903.
Anderson, Ray S. *Shape of Practical Theology: Empowering Ministry with Theological Praxis*. Downers Grove, IL: InterVarsity, 2001.
Armstrong, A. H. *An Introduction to Ancient Philosophy*. Westminster, MD: Newman, 1949.
Armstrong, John H., ed. *Reforming Pastoral Ministry*. Wheaton, IL: Crossway, 2001.
Arndt, William F. and F. Wilbur Gingrich. *A Greek-English Lexicon of the New Testament and Other Early Christian Literature*. Chicago: University of Chicago Press, 1979.
Attwater, Donald. *St. John Chrysostom: Pastor and Preacher*. London: Catholic Book Club, 1959.
Augustine, Saint. *A Treatise on the Spirit and the Letter*. In vol. 5 of *NPNF*. Translated by Benjamin B. Warfield, 103. Grand Rapids: Eerdmans, 1997.
Ballard, Paul and John Prichard. *Practical Theology in Action*. London: SPCK, 2001.
Barr, James. *Comparative Philology and the Text of the Old Testament*. Oxford: Clarendon, 1968.
Barrett, C. K. *The First Epistle to the Corinthians*. In *Black's New Testament Commentary*. Peabody, MA: Hendrickson, 1996.
———. *The Gospel According to St. John*. 2nd ed. Philadelphia: Westminster, 1978.
Barth, Karl. *Church Dogmatics*. Vol. 4. Translated by G. W. Bromiley. Edited by T. F. Torrance. Edinburgh: T. & T. Clark, 2000.
Basil, Saint. *On the Holy Spirit*. New York: St. Vladimir's Seminary Press, 1980.
———. *Letters*. Translated by Roy J. Deferrari. Cambridge: Harvard University Press, 2000.

Bibliography

———. *Way to Paradise*. Edited by Oliver Davies. Translated by Tim Witherow. London: New City, 1991.
Baur, Chrysostomus. *Der heilige Johannes Chrysostomus und seine Zeit*. 2 vols. Munchen: M. Hueber, 1929-30.
———. *John Chrysostom and His Time*, 2 vols. Translated by M. Gonzaga. Westminster, MD: Newman, 1959.
———."Wann ist der hl. Chrysostomus geboren?" In *Zeitschrift fur Katholische Theologie* (1928) 4001-406.
Bavinck, J. H. *An Introduction to the Science of Missions*. Translated by David H. Freeman. Phillipsburg, NJ: Presbyterian & Reformed, 1960.
Baxter, Richard. *The Reformed Pastor*. Portland, OR: Multnomah, 1982.
Benestad, J. Brian. "Chrysostom on Wealth and Poverty." *Diakonia* 23:1 (1990) 201-10.
Blackaby, Henry and Richard. *Spiritual Leadership*. Nashville: Broadman & Holman, 2001.
Blanchard, Ken. "Reflections on Encourage the Heart." In *Christian Reflections on The Leadership Challenge*, edited by James M. Kouzes and Barry Z. Posner. San Francisco: Jossey-Bass, 2004.
Bloede, Louis W. *The Effective Pastor: A Guide to Successful Ministry*. Minneapolis: Fortress, 1996.
Bock, Darrell L. *Jesus According to Scripture: Restoring the Portrait from the Gospels*. Grand Rapids: Baker Academic, 2002.
Bosch, David J. *Transforming Mission: Paradigm Shift in Theology of Mission*. New York: Orbis, 1999.
Bouchier, E. S. *A Short History of Antioch*. London: Basil Blackwell, 1921.
Brandle, Rudolf. *Johannes Chrysostomus: Bischof, Reformer, Martyrer*. Stuttgart: Kohlhammer, 1999.
———. "Gott wird nicht allein durch richtige Dogmen, sondern auch durch einen gutten Lebenswandel verrlicht." *Theologische Zeitschrift* 55 (1999) 121-36.
Brock, Sebastian P. *Spirituality in the Syrian Tradition*. Kerala, India: St. Ephrem Ecumenical Research Institute, 1989.
Brown, Raymond E. and John P. Meier. *Antioch and Rome: New Testament Cradles of Catholic Christianity*. New York: Paulist, 1983.
———. *The Gospel According to John*. In *The Anchor Bible* 29. New York: Doubleday, 1970.
Browning, Robert. "The Riot of AD 387 in Antioch," *Journal of Roman Studies* 42 (1952) 13-20.
Bruce, F. F. *1 & 2 Thessalonians*. In *Word Biblical Commentary* 45. Waco, TX: Word, 1982.
Buber, Martin. *Israel and the World: Essays in a Time of Crisis*. New York: Schocken, 1948.
Bultmann, Rudolf. *The Gospel of John: A Commentary*. Translated by G. R. Beasley-Murray. Philadelphia: Westminster, 1971.
Burger, Douglas Clyde. *A Complete Bibliography of the Scholarship on the Life and Works of Saint John Chrysostom*. Evanston, IL: Self Published, 1964.
Bush, R. Wheler. *The Life and Times of Chrysostom*. London: Religious Tract Society, 1885.
Buttrick, David. *Homiletic*. Philadelphia: Fortress, 1987.
Calvin, John. *Calvin's Commentaries: The Gospels*. Vol. 7. Grand Rapids: Associated Press, 1965.
———. *Institutes of the Christian Religion*. Translated by Henry Beverridge. Grand Rapids: Eerdmans, 1970.

Bibliography

Carroll, Jackson. "Leadership and the Study of the Congregation." In *Studying Congregations*, edited by Nancy T. Ammerman, 167–95. Nashville: Abingdon, 1998.

Carroll, Jackson et al., eds. *Handbook for Congregational Studies*. Nashville: Abington, 1987.

Carter, Robert. "The Chronology of Saint John Chrysostom's Early Life," *Traditio* 18 (1962) 357–62.

———. "The Future of Chrysostom Studies: Theology and Nachleben." In *Symposium: Studies on St. John Chrysostom*. Thessaloniki: Patriaxikon Ilryma Paterikon Meleton, 1973.

Castelli, Elizabeth A. *Imitating Paul: A Discourse of Power*. Louisville, KY: Westminster John Knox, 1991.

Chae, Young Chang. *The History of the Korean Community of Washington, D.C.* Washington D.C.: Korean Society of Washington, D.C., 1994.

Chambers, Paul. *Religion, Secularization, and Social Change in Wales*. Cardiff: University of Wales Press, 2005.

Chapell, Bryan. *Christ-Centered Preaching*. Grand Rapids: Baker, 1994.

Chase, Frederic Henry. *Chrysostom: A Study in the History of Biblical Interpretation*. London: George Bell, 1887.

Childs, Brevard S. *The Book of Exodus*. Louisville, KY: Westminster John Knox, 1974.

Christo, Gus George. *Bishop as Successors to the Apostles according to John Chrysostom: Ecclesiastical Authority in the Early Church*. Lewiston, NY: Mellen, 2008.

———. *The Church's Identity: Established through Images according to Saint John Chrysostom*. Rollinsford, NH: Orthodox Research Institute, 2006.

———. *Martyrdom According to John Chrysostom*. Lewiston, NY: Mellen University Press, 1997.

Chrysostom, St. John. *Apologist*. Translated by Margaret A. Schatkin and Paul W. Harkins, the Fathers of the Church. Edited by Thomas P. Halton. Vol. 73. Washington, D.C.: Catholic University of America Press, 1985.

———. *Baptismal Instructions*. In Ancient Christian Writers 31. Translated by Paul W. Harkins. Edited by Johannes Quasten. New York: Paulist, 1963.

———. *Chrysostom and His Message: A Selection from the Sermons of St. John Chrysostom of Antioch and Constantinople*. Edited by Stephen Neil. London: Lutterworth, 1963.

———. *Commentary on the Psalms*. Translated by Robert C. Hill. 2 vols. Brookline, MA: Holy Cross Orthodox Press, 1998.

———. *A Comparison between a King and a Monk / Against the Opponents of the Monastic Life*. In Studies in the Bible and Early Christianity 13. Translated by David G. Hunter. Lampeter, Wales: Mellen, 1988.

———. *Concerning Lowliness of Mind*. In vol. 9 of *NPNF*, Series 1. Translated by R. Blackburn. Edited by Philip Schaff, 147–55. Peabody, MA: Hendrickson, 1994.

———. *Discourses against Judaizing Christians*. In Fathers of the Church, translated by Paul W. Harkins. Vol. 68. Washington, D. C.: Catholic University of America Press, 1979.

———. *An Exhortation to Theodore after His Fall*. In vol. 9 of *NPNF*, Series 1. Translated by W.R.W. Stephens. Edited by Philip Schaff, 91–116. Peabody, MA: Hendrickson, 1994.

———. *Letter to a Young Widow*. In vol. 9 of *NPNF*, Series 1. Translated by W.R.W. Stephens. Edited Philip Schaff, 121–28. Peabody, MA: Hendrickson, 1994.

———. *In Praise of Saint Paul*. Translated by Thomas Halton. Boston: St. Paul, 1963.

Bibliography

———. *The Homilies on the Acts of the Apostles*. In vol. 11 of *NPNF*, Series 1. Translated by J. Walker, J. Sheppard and H. Browne, 1–328. Grand Rapids: Eerdmans, 1997.

———. *The Homilies on the Epistle of St. Paul the Apostle to the Romans*. In vol. 11 of *NPNF*, Series 1. Translated by J. R. Morris and W. H. Simcox. Edited by Philip Schaff, 335–572. Grand Rapids: Eerdmans, 1997.

———. *The Homilies on the Epistles of Paul to the First Corinthians*. In vol. 12 of *NPNF*, Series 1. Translated by Talbot W. Chambers. Edited by Philip Schaff, 1–269. Grand Rapids: Eerdmans, 1997.

———. *The Homilies on the Epistles of Paul to the Second Corinthians*. In vol. 12 of *NPNF*, Series 1. Translated by Talbot W. Chambers. Edited by Philip Schaff, 271–420. Grand Rapids: Eerdmans, 1997.

———. *The Commentary on the Epistle of St. Paul to the Galatians*. In vol. 13 of *NPNF*, Series 1. Translated by Gross Alexander. Edited by Philip Schaff, 1–48. Grand Rapids: Eerdmans, 1994.

———. *The Homilies on the Epistle of St. Paul to the Ephesians*. In vol. 13 of *NPNF*, Series 1. Translated by Gross Alexander. Edited by Philip Schaff, 49–172. Grand Rapids: Eerdmans, 1994.

———. *The Homilies on the Epistle of St. Paul to Philippians*. In vol. 13 of *NPNF*, Series 1. Translated by Gross Alexander. Edited by Philip Schaff, 181–255. Grand Rapids: Eerdmans, 1994.

———. *The Homilies on the Epistle of St. Paul to Colossians*. In vol. 13 of *NPNF*, Series 1. Translated by Gross Alexander. Edited by Philip Schaff, 257–321. Grand Rapids: Eerdmans, 1994.

———. *The Homilies on the Epistle of St. Paul to the First Thessalonians*. In vol. 13 of *NPNF*, Series 1. Translated by Gross Alexander. Edited by Philip Schaff, 324–75. Grand Rapids: Eerdmans, 1994.

———. *The Homilies on the Epistle of St. Paul to the Second Thessalonians*. In vol. 13 of *NPNF*, Series 1. Translated by Gross Alexander. Edited by Philip Schaff, 377–98. Grand Rapids: Eerdmans, 1994.

———. *The Homilies on the First Epistle of St. Paul to Timothy*, In vol. 13 of *NPNF*, Series 1. Translated by Gross Alexander. Edited by Philip Schaff, 407–73. Grand Rapids: Eerdmans, 1994.

———. *The Homilies on the Second Epistle of St. Paul to Timothy*. In vol. 13 of *NPNF*, Series 1. Translated by Gross Alexander. Edited by Philip Schaff, 475–518. Grand Rapids: Eerdmans, 1994.

———. *The Homilies on the Epistle of St. Paul to Titus*. In vol. 13 of *NPNF*, Series 1. Translated by Gross Alexander. Edited by Philip Schaff, 519–34. Grand Rapids: Eerdmans, 1994.

———. *The Homilies on the Epistle of St. Paul to Philemon*. In vol. 13 of *NPNF*, Series 1. Translated by Gross Alexander. Edited by Philip Schaff, 545–65. Grand Rapids: Eerdmans, 1994.

———. *The Homilies on the Epistle to the Hebrews*. In vol. 14 of *NPNF*, Series 1. Translated by Frederic Gardiner. Edited by Philip Schaff, 363–522. Grand Rapids: Eerdmans, 1996.

———. *The Homilies on Genesis 1–17*. Translated by Robert C. Hill, the Fathers of the Church. Edited by Thomas P. Halton. Vol. 74. Washington, D.C.: Catholic University of America Press, 1986.

Bibliography

———. *The Homilies on Genesis 18–45*. Translated by Robert C. Hill, the Fathers of the Church. Edited by Thomas P. Halton. Vol. 82. Washington, D.C.: Catholic University of America, 1990.

———. *The Homilies on Genesis 46–67*. Translated by Robert C. Hill, the Fathers of the Church. Edited by Thomas P. Halton. Vol. 87. Washington, D.C.: Catholic University of America, 1992.

———. *Homilies on the Gospel of St. Matthew*. In vol. 10 of *NPNF*, Series 1. Translated by George Prevost Barronet. Edited by Philip Schaff, 1–545. Grand Rapids: Eerdmans, 1998.

———. *The Homilies on the Gospel of St. John*. In vol. 14 of *NPNF*, Series 1. Edited by Philip Schaff, 1–334. Grand Rapids: Eerdmans, 1996.

———. *The Homilies on the Statues to the People of Antioch*. In vol. 9 of *NPNF*, Series 1. Translated by W.R.W. Stephens. Edited by Philip Schaff, 331–489. Peabody, MA: Hendrickson, 1994.

———. *On Incomprehensible Nature of God*. In Fathers of the Church, translated by Paul W. Harkins. Vol. 72. Washington, D. C.: Catholic University of America Press, 1984.

———. *On Living Simply*. Edited by Robert Van de Weyer. Liguori, MO: Triumph, 1996.

———. *On Marriage and Family Life*. Translated by Catherine P. Roth and David Anderson. New York: St Vladimir's Seminary Press, 2000.

———. *On Repentance and Almsgiving*. Translated by Gus George Christo, The Fathers of the Church. Edited by Thomas P. Halton. Vol. 96. Washington, D.C.: Catholic University of America Press, 1998.

———. *On the Priesthood: A Treatise in Six Books*. Translated by Patrick Boyle. Westminster, MD: Newman, 1943.

———. *On Wealth and Poverty*. Translated by Catharine P. Roth. New York: St Vladimir's Seminary Press, 1999.

———. *The Preaching of Chrysostom: Homilies on the Sermon on the Mount*. Edited by Jaroslav Pelikan. Philadelphia: Fortress, 1967.

———. *Priesthood*. Translated by W. A. Jurgens. New York: Macmillan, 1955.

———. *Six Books On the Priesthood*. Translated by Graham Neville. New York: St. Vladimir's Seminary Press, 2002.

———. *Spiritual Gems from the Book of Psalms*. Translated by Robert Charles Hill. Boston: Holy Cross Orthodox, 2004.

———. *Treatise Concerning the Christian Priesthood*. In vol. 9 of *NPNF*. Translated by W.R.W. Stephens. Edited by Philip Schaff, 33–83. Peabody, MA: Hendrickson, 1994.

Chung, Peter H., Harold Kim and Sara Yoon, "The Providence of God in the Life of Rev. Won Sang Lee." In *The Keimyung Pioneers*, edited by Jung Hwan Kim, 415–25.

Clarke, Andrew D. *Serve the Community: Christians as Leaders and Ministers*. Grand Rapids: Eerdmans, 2000.

Clowney, Edmund P. *The Church: Contours of Christian Theology*. Downers Grove, IL: InterVarsity, 1995.

Coleman, Robert E. *The Mater Plan of Evangelism*. Old, NJ: Revell, 1981.

Coleman-Norton, P. R. "St. Chrysostom and Greek Philosophers," *Classical Philology* 25 (1930) 305–17.

Collins, Jim. *Good to Great: Why Some Companies Make the Leap and Others Don't*. New York: HarperCollins, 2001.

Collins, Jim, and Jerry Porras. *Built to Last: Successful Habits of Visionary Companies*. New York: Harper Business, 1994.

Bibliography

Comiskey, Joel. *Groups of 12: A New Way to Mobilize Leaders and Multiply Groups in Your Church*. Houston: Touch, 1999.

———. *Leadership Explosion: Multiplying Cell Group Leaders to Reap the Harvest*. Houston: Touch, 2000.

Cooper, John M., ed. *Plato*. Translated by G. M. A. Grube. Indianapolis: Hackett, 1997.

Cornick, David. *Letting God Be God*. London: Darton, Longman, & Todd, 2008.

Covey, Stephen R. *The 7 Habits of Highly Effective People: Powerful Lessons in Personal Change*. New York: Simon & Schuster, 2013.

Craddock, Fred B. *Overhearing the Gospel*. St. Louis, MO: Chalice, 2002.

Cranfield, C. *Romans*. Edinburgh: T & T Clark, 1989.

Croft, Steven. *Ministry in Three Dimensions: Ordination and Leadership in the Local Church*. London: Darton, Longman, & Todd, 1999.

———. *Transforming Communities: Re-imaging the Church for 21st Century*. London: Darton, Longman, & Todd, 2002.

Crouzel, Henri. *Origen*. Translated by A. S. Worrall. Edinburgh: T. & T. Clark, 1999.

D'Alton, J. F. *Selections from St. John Chrysostom*. London: Burns, Oates, & Washbourne, 1940.

Davies, Daniel M. *The Life and Thought of Henry Gerhard Appenzeller (1858–1902), Missionary to Korea*. Lewiston, NY: Edwin Mellen, 1988.

Davies, Eryl. *The Ultimate Rescue: Christ's Saving Work on the Cross*. Durham, NC: Evangelical, 1995.

De Boer, Willis Peter. *The Imitation of Paul: An Exegetical Study*. Kampen: Vrije Universiteit Te Amsterdam, 1962.

De Mendieta, Emmanuel Amand. "The Unwritten and Secret Apostolic Traditions in the Theological Thought of St. Basil of Caesarea." In *Scottish Journal of Theology Occasional Papers*. Vol. 13. Edinburgh: Oliver and Boyd, 1965.

De Paverd, Frans van. *St. John Chrysostom: The Homilies on the Statues*. Roma: Pont. Institutum Studiorum Orientalium, 1991.

Delitzsch, Franz. *Biblical Commentary on the Prophecies of Isaiah*. Vol. 2. Edinburgh: T & T Clark, 1890.

Dever, Mark. *Nine Marks of a Healthy Church*. Wheaton, IL: Crossway, 2004.

Dorr, Donald. *Faith at Work: A Spirituality of Leadership*. Collegeville, MN: Liturgical, 2006.

Downey, Glanville. *Ancient Antioch*. Princeton: Princeton University Press, 1963.

———. *Antioch: In the Age of Theodocius the Great*. Norman, Oklahoma: University of Oklahoma Press, 1962.

Dreyfus, Francois. "Divine Condescendence as a Hermeneutic Principle of the Old testament in Jewish and Christian Tradition." *Immanuel* 19 (1984) 74.

Drucker, Peter F. *Management Challenges for the 21st Century*. New York: Harper Business, 1999.

Dudley, Carl. *Building Effective Ministry: Theory and Practice in the Local Church*. San Francisco: Harper & Row, 1983.

Dudley, Carl, et al., eds. *Carriers of Faith: Lessons from Congregational Studies*. Louisville, KY: Westminster John Knox, 1991.

Dunn, James D. G. *The Christ & The Spirit: Christology*. Vol. 1. Grand Rapids: Eerdmans, 1998.

Bibliography

―――. "Christ, Adam, and Preexistence." In *Where Christology Began: Essays on Philippians 2*, edited by Ralph P. Martin and Brian J. Doo, 74–83. Louisville, KY: Westminster John Knox, 1998.
―――. *Christology in Making*. London: SCM, 1992.
Esler, Philip F., ed. *The Early Christian World*. 2 Vols. London: Routledge, 2000.
Ettlinger, Gerald H. Review of *John Chrysostom*, by Wendy Mayer and Pauline Allen. *Theological Studies* 62 (2001) 422–23.
―――. "Some Historical Evidence for the Date of St. John Chrysostom's Birth." *Traditio* 16 (1960) 372–80.
Eusebius, Pamphilus. *The Ecclesiastical History*. Translated by Christian Frederick Cruse. Grand Rapids: Baker, 1988.
Fairweather, Janet. "The Epistle to the Galatians and Classical Rhetoric." *Tyndale Bulletin* 45 (1994) 213–42.
Fantham, Elaine. "Imitation and Decline: Rhetorical Theory and Practice in the First Century after Christ." *Classical Philology* 73 (1978) 102–16.
Fee, Gordon D. *The First Epistle to the Corinthians*. Grand Rapids: Eerdmans, 1987.
―――. *Paul's Letter to the Philippians*. Grand Rapids: Eerdmans, 1995.
Ferguson, Everett. *Background of Early Christianity*. Grand Rapids: Eerdmans, 1987.
Fong, Ken Uyeda. *Pursuing the Pearl: A Comprehensive Resource for Multi-Asian Ministry*. Valley Forge, PA: Judson, 1999.
Ford, David C. *Women and Men in the Early Church: The Full Views of St. John Chrysostom*. South Canaan, PA: St. Tikhon's Seminary Press, 1999.
Forshaw, B. "Doctor of the Church." In *The New Catholic Encyclopedia*, edited by William J. McDonald, 938. Vol. 4. Washington, D.C.: Catholic University of America, 1967.
Gardner, John W. *On Leadership*. New York: The Free Press, 1990.
Garrett, Duane A. *An Analysis of the Hermeneutic of John Chrysostom's Commentary on Isaiah 1–8*. 12 vols. Lewiston, NY: Mellen, 1992.
George, Carl F. *The Coming Church Revolution: Empowering Leaders for the Future*. Grand Rapids: Fleming H. Revell, 1994.
Gerkin, Charles V. *An Introduction to Pastoral Care*. Nashville: Abingdon, 1997.
Gibbs, Eddie. *Church Next: Quantum Changes in How We do Ministry*. Downers Grove, IL: InterVarsity, 2000.
―――. *I Believe in Church Growth*. Grand Rapids: Eerdmans, 1981.
Gibbs, Eddie, and Ryan Bolger. *Emerging Churches: Creating Christian Community in Postmodern Cultures*. Grand Rapids: Baker, 2005.
Gilchrist, Paul R., ed. *The Book of Church Order*. Atlanta: Office of the State Clerk of the General Assembly of the Presbyterian Church in America, 1995.
Gillard, Geoffrey V. "God in Gen. 1:26 according to Chrysostom." *Studia Biblica* 1 (1978) 149–56.
Glasser, Arthur. *Announcing the Kingdom*. Grand Rapids: Baker, 2003.
Goleman, Daniel. *Emotional Intelligence*. New York: Bantam, 1997.
―――. *Primal Leadership: Realizing the Power of Emotional Intelligence*. Cambridge: Harvard Business School Press, 2002.
Goodall, Blake. *The Homilies of St. John Chrysostom on the Letters of St. Paul to Titus and Philemon*. Vol. 20. Berkeley: University of California Press, 1979.
Greeley, Dolores. "The Church as Body of Christ According to the Teaching of Saint John Chrysostom." PhD diss., University of Notre Dame, 1971.

Bibliography

———. "St. John Chrysostom: Prophet of Social Justice." *Studia Patristica* 17 (1982) 1163–68.
Greer, Rowan A. "The Antiochene Christology of Christology of Diodore of Tarsus." *Journal of Theological Studies New Series* 16 (1966) 341.
———. "Reflection on Priestly Authority." *Saint Luke's Journal of Theology* 34 (1991) 103–13.
Gregory the Great. *Pastoral Practice*. Translated by John Leinenweber. Harrisburg: Trinity Press International, 1998.
Gregory of Nazianzus. "On the First Principles." In *Poemata Arcana*, translated by D. A. Sykes. Oxford: Clarendon, 1997.
———. "On Silence at the Time of Fasting." In *Gregory of Nazianzus Autobiographical Poems*, translated by Carolinne White. Cambridge: Cambridge University Press, 1996.
———. *Oration II (In Defense of His Flight to Pontus, Apologeticus de fuga)*, In vol. 5 of *NPNF*, Series 2. Translated by Charles Gordon Browne. Grand Rapids: Eerdmans, 1958.
Gregory of Nyssa. *The Great Catechism*. In vol. 5 of *NPNF*. Translated by William Moor. 501–02. Grand Rapids: Eerdmans, 1997.
———. *The Lord's Prayer and the Beatitudes*. In *Ancient Christian Writers* 18. Translated by Hilda C. Graef. New York: Paulist, 1954.
Gredanus, Sidney. *Preaching Christ from the Old Testament: A Contemporary Hermeneutical Method*. Grand Rapids: Eerdmans, 1999.
Grierson, Denham. *A People on the Way: Congregation, Mission & Australian Culture*. Melbourne, Australia: D. Lovell, 1991.
———. *Transforming a People of God*. Melbourne, Australia: Board of Christian Education of Australia, 1984.
Grillmeier, Aloys. *Christ in Christian Tradition*. Translated by J. S. Bowden. New York: Sheed & Ward, 1965.
Groothuis, Douglas R. *Unmasking the New Age*. Downers Grove, IL: InterVarsity, 1986.
Grudem, Wayne. *Systematic Theology*. Grand Rapids: Zondervan, 1994.
Guest, Mathew, Karin Tusting, and Linda Woodhead. *Congregational Studies in the UK: Christianity in a Post-Christian Context*. Burlington, VT: Ashgate, 2004.
Gundry, Robert H. *Mark: A Commentary on His Apology for the Cross*. Grand Rapids, Eerdmans, 1993.
Gunton, Colin E. *Father, Son and Holy Spirit*. London: T. & T. Clark, 2003.
Hahnenberg, Edward P. *Ministries: A Relational Approach*. New York: Crossroad, 2003.
Hall, Christopher A. *Reading Scripture with the Church Fathers*. Downers Grove, IL: InterVarsity, 1998.
Hamell, Patrick J., *Handbook of Patrology*. Staten Island, NY: Alba House, 1968.
Hartney, Aideen M. *John Chrysostom and the Transformation of the City*. London: Duckworth, 2004.
Hawthorne, Gerald F. *Philippians*. In *Word Biblical Commentary* 43. Waco, TX: Word, 1983.
Hays, Richard B. *The Moral Vision of the New Testament*. New York: Harper Collins, 1996.
Heath, Malcolm. "The Influence of Contemporary Rhetoric and Galatians." *Biblical Interpretation* 12 (2004) 369–4000.
Heather, Peter and John Matthews. *The Goths in the Fourth Century*. Liverpool: Liverpool University Press, 1991.

Bibliography

Hedahl, Susan K. *Listening Ministry: Rethinking Pastoral Leadership.* Minneapolis: Fortress, 2001.
Hiebert, Paul G. and Eloise Hiebert Meneses. *Cultural Anthropology.* Grand Rapids: Baker, 1983.
———. *Incarnational Ministry.* Grand Rapids: Baker, 1995.
Hill, Robert C. "The Spirituality of Chrysostom's Commentary on the Psalms." *Journal of Early Christian Studies* 5 (1997) 569–79.
———. "St. John Chrysostom: Preacher on the Old Testament." *Greek Orthodox Theological Review* 46 (2001) 268–86.
Hiltner, Seward. *Preface to Pastoral Theology: The Ministry and Theology of Shepherding.* New York: Abingdon, 1958.
Hoehner, Harold W. *Ephesians: An Exegetical Commentary.* Grand Rapids: Baker, 2002.
Hooker, Morna D. "Interchange in Christ." *The Journal of Theological Studies* 22 (1971) 349–61.
Hopewell, James. *Congregation: Story and Structure.* Philadelphia: Fortress, 1987.
Hubbell, H. "Chrysostom and Rhetoric," *Classical Philology* 19 (1824) 261–76.
Hull, Bill. *The Disciple Making Church.* Grand Rapids: Fleming H. Revell, 1998.
Hunger, Herbert. *On the Imitation of Antiquity in Byzantine Literature.* Washington, D.C.: Dumbarton Oaks Center for Byzantine Studies, 1969.
Hurtado, Larry W. "Following Jesus in the Gospel of Mark—and Beyond." In *The Patterns of Discipleship in the New Testament,* edited by Richard N. Longenecker, 9–29. Grand Rapids: Eerdmans, 1996.
Hybels, Bill. *Courageous Leadership.* Grand Rapids: Zondervan, 2002.
———. *Rediscovering Church.* Grand Rapids: Zondervan, 1995.
Japhet, Sara. *I & II Chronicles: A Commentary.* Louisville, KY: Westminster John Knox, 1993.
Jellico, Sidney. *The Septuagint and Modern Study.* Oxford: Clarendon, 1968.
Jinkins, Michael and Deborah Bradshaw Jinkins. *The Character of Leadership.* San Francisco: Jossey-Bass, 2000.
Jo, Moon H. *Korean Immigrant and the Challenge of Adjustment.* Westport, CT: Greenwood, 1999.
Johnson, Paul E. *The Psychology of Pastoral Care.* Nashville: Abingdon, 1953.
Johnstone, Patrick. *The Church is Bigger Than You Think.* Ross-shire, UK: Christian Focus, 1998.
Johnstone, Patrick and Jason Mandryk. *Operation World.* Combria, UK: Paternoster Life Style, 2001.
Jones, A. H. M. "St. John Chrysostom's Parentage and Education." *HTR* 46 (1953) 171–73.
Jones, Laurie Beth. *Jesus, CEO: Using Ancient Wisdom for Visionary Leadership.* New York, Hyperion, 1995.
Jun, Sung Chun, ed. *The Korean Church History of Young-Nam Province.* Dae Gu, Korea: The Committee of the Korean Church History of Young-Nam Province, 1987.
Kallistos, Bishop of Diokleia. *The Orthodox Church.* Edited by Timothy Ware. New York: Penguin, 1993.
Kang, Woong Joe. *History of the Korean American in the Washington Metropolitan Area, 1883–2005.* Alexandria, VA: Korean American Foundation in Greater Washington, D.C., 2009.
Keil, C. F. *The Books of the Chronicles.* Translated by Andrew Harper. Grand Rapids: Eerdmans, 1968.

Bibliography

Kelly, Geffrey B. and F. Burton Nelson. *The Cost of Moral Leadership: The Spirituality of Dietrich Bonhoeffer.* Grand Rapids: Eerdmans, 2003.
Kelly, J. N. D. *Early Christian Doctrines.* New York: Harper Collins, 1978.
———. *Golden Mouth: the Story of John Chrysostom—Ascetic, Preacher, Bishop.* Grand Rapids: Baker, 1995.
———. *The Pastoral Epistles: Black's New Testament Commentary.* Peabody, MA: Hendrickson, 1960.
Kennedy, James. *Evangelism Explosion: Equipping Churches for Friendship, Evangelism, Discipleship, and Healthy Growth.* Wheaton, IL: Tyndale, 1996.
Ker, John. *Lectures on the History of Preaching.* New York: A. C. Armstrong, 1889.
Kern, Philip. *Rhetoric and Galatians: Assessing An Approach to Paul's Epistle.* Cambridge: Cambridge University Press, 1998.
Kidd, B. J. *A History of the Church.* Oxford: Clarendon, 1922.
Kim, Heung Kyu. *The Naeri Methodist Church Handbook.* Inchon, Korea: Naeri Methodist Church, 2006.
Kim, Jung Hwan, ed. *The Keimyung Pioneers.* Dae Gu, Korea: Kyung, 2004.
Kim, Seyoon. *Paul and the New Perspective: Second Thoughts on the Origin of Paul's Gospel.* Grand Rapids: Eerdmans, 2002.
Kittel, Gerhard, et al. *Theological Dictionary of the New Testament.* Vol. 8. Grand Rapids: Eerdmans, 1964.
Knight, George W. *Commentary on the Pastoral Epistles: New International Greek Testament Commentary.* Grand Rapids: Eerdmans, 1992.
Ko, Yoo Kyung. "A Comparative Analysis of the Interrelation of the Pastoral Leadership and the Church Growth from 1977 to 2007 among the Korean Churches in Greater Washington, D. C. Area." Personal Paper. July 31, 2007.
Kouzes, James M. and Barry Z. Posner. *Credibility: How Leaders Gain and Lose It, Why People Demand It.* San Francisco: Jossey-Bass, 1993.
———. *Encouraging the Heart: A Leader's Guide to Rewarding and Recognizing Others.* San Francisco: Jossey-Bass, 1999.
———. "Leadership is a Relationship." In *Christian Reflection on Leadership Challenge,* edited by Jaea M. Kouzes and Barry Z. Posner. San Francisco: Jossey-Bass, 2004.
Krstitch, Daniel S. B. "St. Chrysostom as the Theologian of Divine Philanthropy." *Harvard Theological Review* 62 (1969) 433–34.
Krupp, R. A. *Saint John Chrysostom: A Scripture Index.* Lanham, MD: University Press of America, 1984.
———. *Shepherding the Flock of God: The Pastoral Theology of John Chrysostom.* New York: Peter Lang, 1991.
Kurz, William S. "Kenotic Imitation of Paul and Of Christ in Philippians 2 and 3." In *Discipleship in the New Testament,* edited by Fernando F. Segovia. Philadelphia: Fortress, 1985.
Lane, William L. "Standing before the Moral Claim of God: Hebrews." In *Patterns of Discipleship in the New Testament,* edited by Richard N. Longenecker, 203–24. Grand Rapids: Eerdmans, 1996.
Latourette, Kenneth Scott. *A History of Christianity.* 2 Vols. Peabody, MA: Prince, 1999.
Lawrenz, Melvin E. *The Christology of John Chrysostom.* Lewiston, NY: Mellen University Press, 1996.
Lee, Eun Hye. "John Chrysostom, A Glorious Failure: The Poor, The Rich and The Authentic Christian Community." PhD diss., Drew University, 2003.

Bibliography

Lee, Seung Hee. "Edward Adams, A Fifty-Year Dream." In *The Keimyung Pioneers*, edited by Jung Hwan Kim. Taegu, Korea: Keimyung University, 2004.
Lefroy, William. *Lectures on Ecclesiastical History*. New York: Thomas Whittakerm, 1897.
Levering, Matthew, ed. *On the Priesthood: Classic and Contemporary Texts*. Lanham, MD: Rowman & Littlefield, 2003.
Leyerle, Blake. "Ascetic Pantomime: John Chrysostom against Spiritual Marriage." PhD diss., Duke University, 1991.
———. "John Chrysostom on Almsgiving and the Use of Money." *Harvard Theological Review* 87/1 (1994) 29–47.
———. *Theatrical Shows and Ascetic Lives: John Chrysostom's Attack on Spiritual Marriage*. Berkeley: University of California Press, 2001.
Liddell, Henry George, et al. *A Greek-English Lexicon*. Oxford: Clarendon, 1940.
Liebeschuetz, J. H. *Barbarians and Bishops: Army, Church, and State in the Age of Arcadius and Chrysostom*. Oxford: Clarendon, 1990.
———. "The Fall of John Chrysostom." In *Nottingham Medieval Studies*. Edited by Antonia Gransden. Vol. 29. South Kelsey, UK: Winghale, 1985.
———. "Friends and Enemies of John Chrysostom." In *Classical, Byzantine, and Renaissance Studies for Robert Browning*, edited by Ann Moffatt, 85–111. Canberra: Australian Association for Byzantine Studies, 1984.
Lightfoot, J. B. *Saint Paul's Epistle to the Philippians*. Grand Rapids: Zondervan, 1970.
Lindner, Eileen, ed. *Yearbook of American & Canadian Churches, 2007*. Nashville: Abingdon, 2007.
Lodge, R. C. *Plato's Theory of Ethics*. London: Routledge & Kegan, 1950.
Long, Thomas G. *The Witness of Preaching*. London: Westminster, 1989.
Longenecker, Richard N. "The Foundational Conviction of New Testament Christology: The Obedience/ Faithfulness/Sonship of Christ." In *Jesus of Nazareth: Lord and Christ*, edited by Joel B. Green and Max Turnr, 473–88. Grand Rapids: Eerdmans, 1994.
Loukakis, Constantine. *The Works of St. John Chrysostom*. Athens: The Word, 1970.
Luther, Martin. *Luther's Works*. In *Word and Sacrament* 35. Translated by E. Theore Bachmann. Edited by Helmut T. Lehmann. Philadelphia: Fortress, 1960.
———. *Luther's Works*. In *The Catholic Epistles* 30. Translated by Martin H. Bertram. Edited by Jaroslav Pelikan. St. Louis: Concordia, 1967.
Lyon, Brynolf. "What is the Relevance of Congregational Studies for Pastoral Theology?" In *Pastoral and Practical Theology*, edited by James Woodward and Stephen Pattison. Malden, MA: Blackwell, 1999.
Maat, William A. "A Rhetorical Study of St. John Chrysostom's De Sacerdotio." PhD diss., Catholic University of America, 1944.
MacNair, Donald. *The Practices of a Healthy Church: Biblical Strategies for Vibrant Church Life and Ministry*. Phillipsburg, NJ: P&R, 1999.
Malingrey, A. M. "John Chrysostom." In *Encyclopedia of the Early Church*, edited by A. Di Berandino. Edinburgh: James Clark, 1992.
———. *Sur la vaine Glorie et l Education des Enfants by John Chrysostom*. Paris: Cerf, 1972.
Malphurs, Aubrey. *Being Leaders: The Nature of Authentic Christian Leadership*. Grand Rapids: Baker, 2003.
———. *Planting Growing Churches: A Comprehensive Guide for New Churches and Those Desiring Renewal*. Grand Rapids: Baker, 2004.

Bibliography

Marshall, I. Howard. *Acts.* Tyndale New International Commentaries. Vol. 5. Grand Rapids: Eerdmans, 1992.

Martin, Ralph P. and Peter H. Davids, eds. *Dictionary of the Later New Testament & Its Developments.* Downers Grove, IL: InterVarsity, 1997.

Maxwell, Jaclyn LaRae. "Preaching to the Converted: John Chrysostom and His Audience in Antioch." PhD diss., Princeton University, 2000.

Maxwell, John C. *The 21 Irrefutable Laws of Leadership.* Nashville: Thomas Nelson, 1998.

Mayer, Wendy and Pauline Allen. *John Chrysostom.* London: Routledge, 2000.

———. "John Chrysostom and His Audiences: Distinguishing different Congregations at Antioch and Constantinople." *Studia Patristica* 31 (1995) 70–75.

———. "John Chrysostom: Extraordinary Preacher, Ordinary Audience." In *Preacher and Audience: Studies in Early Christian and Byzantine Homiletics,* edited by May B. Cunningham and Pauline Allen. Leiden, Holland: Brill, 1998.

———. "Manuscripts and Sources: Traditions of Constantinopolitan Preaching: Towards a New Assessment of Where Chrysostom Preached What." *Byzantinische Forsuchungen* 23 (1996) 93–114.

———. "Patronage, Pastoral Care and the Role of the Bishop at Antioch." *Vigiliae Christianae* 55 (2001) 58–70.

———. "Provenance of the Homilies of St. John Chrysostom. Towards a New Assessment of Where He Preached What." Ph.D. diss., University of Queensland, 1996.

———. Review of *Golden Mouth: The Story of John Chrysostom—Ascetic, Preacher, Bishop,* by J. N. D. Kelly. *Sobornost* 18:1 (1996) 79–82.

McGavran, Donald A. *Understanding Church Growth.* Grand Rapids: Eerdmans, 1994.

McGrath, Alister E. *Christian Spirituality.* Maldem, MA: Blackwell, 1999.

McKenzie, John L. "Annotation on the Christology of Theodore of Mapsuestia." *Theological Studies* 19 (1958) 345–73.

McLeod, Frederik G. *The Image of God in the Antiochene Tradition.* Washington, D.C.: Catholic University of America, 1999.

Meredith, Anthony. *The Cappadocians.* New York: St. Vladimir's Seminary Press, 2000.

Meyendorff, John. *Christ in Eastern Christian Thought.* New York: St. Vladimir's Seminary Press, 1987.

Migne, Jacques Paul. *Patrologia Graeca.* Ridgewood, NJ: Gregg, 1965.

Miller, Timothy S. *The Birth of the Hospital in the Byzantine Empire.* Baltimore: Johns Hopkins University Press, 1997.

———. "Byzantine Hospitals." *Dumbarton Oaks Papers* 38 (1984) 53–63.

Mindell, Arnold. *Sitting in the Fire: Large Group Transformation Using Conflict and Diversity.* Portland, OR: Lao Tse, 1995.

Mitchell, Margaret M. *The Heavenly Trumpet: John Chrysostom and the Art of Pauline Interpretation.* Louisville, KY: Westminster John Knox, 2002.

Mock, Dennis J. *Bible Training Centre for Pastors and Church Leaders.* Atlanta: np, 1989.

Moltmann, Jurgend. *The Church in the Power of the Holy Spirit.* Translated by Margaret Kohl. Minneapolis: Fortress, 1993.

Morrison, Karl F. *The Mimetic Tradition of Reform in the West.* Princeton: Princeton University Press, 1982.

Mullen, William L. "The Polemical Sermons of John Chrysostom against Judaizers: A Dramatistic Analysis," PhD diss., University of Nebraska, 1990.

Nanus, Burt. *Visionary Leadership: Creating a Compelling Sense of Direction for Your Organization.* San Francisco: Jossey-Bass, 1992.

Bibliography

Nassif, Bradley. "Antiochene Theoria in John Chrysostom's Exegesis." In *Exegesis and Hermeneutics in the Churches of the East*, edited by Vahan S. Hovhanessian. New York: Peter Lang, 2009.
Neander, August. *The Life of St. Chrysostom*. Translated by J. C. Stapleton. London: R. B. Seeley & W. Burnside, 1845.
Neighbour, Ralph W. *Where Do We Go from Here? A Guidebook for the Cell Group Church*. Houston: Touch, 2000.
Norman, A.F. *Labanius*. Cambridge: Harvard University Press, 1987.
Norris, R. A. *Manhood and Christ: A Study in the Christology of Theodore of Mopsuestia*. Oxford: Clarendon, 1963.
O'Brien, Peter T. *Epistle to the Philippians: A Commentary on the Greek Text*. In *NIGTC*. Grand Rapids: Eerdmans, 1991.
Oak, John H. *Healthy Christians Make a Healthy Church*. Translated by Sam Ko and Jerry Vreeman. Seoul, Korea: DMI, 2001.
Oden, Thomas C. *Pastoral Theology*. New York: Harper & Row, 1983.
Origen, *Spirit and Fire*. Edited by Han Urs von Balthasar. Translated by Robert J. Daly. Washington, D.C.: Catholic University of America Press, 2001.
Osborne, Kenan B. *Priesthood*. New York: Paulist, 1988.
Packard, A. Appleton. "Chrysostom's True Christian Philosophy." *Anglican Theological Review* 45 (1963) 396–406.
Paik, Soon, ed. *Thirty-Year Anniversary Publication*. Vienna, VA: KCPC, 2003.
Paik, George Nak-Joon. *The History of Protestant Mission in Korea 1832–1910*. Seoul, Korea: Yonsei University Press, 1998.
Palladius, *Dialogue on the Life of St. John Chrysostom*. Translated by Robert T. Meyer. New York: Newman, 1985.
Pannenberg, Wolfhart. *Systematic Theology*. Translated by Geoffrey W. Bromiley. Vol. 1. Grand Rapids: Eerdmans, 2001.
Papageorggiou, Panayiotis E. "A Theological Analysis of Selected Themes in the Homilies of St. John Chrysostom on the Epistle of St. Paul to the Romans." PhD. diss., Catholic University of America, 1995.
Parkes, James. *Anti-Semitism*. London: Valentine, Mitchell, 1963.
———. *The Conflict of the Church and the Synagogue: A Study in the Origin of Anti-Semitism*. New York: Atheneum, 1974.
Patsavos, Lewis J. "The Image of the Priest according to the Three Hierarchs." *Greek Orthodox Theological Review* 21 (1976) 53–70.
Patterson, L. *Theodore of Mopsuestia and Modern Thought*. London: Society for Promoting Christian Knowledge, 1926.
Payne, Robert. *The Holy Fire*. New York: St. Vladimir's Seminary Press, 1980.
Pelikan, Jaroslav. *Divine Rhetoric: The Sermon on the Mount as Message and as Model in Augustine, Chrysostom and Luther*. New York: St. Vladimir's Seminary Press, 2000.
Peterlin, Davorin. *Paul's Letter to the Philippians in the Light of Disunity in the Church*. Leiden, Holland: E. J. Brill, 1995.
Peters, George W. *A Biblical Theology of Missions*. Chicago: Moody, 1972.
Pfeiffer, Robert H. *Introduction to the Old Testament*. New York: Harper & Row, 1948.
Philo, "On the Life of Moses." In *The Works of Philo*, translated by C. D. Yonge. Peabody, MA: Hendrickson, 1993.
Pinsky, Robert. "Poetry and American Memory," *The Atlantic Online* (1999). http://www.theatlantic.com/issues/99oct/9910pinsky.htm.

Bibliography

Platt, Daryl. "A Call to Partnership in the Missionary Selection Process." In *Too Valuable to Lose: Exploring the Causes and Cures of Missionary Attrition*, edited by William D. Taylor, 200-01. Pasadena: William Carey Library, 1997.
Proudfoot, C. Merrill. "Imitation or Realistic Participation?" *Interpretation* 17 (1963) 140-160.
Puech, Aime. *Saint John Chrysostom*. Translated by Mildred Partridge. London: R. & T. Washbourne, 1917.
Purves, Andrew. *Pastoral Theology in the Classical Tradition*. Louisville, KY: Westminster John Knox, 2001.
―――. *Reconstructing Pastoral Theology: A Christological Foundation*. Louisville, KY: Westminster John Knox, 2004.
Quasten, Johannes. *Patrology*. Vol. 3. Allen, TX: Christian Classics, 1995.
Rainer, Thom S. *Breakout Churches: Discover How to Make the Leap*. Grand Rapids: Zondervan, 2005.
Rice, Tamara Talbot. *The Scythians*. New York: F. A. Praeger, 1957.
Ridderbos, Herman. *The Gospel of John*. Translated by John Vriend. Grand Rapids: Eerdmans, 1997.
Riley, Gregory J. "Mimesis of Classical Ideas in the Second Christian Century." In *Mimesis and Intertexuality in Antiquity and Christianity*, edited by Dennis R. MacDonald. Harrisburg: Trinity, 2001.
Ritter, Adolf Martin. "John Chrysostom as an Interpreter of Pauline Social Ethics." In *Paul and the Legacies of Paul*, edited by William S. Babcock. Dallas: Southern Methodist University Press, 1990.
Ro, Danny, ed. *The Korean Central Presbyterian Church Handbook*. Vienna, Virginia: KCPC, 2004.
Robertson, A. T. *A Grammar of the Greek New Testament in the Light of Historical Research*. Nashville: Broadman, 1934.
Robinson, Haddon W. *Biblical Preaching: the Development and Delivery of Expository Messages*. Grand Rapids: Baker, 1980.
Roux, R. "The Doctrine of the Imitation of Christ in the Liber Graduum: Between Exegetical Theory and Soteriology." *Studia Patristica* 30 (1997) 259-64.
Rueter, Rosemary Radford. *Gregory of Nazianzus: Rhetor and Philosopher*. Oxford: Clarendon, 1969.
Russell, D. A. *Criticism in Antiquity*. Berkeley: University of California Press, 1981.
Rylaarsdam, David M. "The Adaptability of Divine Pedagogy: Sunkatabasis in the Theology and Rhetoric of John Chrysostom." PhD diss., The University of Notre Dame, 1999.
Sanders, Oswald J. *Spiritual Leadership*. Chicago: Moody, 1994.
Schaff, Philip. *The Creeds of Christendom*. Vol. 2. Grand Rapids: Baker, 1919.
―――. *History of the Christian Church*. Vol. 3. Grand Rapids: Eerdmans, 1968.
―――. *Saint Chrysostom and Saint Augustine*. New York: Thomas Whittaker, 1891.
―――. "Prolegomena: Life and Work of St. John Chrysostom." In vol. 9 of *NPNF*, First Series. Edited by W.R.W. Stephens. Grand Rapids: Eerdmans.
Schatkin, Margaret Amy. *John Chrysostom As Apologist*. Thessaloniki: Patriarchal Institute for Patristic Studies, 1987.
Schwarz, Christian A. *Natural Church Development: A Guide to Eight Essential Qualities of Healthy Churches*. Carol Stream, IL: Church Smart Resources, 1998.

Bibliography

Schwarz, Christian and Chrsitoph Schalk. *Implementation Guide to Natural Church Development*. Carol Stream, IL: Church Smart Resources, 1998.
Scott, Charles A. *Ulfilas Apostle of Goths: the Gothic Churches and their Decline*. Cambridge: Macmillan, 1885.
Shapiro, David S. "The Doctrine of the Image of God and Imitatio Dei." *Judaism* 12 (1963) 53.
Shedd, William G. T. *Homilectics and Pastoral Theology*. London: Banner of Truth, 1965.
Simonetti, Manlio. *Biblical Interpretation in the Early Church*. Edinburgh: T. & T. Clark, 2001.
Slee, Michelle. *The Church in Antioch in the First Century*. London: T & T Clark, 2003.
Smith, Morton. *Commentary on the Book of Church Order*. Greenville, SC: Greenville Seminary Press, 1990.
Socrates. *Ecclesiastical History*. In vol. 2 of *NPNF*, Series 2. 1–178. Grand Rapids: Eerdmans, 1997.
Song, Joshua YunBum. "An Historical and Theological Analysis of Schism in Presbyterian Churches in Korea, 1969–2005." PhD diss., University of Wales, 2006.
Sozoman. *Ecclesiastical History*. In vol. 2 of *NPNF*, Series 2. 179–427. Grand Rapids: Eerdmans, 1997.
Stanley, D. M. "Become Imitators of Me: The Pauline Conception of Apostolic Tradition." *Biblica* 40 (1959) 859–77.
Stapleton, J. C. *The Life of St. Chrysostom*. London: R. B. Seeley and W. Burnside, 1845.
Steiman, Sidney. "Imitation of God." In *Encyclopedia Judaica*. Vol. 8. New York: Macmillan, 1971.
Stephens, W. R. W. *Saint Chrysostom: His Life and Times*. London: John Murray, 1872.
Sterk, Andrea. *Renouncing the World Yet Leading the Church: The Monk-Bishop in Late Antiquity*. Cambridge: Harvard University Press, 2004.
Stetzer, Ed, and Mike Dodson. *Comeback Churches*. Nashville: B & H, 2007.
Stewart, Colomba. *Working the Earth of Heart: The Messalian Controversy in History, Texts, and Language to AD 431*. Oxford: Clarendon, 1991.
Stitzinger, James F. "Pastoral Ministry in History." In *Rediscovering Pastoral Ministry: Shaping Contemporary Ministry with Biblical Mandates*, edited by John MacArthur. Nashville: The Word, 1995.
Stott, John. *Basic Christian Leadership: Biblical Method of Church*. Downers, IL: InterVarsity, 2002.
———. *Between Two Worlds: The Art of Preaching in the Twentieth Century*. Grand Rapids: Eerdmans, 1982.
Stylinaopoulos, Theodore G. *The Way of Christ: Gospel, Spiritual Life and Renewal in Orthodoxy*. Brookline, MA: Holy Cross Orthodox, 2002.
Sullivan, Francis A. *The Christology of Theodore of Mopsuestia*. Analecta Gregoriana Vol. 82. Rome: Universitatis Gregoriana, 1956.
Swete, Henry Barclay. *Patristic Study*. London: Longmans, 1909.
Swinton, John, and Harriet Mowatt. *Practical Theology and Qualitative Research*. London: SCM, 2006.
Tate, J. "Plato and Imitation." *Classical Quarterly* 26 (1932) 162–64.
Tidball, Derek. *Skillful Shepherds: Explorations in Pastoral Theology*. 1986. Reprint, Leicester: Apollos, 2003.
Theodoret. *History of the Church*. Translated by Edward Walford. London: Henry G. Bohn, 1854.

Bibliography

Thomas a Kempis. *The Imitation of Christ.* Translated by Joseph N. Tylenda. New York: Random, 1998.
Thuren, Lauri. "John Chrysostom as a Rhetorical Critic: The Hermeneutics of an Early Father." *Biblical Interpretation* 9 (2001) 180–214.
Thurneysen, Eduard. *A Theology of Pastoral Care.* Translated by Jack A. Worthington. Richmond: John Knox, 1962.
Tinsley, E. J. *The Imitation of God in Christ: An Essay on the Biblical Basis of Christian Spirituality.* London: SCM, 1960.
Torrance, Thomas F. *The Christian Doctrine of God, One Being Three Persons.* Edinburgh: T. & T. Clark, 1996.
———. *The Trinitarian Faith.* London: T. & T. Clark, 2003.
Towner, Philip H. *The Goal of Our Instruction: The Structure of Theology and Ethics in the Pastoral Epistles.* Sheffield: JSOT, 1989.
Valantasis, Richard. "Body, Hierarchy, and Leadership in Chrysostom's *On The Priesthood.*" *Greek Orthodox Theological Review* 30/4 (1985) 455–71.
Van Engen, Charles. *God's Missionary People: Rethinking the Purpose of the Local Church.* Grand Rapids: Baker, 1991.
Vandenburghe, Bruno H. *John of the Golden Mouth.* Westminster, MD: Newman, 1958.
Vasiliev, Alexander A. *The Goths in the Crimea.* Cambridge, MA: Medieval Academy of America, 1936.
Verdenius, W. J. *Mimesis: Plato's Doctrine of Artistic Imitation and Its Meaning to Us.* Leiden: E. J. Brill, 1949.
Volf, Miroslav. "Theology for a Way of Life." In *Practicing Theology: Beliefs and Practices in Christian Life,* edited by Miroslav Volf and Dorothy C. Bass. Grand Rapids: Eerdmans, 2002.
VooBus, Arthur. "Celibacy, A Theological Requirement for Admission to Baptism in the Early Syrian Church." In *Papers of the Estonian Theological Society in Exile.* Vol. 1. Stockholm: Este, 1951.
———. *History Asceticism in the Syrian Orient: A Contribution to the History of Culture in the Near East.* Vol. 2. Louvain, Belgium: Secretariat Du CorpuSco, 1974.
Wagner, C. Peter. *The Healthy Church.* Ventura, CA: Regal, 1996.
———. *Your Church Can Grow: Seven Vital Signs of a Healthy Church.* Ventura, CA: Regal, 1984.
Wallace-Hadrill, D. S. *Christian Antioch: A Study of Early Christian Thought in the East.* Cambridge: Cambridge University Press, 1982.
Walls, Andrew F. *The Missionary Movement in Christian History: Studies in the Transmission of Faith.* Edinburgh: T. & T. Clark, 2000.
Warner, R. Stephen. "The Korean Immigrant Church as Case and Model." In *Korean Americans and Their Religions: Pilgrims and Missionaries from a Different Shore,* edited by Ho-youn Kwon, Kwang Chung Kim, and R. Stephen Warner. University Park, PA: Pennsylvania State University Press, 2001.
Warren, Rick. *The Purpose Driven Church.* Grand Rapids: Zondervan, 1995.
Warren, Robert. *Building Missionary Congregations: Towards a Post-modern Way of Being Church.* London: Church House, 1995.
Wenger, Antoine. Hui catecheses baptismales inedites by John Chrysostom. Paris: Cerf, 1957.

Bibliography

Wickham, Lionel. "Teachings about God and Christ in *the Liber Graduum*." In *Logos: Festschrift fur Luis Abramowski*, edited by Hans Christof Brennecke, et al, 486–98. Berlin: Walter de Gruyter, 1993.
Wilken, Robert L. *John Chrysostom and the Jews*. Berkeley: University of California, 1983.
———. *Remembering the Christian Past*. Grand Rapids: Eerdmans, 1995.
———. *The Spirit of Early Christian Thought*. New Haven, CT: Yale University Press, 2003.
Wiles, M. F. "Theodore of Mopsuestia as Representative of the Antiochene School." In *The Cambridge History of the Bible*, edited by P. R. Ackroyd and C. F. Evans. Vol. 1. Cambridge: Cambridge University Press, 1970.
Willard, Dallas. "Personal Soul Care." In *Pastor's Guide to Effective Ministry*, edited by William Willimon. Kansas City, MO: Beacon Hill, 2002.
Willey, John H. *Early Christian Portraits*. Edinburgh: T. & T. Clark, 1927.
Williams, Donald Manly. "The Imitation of Christ in Paul with Special Reference to Paul as Teacher." PhD diss., Columbia University, 1967.
Winslow, Donald F. "Christology and Exegesis in the Cappadocians." *Church History* 40 (1971) 390.
Wolfson, Harry A. *Philo: Foundation of Religious Philosophy in Judaism, Christianity and Islam*. Vol. 1. Cambridge: Harvard University Press, 1948.
Womack, Morris M. "A Study of the Life and Preaching of John Chrysostom." PhD diss., Wayne State University, 1967.
Woods, Richard. *Christian Spirituality: God's Presence through the Ages*. Allen, TX: Christian Classics, 1996.
Woodward, James, and Stephen Pattison, eds. *The Blackwell Reader in Pastoral and Practical Theology*. Oxford: Blackwell, 2007.
Yanney, Rudolph. "Priesthood between St. Gregory the Theologian and St. John Chrysostom." *Coptic Church Review* 20 (1999) 135–41.
Yates, Timothy. *Christian Mission in the Twentieth Century*. Cambridge: Cambridge University Press, 1994.
Yeakley, Flavil. "Recent Patterns of Growth and Decline among Heirs of the Restoration Movement." *Restoration Quarterly* 37/1 (1995) 1–6.
Young, Edward J. *The Book of Isaiah*. Vol. 3. Grand Rapids: Eerdmans, 1976.
Young, Frances. "John Chrysostom on First and Second Corinthians." *Studia Patristica* 18/1 (1986) 349–52.
———. Review of *Shepherding the Flock of God: The Pastoral Theology of John Chrysostom*, by R. A. Krupp. *JTS* 46 (1995) 825–26.
———. *The Theology of the Pastoral Letters*. Cambridge: Cambridge University Press, 1994.
———. "They Speak to Us across the Centuries: John Chrysostom." *Expository Time* 109 (1998) 38–41.

About the Author

Won Sang Lee is Senior Pastor Emeritus of the Korean Central Presbyterian Church, Centreville, Virginia which he has served for twenty-six years. He is also currently serving as President of SEED International (a member of Missio Nexus) since 2000, and as a founding President of PRASSION International (Prayer is Mission). He holds a BA (Philosophy) and an honorary PhD from Keimyung University, Daegu, Korea, an MA from Kyungpook National University (Philosophy), Daegu, Korea, a ThM from Dallas Theological Seminary (Old Testament), an MA from University of Pennsylvania (Near Eastern Studies), and a PhD from University of Wales (Pastoral Theology).

Index

Adams, Edward, 12
Adams, Jay E., 148
Adopt-a-People Clearinghouse, 93
AD 2000 and Beyond Movement, 93
Aetius, 115n119
Against the Enemies of Monasticism (Chrysostom), 110-11
Ahn, Peace Sung-Sik, 92n85
Alexandrian school, 188n130
Allen, Pauline, 121, 127, 130, 145, 148, 166
almsgiving, 105, 170-75, 199, 223, 224-25
Ameringer, Thomas Edward, 126
Ammerman, Nanfy T., 30-31
Analysis of the Hermeneutics of John Chrysostom's Commentary on Isaiah 1-8, An (Garrett), 127
Andragathius, 98, 99n22, 138, 231
anger, 156
Anomoeans, 115
Anthusa, 97-98
Antioch. *See also* Chrysostom, service in Constantine
   Christianity's development in, 3
   as model for church planting, 3
   riot in, 102-3, 114, 147-48, 184, 188n135
   unique position of in church history, 4
Antioch school, 3, 99, 139, 185, 188, 190, 231
Apologetic Composition (Gregory of Nazianzus), 141
Apostles, as archetypes, 203

Appenzeller, Henry G., 69
applied theory, 94n2
Arcadius, 103, 108, 167
Arianism, 195-96, 233
Arians, 119, 122, 212, 214
Aristobulus, 188n130
asceticism, 99-100
Asketerion, the, 99, 138
associates, 135
Athanasius the Great, 103, 106, 108
Attwater, Donald, 101-2, 125-26, 138-39, 165
Aubineau, Michel, 127

Babylas, 115, 121
Baeq, Daniel, 93
Baeq, Esther, 93
Ballard, Paul, 5, 94
baptism, 133, 151-52, 218
Baptismal Instructions (Chrysostom), 112-13, 182, 183
Barrett, C. K., 10
Basil of Caesarea, 108, 115, 142-43, 144, 145-47, 150, 158
Baur, Chrysostomus, 118n143, 126, 175, 188, 195, 197, 199, 221n292
BCF. *See* Biblical Counseling Foundation
Beasley-Murray, George B., 10
Benestad, J. Brian, 173n45
Bernard de Montfaucon, 122
Bible Training Centre for Church Leaders, 91
Bible Training Centre for Pastors, 91
biblical counseling, 227

261

Index

Biblical Counseling Foundation, 73
biblical preaching, Chrysostom and Lee compared, 230–32
Biblical Preaching (Robinson), 89
bishop, office of, 134–35
Blackaby, Henry, 82, 229
Bolger, Ryan, 61–62, 63
Book of Church Order of the Presbyterian Church in America, 1, 14n35, 56, 57, 136–37, 231
Book on Pastoral Rule (Gregory the Great), 141
Brandle, Rudolf, 128, 136
breakout churches, criteria for, 33–34
Breakout Churches (Rainer), 17, 18, 20, 31–33
Brewin, Kester, 63
Brottier, Laurence, 127
BTCP. *See* Bible Training Centre for Pastors
Buddha, 6
Buddhism, 76
Building Effective Ministry: Theory and Practice in the Local Church (Dudley), 30
Built to Last (Collins and Porras), 26–27
Bultmann, Rudolf, 10
Bush, George W., 19, 68
business management, leadership principles and, 26, 27

Calvin, John, 84n55, 133, 152n75, 192n152
caring, ministries of, 73–75
Carroll, Jackson W., 30–31, 227, 236
Carter, Robert, 126, 128, 130
Carterius, 99
Castelli, Elizabeth, 178–79
cells, 28, 226, 227. *See also* small groups
as church foundation, 72
division among, 71
Central Missionary Fellowship, 14n36, 32, 92, 234
Central Senior Center, 73, 225
Cha, Moon Jae, 36
Cha, Young Joon, 35
Chang, In Kyu, 36

Chang, Jin Myung, 91
Chang, Jin Pil, 43n34
Chang, Raymond, 21, 51
Chapell, Bryan, 192n152
character, building influence and, 8
Charm people, 93
Chase, Frederic Henry, 117–18, 126
Cho, Young Jin, 25n70, 26, 80–81
Choi, Dong Jin, 12, 46, 86
Christ. *See* Jesus Christ
Christ Central Presbyterian Church, 21–22
Christ-hymn, 84
Christlike character
development of, 2
as element of pastoral leadership, 43
goal of, seeking, 4
Christo, Gus George, 129, 134, 220, 221
Christology
Chrysostom's, 128, 191, 209, 210–11, 213
pastoral theology and, 8–9
Christology of John Chrysostom, The (Lawrenz), 128
Chrysostom, John, vii–viii
advocating values of monastic life, 111
on almsgiving, 114, 170–75
apologizing for seeking the priesthood, 142
on apostles' authority, 151–52
asceticism of, 99–100, 177, 231
attitude of, toward the Jews, 129–30, 234
baptism of, 98
on baptism, 112–13
on church reform, 173–74
character of, 97, 101–2, 106–7, 156–57, 188
on Christian theology, 120
church reformation of, 105
comparing priesthood in Judaism and Christianity, 153–54
criticism of, 159
cross-cultural mission and, 192–200, 232–34
death of, 108, 220–21

262

Index

on declining ordination, 150, 154–55
defending Christ's deity, 123–24
defending Christ's simultaneous
  divinity and humanity, 122
defending Christian philosophy of
  life, 110
defending the doctrine of the Incarnation, 122
dialogue with Basil, 142–48, 150
discipleship training from, 113
ecclesiology of, 132–34
education of, 4, 98, 99, 138–39,
  231–32
emphasizing Christ in his preaching,
  190–92
emphasizing unity of the church, 134
on the essence of Christ in the flesh,
  115
establishing hospitals, 174
exegetical homilies of, 116–22
exile of, 106–8, 124, 125
founding German national church in
  Constantinople, 197
on the fullness of the church, 134
on Genesis, 116–17
on heretical beliefs, 119, 120, 122,
  196
on the Holy Spirit's significance for
  Christians, 181–83
homilies of, 2, 109, 110
on husband's and wife's responsibilities, 121n172
influence of, 102–3
on leadership through example,
  175–83
letters of, 125
as martyr, 220–21
ministry of, 100–101, 109
mission policy of, 197–99
multiracial congregations of, 226
on the nature of the priesthood, 143
New Testament homilies of, 140
opposition to, 104, 105–8, 112, 167
ordination of, 100, 101, 109, 140
panegyrics of, on the Saints, 115–16
pastoral leadership of, 3, 4, 130–31
on pastoral leadership, 135
on the pastoral office, 142

pastoral theology of, 4, 130
on Paul, 116, 152, 154, 163, 176–80,
  202–4, 206–7
personality of, 223–24
on prayer, 85, 182–83
preaching of, 101–2, 103, 104–6,
  113–14, 116–22, 127, 183–92,
  199–200
on preaching, 90, 143, 161–64
preserving theological orthodoxy,
  115
on the priesthood's importance,
  142–43
on the Psalms, 117
reaching out to Jews and Gentiles,
  198–99
on repentance, 114
rhetorical techniques of, 189–90
on salvation, 159–60, 194
on salvation history, 117
service in Antioch, 27, 100–104, 109,
  110–13, 114, 116–25, 139–40,
  147, 148, 165–67, 169
service in Constantinople, vii, 103–7,
  119, 123–28, 137, 144, 145, 159,
  167–70, 175
serving the poor, 160–61
on social issues, 117, 129–30
on spirituality, 182–83
studies of, 126–28, 143–45
on unity in the church, 121n171
on wealth distribution, 169–70
writings of, 96–97, 101, 108–28
*Chrysostom: A Study in the History of
  Biblical Interpretation* (Chase),
  126
Chung, Hae Sun, 43n34
Chung, Kang Hyun, 43n34, 93
Chung, Sam Hyun, 43n34
church. *See also* church growth
  consensus within, 226–27
  considering potential pastors and
    leaders, suggestions for, 239
  definition of, 74
  functional divisions of, 72
  government, Presbyterian form of,
    29
  health of, 47, 90n78

Index

Chrysostom, John *(continued)*
   individualism of, 76
   inseparable from mission, 4
   multiple contexts for, recognizing, 239–40
   self-critical approach for, 239–40
   structure of, 228
   unity in, 183
Church of Antioch, 117
church growth
   goal of, vii
   laity's mobilization and, 48
   pastoral integrity and, 78
   pastoral leadership and, 23–24, 48, 78, 79
   qualitative, 240–41
   reasons for, 45
   revival and, 45–46
   vital signs for, 48n44, 65
church leaders, choosing, suggestions for, 239
church officers, 135
church shopping, 43–44, 77
church-state relations, 137, 175
classic leaders, 7
Clement of Alexandria, 172
clergy, 5
   understanding their congregations, 236
CMF. *See* Central Missionary Fellowship
Collins, James, 17–18, 26, 27
Commentary on Galatians (Chrysostom), 120
Commentary on the Gospel of John, The (Chrysostom), 119
Commentary on the Gospel of Matthew, The (Chrysostom), 119
Commentary on Romans (Chrysostom), 120
Community Center, 21
community formation, 227
Community Service Center (Washington, DC), 32
companies
   exceptional, qualities of, 26–27
   ideology of, 26

Comparison between a King and a Monk, A (Chrysostom), 110
condescension, 208–11
conflict
   management of, suggestions for, 238
   response to, 66
   usefulness of, 227
Confucianism, 75, 76
congregation, 5
   clergy's understanding of, 236
   as context and agent for pastoral care, 66
   life of, otherness within, 227–28
   studies of, 30–31
Congregation: Story and Structure (Hopewell), 30
Connolly, Gerald E., 16
Constantine, 137
Constantinople. *See also* Chrysostom, service in Constantine
   Chrysostom's preaching in, 104–6
   importance of, 103
   unethical church practices in, 105
contemporary enquiry, 95
Cornick, David, 85, 88
Council of Nicaea, 103
courtesy, 75
Covey, Stephen, 206n216
critical conversation, model of, 94–96
critical correlation, 94
Croft, Steven, 60–61, 82, 88, 229
cross-cultural mission, 2, 91–93, 192–200, 223
   Chrysostom and Lee compared, 234
   Chrysostom's attention to, 232–34
Culpeper Prayer House, 21
Cyprian, 172

Daily Morning Prayer, 86
Davis, Tom, 15
De Boer, Willis Peter, 205
deaconesses, 135, 136
deacons
   office of, 134, 135–37
   role of, in Chrysostom's day, 136
   structure of, 228
de fuga. See Apologetic Composition
Delitzsch, Franz, 217n272

Index

Der heilige Johannes Chrysostomus und seine Zeit (Attwater), 126
Dever, Mark, 90
diakonos, 216–17
dialogic methodology, 145–47
Dialogues, 125
Didache, 3–4
diligent enquiry, 96
Diodore of Tarsus (Diodorus), vii, 99, 138, 139, 177, 231
discipleship, 218
discipleship training, 2
Discipleship Training for the Laity, 72
Discourse on Blessed Babylas and against the Greeks, The (Chrysostom), 115
Discourses against Judaizing Christians (Chrysostom), 112
Doctors of the Church, 108
Dorr, Donald, 6–7, 8, 60, 82–83, 229
Drucker, Peter F., 11
DTL. *See* Discipleship Training for the Laity
Dudley, Carl, 30–31

Eastern Orthodox Church, hierarchy in, 134
Ecumenical Councils, 103
Edict of Milan, 137
EE. *See* Evangelism Explosion
elderly, pastoral care for, 73
elders
  integrity of, 81
  role of, 64
  types of, 135
Elders' Session, 135
emergent leaders, 7
emerging churches, 28, 29
  characteristics of, 61–62
  pastoral leadership model for, 61–64
  philosophy of, 49
  rejecting traditional forms, 74–75
Emerging Churches (Gibbs), 74
envy, 156
Ettlinger, Gerard, 127
Eucharistic ministry, and caring for the soul, 159–60

Eudoxia, 106, 107, 108, 167, 168, 175, 221
Eutropius, 103–4n55, 166
Evangelical Alliance (UK), clergy survey by, 87–88
Evangelical Fellowship Mission Agencies, 14n36
evangelical leaders, church fathers and, vii
evangelism
  personal, 92
  worldwide, 10
Evangelism Explosion, 92
expository preaching, 2, 89–90
  Chrysostom and Lee compared, 232
Ezra Leadership Institute, 14

Facundus de Hermiane, 101
Fairweather, Janet, 190
fasting-prayer retreat, 86
Fee, Gordon D., 84, 203
fellowship circle, 72
Fifty-five Homilies on the Acts of the Apostles (Chrysostom), 123
First Korean Presbyterian Church of Maryland, 23, 24, 78, 79
Flavian, 101, 103, 113, 135, 139
forgiveness, 152, 201
Francis of Assisi, 6
Fronton le Duc, Sancti Joanis Chrysostomi Opera omnia in 12 tomos didtributata (Morel edition, Chrysostom), 109–10
funerals, 73–74

Gainas, 197–98
Gandhi, Mahatma, 7
Gardner, John, 7
Garrett, Duane A., 108, 117, 127, 184
gender, 129
George Alexandrius, 125
Gerkin, Charles V., 65–66, 69–70, 81, 85, 89
Gibbs, Eddie, 48, 61–62, 63, 74
Global Mission Church, 23, 24, 25, 78, 79, 80, 81
Global Mission Church (Seoul), 26, 80
Gnosticism, 85

265

Index

God, self-disclosure of, in history, 5
Golden Mouth: The Story of John Chrysostom—Ascetic, Preacher, Bishop (Kelly), 126
Good to Great: Why Some Companies Make the Leap and Others Don't (Collins), 17–18
Goodall, Blake, 127
Goths, 196–97
government, assistance from, 224
Great Commission, 10, 91, 194
greatness, principles of, 17
Greeley, Dolores, 129, 150n60
Greer, Rowan, 155
Gregory the Great, 141, 144, 164
Gregory of Nazianzus, 108, 141, 144, 151n69, 158, 164
Gregory of Nyssa, 115
Grierson, Denham, 30, 226–27, 236
Gundry, Robert H., 83

Ha, Yong Jo, 46
habitus model, 95n
Hahm, Hank Hyun-Ku, 21
Hahn, Jin Kwan, 46
Hahnenberg, Edward P., 47
Halton, Thomas, 115
Harkins, Paul W., 112
Hartney, Aideen M., 130, 144–45, 175
hastiness, 77
Hawthorne, Gerald F., 84, 208
Hays, Richard, 218
Heath, Malcolm, 190
Heavenly Trumpet, The (Mitchell), 127–28
Hedahl, Susan K., 168
heuristic clarity, 96
hierarchies, 48n46, 62, 228
Hill, Robert Charles, 117n139, 127, 183
Hiltner, Seward, 68
Hitler, Adolf, 7
holiness, maintaining, 235
holistic care, 225
holistic small groups, 70–71, 226. See *also* small groups
Holy Communion, 133
Holy Spirit, significance of, 181–83
Holy Trinity, relationship within, 62–63

Home Cell groups, 72
Home Visitation Ministry, 68, 69, 226, 227
Homiliae 7 de laudibus S. Pauli (Chrysostom), 115
Homilies on the Epistle to the Colossians (Chrysostom), 123
Homilies on First and Second Corinthians (Chrysostom), 120
Homilies on the First and Second Epistles to the Thessalonians (Chrysostom), 124
Homilies on the Epistle to the Ephesians (Chrysostom), 120–21
Homilies on the Epistle to the Hebrews (Chrysostom), 124
Homilies on the Epistles to Timothy, Titus, and Philemon (Chrysostom), 122
Homilies of the Philippians, The (Chrysostom), 121–22
Homilies of St. John Chrysostom on the Letters of St. Paul to Titus and Philemon, The (Goodall), 127
Hong, Seung Ha, 69
Hopewell, James, 30
Hort, Fenton John Anthony, 119
hospitality, 47
House for Homeless Wounded Soldiers (Kung San), 14
How Parents Should Bring Up Children (Chrysostom), 111
Hubbell, H., 190
human dynamics, viii
humility, 48, 83–84, 162, 183, 206–7, 208, 209–20, 229
  as element of pastoral leadership, 41
  prayer and, 85
Huns, 197
HVM. See Home Visitation Ministry

ICMS. See Imitating Christ Missionary Training School
ideology, and visionary companies, 26
Ignatius of Loyola, 83
Illert, Martin, 128
Imitating Christ Missionary Training School, 238

Index

imitation, learning by, 203-4
Imitation of Christ, The (Thomas a Kempis), 208n229
individualism, pietistic, 65-66
individuals, taking personal interest in, 2
influence
  law of, 7
  power of, earning, 7-8
Ingoo, Kang, 12
Innocent, 125
integrity, 78, 81-83, 183, 228, 229-30, 240
  as element of pastoral leadership, 41
  maintaining, 235
  pastoral leaders and, 75, 76
introspection, 76
Isaac (monastic leader), 107
Isidore, 103, 106

Jaehwa, Choi, 12
Jesus CEO (Jones), 10-11
Jesus Christ
  archetypal image of, 203
  attitude of, 212-13
  character of, 82
  commanding Peter to establish the church, 10
  condescension of, 208-11
  demonstrating pastoral leadership, 9
  distinct natures of, 212-13
  divinity of, 212
  emphasized in Chrysostom's preaching, 190-92
  emphasizing world mission, 193-94
  Great Commission of, 10, 91, 194
  headship of, 62
  humility of, 83-84, 206-7, 208, 209-20
  imitation of, 84, 116, 170-71, 175-76, 178, 181, 183, 186, 192, 199, 200-221, 228-29. *See also* leadership through example
  incarnation of, 200, 207-10, 213-15
  leadership example of, 8, 10-11
  mind of, developing, 211-12
  obedience of, 216-19
  prayer life of, 86

revelation of, 210
servanthood of, 217
shepherd motif in ministry and ascension of 9-10
as source of preaching's power, 90
spiritual union of, with believers, 191-92
Jin, Ki Chan, 35
Johannes Chrysostomus: Bischof, Reformer, Martyr (Brandle), 128
Johannes Chrysostomus in Konstantinopel (398-404) (Tiersch), 126
Johannes Chrysostomus und das antiochenisch-syrische Monchtum (Illert), 128
John Chrysostom (Mayer and Allen), 127
John Chrysostom and the Transformation of the City (Hartney), 130
Johnson, Paul E., 66-67
Jones, Laurie Beth, 10-11
Julian, 121
Jurgens, W. A., 162

Kang, Joon Min, 22n62, 55n
Kang, Ok Hwa, 86
kawnsa, 135
KCPC. *See* Korean Central Presbyterian Church
Keimyung Pioneers, The, 11-12
Keimyung University, 11-12
Kelly, J. N. D., 111, 112, 126, 138, 145
Kennedy, James, 92
kenosis, 207-19, 218-19
Ker, John, 186-87
Kern, Philip, 189, 190
Kim, Dong Soo, 43n34
Kim, Harold Hyung-Yoon, 21
Kim, Jae Dong, 24n67, 36, 79n42
Kim, James Young-Yong, 23n65, 79n
Kim, Joong Shik, 32
Kim, Seung Hak, 24n66, 79n41
Kim, Seyoon, 4
Kim, Wayne, 57n60
Kim, Yong Hoon, 36
kinship circle, 72
Ko, Yoo Kyung, 24, 42, 79

267

Index

Korea
  American missionaries in, 92
  mindset of, 76
Korean-American immigrant churches
  church officers' election in, 39
  church shopping at, 43–44
  church splits at, and Sunday attendance, 44
  competitiveness among, 76
  conflicts and divisions in, 37, 75–78
  context for, 75
  pastoral changes at, turmoil resulting from, 54
  short-term ministries in, 81
  uniqueness of, 68, 69
  wanting their own buildings, 50
Korean Baptist Church of Montgomery, 24, 25, 79
Korean Baptist Church of Washington, 23, 24, 44, 78, 79
Korean Capital Presbytery of PCA, 22
Korean Central Presbyterian Church (Centreville, VA), 16, 23, 24, 78, 79
  adding worship services, 32
  Bible Training Centre for Pastors at, 91
  Biblical Counseling Foundation at, 73
  care ministry at, 58
  Central Missionary Fellowship at, 92, 234
  Central Senior Center at, 73
  Children and Youth Ministries at, 21
  christology and theology of, 133
  church officers at, 39–41, 49, 135
  commissioning first missionary families, 21
  committees of, 37
  construction at, 20
  cross-cultural missions at, 234
  Discipleship Training for the Laity at, 72
  diversity at, 21
  divisions in, 20, 35–36, 228, 229
  English-speaking ministry at, 51–52
  establishing Central Missionary Fellowship, 32
  establishing worship for English-Speaking Congregations, 21
  Evangelism Explosion at, 92
  fitting criteria for a breakout church, 33
  formally affiliating with PCA, 33
  founding of, 34
  free of government control, 138
  growth factors at (1981–85), 45–47
  growth of, viii, 16–17, 20–21, 22, 25, 32, 34, 38, 41–42, 44–45, 50–51, 52–54, 55, 70, 80
  history of, 19–23
  Home Cell groups at, 72
  Home Visitation Ministry, 68, 69
  identified as a good-to-great church, 18
  missionaries sent from, 32, 93
  Mission Board, 93
  mission-focused locally, 32
  Mutual Aid Association at, 73–74
  new building for, 49–51
  nurturing the congregation, 21
  organizing Board of Deacons, 21
  pastoral leadership at, 2
  pastoral organization of, 49
  peace in, 54
  prayer at, 86
  promoting fellowship within, 37
  property purchases by, 32
  purchasing Community Service Center (Washington, DC), 32
  relocation of, 21, 38
  renaming English Ministry at, 21–22
  retention rate at, 44
  SEED International, 234
  senior pastor transitions at, 22
  small groups at, 70, 90
  speakers at, 46
  split of, 16, 31–32
  stability of, 39, 44–45
  Stephen Ministry at, 73
  Timothy Bible Institute at, 90
  training programs at, 20–21
  unity in, 54
  Vision 2020, 58, 72, 90, 92–93
  weaknesses in, regarding unity and stewardship, 38

Index

world mission vision developing at, 21
youth ministry at, 51
Korean churches (Washington, DC, area), growth of, 23
Korean Church of Fairfax, 23n65, 79n
Korean Church of Houston (TX), 22n62
Korean Day (US), 19
Korean Nazarene Church, 23, 24, 78, 79
Korean Orthodox Presbyterian Church, 36
Korean Presbyterian Church, women in, 135
Korean Presbyterian Church of Maryland, 23, 24, 78, 79
Korean Presbyterian Church of Northern Virginia, 23, 24, 78, 79
Korean Presbyterian Church of Washington, 23, 24, 78, 79
Koreans
  immigrating to the United States, 19, 68–69
  leaders among, growing disrespect for, 75, 230
  as percentage of US population, 19
Korean United Methodist Church of Greater Washington, 23, 24, 25, 26, 34, 51, 78, 79, 80–81
Korean United Presbyterian Church of Washington, 23, 24, 78, 79
Korean World Commission for Christ, 15
Krupp, R. A., 130, 134–35, 136, 143–44
KUMC. *See* Korean United Methodist Church
Kurds, Turkish, 93

laity
  leadership of, relations with clergy, 47
  ministry of, 48
  mobilization of, 49
  pastoring gift among, 71
Lawrenz, Melvin E., 128, 210–11, 212–13n251
lay orders, 134

Lay Visitation Teams, 70
leader, term used in religious context, 60–61
leaderless groups, 62, 63
leaders
  cultic, 63
  possessing godly moral character, 7
leadership
  alternative model for, 29
  defined, 6, 60
  through example, 175–83
  influence of, 7
  intra-Trinitarian relations and, 62–63
  Jesus' example of, 7, 8
  lacking, in 21st century, 11
  models of, 48
  on moral issues, 8
  nature and expression of, 27–28
  persuasion and, 7
  respect for, in Asiatic cultures, 75
  transitions of, problems accompanying, 22
  types of, 6–7
Lee, Byung Hee, 22n62, 55n
Lee, Byung Ik, 14n37
Lee, Byung In, 36
Lee, Dong Won, 25–26, 80, 81
Lee, Eun Hye, 172
Lee, Eunice, 16
Lee, James Kwang-Jin, 21
Lee, Joseph, 16
Lee, Sang Keun, 46, 89
Lee, Sung-Bong, 12
Lee, Won Sang, 58
  assuming pastoral duties at KCPC, 37–39
  biography of, 12–14
  calling of, 12
  considering affiliation with Presbyterian Church, USA, 33
  developing Home Visitation Ministry, 70
  discipleship of, xii
  education of, 12–13, 15, 89, 139
  KCPC during pastorate of, 31–32. *See also* Korean Central Presbyterian Church

269

Index

Lee, Won Sang *(continued)*
 life of, viii
 nonclerical leadership positions of,
  14, 15
 ordination of, challenged, 39–40
 pastoral effectiveness of, 42–43,
  86–87
 pastoral experience of, 13–14
 pastoral situation of, 225–26
 personality of, 223–24
 preaching ministry of, 88, 90
 principles of, xii, 2
 prioritizing prayer, 12, 85–87
 retirement of, 21, 55, 56–57
 tributes for, 14–16
Lee, Young Hee, 14n36
Lee, Young Ja, 46–47, 70, 74, 85
Lee, Young Ki, 34, 43n34
Leo Imperator, 125
Letter to a Young Widow (Chrysostom),
 111
Lewinsville Presbyterian Church, 38
Lewis, James W., 66
Leyerle, Blake, 129, 173
Libanius, vii, 98, 99n22, 138, 139, 231
Liebeschuetz, J. H., 168, 169, 197
Life of St. Chrysostom (Neander), 125
Lim, Chang Ho, 47
Lim, Dong Sun, 22n62, 54–55n55
listening, 66, 168–69
lone leaders, 6
Lonergan, Bernard, 83
Loukakis, Constantine, 114
Lucian, 99
Luther, Martin, 153
LVT. *See* Lay Visitation Teams
Lyon, Brynolf, 30, 227

Maat, William, 189–90
Machiavelli, Niccolo, 8
MacNair, Donald J., 47
Malingrey, Anne Marie, 126–27, 185
Manichaeism, 119n151, 120n162
Manicheans, 119
Mani the Persian, 119n151, 120n162
Marcion, 122n176
Marcionites, 122
marriage, 129

Marshall, Howard, 9
martyrdom, 219–21
Martyrius Antiochenus, 125
Matthew, Gospel of, written in Antioch, 3–4
Maxwell, John, 7
Mayer, Wendy, 118–19, 121, 126, 127,
 128, 130, 145, 148, 166
McGavran, Donald A., 45–46
McKinney, William, 30–31
McLean Korean Presbyterian Church,
 24, 25, 79, 80
mega-churches, 76
Meir, John P., 3
Meletius, 98, 99, 100, 109, 112, 115,
 139, 231
membership circle, 72
mentoring, personal, 235
mercy, 47, 201
mercy ministry, 160–61, 167
Migne, Jacques Paul, 110
Miller, Timothy S., 174n52, 174n54
ministry, 5
 expository, 48
 members' involvement in, 47–48
 pastoral, 67
 for the soul, 159–60
 training for, 138
mission
 biblical theology of, 4
 inseparable from church, 4
 personnel, training for, 238
 theology of, 195
missionary congregations, 91–92
missionary outreach, 192–200
mission church, 14n35
Missio Nexus, 14n36
mission pastor, 93
Mitchell, Margaret M., 116, 127–28,
 145, 177, 190, 202, 203–4
Mock, Dennis J., 91
modernity, 62
Moltmann, Jurgen, 91, 194–95
monasticism, 99–100, 105
Morel, Claude, 110
Morel, Frederick, 110
Mowatt, Harriett, 96
Mullen, William L., 129–30

Murphy, F. X., 171, 173
Mutual Aid Association, 73–74, 225
mutual critical correlation, model of, 96

Naeri Methodist Church (Korea), 69
Natural Church Development (Schwarz), 71
Navigator Mission and Evangelism Explosion, 21
Nazianzus. *See* Gregory of Nazianzus
Neander, August, 112n103, 125
Nectarius of Constantinople, 103, 107n70, 173
needy, providing for, 145, 160–61, 169, 172–73. *See also* almsgiving
neighbors, care for, 171, 175, 200
Neil, Stephen, 116n129
networking, 63
New Age spirituality, 84–85
New Testament Homilies (Chrysostom), 118–22
New York Presbyterian Church, 14n36
North American Presbyterian Board, 11–23
nosokomeia, 174
nurture, 47

obedience, 216–19
observing, capacity for, 66
Oden, Thomas C., 5
On the Education of Children (Chrysostom), 111–12
On the Incomprehensible Nature of God (Chrysostom), 114–15
On the Priesthood (Chrysostom), 101, 109, 110, 112, 130, 131, 140–64, 168, 170, 181, 189, 199
On the Statues (Chrysostom), 148, 184, 186, 188
On Vain Glory (Chrysostom), 111
On Virginity and Widowhood (Chrysostom), 111
Open Door Presbyterian Church, 36
oratory, Chrysostom and Lee compared, 232
ordination, 134

Oriental Mission Church (Los Angeles), 22n62, 54–55n55
Origen, 188n130
otherness, 227–28
outreach, 47

Palladius, 98, 103–4n55, 104, 105n60, 106n65, 107, 125, 167, 174, 195, 220–21
palli-palli, 77
Park, Chae Gon, 36
Park, John Shin-Wook, 92n85
Park, Ju Yong, 86–87
Park, Kwang Chul, 22n62, 55n
Park, Yoon Sam, 36
Parkes, James, 129
Park family (Rev. and Mrs. John Shin-Wook), 21
pastor, character of, 75–88
pastoral care, 65–75. *See also* almsgiving
  Chrysostom and Lee compared, 224–28
  communal model of, 70
  defining, 66–68
  ministries for, 73–75
  spiritual direction and, 85
  strengthening, 236–37
pastoral character, Chrysostom and Lee compared, 228–30
pastoral counseling, 66n17
  almsgiving and, 105, 170–75, 199, 223, 224–25
  and caring for people, 148–50, 157–60
  Christological perspective on, 8
  church discipline and, 161
  cross-cultural mission and, 91–93, 192–200
  demanding holistic practice of faith, 97
  effects on transition, 22
  through example, 175–83
  functions of, 63, 157–64
  fundamental task for, 9
pastoral counseling *(continued)*
  goals for, 93
  humility of, 83–84

271

Index

ingredients of, 41
listening and, 168–69
maintaining contact with God, 181
model for, 9
personal character and, 154–57, 180, 183
personality and, 6
practitioners of, 5
prayer and, 85
preaching and, 161–64, 183–92
principles of, 2, 27
secular models for, 61
and serving the poor, 160–61
spirituality and, 182–83
theological response to, 95
training for, 237–38
transparency of, 78
triangle relationships in, 8n19
visitation and, 161
pastoral ministry
  core concepts of, 67
  Jesus' example for, 8
  outcome of, 6
  as salvation and sanctification of a person in Christ, 141
pastoral studies, 5
pastoral theology
  defined, 6
  elements of, 5–6
  field of, 5
  growing interest of, in groups and communities, 30
  reconstructing through Christological perspective, 8–9
  scope of, 5–6
  shepherding in, 68
  US context for, 236
Pastoral Theology in the Classical Tradition (Purves), 130, 144
pastoral training, suggestions for, 237–38
pastoral visitation, 161
pastoral work, purpose of, 9
pastoring, gift of, 71
pastors
  authority of, 75
  change of, leading to turmoil, 54
  character of, challenged, 83

election procedures for, 56, 57
first-generation Korean vs. second-generation Korean-American, 52
integrity of, 81–83
length of tenure, and church stability, 44
in Presbyterianism, 135
role of, 135
succession of, 77
tenure of, average, 81
Patsavos, Lewis, 162
Pattison, Stephen, 94–96, 132
Patton, John, 236
Paul
  apostolic call of, 4
  dying daily, 207
  as exemplar, 116, 229
  exemplar theory of, 179
  imitating Christ, 4
  imitation of, 176–81, 199, 202–4
  pastoral leadership of, goal of, 180
Paul of Samosata, 122
PCA. *See* Presbyterian Church in America
Pelikan, Jaroslav Jan, 129, 188n135, 190
Pennsylvania Presbytery, 39–40
people
  spiritual care for, 65–75, 145, 147, 148–50, 157–60
  understanding the value of, 145, 148–50
people-centered ministry, 67
People on the Way, A (Grierson), 30
personal dialogue, 146, 168
personality, pastoral leadership and, 6
persuasion
  by example, 146
  leadership and, 7
Philo, 118n141, 188n130
piety, filial, 76
Pinsky, Robert, ix
poor. *See also* almsgiving; needy
  care for, 223
  serving, 200
Porras, Jerry, 26
power-hungry leaders, 7
practical theory, 95n
prayer, 2, 46, 240

Index

as element of pastoral leadership, 43
humility and, 85
importance of, 12, 85, 182–83
preaching, 183–92, 199, 200
   Christ emphasized in, 190–92
   Chrysostom and Lee compared, 230–32
   duty of, 145, 161–64
   as element in pastoral care, 226
   exegetical, 185–86
   expository, 89–90, 184–85, 186
   healing qualities of, 184
   importance of, 142
   pastoral, 184
   pastoral leadership and, 88–91
   as pastor's main duty, 143
   rhetorical, 189–90
   training for, 230–31
   Word and deed related to, 162–63
Presbyterian Church in America, 1, 136–37
   constitution of, 1–2
   founding of, 1
   ministers in, training for, 231
   ordination in, 231
Presbyterian Churches of Korea, General Assembly of, 40
Presbyterian Church, USA, 33
Presbyterianism
   church officers in, 135–36
   governance model, 29
   leadership model of, 64
present blessing, 76
pride, 155
priesthood
   character of, 141, 145, 154–57
   dignity of, 142–43, 145, 150–54
   duties of, 145, 157–64
   integrity of, 199
   nature of, 145
   personal character of, 145
   piety of, 143
   qualification for, 101, 141–42
   sacred soul of, 158
   seeking, apology for, 141, 142
   standards for, 159
   training for, 138–39
priesthood of believers, 62, 153

Pritchard, John, 5, 94
Protestant spirituality, 85
Ptolemy II Philadelphus, 118n141
Purves, Andrew, 4, 8–9, 67–68, 130, 144, 159
Pusey, P. E., 124
Pyung-San Presbyterian Church (Kyung-San City), 13–14

Quasten, Johannes, 118n144, 125n198, 143, 146, 184, 186, 188

Rainer, Thomas S., 17, 18, 20, 27, 31–34, 81
Reformed spirituality, 85, 88
regeneration, 133, 151–52
Renouncing the World Yet Leading the Church (Sterk), 131
repentance, 129
repetition, imitation and, 204
respect, mutual, 64
revival, church growth and, 45–46
rhetoric, 189–90
Rice, Tamara Talbot, 196
Ridderbos, Herman, 10, 88
Ritter, Adolf Martin, 129
Ro, Danny Chang-Soo, 21, 22, 23, 32, 55, 56–58, 72, 77–78
Roberts, Paul, 63
Robinson, Haddon, 89
ROW (Reaching to the World), 14n36
ruling elder, 135
Ryoo, David Eungyul, 22–23

Saint Chrysostom, His Life and Times (Stephens), 125
Saint Johannis Chrysostomi Opera Omnos (Chrysostom), 109
Saint John Chrysostom: A Scripture Index (Krupp), 144
salvation, 194, 214
   almsgiving and, 171–72
   humility and, 217n18
   scriptural knowledge and, 186
Sancti Joannis Chrysostomi Opera omnia quae extant vel eius nomine circumferunter (Benediction

Index

Edition of Bernard de Montfaucon; Chrysostom), 110
Sa Rang Presbyterian Church (Los Angeles), 22
Savile, Henry, 109, 125
Schaff, Philip, 109, 110
Schwarz, Christian A., 70–71, 226
Scott, Anderson, 197
Scripture
   infallibility of, 185
   priority of, 185n119
   salvation and, 186
Scythians, 196
Secundus, 97
SEED International, 14, 15, 21, 92, 234, 238
selfishness, 76
Seoul Presbyterian Church, 16, 24, 25, 35–36, 79, 80
Seoul Theological Seminary, 22n62
Septuagint (LXX) or *Interpretation of the Seventy Men*, 118n141
Serapion, 106n
sermons. *See also* preaching
   characteristics of, 186, 187n126
   preparation of, 90
servant, ideal, 9
servanthood, 63, 217
servant leadership, 83–84, 229
session, 137
   as congregational role model, 41
   role of, 64
Seven Homilies on Wealth and Poverty (Chrysostom), 113
Shamanism, 76
shepherding, 67–68, 88–89
   God as true example of, 10
   ideal, 9
   motif of, 9–10
Shepherding the Flock of God: The Pastoral Theology of John Chrysostom (Krupp), 130, 143–44
sin, forgiveness of, 171–72
Skillful Shepherd: An Introduction to Pastoral Theology (Tidball), 144
small groups, 58, 90, 226. *See also* cells
   cell division among, 71
   holistic, church growth and, 70–71

ongoing training for, 71–72
Social Gospel, 65–66
Socrates, 99, 106n65, 107, 109, 125, 167–68n13, 195
souls, caring for, 157–60
Sozomen, 105, 106n65, 107n72, 167, 174–75, 195, 197, 198
speaking, fluency in, 162–63
spiritual care, 142, 236–37
spiritual character, as element of pastoral leadership, 43
spiritual direction, 85
spiritual gifts, 43n34
Spirituality of Chrysostom's Commentary on the Psalms, The (Hill), 127
spirituality, 48, 84–88, 182–83, 228, 240
   hybrid, 85
   pastoral leaders and, 75, 236
spiritual marriage, 129
Stalin, Joseph, 7
Stapleton, J. C., 125
Stephen Ministry, 73
Stephens, W. R. W., 125, 160
Sterk, Andrea, 131, 144, 157
Stevens, George B., 136
St. John Chrysostom: The Homilies on the Statues (van de Paverd), 127
St. John Chrysostom: Pastor and Preacher (Attwater), 126
St. John Chrysostom's Commentary on the Psalms (Hill), 127
Stott, John, 162
Studying Congregations: A New Handbook (Ammerman et al., eds), 30–31
subordination, 62
Suh, Jong Dae, 13n33
sunkatabasis, 208–9
Swete, H. B., 108–9
Swinton, John, 96
Synn, Ilhi, 12
Synod of the Oak, 102, 104, 107
Syrus, 99–100, 231

Tall Brothers, 106
tapeino, 211
teaching elder, 135

Index

Ten Homilies on Repentance and Almsgiving (Chrysostom), 114
Theatrical Shows and Ascetic Lives (Leyerle), 129
Theodoret, 106n65, 125, 195-96, 197
Theodosius, 102-3, 113, 122, 147
theological politics, 120
theology
  mission of, 4
  of missions, 195
Theophilus, 103-4, 106, 107, 175
Thirty-Year Anniversary of KCPC, The, 54
Thomas à Kempis, 208n229
Thornton, Andy, 63
Thumma, Scott L., 43n35
Thuren, Lauri, 190
Tidball, Derek J., 67, 144
Tiersch, Claudia, 126
Tillich, Paul, 94
time, management of, 205-6
Timothy
  demonstrating Christlike character, 205
  following Paul, 180-81
  personal character of, 179-80
Timothy Bible Institute, 90
triangle relationships, 8n19
Trinitarian theology, 133
Twenty-One Homilies Concerning the Statues (Chrysostom), 113
Two Letters: An Exhortation to Theodore after His Fall (Chrysostom), 111
2:7 Disciple Training Series, 21

United Methodist Church of USA, 136
United States
  Constitution of, 137
  Korean churches in, 19n52
  pastoral theology in, 236
unity, 64, 211
unity in love, maintaining, as element of pastoral leadership, 41
University of Wales, Lampeter, PhD program at, xi

vainglory, 183

Valantasis, Richard, 131, 159
Vandenburghe, B. H., 105
van de Paverd, Frans, 126, 127
Virginia Korean Baptist Church, 23, 24, 44, 78, 79
Vision 2020: "Training the Saints to Transform the World," 21, 58, 72, 90, 92-93
visitation, 2, 46, 68
Visitation Ministry, 47
Volf, Miroslav, 169-70n24
Voobus, Arthur, 195n166

Wagner, C. Peter, 48, 65, 72
Ware, Timothy, 134
Warner, Stephen, 77
Warren, Robert, 91
Washington, DC, Korean churches in, 78-81
Wei, Sung Yong, 43n34
Wenger, Antoine, 112
Westcott, Brooke Foss, 119
Westminster Confession of Faith, 1-2
White, Edward, 35
Wilken, Robert L., 129, 190, 198
Wind, James P., 66
Word of God
  centrality of, 85, 133
  preaching of, 88-91, 230-32
world mission, 193-200
worship, 47, 58

Yang, David Choon-Ho, 21, 51
Yang, Kwang Ho, 23n65, 79n
Yoo, Suk Hee, 75-76
Yoon, Myung Ho, 16, 20, 24, 34-36, 58, 79n42, 81
Young, Frances, 130

Zoroastrian Dualism, 119n151, 120n162
Zur Geschichte Der Messliturgie (van de Paverd), 126

www.ingramcontent.com/pod-product-compliance
Lightning Source LLC
Chambersburg PA
CBHW070237230426
43664CB00014B/2338